Three Grains of Wheat

Three Grains of Wheat

A Memoir of Inspiring Journeys to One-Way Destinations

Mike Papasavas

Mill City Press

Copyright © 2010 by Mike Papasavas

Mill City Press, Inc.

212 3rd Avenue North, Suite 290

Minneapolis, MN 55401

612.455.2294

www.millcitypublishing.com

All rights reserved. No part of this publication may be reproduced, stored in a retrieval system,

or transmitted, in any form or by any means, electronic, mechanical, photocopying, recording, or

otherwise, without the prior written permission of the author.

ISBN - 978-1-936400-68-3

LCCN - 2010939869

Cover Design & Typeset by Nate Meyers

Printed in the United States of America

To my wonderful wife Angela, who truly shaped my life and also played a significant role during the entire process of the writing and editing of the book.

My son Alex, whose encouragement and support helped me bring this project to fruition.

My son Paul, whose persistence and frequent reminders for me to start writing have finally laid the foundation and energized my commitment to write.

My daughter-in-law Stacia, who believed in my writing ability and also helped with the book proposal process.

My little granddaughter Ashlin, who was the inexhaustible fueling energy during the writing process.

Acknowledgments:

First and foremost I would like to thank my wife Angela who since I met her has been the most important person in my life, always standing by my side in good and bad times. While maintaining an unwavering approach and a positive attitude, she was continuously discovering and evoking my dormant talents, one of which was writing. Angela became the reason for the confidence I needed to believe in my self-worth.

I owe special recognition and gratitude to my editor Pamela Guerrieri (prooftoperfection.com) whose professional ability, creative thinking, and constructive comments gave the book a unique synthesis and smooth flow. On a personal level, over and above her editing credentials, Pamela is a wonderful human being whose soothing voice, encouraging words, and even-tempered attitude made me feel as if I had known her since childhood. Also, special thanks to Kevin Cook and Kim Jace who worked with Pamela during the editing and proofreading phase. Kevin's insightful and clever comments really made a difference!

I would like to thank one of my best friends Mary Haniotis, who was my adviser and personal "thesaurus" during the entire writing period. As a final proofreader, her feedback and comments were invaluable.

Also, special thanks to Beata Smith, whose exceptional knowledge of the English language helped me define or redefine some sticky situations in the book.

To my friend and ex-coworker Celia Backer, who found the time to read the first two parts of the book and came up with a constructive feedback.

I owe special thanks to my friend Paul Thimou who, besides being a key character in the book, is now a professor at FIT in New York as well as an author himself. After he read the first part of the book he commented that it was like "watching a movie."

And finally, I would like to thank my entire extended family and friends, as well as the rest of the characters in the book that definitely played a major role in shaping my personality.

Thank you all.

Foreword

Over the years I've known Mike Papasavas, he has shared many stories from his remarkable life. I thought I had heard it all, but what an incredible and delightful surprise it was to find out that there was so much more I didn't know—so much that amazed me. Through this book, Mike takes us on the incredible journey of a discontented youngster and brave young man as he searches for happiness.

I met Mike when I applied for one of his open positions at the bank. We discussed the position, and he proceeded to give me the toughest technical interview I had ever had. Lucky for me, Mike offered me the position. I jumped at the chance to work for him, for I saw in him a very intelligent and forward-thinking person from whom I could learn much.

It wasn't long before we formed quite a professional bond and a dynamic team, and more importantly, the beginning of an everlasting friendship. What I found most unique about Mike was his uncanny ability to be both avant-garde without missing the opportunity to embrace and appreciate the moment. He began each and every day with enthusiasm. If I had a dollar for every movie he saw, every book he read, every meal he ate being the "**best** he'd ever seen/read/eaten…"

It was this pure unadulterated pleasure for all that life had to offer that impressed me so much. And I now see that this passion has been a driving force throughout his life. His fervor, combined with his many other attributes, are what have molded Mike into the incredible person he is today.

Besides being one of the most intelligent men I had ever met, he slowly unveiled to me his many other talents. During one of our casual meetings in his office, he appeared to be doodling on a 4x6 piece of scrap paper. At the end of our meeting, he handed me a beautiful landscape scene—which I promptly framed and still have on display.

Mike lived through some very difficult times and experienced a number of adventures. In retrospect, he may not have always made correct choices, but right or wrong, he learned from every one of them, and every one of them helped make him the incredible person he is today. With the exception of the divine intervention that often shaped his destiny, he is truly a self-made man who has never taken anything for granted. He realizes that he has been blessed in life, especially for his beautiful family, and feels very strongly about "giving back." I am extremely fortunate to have been a recipient of Mike's generosity—both tangible and intangible—and for that I will always be eternally grateful.

May you enjoy reading the journey of this remarkable man.

Mary Haniotis

Introduction

It's an amazing thing to look back on your life and consider the moments that shaped who you are at this point in time. Some were good moments, and some were bad. When I set out to write my memoir, I didn't do it for my own personal glory or to fill up empty hours. I wrote it in order to leave a vivid remembrance of my life so that my children and grandchildren would have a better understanding of who I was, what I have done, and where I ended up. Perhaps my life could be a lesson learned or an inspiration of some sort. Who knows? I do know that the journey of reliving my old memories and documenting them has been almost as exciting as living out the experiences the first time around. I've had many adventures since I left my small, Greek village so long ago.

After reading and being influenced by all the books Wayne Dyer wrote, it was Elizabeth Gilbert's book *Eat, Pray, Love* that instilled in me the emotional energy I needed to finally start writing. Two years later, I had completed my memoir, an accomplishment that I didn't think I would ever bring to a satisfactory outcome. I hope my children and their children will accept this book as both a gift and the means by which to see what sparked my determination and fueled my curiosity to explore new horizons.

At the tender age of eleven, I determined that there must be real life beyond the horizons of the village—along with dormant, limitless possibilities deep within me. My heart yearned to discover my own identity. Something inside me told me to search for it. During my first school trip around the island of Rhodes, the marvel of the city, the picturesque harbor, and the sandy beaches awakened my curiosity to seek a life other than that of the village. I soon discovered that I had total control of steering toward a direction of my liking. That trip became a profound learning experience, giving me the inspiration I needed to shift my imagination toward bigger and better possibilities.

But life didn't change all at once. One day when I was working in the fields, I was suddenly overtaken by a strange sensation of depression, fear, anxiety, and desperation. At that moment, I stopped the animals in the middle of the path. I took three grains of wheat from one of the bags and placed them under a stone. That act—those three grains of wheat beneath the rock—symbolized my commitment to one day abandon the village life and seek my own path. Those three grains of wheat have served as a reminder that there will always be opportunities beyond the familiar.

It was something of an epiphany as I considered the new worlds out there waiting for me to take the first step. And during the adventures that followed, I never forgot those precious moments on that dirt-trodden path. They would serve as an invisible source of energy behind every decision I made or risk I took from that point on. No longer would I take the easy way out when confronted with tough choices and dangerous challenges.

If I had to live my life all over again, I wouldn't change anything in terms of the big picture, as I have never regretted any decision I made. Instead, whatever path I took at the fork of a road, I kept going with a conviction that it was the right choice. This mentality ultimately yielded successful results and generated even more exciting, new opportunities. However, there were several occasions during my younger years where my immature emotional behavior overrode my logic. Thus is the way with youth, I suppose. But I did grow up and grow into myself. And I did end up finding my self-identity. Although even now, in my golden years, I'm still learning, still changing, I can rest easy knowing that I lived my life the way I wanted to—fully and without regret.

Chapter 1

A One-Way Ticket Going Anywhere

On a cloudy mid-morning in April of 1959, at twenty years of age—trembling with great anticipation, fear, anxiety, and a mixed bag of other emotions—I found myself standing on the platform in the Athens train station. I clutched a battered suitcase and a one-way ticket to Bonn, Germany. A happy young couple stood next to me, holding hands and gazing lovingly into each other's eyes. These lovebirds were clearly looking forward to their selected destination, perhaps their honeymoon or a long-anticipated vacation. An envious thought crossed my mind. I fantasized about the day when I would have the financial means to take someone I love on a dream vacation. *Maybe someday*, I thought, glancing at the lovebirds with a wistful sigh.

For the most part, my fellow passengers were traveling with family members or other companions. They were going either to the northern parts of Greece or beyond the borders of Yugoslavia. At the far corner of the platform, I noticed a stray dog curled up in a cozy ball. He seemed contented and appreciative for the food and goodies the passengers threw his way. *Ah*, I thought, *what a carefree life a dog leads!* But I also wondered: did he really have a choice to be born as a dog? Who knows?

We waited for what seemed to be an eternity for the train to arrive. I was overtaken by a confusing mixture of emotions. At one point, I even pinched my arm to remind myself that I was determined to reach my goal: to go to a new country and try to make it on my own.

My mother and father truly believed in me. When we had exchanged good-byes, my father had hugged me. "Son, go for it," he said. "I know you can do it!" I believed he meant what he said, and his comment had raised my confidence and self-esteem. He said he was willing to pay for a two-way ticket, but I knew he would have to borrow the money. I refused.

"I only want a one-way ticket," I replied. "I don't have to have any choice but to succeed." I knew that if I had a return ticket and some obstacles or difficulties came my way, I might be tempted to give up and return to my homeland. This is why I categorically dismissed this alternative and moved forward, as planned.

The shrill whistling of the train as it chugged into the station rudely interrupted my thoughts. I took my place in line and waited until the train came to a full stop. I hoisted my only suitcase, entered the train, and found a seat in a six-passenger compartment. A family of four—a couple and their two boys—were to be my traveling companions; the last seat remained empty. We began exchanging a few words and I found out they were traveling to Thessaloniki in northern Greece.

When they asked me why I was going to Germany, I didn't know how to answer. *Should I tell them that I'm going to remold my life, or find my destiny?* I wondered. In the end, I said the first thing that came to mind: that I was going to study at the University of Bonn. This wasn't an outright lie, because one of my secondary goals was to continue my higher education as soon as I was comfortable with the German language. Fortunately, they did not ask me any other questions, but their question started me thinking about how difficult it would be to become fluent in German, which is one of the most difficult languages to learn.

I had already purchased a Greek-German tutorial textbook and had started learning the basics. I had memorized a few words, but I was mainly concentrating on grammar rules and sentence structure. To my surprise, I realized that the German syntax of a sentence was similar to the classic Greek I had taken in high school for six years. *Wow,* I told myself, *that part of the language should be easy!* This turned out to be true.

The family was chattering away amongst themselves as the train's whistle blew, announcing our departure. The two little boys applauded this thrilling event with obvious glee. Meanwhile, I was staring quietly out the window, watching the buildings and fields disappear behind me.

Did I mention that this was my very first train ride? It was, indeed—my first experience with a train that long. To me, it seemed like a gleaming, metallic snake, with its many cars attached to one another. The only other means of transportation I had ever used were bicycles, cars (not mine), and boats that I took from Rhodes to Athens. Airplane travel had always been out of the question, because the cost was excessively high.

For the next thirty to forty-five minutes, I gloried in the view of the Athenian suburbs and beyond, feeling gratified that the Lord had granted me the privilege of experiencing this exciting new spectacle. I looked heavenward and silently said, "Thank you!"

It would take us three days to arrive in Bonn, and the only train accommodation at my disposal was a single window seat. Seated there, I could eat my meals and also sleep—that is, if I were able to make myself comfortable enough by resting my head on the windowsill. The food offered at the cantina was too expensive for my budget. I wanted to preserve as much money as I could, because I did not know what surprises would come my way when I arrived in Germany. In my suitcase, I had some homemade bread and cheese my mother had packed for me, as well as some preserved foods. From those, I made my meals during the train ride.

When there were some quiet moments in the compartment, many parts of my youth flashed before my eyes, filling my mind with pictures, events, actions, reactions, and repercussions. This was the perfect time to review and reflect upon the good, the bad, and the most unusual moments I had experienced since childhood. I was only twenty years old, but in that short time, I felt that I had already lived a long and eventful life.

I was traveling alone, but the original plan had been for me to travel with two other friends (so to speak). However, the other two had backed out a few days before our pre-arranged departure to Germany. I sincerely understood their fears of the unknown and their limited courage for risk-taking, so I never held any grudges about their decision to stay behind.

Just one day before I left Rhodes, I met an acquaintance named Manolias, a name that is a modified derivation of the name Emmanuel. Manolias was a world traveler who possessed a vast array of knowledge regarding foreign countries; he knew about everything related to getting work visas, as well as so many other facets of globetrotting. He was a United States citizen and had just arrived from Belgium, driving a car through Germany.

Manolias told me that I should not even *think* about taking a risk of this magnitude—going to a country without any definite plans or assurances. He was emphatic that I was setting myself up for a colossal failure.

"Don't go! Cancel your trip!" he had warned me.

I remember that afternoon conversation, which took place in my friend Dimitri's store, as if it happened yesterday. I have to admit, I was shaken by this veteran world traveler's comments. Yes, I thought of chickening out. I thought that he might be right—that I was probably heading toward a brick wall. I remember staring at the ceiling of the store, looking for strength, when I thought of the last words my father had said to me:

"Son, go for it!" Who knew me better than my father? Manolias, the world traveler, did not know me very well; he did not know my strengths, my tenacity, and my determination to go all the way, taking any and all risks to reach my goal.

With my father's words to guide me, I was able to dismiss Manolias' comments and move forward with my plans.

Chapter 2

Humble Origins

The train was steadily chugging along the railway in the lower continental region of Greece, passing through green valleys filled with manicured orchard groves in full bloom and all sorts of fresh-grown vegetables. Gazing out the window, I noticed some farmers riding their cultivating tractors as they tilled the rich earth or spread fertilizers. What a peaceful, scenic sight! I had never seen such a vast expanse of lush, cultivated farmland.

My hometown was the small village of Agios Isidoros, was where I was born in 1938. I spent the first twelve years of my life there. The village is located in the middle of the island of Rhodes at the bottom of Mount Ataviros. Because of its location, the village is at least twenty to thirty kilometers away from any seashore.

My father owned six or seven small parcels of land scattered in separate locations throughout the village's territorial compounds. Their average size was a little more than one acre each, and the distance between the parcels was about two to three kilometers. As a result, my father could only work in one parcel at a time within the same day. He used the land to grow wheat so we would have an ample supply of bread to feed the family for an entire year. He also sowed and grew rye and barley, which he mainly used as supplemental fodder. These grains were mixed with chaff for the working animals: a mule, a donkey, and a cow.

Our house in the village resembled a duplex, with one large room on one side and two rooms on the other. Twelve of us lived in the two-room housing structure. I was the oldest of eight children. Next was my sister, Vasilia, then Despina, Mary, Anastasia, Katina, George, and Anna. Half of the children slept in one of the rooms with my parents, and the rest, including me, with my grandmothers in the other room. The third room was used to store all the dry goods and to accommodate the animals during the cold winter months.

We had no indoor or outdoor plumbing facilities. When nature called, we used the fields, which were a short distance from the house. Even the drinking water had to be brought in on the shoulders of family members, who carried it in large, earthen pots from springs located two or three kilometers away. Health department experts had tested the water from the fountain in the center of the village and determined it was not potable.

My great-grandmother was the only adult who did not work in the fields. As our "nanny," so to speak, she took care of the children and all of the household chores, including the daily cooking for the entire family. She was our first-aid doctor, too. But most of all, she was a strict disciplinarian.

My grandmother, on the other hand, was the "shepherd" who took care of our more than one hundred sheep, all year round. She was responsible for selecting the fields and guiding the sheep out for their daily grazing, and protecting them in our farmhouse when the weather turned foul.

In the spring, she collected the sheep's milk, which ultimately was made into cheese or butter, or just served as milk for everyday drinking. I can attest that the sheep's milk is richer and creamier than cow's milk and doesn't have the faint tanginess of goat's milk. If you've only drunk cow's milk, switching over to sheep's milk may take an initial adjustment period, but many people prefer its rich taste once they make the change. We had no refrigeration; therefore, we could not preserve milk for more than a day or so.

At the beginning of summer, my grandmother sheared the sheep's wooly fur, most of which we sold to wholesalers. A small portion of the wool was refined by my great-grandmother, who used it to make homespun clothing and quilts for our beds.

My mother (in Greek, we called her *Mana*) seemed to be everywhere at once. At times, she helped my father (we called him *Patera*) out on the fields. Other times, she helped my grandmother (*Yayia*) with the sheep. When any of the children needed her help, my mother was always there for us. She would assist us with our homework or tell us a story before bedtime. None of the adults took a day off except for some Sundays—and even then, after the Liturgy, they always found something that had to be done.

Despite the bleak quality of life and the never-ending, hard work for a slice of bread and a piece of cheese, we were a close family. We cared deeply for one another, no matter how harsh our situation. The respect my siblings and I had for our parents and grandmothers was one of our most important attributes. That quality was engraved on our characters, and I'm proud to say we all lived by that principle in our everyday lives.

Chapter 3

The Farming Cycle

U nlike the farmers on tractors that I was observing through the train window, my father worked his land using archaic methods: home-made tools and the strong backs of a cow, a mule, and a donkey. During the fall months, he prepared the field by removing all the wild shrubs and weeds with a hoe, and using an ax when the trunk of a shrub was overgrown.

After fertilizing the soil—mostly with organic material like cow manure—the fields were ready for the next phase. In the latter part of the winter months, he plowed the fields using a homemade plow dragged by a mule and a cow, guiding them back and forth until the soil of the entire parcel was freshly turned over. He then proceeded to spread the wheat, rye, or barley seeds by hand.

At the beginning of spring, after the sowing of the wheat and rye was complete, my father worked on the vegetable gardens and vineyards. These were located in four different sites, far apart from each other. He planted all sorts of vegetables including lentils, corn, and various beans, enough to feed the family for the entire year. He also planted many seasonal fruit trees as well as almond, walnut, and olive trees.

I remember that during the summer and fall months, we had all the different kinds of fruits and vegetables that could be grown in that region of the island. In the winter months, the citrus fruits, such as oranges, grapefruits, tangerines, and lemons, ripened and were ready to be picked.

I will never forget the garden we owned in a location called Mylos, four kilometers from the village. There was plenty of spring water there, which initially had been used to run a watermill to grind wheat flour. The

Greek word for watermill is *mylos*—which became the name of the locale. The water was distributed to gardens throughout the immediate area.

Our garden in Mylos was as splendid and bountiful as the Garden of Eden—at least, that's how I thought of it. We had every fruit tree you can imagine, and we grew all sorts of vegetables. Every time I went there to water our garden, a huge smile bloomed on my face as I imagined myself in paradise. What an awe-inspiring feast for the eyes that garden was!

Around the end of June, the wheat, rye, and barley crop was ready to be reaped. Using a sickle, my father and mother would cut the stalks and tie them into bundles to get them ready to be transported to a threshing floor, which is called an *aloni*. This threshing floor was a round arrangement of flagstones measuring about thirty feet in diameter, and was prepared with tightly packed cement-like dried clay.

I clearly remember all these details because, when the school year was over, I was the one who transported the bundles from the fields to the threshing area and stacked them around and outside the perimeter of the floor. We would load two bundles each on the mule and the donkey, and I would guide them through narrow paths to our designated area of the threshing grounds.

Each of the village's 200 farmers had their own ground. The entire compound was surrounded by a fence made out of dry, thorny shrubs to keep the animals out during the night. At the end of the threshing day, all the working animals were left free outside the prickly fence, where they would wander all night and graze to their hearts' content. The facility had also a twenty-four- hour guard whose compensation was the responsibility of all the farmers.

I dreaded the summer months. Instead of getting to enjoy a vacation from school, my father scheduled chores for me six days a week from dawn to dusk for the entire summer. I was jealous of some of my friends and fellow students who were free all summer to do whatever they pleased. I never had that luxury. Many times, I found myself resenting the way my father treated me.

On the other hand, doing this hard work made me a stronger person, both physically and emotionally. Could it also be that this was one of my main reasons for seeking my fortune outside my familiar horizons? Well, during this period I was clearly convinced that everything happens for a reason. The events that followed were to become the stronger links that formed, and continue to form, the unbreakable and long-lasting chain of life.

From the time I was eight years old until I was through with high school, my summers were spent working with my father. A typical workday was waking up at 5:00 a.m., grabbing a slice of bread and a piece of cheese, and ambling off to the fields—yawning all the way—to locate our mule and donkey, which had been left to roam free the evening before. I always took my homemade slingshot with me, which I wielded expertly in one of my favorite pastimes: chasing and killing birds.

Most young people had a slingshot that was made by using the V-section of a tree branch, two thin slices of an inner tube from a tire (red tubes were better), and a piece of leather to hold the stone that would hit the target. All three pieces were tied together with rubber-band-like thin cuts and ... *voilà*, a perfect slingshot! With my pocket filled with half a dozen round stones, I was primed and ready to spot and pick off any bird within shooting distance.

Within an hour or so, I would locate the animals a few miles away from the *aloni*. Riding the mule and pulling the donkey behind me by its reins, I ultimately arrived at the destination. Many times, my father was angry with me for arriving later than all the others. His usual comment was, "Were you chasing birds again?"

Of course I was! I thought to myself. *It's the only enjoyment I get the whole summer while I'm made to do this slave-like, tortuous work.* But I just kept my head down and did not say a word.

My morning animal-locating chore wasn't that bad. Even though I had to wake up early in the morning, the breathtaking sight of the lush, green scenery, stretching away toward the horizon in the orange glow of the rising sun, made it all seem worthwhile. I never tired of this daily phenomenon. I felt that nature and I were connected. In addition, I was holding my trusty slingshot. The morning spectacle made my tiresome chore bearable, if not exactly enjoyable.

Now the work began. Tying up the animals to a center post, through a rope loop, we walked behind the animals, forcing them to go around the circular threshing floor, which was filled with a layer of stalked wheat. I always wore a straw hat, but the hot sun would pierce through my entire body anyway. My clothes would be drenched with perspiration as I went around and around in what it seemed a never-ending journey. The heavy animals would thresh the stalked wheat.

Periodically, throughout the day, we would spread a fresh layer over the threshed one. At fifteen-minute intervals, my father and I would take turns walking and directing the animals, as it would have been too much for one person to do this all day long.

Our resting period took place under a homemade umbrella made out of straw and twigs secured on a precut, small tree with wide, dry branches. This structure was sufficient to give us the shade we needed. We continued this routine for about five or six hours; by noon, both people and animals needed their lunch breaks.

The first task at noon was to take the animals to a nearby location—about a kilometer away—to drink water. It was amazing how many gallons of water these beasts of burden could consume! When lunch was over for man and beast, the wheat threshing routine continued until sundown, at which time I would take the animals for another water-drinking session and then let them free in the open fields.

When the threshing process was completed, the next phase was the separation of the grain from the chaff. First, the entire mixed crop was pushed and amassed toward the west side of the ground, making a small, mound-like shape. When the west wind was gusting favorably at about seven to ten miles an hour, we would throw the crop in the air using a shovel-like tool. We could toss it about two meters high, depending on the strength of the wind. Being lighter, the chaff was blown to the left side of the mass, whereas the wheat grains would fall straight down, thus accomplishing the separation. The grains were then put into bags and transported to the house, where they were stowed in large, wooden storage bins.

During this mid-summer phase, I made ten to twelve trips a day using a donkey and a mule, to transport the grain. I worked for as many days as it took to accomplish the grain separation process. But one day, something changed.

It was around noontime. I felt a sensation of nervousness and an unknown fear as I guided the animals towards the village. I suddenly stopped the animals and looked upward, as if I were pleading for help. I can't possibly describe that alarming feeling I was experiencing at that moment. It was a blend of boredom, panic, and anxiety.

I had suddenly realized that I truly hated that chore, and that there was nothing and nobody that would be able to keep me in the village for the rest of my life. I didn't want to follow in my father's footsteps. I knew I had to make a promise to myself that I would leave the fields behind and find a new life.

I took three grains of wheat from one of the loaded bags and placed them under a rock on the side of the pathway. I thought to myself, *I will remember this unhappy and miserable moment as one of the worst in my life*. That feeling would serve as a yardstick for comparison with future calamities or difficulties that might befall me. I labeled that thought the "Three Grains of Wheat." I knew it was a significant milestone. It became a turning point in my life.

Many times after that day, I found myself trying to analyze and understand the quality of life my parents had. I did not even call it "living."

It was a survival process that repeated itself, year in, year out, onward toward the grave. On the other hand, based on some significant events that had preceded my father's birth, I considered the possibility that divine intervention was involved in arranging this life for them. I believed that, by living this life, an unknown master plan would be satisfied and kept in its natural, preplanned order.

Let me explain as we examine the following events. My grandmother got married when she was fourteen years old, and my father was born one year later. My grandfather died during the Spanish flu epidemic. He was twenty years old. As I had been told, my father had one of the brightest minds in the village.

After completing the sixth grade in the village, he attended a six-year high school in the city. In the middle of the first year, his teachers determined that he was too advanced for the first class level, so they enrolled him in the third year. Even there, he finished first in his class.

At the end of the school year, he went to the village and spent all summer helping his mother with the farming chores. But one summer, my grandmother decided to keep my father in the village instead of letting him return to school, because she could not handle all of the responsibilities single-handedly. A few years later, my father married my mother. During a span of twelve years or so, their eight children—including me—were born.

So many possibilities could have altered the outcome of what we are today. Eight children, many grand- and great-grandchildren, were born out of a single person, who was barely brought into this life before his father died. Why did my grandmother have to get married at the tender age of fourteen? Even in 1913, this was not customary or the average age for a woman to wed. Why did my grandfather, a strong and healthy farmer, have to die so young? His death meant that my father, who was one of the brightest students of his time, had to abandon a promising education. Perhaps, someday, all of us will know the answer.

During a period of eleven years, my six younger sisters and my brother were born. With my parents, grandmother, and great-grandmother, it became a very crowded house. Half of us slept in one room, while my parents, with four of the girls, bedded down in the other. We slept on woven straw mats on the packed, dry clay floors that were covered with thick, homemade wool blankets instead of mattresses.

In the wintertime, we also used wool blankets as covers. The fireplace was built in one of the outer corners of the raised part of the living area. It was always ablaze. We used it for cooking during the day and for keeping the house warm on chilly nights.

Our diet was vegetarian, for the most part. However, once a month or so, we had meat, fish, or chicken. My family produced all the vegetables, fruits, eggs, bread, oil, meat, and dairy products. All pasta dishes were made from scratch. For breakfast, we usually had a slice of bread with pork fat and honey. For a typical lunch, we had either a boiled egg or feta cheese with bread, followed by seasonal fruits and dry nuts.

Dinner was the only time that the entire family was together. The adults sat at a small, rectangular, four-chair table, and the rest of us gathered around a low, round table with small benches, much like a traditional Japanese table setting. Next to the adult table was a wooden cabinet used to hold four homemade, earthen water jugs. The cabinet was aptly named *stamno-thiki*—a Greek compound word meaning "jug-case" or "jug-holder." The upper level of the case held the drinking water jugs while the lower level housed the other two jugs, which were filled with the non-potable water we carried from local fountains.

In the evening, the children did their homework with the aid of a few petroleum lamps or the light from the fireplace. There was plenty of interaction between the family members, including lively discussions about village gossip or farming. I listened to stories my mother or grandmother recited. Sometimes we played games: we would spin homemade tops, make paper-folding creations, and play hide-and-seek.

A few hours after dinner, everyone went to bed. Everyone worked so hard during the day, we had no problem falling asleep and resting peacefully at night.

Chapter 4

My Father the Jailbird

My train ride continued. We were now in Thessaly, one of the thirteen regions located in the central part of Greece, passing through plains surrounded by tall mountain ranges. Fortunately, the other passengers in the compartment were quiet, mostly napping, so I had ample time to think and on many past events of my life in the village and during my high school years in the city.

As I daydreamed, glimpses of concern jumped in and interrupted my imaginary journey down memory lane; these somewhat disturbing thoughts magnified my fear of the unknown. I would be in a strange land.

I tried to dismiss these negative thoughts, because I had already made up my mind and was determined to face any obstacles or difficulties that might come my way. After all, those few who knew me well enough had characterized me as an "eternal optimist," always looking at the bright side of any undertaking, no matter the risk or the level of difficulty.

I was headed for Germany, a country we had been at war with not too long ago. The Germans had invaded Greece. While Mussolini's fascists were defeated and stopped from entering the Greek mainland at the Albanian border, the German invasion spread throughout the country and even reached our small village of about one thousand residents.

I was just a little boy of three or four. I vividly remember the harsh language of the German soldiers and the echo of their spike-soled boots. Their ominous footfalls on the village's cobblestone streets could be heard and recognized from 300 to 400 feet away.

The soldiers would try to be nice to the village children. In fact, one day, a soldier offered me a chocolate bar. But even at that young age, I could understand that I should not take something from the enemy, so I said *"Nein."* I did not accept the chocolate bar. Later, I felt good that I had been able to refuse such a rare treat, which a poor farm boy like me could only dream about.

Another time, in the center of the village, I watched soldiers escorting a line of about ten handcuffed villagers who were ready to be put to death by a firing squad. At the last minute, a shiny black Mercedes—a Nazi staff car—pulled up and a high-level German official stepped out and ordered the cancellation of the execution.

I have many other memories of the German invasion, but the one incident that clearly sticks out was the time when they issued an order demanding that all households must surrender their dry goods to the German authorities. My father gave them a few bags of wheat, but the bulk of our supply was hidden in a brick-covered, secret compartment in the back portion of the house.

One of our neighbors knew that my father hid most of the dry goods, so he told the Germans to search the house for more wheat and rye. After a thorough search, they did not find anything. Still, the neighbor insisted. He reassured the Germans that the wheat was hidden behind a brick wall and suggested that they access this hidden compartment through the roof of the house; when they did, they located our storage compartment.

While this was going on, my father was working in one of the vineyards a few miles from the village. When he arrived in the front yard of the house, the Germans were waiting and immediately handcuffed him. They asked him a few questions and then took him toward the center of the village, where a black car was waiting to take him to jail or to be executed by a firing squad.

He was charged with concealing part of our own dry goods, instead of turning every food-related product over to the Germans. What nerve, what audacity! What did the Germans do to deserve the little food we had, which barely kept us alive through the trying years of war?

That awful scene is permanently etched in my memory. I can still see the curious onlookers asking questions and the German soldiers who were handcuffing my father. I remember my mother's nervous pacing back and forth and my father's puzzled expression as he faced all this commotion. "What did I do?" he protested.

I was truly shaken by all this, and my tear-filled eyes were glued on my father, who surprisingly maintained a calm disposition. I even noticed a tinge of a forced smile when he came close to me and, while putting his handcuffed hands on my head, he said, "Don't worry son, everything is going to be fine."

15

My mother was weeping and crying out hysterically, uttering a few words of hopelessness and despair. "Where are they taking you?" she asked my father. To the soldiers, she shouted, "No, no, don't take him! He did not do anything wrong!" All the while, she was trying to pull her dear husband away from the soldiers, crying out loud, "Am I going to see you again?"

Then she turned her head upwards, stretched her arms wide open, and seemed as though she were going to begin to pray. Instead, she uttered the neighbor's name aloud. "V——you are a traitor who betrayed us for no reason! I never hated anyone in my life, I never wished harm for anybody, but now I wish that you pay and feel the pain that I'm feeling at this moment! I don't want to do this, but my curse is …"

She paused for a moment and then went on in a sobbing voice: "*I wish and pray that you lose your eyesight, as I'm losing my husband, so that you experience the pain and suffering when they take away the most valuable part of your livelihood.*" The curse about one's eyesight was one of the most common outbursts used in the village as a wishful punishment for those who had done harm to others.

I don't know if my mother's curse had any power, but some years later, V—— lost his left eye when his shotgun misfired while he was hunting. Was this divine justice? Who knows!

After my father was taken to jail, my hatred for the German soldiers peaked to an intense, white-hot anger. I wanted revenge! I was willing to do anything to get even with those black-hearted bullies who *took* my father away. His absence had forced my mother to assume all of the farming responsibilities. If I'd gotten an opportunity to kill one of those goose-stepping cowards, I would not have felt any remorse. On the other hand, how could I, a five- or six-year-old kid, attempt to take any type of revenge without risking my own life?

Even at that age, my friends, Michalis and Tasos, and I knew a lot about weapons and ammunition. So I convinced my two friends to try something dangerous. The three of us stole a huge, wooden box of ammunition from the German base in Atria by sneaking under the barbed wired fence.

Atria was located about three kilometers east of the village. The box was too heavy to lift, so we dragged it about one kilometer away and placed it in the middle of the road. We knew that around noontime, a German soldier would be passing that spot on his motorcycle to deliver mail to the base. We gathered and placed some dry grass and twigs around the wooden box and set it on fire a few minutes before the soldier was scheduled to pass.

16

As we ran uphill toward the mountain, we heard the loud purr of an engine. Then we saw the motorcycle approaching the burning box with the ammunition inside. All of a sudden, we heard multiple explosions. Bullets were flying in all directions! My co-conspirators and I kept running uphill, occasionally turning around to see if any of those bullets had hit the soldier. But to our dismay, we saw that the soldier had taken cover behind a rock—and then he began shooting at us!

I remember that I was barefoot and it was difficult for me to run as fast as my friends could because I had a blister on one heel. To avoid the bullets that zinged past me, I crouched behind the trunk of an olive tree until the soldier stopped shooting. I watched as he rode his motorcycle away from the burning box, heading toward the village.

A week or so later, I witnessed an event that took place in the village church. It involved a man named Nikolas, whose house was next to the church grounds. Nikolas was a tall, rugged, and heavily muscled individual whose impressive physical attributes had justifiably earned him the reputation of being the strongest man in the village.

When Nikolas came home from the fields early one evening, he was told that his two daughters had been abducted by three Germans and taken inside the church. The puffed-up veins on his face, which was redder than an overripe tomato, looked like they were going to explode. My mouth dropped open as he screamed with all his might, "I will kill those bastards! I will definitely kill them!"

He immediately ran toward the church entrance as a parade of onlookers ran right behind him. There was a soldier, armed with a rifle, on guard in front of the door to stop anyone from entering the church. Without fear of the rifle and despite the warnings shouted by the German, Nikolas charged forward and swiftly grabbed the gun. He began striking the soldier in the face with the stock of the rifle until the German fell down, unconscious.

Nikolas then took the rifle and broke it into two pieces by slamming it against his thigh, thus separating the stock from the barrel. Consumed with rage and anger, he stalked inside the church and saw two soldiers trying to rape his daughters.

He stormed toward the soldier closest to him and went into a frenzy, throwing punches at his face. Then this mighty colossus picked the soldier up as if he were a doll, lifted him high in the air, and deliberately dropped him on the marbled floor, where he lay in a crumpled heap.

The other soldier came to his bleeding friend's rescue, but as we had expected, he suffered the same consequences. Both soldiers remained on the floor, unconscious, while Nikolas escorted his beloved daughters home. Fortunately, he had gotten there in time to prevent the actual rapes. As the girls exited the church, they covered their upper bodies with the shreds of their torn blouses. I never found out if that heinous act left any permanent emotional scars on the father and those lovely girls.

Chapter 5

The Letter That Changed My Life

Although I had witnessed firsthand several unpleasant experiences of war involving both the Germans and the Italians, I still thought that Germany was my best choice of destination because the decision had an interesting twist.

As I mentioned earlier, two other friends and I were considering emigrating to one of the northern countries in Europe—Sweden, Norway, or Germany. After both of them backed out of the trip, I came across a personal ad in a magazine. A young man from Germany named Niko wished to correspond with a young Greek lady "for friendship or whatever results in the future."

I thought about that personal ad, and a few days later, it hit me! I screamed, "Eureka!" I asked my sister, Despina, to write to Niko to see if she would get a response. She wrote a letter and, sure enough, Niko wrote back. In a sort of a pleading tone, he asked Despina if she were willing to continue the correspondence. In the third letter, following my instructions, Despina wrote, "By the way, my brother is planning a trip to Germany—would you mind if you two meet? He might need some help with housing, his visa, etc."

Niko's response was encouraging: "I would be more than happy to help your brother, depending on what city he would be traveling to. I live about ten kilometers from Bonn."

Upon hearing that, my eyes darted to a nearby map, and I studied Germany and its many cities. I looked up and said to Despina, "Guess what? I'm going to Bonn!"

Chapter 6

Mount Ataviros

The train was passing through a narrow valley between two tall mountain ranges. This scene reminded me of the mountain that stood tall above my village's upper boundaries. On many occasions, I had climbed to the top of Mount Ataviros (about 1600 meters high) and spent countless carefree hours enjoying the panoramic view of the Aegean Sea and the sight of the many islands that beckoned to me, stretching all the way to the end of the horizon.

Perhaps the most noteworthy landmark on this lofty plateau was the ancient ruins of an old settlement. I often wondered how the massive stones that remained had been moved to the top of that mountain. Where did they move them from? It's puzzling, because the makeup of the immediate terrain does not in any way resemble the limestone-like rocks of the ruins. That mystery is similar to that of the Egyptian pyramids.

I later learned the legend of that settlement. According to the www.greecetravel.com web site, Katreus was the son of Minos, who was the king of Crete. Katreus had three daughters—Airope, Klymene, Apemosyne—and a son, Althaimenes. When Katreus asked the oracle how his life would end, he was told that one of his children would be the cause of his death.

Kateus hid the oracle in a secret place, but Althaimenes learned of it and, not wanting to be the killer of his father, went with his sister, Apemosyne, to a place in Rhodes that he called Kretinia. From a mountain named Mount Ataviros, he could see all the way to Crete. He erected an altar there to Zeus Ataviros.

The walk to the top of the mountain—especially the last, steep peak—was fatiguing and took about three hours. On the other hand, the return trip to the village at the foot of the mountain was an easy downhill walk and took less than an hour.

I know that people have written detailed books about the village of Agios Isidoros. In fact, my mother's uncle, Emmanuel, who was a lawyer, wrote several books, including one specifically dedicated to the village of Agios Isidoros. In that book, which was published in 1996, he wrote about the various customs, dialectic expressions, food, and overall behavior of the inhabitants.

Once in a while, I read parts of this book, which includes some pictures of our ancestors going back several generations. Rather than explore these facts, however, I will try to limit my writing to the description of some of the significant events that affected me personally during my twelve years in the village.

It is hard to believe, but the first event I remember was when I was only thirteen months old. The living space of our house had two levels, one of which was raised a little more than a foot and was extended to the fireplace in the left corner of the outer wall. My mother was sitting on the edge of the raised level, holding and breast-feeding my sister, Vasilia, who is one year younger than I am. At that moment, I clambered up onto her lap and tried to get breast-fed as well, but my mother pushed me away and I fell from her lap to the first level floor.

I remember the pain when I hit the floor, but her rejection of me was more emotionally hurtful than the physical pain. This incident was deeply engraved in my memory. Even today, I can recall all the details of the scene, as well as my first emotional experience.

Another time, when I had barely learned to walk, my mother picked me up and stopped in front of a full-length mirror. I saw my mother in the mirror, of course, but I did not recognize the smiling toddler who looked back at me; it was perhaps the first time I had seen myself. I don't know which of these two incidents occurred first. Nevertheless, I'm convinced that it is possible for our mind to record and recall all the details of our past, from birth and perhaps even before.

Chapter 7

The Third Grade Teacher and the Grenades

The island of Rhodes was under Italian rule since 1912, when Italian troops took over the island, along with the rest of the Dodecanese Islands. They had established an Italian colony known as *Isole Italiane del Egeo*—meaning "Italian Islands of the Aegean"— in 1923.

The islands were formally united with Greece in 1947. During this period, both Italian and Greek languages were taught in all levels of school. I remember some first grade Italian textbooks, especially one in particular that contained a large picture of a small, yellow chick. The words under the picture were *piccolo pulcino*, which means "small chick" in English.

I must have been three years old, yet that page has remained vividly clear in my memory—even the Italian words. But how did I learn how to read and understand both Greek and Italian at such a young age? My parents did not remember giving me any reading instructions in either language.

I recall that, one day, I walked into a first grade classroom, sat down in an empty desk, and opened a textbook. The teacher approached me and asked me to leave because I was too young to attend first grade. Even when I proved to her that I could read any textbook with ease, she did not let me stay in her class.

A few years later, I began attending elementary school. According to my teacher, Mrs. Anna, I was one of her best students during the first few years. However, one disturbing incident that occurred in third grade left a permanent scar on my emotional makeup and changed the way I viewed the behavior of others, especially adults.

At the beginning of the year, when the teacher asked for a show of hands, I was the only one who volunteered to give a synopsis on what we had learned the previous year. The teacher was impressed with my description; as a reward, he gave me a thick, hardbound notebook. I was so pleased and my parents were proud of my achievement.

I began using the notebook—in fact, I clearly remember that I had already written notes on the first four pages. But no more than a week after I received the notebook, the same teacher took it away from me and gave it to someone else. His reason was that I had come to school that day with my fingernails uncut and dirty.

Perhaps it was this incident that made me aware of the notion of injustice, because after that episode, I became somewhat rebellious. Most of my decisions were risky and of a radical nature overall. At the young age of eight or nine, I was looking for ways to occupy my free time as well as satisfying my restless and curious mind.

In the absence of toys or games suitable for children, we substituted whatever we could find at the abandoned army base that the Italians and the Germans had left behind. There were plenty of unexploded bombs, broken rifles, and grenades scattered in and around the base.

I was not afraid of guns, bombs, or hand grenades. I knew how to hold and release the safety pin of the grenade and, while standing behind a rock, I would hurl the grenade, either to kill some birds or just for fun. In fact, I remember one day I made a necklace and hung a dozen grenades and began my bird hunting. My father spotted me and— horrified, of course—he tried to catch me, but I ran away from him. He finally stopped chasing me, lest I should slip and fall, whereupon the grenades might have exploded.

Apparently, I developed a gravitational pull towards explosives at a young age, for when I was four or five years old, I found an oval metal object, picked it up, and took it home. I wanted to break it open to see what was inside, so I found a large stone in our front yard and began hitting the object hard, determined to break its thick, pineapple-like shell.

I sat down and continued striking the un-budging object. My curiosity was unbearable as I pummeled the shiny thing, and I nearly drooled at the prospect of what treasures it might contain.

When the rock finally broke to pieces, I realized the accursed thing was unbreakable and gave up. Having lost interest in cracking the impenetrable hull—or was it just sour grapes?—I took the oval object and left it outside a café in the center of the village.

A few minutes later, an adult named Yanni picked it up and exclaimed loudly, "Look at this, fellows! Some kid must have been playing with this grenade! Wow, let me take a look." He examined it carefully and observed,

"This thing must have been either underwater or in a wet, muddy place, because there's quite a bit of rust accumulated around the knob."

The crowd of fascinated bystanders listened intently as Yanni explained that this type of German grenade has a knob on one end that must be unscrewed first, and then the igniter must be pulled to activate the detonator. "It could explode, because by loosening up the rust, the knob will turn slowly—see?" said Yanni, deftly twisting the knob as the people in the crowd craned their necks warily to see.

Yanni invited his admirers to follow him to a nearby, steep cliff, where he planned to throw the grenade over the edge to see if it would explode. With great anticipation, I also followed the crowd and waited to see if Yanni's claim was true. The knob of the grenade was already unscrewed, so he just pulled it and threw the grenade over the edge of the yawning chasm. As he had promised, it exploded with a reverberating *pow* as soon as it hit the ground—a drop of about 200 meters. Yanni held his nose high in the air, pleased that his assumptions had been correct.

The thrilled bystanders shook their heads appreciatively and exchanged breathless comments, such as, "There must have been a guardian angel standing next to the fool who was pounding on that grenade." I left quietly without revealing to anyone that I was that lucky kid whose life fate had spared.

Chapter 8

Sixty Kilometers to Thessaloniki

It was late afternoon and the sun had just come out of the clouds just above the west horizon line. The train was approaching the northern part of Greece as we passed the "60 kilometers to Thessaloniki" sign. I gazed wistfully at the family in my compartment, knowing they were scheduled to get off soon.

My thoughts came rushing back to the present. I wondered what other kinds of passengers would join me in my cozy little compartment. Would they be Greeks traveling to another country, or people who were returning home to their own country?

I thought it would be nice if I were able to communicate with someone during the remainder of my journey. I decided to take out my German instruction handbook and continued studying the different grammar rules as they apply to sentence structure. I realized that, in German, you couldn't differentiate the gender of a noun based on its suffix, as in many other languages. For example, in Italian, French, or Greek, when a noun ends in "a," the gender, in most cases, is feminine. In German, you just have to learn and memorize which of the three genders—*der, die, das*—represents a given noun, with no rhyme or reason. Anyway, I took a deep breath and carried on reading until the train stopped in the Thessaloniki station.

The family said good-bye, wished me good luck, and exited the compartment. The platform was crowded with people who were waiting to pick up relatives and others who were holding luggage and about to board the train. A few minutes later, two men and three women entered my compartment, stored their luggage in the overhead shelves, and introduced themselves in either German or English, neither of which I could speak or understand, except for a few words and phrases.

During the introductions, I understood that the two men were accompanying two of the women and the third woman was a German, traveling alone to Munich. When she told me that she spoke a little French, I drew a heavy sigh of relief. My understanding of French was also meager, despite five years of studying the language in high school, but it was good enough to carry on a conversation.

So, speaking in broken French, we managed to understand one another. Her name was Edith and she was an English teacher returning to Germany after a two-week stay in Greece.

In the early evening, the train left the Thessaloniki station and headed for the Yugoslavian border. Given the sound of the language the other two couples were speaking, I assumed they were either Serbs or Czechs. Edith, who sat next to me, was not what I would call a pretty woman, but she had a pleasant personality. Every time I asked her, "How do you say so-and-so in German?" she was eager to help.

Later on that evening, she had asked me if I wanted to go with her to the dining car to have dinner. I politely said no, I wasn't hungry, and she went alone. In truth, I was quite hungry, but I could not possibly afford dinner on the train. Furthermore, if I went to dinner with Edith, I probably would have had to pay for both of us, as I had been taught that a gentleman would never let a female companion pay for a meal. My funds were so limited that I had to be frugal.

I was so jealous when Edith and the two couples began conversing effortlessly in fluent English. The only word I understood was "okay." Back in high school, I had decided to take French instead of English—not that I particularly liked French, but I honestly disliked English because I could not clearly identify the separation of words. To my ears, it sounded as though all the words were monotonously bunched together.

Unfortunately, the school did not offer classes in Italian, a language so melodically romantic with succinctly pronounced words that its phrases tripped off the tongue like music. I called it *la lingua del'amore*—the language of love.

My French vocabulary was about average, but the only English words I knew could be counted on one hand. I had phonetically memorized the English lyrics of Doris Day's song "Que Sera, Sera," although I had no idea what the translation or the meaning was! I was sure that I possessed a definite aptitude for learning foreign languages rather quickly, my past deficiencies notwithstanding.

THREE GRAINS OF WHEAT

This time, I made a promise to myself that I would definitely make every effort to learn the German language and speak it fluently. When the two couples and Edith went to the dining car, I managed to have a little snack—bread and cheese that I kept in my suitcase. Well, this was really my dinner—and for the next three or four days, it would be the same menu choice for breakfast, lunch, and dinner. I did not mind it, because I had lived and survived in much worse situations, such as the period when I was sixteen years old, in the fifth year of high school.

Chapter 9

The Homeless Year

My fifth year in high school did not start on solid ground. During the first few weeks, my math teacher kept telling me repeatedly that he would not give me a passing grade at the end of the school year. I don't know what I had done to him to make him form such a negative opinion of me, but I must have annoyed him to the point that he had already stamped me with a failing grade. I did not want to go through the year under these conditions, so I decided to transfer to a night school.

In night school, I took the same fifth grade program that was designed for the working students, mostly adults who wanted to finish high school. The only difference—which was a big problem for me—was the mandatory tuition. The night school was not funded by the city.

When I told my father of my decision, he was utterly against it and insisted that I stick it out in day school, no matter the circumstances. He said emphatically, "If you go to night school, do not expect me to pay for it! You won't get any help from me; you will be on your own, and that's my final word."

I knew that if I carried out my decision, I would have to find a job to earn enough money to pay for rent, food, and tuition. Fortunately, within a few days, I found a job in a print shop. It paid just enough to cover my essential expenses, but I went ahead and transferred to night school.

For a period of four months, I was able to work and had time to study and attend school with ease and contentment. But alas, one day my boss told me that he had to let me go because he had been warned, after an official audit, that he had an under-aged sixteen-year-old in his employ. So ended my brief career as print shop apprentice!

Back in the village–which was sixty-five kilometers outside the city–my parents were not aware of my situation, for we'd had no communication since my last conversation with my father. So, I went back to job searching again.

Just before my hoarded funds were depleted, I found a job at a bookstore, selling books for a 20 percent commission. My customers were bi-monthly subscribers who had good paying jobs at various downtown establishments. In fact, most of my clients were executives who worked in the governor's building. In this much more lucrative job, I carried and sold new books via bicycle. Once a week, I met with my boss to hand over the proceeds, minus my commission.

Everything was going well until I woke up one morning to discover that the money I had collected the day before was missing from my wallet. I had counted the money oh-so-carefully and put it back in my wallet before I went to bed.

When I asked my roommate if he knew what had happened to the money, he said he had no idea. I reported the incident to my landlords, who were somewhat distant relatives, but they became defensive and began attacking me with abusive comments. I backed off and let it go—but how would I explain to my boss that I had not collected any money?

Out of desperation, I started altering the customer payment books by keeping two sets. I was certain that my roommate was the one who stole the money, and after he left to share a room with someone else, I was relieved. This time, I kept the gross proceeds in my pants pocket, always counting it before I went to bed. Despite my precautions, one morning, the money was again missing! This time I confronted the landlord's daughter and told her that someone in this house was stealing my money. Slamming the door behind me, I walked out of the house.

Things got worse. I decided to confide in my boss and try to explain to him calmly and rationally how someone in my boarding house was stealing the bulk of the gross proceeds. To my astonishment, he was waiting for me with a face full of rage and viciousness, as though he were ready to kill someone—probably me!

"What did you do?" he yelled, his wild eyes blazing. "I contacted a few of the customers, who claim that their payments are up to date. Why are you showing a balance in your ledger?

"Well, that's what I came here to explain ..." I said, my voice trembling.

"I don't want to hear your sniveling lies!" he hissed. "You stole the money and spent it with the so-called friends you've been hanging out with!"

"But, but ... p-please give me a chance to explain ..." I stammered.

By now, I was almost crying and begged him to listen. I will never forget how his daughter, who was sitting in the far corner of the store, broke down in tears and begged her father to stop treating me so viciously, but to no avail. He continued to threaten to call the police on me, and said that I would definitely be arrested. He said that I owed him 1000 drachmas, which was an astronomical amount for me at that time. He also made me sign an IOU acknowledging that I would return this kingly sum by September 30, which was less than six months from that day. Then he literally kicked me out of the store, spitting at me and yelling that he never wanted to see my hated face again.

Well, if I were in his position, I probably would have reacted similarly, but I could not forgive the fact that he had refused to give me a chance to explain the reason for the missing money. Deep down, he was a good man, I suppose, but the damage I had inadvertently caused to his established clientele was a big blow to his business.

I left the store that evening and skulked home like a wounded animal. I was frightened and worried about how I would find the money to pay back my boss in such a short time. What if my father found out? He would freak out, and I would face a second round of attacks. I feared that his wrath would be even worse than that of my boss.

On the way home, I remembered that I had confronted the landlord's daughter and held her family categorically accountable. I had insisted that someone in that household was stealing my money. I guess this was the final straw. Her parents were waiting for me when I got home from the bookstore.

Pointing his finger at me, her father shouted, "Gather your belongings and get out of here *right now!* You cannot call us thieves! God knows where you spent the money, and now you try to accuse us!" He was beside himself with anger, gesturing like a madman. "Out, out, get out of here!" he screeched, his voice rising to a fever pitch. "And go to hell!"

Get out I did. I hurriedly shoved all my belongings in a small bag and left at around 11:00 p.m. that night. I walked toward the beach and ended up in an old, abandoned shipyard. I sat on a broken wooden box, utterly confused and without any clear idea of what to do next. I was tired, both physically and emotionally, thinking that there was no justice in this world. What did I do to deserve this kind of treatment? I briefly reviewed the options I had. The first thought that crossed my mind was that perhaps my father had been right when he'd asked me to stick it out in the day school. I recalled his last words: "You're on your own."

Indeed, I was on my own—nowhere to go, nowhere to sleep, and nothing to eat that night. I dismissed the option of going back to my parents and apologizing for my decisions. I considered committing suicide, but this choice would even be more cowardly than going back to my parents.

I got up and headed toward a nearby park. Walking aimlessly through its lush avenues, I came across a bench in front of a thick row of bushes. Overtaken by all sorts of emotions, I sat down for a few minutes, ruminating over how best to face my uncertain future. I girded my loins and decided to confront first things first.

Okay, stay calm and take one problem at a time, I thought to myself. *First off, where will I spend the night, tonight?* I looked around and noticed a small clearing, covered by a layer of dry leaves, in the hedge of bushes behind the bench. That little clearing was adjacent to the medieval wall that surrounded the ancient city of Rhodes. I thought this natural, nest-like refuge would have to suffice as my temporary sleeping quarters.

Since I had no other choice, I crawled into my shelter and tried to make myself a little more comfortable by gathering handfuls of dry leaves to make a thicker base. I used my book bag as a pillow and tried to go to sleep.

I spent more than forty nights in this natural shelter. Sleeping outdoors, without any overcoat or blanket for protection during the frigid April nights, was almost unbearable. The cold wind pierced my shivering body, waking me up every five to ten minutes. Every night, I listened to the town clock and knew what time it was by the number of dings of the lonely-sounding bell.

I remember that one night, it was so cold that no matter how much I tried, I could not fall asleep. My sorrow and misery got the better of me, and I cursed my situation, pleading to God for mercy. *How many people at this moment are sleeping in comfortable beds?* I wondered, feeling supremely sorry for myself. *What about me? Don't I deserve it?*

Just then, I harkened to the melancholy tolling of the tower clock as it rang three times. I promised myself that, if I survived this ordeal, I would never forget this particular moment. I would remember it as the "three tower clock rings" and, similar to the grains of wheat, compare it with any future difficulty or obstacle, to remind me how much suffering or misery a person can endure. I will never, never forget that moment, as the echo of the pealing chimes has been permanently recorded in a non-erasable section of my memory!

I recall another time when a couple made out on the bench next to where I slept, and I witnessed the entire scene of their lovemaking. The reason that I'm mentioning this incident is because I knew the girl—she

31

was my ex-neighbor. When I met her a few days later, I told her that I'd had a dream in which I had seen and heard almost everything they said and did that night. To my amusement, she turned white as a ghost and almost fainted.

"This is spooky!" she said, her eyes wide as saucers. "Go away, go away! I'm afraid of you!"

I started my days by getting some decent sleep on the park bench when the sun was out and the temperature was just right for a late morning nap. Then I spent some time studying the day's homework. My food supplies were limited. In fact, there was a period of five to seven days during which I lived on a bag of peanuts.

Occasionally, I made a point to visit some friends or schoolmates around lunchtime so that they might offer me something to eat or invite me to lunch. However, most of the time, I was hungry, tired, exasperated, and disgusted with myself overall. I'd realized that I was hitting bottom and there was no light at the end of the tunnel. Despite all the difficulties I was going through, I managed to attend school regularly and kept my grades above average.

There was a water fountain near the bench, which I took advantage of to wash out my meager wardrobe: three sets of underwear, two pairs of socks, and two shirts. I did not bother washing my only jacket and pants because they would have shrunk and wrinkled to the point where I would have looked like a clown.

When I had a few drachmas to spare, I went to the Turkish baths and savored a couple of hours of bathing and relaxation in the cleansing steam. This was my one luxury, but I could not afford to do it often.

I will not forget one fateful afternoon when I bumped into Kostas, an acquaintance and ex-schoolmate from my previous year's day class. I hadn't seen him for a while. To my shock and surprise, he gave me a twenty-drachma bill that he supposedly owed me.

Although I did not remember lending him any money, I took it—after muttering a thousand thank-yous—and immediately ran to a delicatessen. I bought a large, freshly baked loaf of bread and a kilo of feta cheese and headed for my park bench, where I had my own version of a feast. The food tasted incredibly flavorsome to my deprived taste buds. I actually enjoyed it so much that it went down in history as the best meal I had during my homeless period!

Besides the mental and physical exhaustion I was going through, I also had to face my school tuition issue and come up with the money necessary to pay for the last two months of the year, May and June. It wasn't easy, but in order to make enough money to pay the tuition, I was forced to go around to the rundown tenements on the outskirts of the city, scrounging for scraps of metal, such as aluminum, copper, or bronze. I sold my findings to junkyard dealers for whatever cash I could get.

Fortunately, I managed to accumulate the two months' tuition and paid it in full. When I had some leftover money, I would go to a restaurant to have a bowl of bean soup with a few slices of bread. What a treat! I would devour it like a wolf, savoring every delicious spoonful. Unfortunately, the restaurant visits were not a daily event—perhaps once a week at the most.

There was another period when the only food I had to my name was a medium-sized bag of peanuts. For about six or seven days, I limited myself to a few peanuts a day, because I did not know how or when my next morsel would come.

One of the close friends I was hanging around with was my ex-neighbor, Takis, who was a person with great confidence and conviction. I always looked up to Takis, a city boy who was socially much more advanced than those of us who had been brought up in the village. One evening toward the end of May, my friend Takis' curiosity and suspicions about my true circumstances had become aroused.

He had noticed that I always found an excuse to avoid taking him to my place, which I had led him to believe was an apartment. He followed me to the park and almost broke into tears when he saw me crawling under the bushes and into my refuge. Well, that was the end of my outdoor living. He dragged me out of my lair, took me to his house, and arranged for me to stay with him for the rest of the school year. I asked him not to say anything to my parents until school was over, and he agreed.

At the end of the school year, my mother was beside herself when my good friend Takis told her everything. I had to calm her with my own explanation. "It was a good lesson I needed to learn for myself," I told her. "Fortunately, I survived this ordeal. I think it made me a stronger person." That same day, my mother and I took the bus headed for the village, where I spent the rest of the summer.

My father was made aware of the events that took place during that year, including the IOU for 1000 drachmas I had signed and had to pay by the end of September. To my surprise, he reacted calmly and assured me that he would take care of the debt. He said he believed that things would be fine from now on.

"The lessons you must have learned will have a much greater value than any amount of money or anything you could have learned in school," he said solemnly. "I'm convinced that you have just added another cornerstone block in the structure of your life." I was moved by his comments. Once again, I was reassured that my father was, in fact, a wise man!

Chapter 10

What's in Yugoslavia?

My agonizing memories of that dreadful year were interrupted when Edith and the two couples came back to the compartment and continued conversing in English. Again, the only words I could understand were "yes" and "okay."

At one point, Edith turned toward me and began conversing in French, trying to tell me that she was willing to offer any help I needed when we arrived in Germany. She gave me her personal/business card with her Bonn address and phone number, explaining that she would be visiting some friends in Munich and would be back in Bonn in about ten days. I made a mental note of that and placed her card safely in my wallet.

Early in the morning, the second day we were in Yugoslavia, we were riding through barren fields interrupted by some small, isolated villages here and there. There was not any worthwhile scenery to observe and enjoy on that stretch of the journey. Because I had hardly slept the night before, I attempted to lean on the windowsill to catch forty winks. But it was no use. My mind was again wandering back and forth, from my past experiences to my future prospects in Germany.

I tried to dismiss some negative thoughts, such as my fear that I would fail to get a work visa that would allow me to find a job and stay in the country for more than the allotted tourist visa. After all, I now had two leads in my possession: Edith, from Bonn, and my sister's pen pal, Niko, from Bornheim. Thinking of them sprinkled some optimistic comfort on my insecurities about being a stranger in a strange land.

Around mid-morning, the train stopped in a remote station in the middle of nowhere. We were told that this was a depot and that they had to re-supply the train with diesel fuel, water, food, and so forth. We were allowed to get out and walk around for about thirty minutes, but there wasn't anything worthwhile to see or do.

In the far distance, I could see a man and two dogs that were circling and guiding a flock of sheep in a specific direction, no doubt as part of their daily routine. There was a little candy store alongside the platform. I took a quick look to see if there was anything that I needed, but then I just walked by, hopped on the train, and headed for my compartment.

We still had another twenty minutes before departure. My fellow passengers were either outside or in the cantina having their afternoon coffee or tea break, a luxury I could not afford. My afternoon break was plain water. All of a sudden, a strong sensation of boredom overtook my senses. I did not know how to occupy my time, so I began pacing nervously in and out of the compartment.

At one point, I grabbed my German book and tried memorizing some words from a vocabulary chapter. But I couldn't concentrate, because the realization that I had left my home country overwhelmed my emotions.

A wave of melancholy, anger, and dejection swept over me. I felt it was unfair that I was not given the opportunity to establish a career in my own country. On the other hand, perhaps I was not as qualified as I should have been to compete with others for the few available jobs.

The one job position I had applied for, and truly wanted so much, was at a bank. I had seen an announcement in the newspaper that the bank planned to hire five full-time employees out of eighty-five applicants, who would be tested and evaluated in three different areas: accounting, math, and a written essay in the area of economics.

My first reaction to the ad was positive, for two reasons. First, I had just completed a nine-month course and obtained a diploma in accounting. Second, the president of the bank was my mother's uncle, and I envisioned that he might throw some crumbs my way. Boy, was I wrong!

They announced the results of the test by listing the names of the people who had competed and their final rank. Was it ironic that my name was in the sixth position, while only the first five were hired? Was it coincidence that the person who was placed first on the list had been sitting next to me and had copied some of my answers during the test? Or was it fate, destiny, or whatever intervening power was involved?

And what about my mother's uncle? When I confronted him and asked him to show me the test results, he claimed the papers had been shredded and there was no way to retrieve them.

After this dreadful setback, my self-confidence was shattered. I continued searching for another job, but the few available positions were of lesser social prestige and paid less than the one at the bank would have. At one point, I reluctantly applied for a guard's position at a museum. I could not believe it when I learned that they had selected someone else, who had only a sixth grade education! Again, in retrospect, whoever was watching over me did not let any of these employment possibilities materialize for some unknown reason. Perhaps he had other plans for me!

Having mentally reviewed all these job-related events, I took a deep breath and heaved a sigh of relief. It was as though I had suddenly received an inner boost of self-confidence, reminding me that I had already hit bottom and that the only way available to me was up. In the meantime, all the passengers boarded the train, and the strident whistle announced the train's departure as it headed toward the northern regions of Yugoslavia.

About mid-afternoon, the train stopped in Belgrade, the capital of Yugoslavia in the Serbian region. I thought the two couples in my compartment would get off, but they did not. I found out that they were traveling to Austria. Within fifteen minutes, the train departed, heading toward Zagreb, and then continued toward the Austrian borders.

Around sundown, Edith insisted that I accompany her to the dining car. This time, she was so adamant that I could not politely decline her invitation—she practically dragged me out of the compartment! We sat down and a waiter brought us our menus, which had limited items written in English and a form of Slavic.

I asked Edith to help me understand the menu, and she recommended a few dishes. She placed the order for both of us, but I had no idea what kind of food I was about to get. The only clue I had was when she made the sound of a pig when she was trying to explain my entrée. Because we frequently couldn't understand one another, our conversation—in both French and German—was accompanied by a lot of hand gestures and distinctive vocal inflections to illustrate words or sentences.

When the waiter arrived with the food, he also brought two glasses of red wine. I was caught off guard about the wine; my immediate concern was how much this dinner would ultimately cost. Edith must have sensed my concern, because she immediately said the dinner was her treat.

I was somewhat relieved—after all, I was not prepared to spend a fortune on one meal. But on the other hand, it did not feel right that a woman should pay for my dinner. The bottom line was, I was having a good time and truly enjoyed Edith's company.

The meal was some sort of pork cutlet with gravy over a toasted slice of bread with black beans and potatoes on the side. Despite our communication barrier, Edith made me understand that, when I had settled in

Germany, she was willing to teach me German. In exchange, I could teach her Greek.

What a wonderful idea, I thought! I said, excitedly in German, "*Ja mag ich es,*" which means, "I like it." Edith responded in German, pronouncing each word slowly: "*Sehr gut, mein freund, du sprischt Deutches gut,*" which translates to "Very good, my friend, you speak German well."

I cracked a satisfied smile and looked intently at Edith, who was taking the last sip of her wine from a long-stemmed glass. She was about five feet seven, with short, dirty blonde hair, light blue eyes, and a well-proportioned, slender physique. She was not what I would consider a pretty lady, but her charming, giggly personality made her nothing less than a beautiful person in my eyes.

When she offered me another glass of wine, I told her that I'd had enough, but she went ahead and ordered one for herself. We continued our broken conversation, but there came a point when we were just staring at one another, and our eyes were saying more than the words and sentences we could muster. At one point during the silent conversation, I was certain that she was reading my thoughts—and she had definitely given me a tacit "yes." You've guessed it!

I had a good feeling about that lady. My intuition was leading me to believe that Edith was a worthwhile and splendid individual, someone I would like to know better, if and when I was settled in Germany. She reminded me once more that she would get off the train in Munich before she went home to Bonn. She also told me that she would spend the night in the sleeper car—a little compartment with a bed and shared restroom facilities. This was an optional amenity and another luxury I could not afford.

We left the restaurant and went to our compartment, where Edith stopped to pick up a few things from her suitcase. She said goodnight and headed for the sleeper car.

It was about 10:00 p.m. and, surprisingly, the other two couples were not in the compartment. Perhaps they had decided to spend the night in the sleeper car as well. I thought it would be great to have the entire compartment to myself, using the three seats to stretch out on and try to get some sleep.

I was tired and felt sure I would sleep like a log—but again, I tossed and turned while attempting to dismiss my thoughts and annoying concerns. No matter how hard I tried, I could not sleep. Finally, I sat up and stared out the window. Every now and again, I would spot a few dim lights in the far distance that broke the monotony of the gloomy, nocturnal scene.

While staring at the darkness, my mind started wandering again, drifting back and forth between my early years and my time in high school. I kept thinking of the event when my teacher in the third grade took away the notebook that he had awarded me. I tried to identify the impact this incident had on my behavior and the development of my personality in the following years. I know that, after that incident, I became a bitter person. I was violent at times and had the desire to destroy things or kill animals, without shame or regret.

During a period of two years, between the ages ten and twelve, I was the leader of a gang of three boys that had formed two or three years earlier. When we, the original gang members, were eleven years old, we added two associates who were one or two years younger than we were. Up until we graduated from sixth grade in elementary school, the gang stuck together. We were labeled as the bad guys of the village. We were blamed for every destructive act, catastrophe, and misadventure that befell the village, whether we had done it or not.

Truth to tell, we *were* guilty of most of the accusations. I personally was a restless individual. As a gang, we spent most of our free time out in the fields, hunting birds, or up in the mountains, exploring caves. We did not care who owned a particular vegetable garden, fruit tree grove, or chicken coop. We considered them community property. We took anything we liked and destroyed the things we disliked. My father could not keep up with the complaints he was getting about me, and I felt the stinging wrath of his belt more times than I can recall.

The pleasure of committing these various acts of mischief far outweighed the threat of the known or unknown consequences of my punishment. I was mean to animals and any living thing that moved. The gang and I thought it was an amusing incident when we set a cat on fire and ran into a house with it, causing a lot of damage. When I attended funerals, I felt no sorrow for the deceased or the grieving family. Instead, I just saw death as another ordinary event.

I was fully aware of my bad reputation and the opinion everyone had of me. However, I never stopped exploring new areas of interest. I was convinced that nothing was impossible if I wanted it badly enough.

I will never forget an overwhelming desire I had one night, as I was standing next to the band playing at a wedding reception. I admired the way the violinist, who was named Kyriako, guided the bow so expertly over the strings. I was fascinated by the supple movement of his fingers as they danced upon the frets and the melodic sound that emerged from that magical, little, wooden box. As young as I was, I wanted to have a violin and be able to play like him. That thought and desire overtook my entire existence, and I could not get it out of my mind.

The following day, I began making my own violin, which I called a *lyra* (the name they called the violin in my village). First, I took a flat plank of wood and hammered four nails at each end. Then, I twisted four pieces of wire on the nails at one end, stretched them tightly to the opposite end, and tied them. For the bow, I cut some hairs from our horse's tail and stretched them between the ends of a small stick. Now I was ready to play my lyra. Alas, when I pulled the bow over the strings, just as the violinist had, no sound came out. I was so disappointed! I tried again and again, harder and harder each time, but to no avail.

I decided to take my instrument to Kyriako's, house and ask him why I couldn't get any sound. He looked at my creation and started laughing at first, but then he told me that this was an imaginative creation for my age. He also explained that I needed some rosin to brush the bow hairs a few times to make them coarser, so that they would produce friction.

I didn't understand his explanation, but he used his own rosin stick on my bow. Then a sound came out of my lyra—a tentative sound, certainly, and not particularly pleasant to the ears. But it produced a sound, nonetheless. He also told me that I could use resin, the dry sap of pine trees, to prime my bow. I was so happy and proud of my invention, my homemade lyra, that it kept me occupied and amused for a while. Then, inevitably, I switched to another interesting activity.

As I recall, it was mid-afternoon on a cloudy day in the early spring of 1944 when we heard a loud boom up on the mountain ridge, about a kilometer outside the village. A throng of people ran to the scene and witnessed the carnage of a military plane crash.

The plane was split into two pieces. Three dead German soldiers lay on the ground, their broken bodies twisted into obscene shapes. I observed the scene with amazement. This was the first time I had ever seen a wrecked plane, but what caught my attention was some of the adults, who were searching the pockets of the dead soldiers.

They took their watches and anything valuable the men had been wearing. One man broke two gold teeth from the bloody mouth of one of the soldiers, an act I thought was disgusting. I kept my cool, despite the macabre scene. You see, I was mentally making my own plans to revisit the crash site to take something I could use or play with.

The following day, my gang and I went back to the crash site and observed many other people who were ripping apart and taking parts of the plane, probably for some personal use. My plan was to build a rifle, so we found a few long pipes and took them back to the village.

It took us a few days, but we managed to make the rifle by first securing the pipe on a piece of carved, round wood, which served as the stock.
Then, as a firing pin, we put a long, sharp nail inside a spring; we placed
the spring inside another small pipe, and secured it at the end of the carved
wood.

The rest was simple: we placed a bullet in the chamber of the barrel,
pulled the spring back, and by releasing it, the sharp firing pin hit the bullet, thus engaging the firing mechanism. Toward the end of the war, bullets
were plentiful around the abandoned Italian army base. We used them to
shoot birds and rabbits, or for just plain target shooting.

When the war was over, we visited the army base quite often either to
get ammunition for our homemade gun or to find something valuable that
the soldiers might have left behind. I remember the hapless fellow, seventeen years young, who was not so lucky when he tried to disarm a bomb.
The bomb exploded, blowing his guts and limbs to kingdom come. It goes
without saying, he died instantly. What a tragedy!

His dog ran toward him, licked his bloody face, and, lifting his head
skyward, let loose a long, mournful howl. Then the poor beast dropped on
the ground and died alongside him. I ask you, was that true love for his
master, or what?

As I recollected this grim scene, I shuddered involuntarily. I shook my
head and wondered how I had survived during those dangerous and trying
times. How had I cheated death when I spent my childhood playing with
all sorts of ammunition, guns, grenades, and sundry other surplus explosives from the war? Again, I felt that perhaps someone had always been
beside me, shielding me with a protective wing to keep me out of harm's
way.

It was already early morning. After two full days of traveling, I had
hardly gotten any sleep. I was physically and mentally exhausted. I was
sleepy, but I could not fall asleep while the train was moving. I was always
like this, unable to sleep on any moving form of transportation. I convinced myself to be patient for a little while longer, because in less than
twenty-four hours, I would be arriving in Bonn. There, I would definitely
be able to rest comfortably in the soft bed of a hotel room.

Chapter 11

Restoration in Austria

The train chugged its way toward Salzburg in Austria, a picturesque city located at the northern boundary of the Alps. Salzburg is the birthplace of Wolfgang Amadeus Mozart. In a zigzag manner, the train circled a mountain downward to reach the city, which was situated in the valley below. What a beautiful setting! Nestled in the valley, with a pair of smaller mountains towering overhead, Salzburg looked like a storybook city. It was a truly fascinating and stunning sight.

We pulled into the station, where we would have a thirty-minute layover. I took advantage of the stop to amble through a nearby street in the downtown district, where most of the buildings, including the many churches, were masterpieces of ornate baroque architecture. What a difference from my country's simple building style, influenced by the classic lines of Doric, Ionic, and Corinthian architecture. Unlike the Gothic style in Salzburg, many of the larger churches in Greece, as well as the public official buildings, are distinctive because of their columnar features. Their neoclassical style later influenced many American capital buildings.

I sat on a bench near a narrow waterway, watching the ducks gliding back and forth as if they were powered by batteries. I admired the manicured bushes and the robust, masterfully pruned trees. A little farther away, the tall buildings looked as if they had been landscaped against the tall mountain in the background. This idyllic scene reminded me of the day that I saw the city of Rhodes for the first time.

I was eleven years old when our fifth grade schoolteacher in the village organized a one-day bus trip around the island. Up until that day, I had not ventured farther than six kilometers from the village, which was situated in the middle of the island. Our first stop was at a beach near some ancient ruins, where I saw the Aegean Sea at close proximity for the first time. I'd had no idea—and could not possibly have conceived—that the sea would be such a huge expanse, a vastness of blue water that touched the horizon!

The way I had pictured the sea was based on the only image I could see, twenty kilometers away from the house in the village: a narrow strip of grayish color attached to the end of the horizon. Therefore, I thought the sea was just a fifty- to one hundred-meter waterway where boats and larger vessels would sail around the island. That was how it looked in my geography book, when a map showed water around an island.

The true dimensions of the sea were revealed, as we got closer. I was in awe! Since the water was rather shallow, our teacher let us frolic in the waves, keeping a watchful eye on us from ten meters up the beach. What a sight! I was experiencing amazing discoveries for the first time, which made my imagination run wild to a future full of wonders and wider horizons.

The next stop was the city of Rhodes, where we visited many areas of interest, such as the museum, the castle, a picturesque harbor, and other spots we could fit into our tight schedule. I was truly fascinated, especially by the harbor and all the boats, small and large. I could not stop staring at the small fish that were swimming in the shallow waters, just below the concrete walkway.

We left the city around noontime and headed for the southern part of the island. We stopped at every village. The most interesting spot for me was the acropolis in the village of Lindos; it was another ancient structure, a natural citadel that had been fortified successively by the Greeks and Romans. The acropolis offered us a spectacular view of the surrounding harbors and the coastline.

As we continued our day trip through the rest of the villages along the east coast, my mind focused exclusively on the new places I was seeing and the fascinating moments I was lucky enough to experience. During the remaining bus ride, I was convinced, beyond a shadow of a doubt, that nothing or nobody would be able to keep me in the village. I was not willing to receive the baton passed from my father, as it were, to carry on the traditional family occupation of farming.

The thought of leaving the village repeated itself like a broken record in my memory. I already had concluded that the horizons outside the village were much wider than I had expected. I resolved to make every effort to overcome any obstacles for the sake of exploring new possibilities.

These same types of thoughts were going through my mind during our stopover in Salzburg. Now I had left my country and I was again experiencing wider horizons in a much bigger world. I felt the architectural and natural delights of that wonderful Austrian city were perhaps a small sample of what I would find in Germany.

As I rose from the bench and headed toward the train, I took a deep breath and exhaled a sigh of contentment. I was truly so grateful. I thanked God for granting me the privilege to explore and enjoy all these foreign places.

When I boarded the train and entered my compartment, I noticed that, besides Edith, there were four new passengers. One was a small, handicapped child, three or four years old, who seemed to be traveling with his parents and grandfather. I greeted them with a few words I knew in German, such as *guten tag*, which means "good day," and they responded the same way.

The train left Salzburg, heading north toward the next scheduled stop—Munich, where Edith was to disembark. Edith started conversing with the other passengers in German, but only the husband and wife were talking. The older man remained silent. At one point, Edith told me that the old man was Greek and was traveling with his son, daughter-in-law, and his little grandson, Nicholas, to Cologne. I started talking to the older man in Greek and his overall demeanor changed from quiet to talkative and happy.

He explained that his son had married an Austrian lady and that little Nicholas was born with some kind of brain disorder, leaving him almost paralyzed on his left side. The doctors in Salzburg had encouraged them to pursue a new surgical procedure that was being practiced successfully at a clinic in Cologne, which offered a potentially promising cure for Nicholas' problem. I told him how sorry I was, seeing a helpless child in that condition, and that I would pray for a successful outcome.

I was totally consumed by the little boy's problem the rest of the way to Munich. At one point, I noticed his mother trying to change the boy's wet diaper and assumed that he'd had a little accident while napping. The mother and father tried to apologize for the unpleasant incident, but I told the father, who also spoke Greek, that I was not at all bothered and that I totally understood what the boy was going through.

In the meantime, while the boy was crying, the mother mumbled a few words in German and the father commented exasperatedly, in Greek, "How long will we go through this? When is he going to stop?"

"Please, listen to me for a moment!" I interjected. "I went through the same phase when I was young. Be patient with him; in time he will stop!"

My tone was stern and emphatic and I meant every word, because I had indeed known the humiliation of a weak bladder.

They just nodded and then everyone was quiet, a silence that lasted a long time. Even Edith wasn't talking. I closed my eyes and for a moment or two, I mentally reviewed the incident with the boy and exhaled a sigh of empathy. I silently prayed, wished, and hoped that the boy would not go through what I went through. This incident brought back some unpleasant and distasteful memories of my younger years, a period that had left some permanent scars on my self-esteem.

I have to admit that, up until I was around thirteen or fourteen years old, I was a bed-wetter. I tried almost everything my parents and relatives suggested. I stopped drinking any liquids after dinner and made every effort to wake up before the disgraceful occurrence, but to no avail.

Almost every night, when my grandmother touched my wet pants, I would get a gentle spanking on my behind, and she would force me to get up to change clothes. It was awful. I had to endure this ordeal for many years, the worst of which was in the seventh and eighth grade, when I was in the city and away from my parents.

Since the village did not offer any classes beyond the sixth grade, I had to move to the city to attend six years of high school (seventh through twelfth). During those years, I lived with one or two other roommates, sharing a rented room in private homes. My roommates and the landlady were aware of my problem, and I have to say that all of them were very understanding. They never made any comments about either the odor or the unpleasant sights that resulted from my problem.

The most embarrassing part of the situation was when I came home from school. The first thing I saw was my mattress hanging over the open window. My landlady was so nice to me and treated me as if I were one of her children, so she made sure that my mattress was dry by the end of the day.

I was miserable and ashamed when I had to face people who knew about my problem. Many times, I ran out of clean clothes and was forced to wear long pants without underwear. Though the rental homes had an outhouse, the only available bathing facilities were the Turkish baths that I was using four or five times a month.

To keep me supplied with food, my parents were sending me a package of goods every Sunday; in turn, every Tuesday I was sending back the dirty clothes, empty containers, and so forth. The packages were transported on the crated roof of the bus that traveled from and to the village on a daily basis. Every Sunday, all the students from the village would convene near the bus stop under our usual tree, a place that became our social rendezvous, as we awaited the bus' arrival.

The train whistle interrupted my thoughts and I realized we had arrived in Munich, where Edith was preparing to leave. I was almost certain I would see her again—at least, I would do my best to get in touch with her once she got back to Bonn. When the train finally stopped, Edith got her belongings, put on her raincoat, and stretching her arms wide, engulfed me in a big hug.

"*Auf wiedersehen*," she said, which means, "See you soon again."

I responded, "*Au revoir*," which has the same meaning in French.

Carrying her suitcase, I escorted her to the exit door and then down to the station platform, where two ladies greeted her. She said good-bye again and left with her two friends, slowly disappearing on the crowded platform, which was teeming with humanity.

With Edith gone, I felt sad. She had been my first German connection, my first encouraging link to a new country. Her friendship had been almost like a security blanket.

I slowly reentered the train and went to my compartment. The family with the boy remained, but now there was a new passenger who had taken Edith's seat. I greeted him in German and sat down. It was late afternoon. We had one more stop in Frankfurt, and then we were scheduled to arrive in Bonn around 2:30 a.m.

For some unknown reason, I began to feel that this last leg of the trip was the most agonizing part. Perhaps it was a combination of Edith's absence and the rainy weather during the evening hours. As I rested my chin in my palms, I recollected that I only had a one-way ticket to Germany, which meant that I absolutely had to overcome any challenges and reach my goal.

When the boat had left the harbor in Rhodes and I had waved good-bye to my friends and relatives, I did not feel that I was abandoning anything worthwhile. Despite my efforts to succeed in my hometown, there had always been some obstacles that prevented me from securing a good job and getting settled.

All of a sudden, I had the feeling that our future is predetermined. I convinced myself that there had to be some invisible power that controlled my destiny. These thoughts conjured up memories that have some bearing on the notion that time is flat and that there must be another dimension of life we cannot perceive or comprehend.

******

Young Love

My first "puppy love" was in the village. The girl, named Sevasti, was beautiful. Moreover, she was aware of her desirability and magnetism, because there were four of us who were attracted by her charms and who pursued her with passion and determination. Sevasti was a teaser, but each of us thought that we were the only one she fancied and that we each had her exclusive interest and secret love. Just saying "Merry Christmas" or shaking her hand produced an electrifying sensation that kindled my awakening feelings of romantic love.

When I was in the eighth grade in the city, I wrote a love letter, enclosed it in an envelope, and addressed it to my sister with instructions to give it to Sevasti. I wrote the letter on a Monday night and sent it on Tuesday afternoon. That night, I dreamed I received a letter back from Sevasti in which she expressed her loving feelings for me, saying that she could not wait to see me. In my dream, I was ecstatically in love and considered myself the luckiest person in the world.

However, there was a postscript at the bottom of the letter, a sheet of paper whose upper right corner was torn and missing. She explained: "P.S. Sorry for the torn sheet, this was the last one I had in my possession."

When I woke up, I was deliriously happy and I could not wait for her response. However, in those days, all communication with my family was enclosed in the food bags we sent back and forth by bus. On Sundays, I would receive food supplies and clean clothes from the village. On Tuesdays, I would send back my dirty clothes, along with a letter and any messages.

When I picked up my bag from the bus stop on Sunday, I hurriedly tore open the only letter I found inside the bag, which was from my father. When I opened the envelope, I noticed that the upper right corner of the sheet was missing. With great disappointment, I started reading his harsh and critical words. He explained that he had confiscated the letter I sent to Sevasti and that my brash behavior and my mixed-up priorities made him angry. He almost ordered me to forget all about girls and love letters and concentrate on my studies.

Incredibly, he finished the letter with exactly the same postscript I had seen in my dream: "P.S. Sorry for the torn sheet, this was the last one I had in my possession."

Was that a coincidence? I had seen the missing corner of the letter in my dream on Tuesday night, whereas my father wrote his letter to me the following Saturday. I don't think that such a minute detail can be coincidental. To my mind, this was evidence of some strange, paranormal phenomenon or a cosmic power that logic cannot explain away.

Perhaps my dream of the future was viable proof of a rare ability that enables some of us to see the future, as if time really were flat. I had to agree with Einstein's theory that time is an illusion. Specifically, past, present, and future coexist simultaneously on a flat plane; therefore, some people might possess the ability to access any part of that flat level of reality.

As I thought about the food bags I received every Sunday, a terrible memory flashed through my mind from my last year of high school. That year, my two sisters, Despina and Mary, and Tess—one of their friends who also was attending school—rented a two-room apartment with me. The three girls slept in the larger room and I took the smaller, adjacent room.

As time went on, I started noticing that Tess' interest in me went beyond that of a mere roommate. Oftentimes, she tiptoed into my room and tried to get close and intimate. She even tried to sleep with me one night, but I pushed her away and told her not to bother me again. I explained that she was just my roommate and I had no feelings for her otherwise. She left my room in tears.

Later on that night, I realized I had been too direct and insensitive, but I could not see her as a woman with whom I cared to start any type of relationship. In fact, I found her character and overall behavior repulsive. Besides her direct approach, her physical attributes also lacked a few commonly accepted feminine qualities; she was tall and skinny as a stick, with equal small measurements from the chest to her hips.

After a few weeks, Tess apparently resigned herself to the fact that I was not interested and decided to move to another place for the rest of the school year. Soon after that, I received a letter from my father saying that he was ashamed of me because I had supposedly stolen the money from Tess' bag that her father had sent to her. My father's angry note went on to say that if this claim were true, he did not want to see me again.

Although I had been kind enough to transport her food bag every Sunday, Tess had used this as a way to get even with me for rebuffing her advances. She had informed her father that I took the money before I brought her bag home.

I could not let this deceitful act stick out like a thorn in our family's reputation, so I decided to rent a motorbike and drive to the village to talk to my father, face-to-face. As the motorbike puttered along, I actually looked forward to confronting my father and anyone else who believed that I was capable of stealing. When I finally arrived, I met my father, who started the interrogation with a question. "Why would she claim that the money was missing, if you did not take it?"

I explained that she wanted to get even with me because I had rejected her sexual advances and all her attempts to become intimate with me.
"Please, father!" I pleaded. "Believe me, this is the truth!"

My father leaned slightly toward believing me, but he suggested that
we speak to the priest before he decided what to do. We found the priest in
church, and told him the entire story, including the girl's accusation. The
priest took my hand, led me in front of the icons of Jesus Christ and the
Virgin Mary, and exclaimed aloud, "In the name of our Lord, would you
swear that you did not commit this crime?"

"I swear, and God be my witness, that I did not do it!" I cried righ-
teously. "If I did this foul deed, I'm asking God right now to strike me with
a bolt of fire so that I may die."

"I believe my son," my father said solemnly.

"I believe him, too ," the priest concurred. "He is telling the truth."

After these trying moments, we went home and had a traditional dinner of lamb stew and homemade pasta, customary for the last day before
Lent. The following morning was rainy, and it was a nightmarish ordeal to
ride the rented motorbike back to the city. But my father's restored faith
in me made pedaling the stalled motorbike for twenty-five miserable kilometers bearable.

Tess's father did not speak to my father for several years after this
incident. However, one day he approached my father and apologized for
the accusation and admitted that his daughter had made it all up. My father
told him that he had known that all along.

The Tray Incident

I have digressed from the aforementioned unexplained phenomena, but
the following incident is worth mentioning. After high school graduation, I
found a summer job at a hotel. One of the maids, named Chloe, was beautiful; I developed an infatuation for her that grew stronger as time went on.
In fact, I wrote a lovely poem for her, but I never gave it to her. The poem
is entitled "Her Picture," translated from the Greek "Η Ζωγραφιά της." I
knew she liked me, or perhaps even loved me—but whatever the feeling
was, our relationship remained a warm, platonic affection.

Then one fateful night, everything changed between us. A few minutes
before midnight, I was helping her bring in a few chairs from the patio.
It was her turn to sleep in that evening, but before going to her room, she
headed for the kitchen to get a glass of water. All the lights were off as we
entered a small dining area adjacent to the kitchen.

When Chloe flicked on the light switch, a tray containing a few coffee
cups flew off the table and ended up on the floor, upside down. Chloe be-

came hysterical. She put her arms around my neck and clinched her body against mine, shaking like a leaf and shouting words of fear and desperation. Her soft hair grazed my cheek and I could feel her heart pounding against my chest like a drum beat.

"What was that? Who did it?" she wailed as she squeezed me even tighter.

"Don't worry, it was nothing, I'm here for you," I cooed, trying to calm her down. "I will protect you. Just relax."

I did not know what had caused the tray to fall off the table, but for the time being, this was neither my concern nor a priority. In fact, in some strange way, I was glad that this incident had occurred. I was truly in ecstasy and overjoyed. Holding Chloe against my body was one of the most delightful and passionate sensations I had ever felt.

When she calmed down and I came back to reality from my rapture, we tried to find a logical explanation for what had caused the tray to fall off the table. The surface of the table was not wet; there weren't any animals in the hotel; and the little dining area where the incident occurred had no windows. In other words, neither man nor beast could have gained admittance to the room to upset the tray.

The only remaining conclusion was that the phenomenon had something to do with spirits or ghosts. Understandably, Chloe didn't want to accept the incident as a paranormal episode, because this was the workplace where she spent many nights, alone in the maid's room on the first floor.

When we went to her room, I urged her to lie down and get some sleep. Sitting in a chair next to her bed, I assured her I would stay with her all night. I told her that I would be her personal guard and that nothing and nobody would bother her. After she was settled in bed, I covered her with a light blanket, and ever so gently held her hand for reassurance. Soon, her heavy lids began to flutter, her breathing slowed down, and before long, she drifted off to sleep.

I remember those moments clearly, because I was experiencing one of the most extraordinary nights of my life. Holding the hand of my dream girl, sitting next to her, gazing at her angelic face, admiring her long, golden blonde hair that was spread all over the pillow, was one of the most unforgettable nights—a blissful night I wished would last forever.

I continued sitting next to her, but never, never for even a moment, did I think of taking advantage of her vulnerability and fear by betraying her trust in me. Instead, I took great delight in counting her breaths—one … two … three—and watching the rhythmic rise and fall of her enchanting bosom. When I got to one hundred, I would start all over again.

At one point, she turned toward me for a brief moment, touched my hand, and thanked me for being there with her. I believed I was living through the shortest night ever. I didn't want the night to end, but soon the birds started singing in the neighboring garden and the dawning light was sneaking through a gap in the unevenly drawn curtain.

Chloe woke up and thanked me over and over again, but unfortunately, I knew it was time for me to go home. I told her that I would see her in three or four hours and left with an enormous smile on my face.

After a few hours of sleep, I couldn't wait to go back to the hotel. When I arrived, I went to see my boss to explain what had happened the night before. His first reaction was, "Did you tell anyone about this?"

I said that I hadn't and asked him why he was so concerned about me telling someone, instead of trying to help us understand what actually could have happened. He said that he did not want to scare the hotel guests with any preposterous notions that the hotel might be haunted.

He paused for a moment and then, wagging his finger in my face, he said, "You know what? On second thought, I don't think I need your services anymore. You're fired!"

I was incredulous. "What did I do? Why are you firing me?"

"Just go, go! I want to protect my business. Go find another job," he said angrily.

And that was the end of my short summer employment at the Ethnikon Hotel. However, a few days later, I met up with the hotel's chef and explained to him that I had been fired right after I'd described the incident with the tray. He said that there had been many other similar, unexplained incidents. He said the boss was aware of the situation but did not want the word to get out that, in addition to guests, ghosts also occupied his hotel.

I was satisfied with the chef's explanation and life went on, as it usually does. The only thing I kept from that hotel was the sweet memory of Chloe and the shortest night of my life. The "tray incident" remains an unexplained mystery I've never been able to unravel.

Chapter 12

Germany, Here I Come

O
ur last stop before Bonn was Frankfurt. When the train stopped, a vendor boarded the train selling assorted bags of chips, pretzels, and other goodies. I indulged myself and bought a bag of what turned out to be very salty pretzels. I was rather hungry and ate plenty of those tasty, salty little curlicues.

I remained in my seat, but after we left the station, I felt extremely tired. I tried desperately to get some sleep. Once again, I could not dismiss my thoughts. The memories of my troublesome high school years popped in and out of consciousness. Sleep just wouldn't come as I leaned on the windowsill, so I let my weary mind traipse back to the past.

I hoped that, by pinpointing the period that was the origin or the pivotal reason behind my many unsuccessful attempts to accomplish something of value or recognition, I might find some long-sought answers. And so, I began reviewing my high school years and the period after graduation.

Starting the Race

In the seventh, eighth, and ninth grades, I was an average student. Although I did my homework every day, I spent many hours either in the city library or at the stadium. In the library, I read hundreds of books that I found to be much more interesting than the school textbooks.

I thought it was a waste of time to have classes in ancient Greek two hours a day, in a format that required students to translate the text from classic to modern Greek. These exercises were easy, because there were plenty of unauthorized translation booklets students could buy and use. My fellow scholars and I passed those classes with flying colors, but we did not learn anything about the essence, the message, or the meaning of the immortal words the great Greek philosophers wrote.

Even at that young age, I realized that this was the wrong method of teaching—not only in ancient Greek, but in other subjects as well. The teachers emphasized memorization, but in doing so, we were losing the meaning of the lesson.

Most students who were from a village were considered second-class citizens, so to speak. We did not have the self-confidence to compete with the city boys in sports or in social or academic activities. Our wardrobe limitations also separated us from the well-dressed city boys, whose families could afford expensive clothes. Their outgoing personalities overshadowed any attempt we made to be included in their circle. The city boys did not accept us "country bumpkins" as part of their elite group; thus we were excluded from all team sports and other social events. Even our gym teacher indirectly influenced that exclusion.

Having accepted this social injustice, I decided to spend a great deal of time in the stadium alone, exercising in various track and field events. My favorites were three- to ten-kilometer races and the pole vault. Sometimes I practiced with experienced runners; they ensured me that I was doing well and that I was ready to compete in a five-kilometer race for adults.

One Sunday afternoon, I was one of ten runners poised five kilometers away from the stadium, ready to begin a race during halftime of a soccer match. There was a light drizzle when the race began. I felt great and I was leading after three kilometers, but all of a sudden, I felt a sharp pain in my stomach and started crouching as I slowed down considerably.

The medics in the emergency vehicle that was following the runners determined that I had stomach cramps; they picked me up and dropped me off outside the stadium. I was so embarrassed when I spotted my friends, who had been waiting to see me, among the other runners, triumphantly entering the stadium. Instead, they saw me staggering out of the car, the picture of humiliation and defeat.

I knew what had caused my stomach cramps—the hearty lunch I had enjoyed before receiving an impromptu invitation to participate in the race—but it didn't matter anymore. I gave up competitive running for good. Now I wondered what impact that period had on the framework of my personality.

Our high school building, named the Venetokleion Boys Gymnasium, was located across from an elementary school building. The high school for girls was one kilometer away. During a class break one day, I spotted a strikingly beautiful girl who was a few years younger than I was.

A few days later, I learned where she lived. Her friends called her Bemba and she was attending sixth grade. During my high school years, I came to know Bemba and her family and tried to get closer to her, but she always kept her distance from me. I wrote many poems for her, but the aloof creature habitually shrugged her shoulders every time I tried to be a little romantic.

As time went on, Bemba blossomed into a breathtakingly beautiful woman whose seductive charms turned the head of every hot-blooded Greek male whose path she crossed. I began to realize that, for the second time, a chord was struck from the harp of Cupid (or was it Eros?), who gently opened a bigger window in the realm of my heart.

My best friend, Dimitri, and I were always consulting one another, no matter the difficulty or the risk level, before we got in and out of trouble. I will supply more details about Dimitri's friendship in later chapters, but just to paint a small picture of him, I can honestly say that he was then, and remains today, a man of his word.

Dimitri had dropped out of school in the ninth grade to go into business with his brother. They succeeded in every step they took and every decision they made and ultimately became wealthy, to say the least. But even with his accumulated wealth, Dimitri remained a down-to-earth person who frequently got together with people regardless of social or economic status, either for dinner or just for a drink.

The Romantic in Me

So, going back to my story, I decided to write a letter to Bemba. I consulted Dimitri to determine how we could send the note without getting her into any sort of trouble with her parents. In addition to many romantic expressions of love about Bemba, the content of the letter included a poem I had written about her, emphasizing her attractiveness by comparing it with Aphrodite's beauty.

Dimitri volunteered to deliver the letter in person, but as this option seemed downright unromantic, we dismissed it right away. We finally decided to mail the letter to the school she was attending. We addressed it simply to "Bemba" in care of her school. (I found out much later that "Bemba" was a nickname. I never learned what her real first name was. My first hunch was "Maria," but even as of this writing, I'm not absolutely sure.)

Anyway, Bemba's older sister later informed me about what had happened to my letter. The school principal had read it aloud, right after the morning prayer gathering in the schoolyard. Her sister said that Bemba had been humiliated in front of all the students and teachers, and did not want to see me ever again.

Dimitri and I realized that sending that letter to Bemba's school had been a foolhardy idea, and both of us tried to find ways to mend fences by going back to square one and starting over again. In spite of my sincere intentions and genuine attempts to approach Bemba, so that I could explain that I had done all those crazy things out of love and desperation, she maintained an unwavering silence for a long, long time. I was not left with any other viable options, so I tried to put her out of my mind. It wasn't easy.

At last, I closed the window that Cupid had opened and placed Bemba in an inactive corner of my heart. Life went on without her, but I will talk about subsequent developments regarding our relationship in later chapters.

I had first noticed Bemba when she was in sixth grade. During this period, our music teacher, whose teaching methods were both enjoyable and effective, had a strong influence on me. For every lesson, Mr. Zygouris accompanied us on his accordion while we read and sang the notes of the day's lesson out loud.

Just to give you an idea how much I enjoyed his classes, I can tell you that, even as of this writing, I still remember and can recite the notes on the tenth page of my music book: sol, fa, mi, fa, sol, do, sol, fa, mi, and so on. I must thank the talented and dedicated Mr. Zygouris, who enabled me to make music a part of my artistic expression, an attribute that I've subsequently shared and passed on to others.

Ever since the time I built my own violin, good ole Lyra, I have considered music one of my artistic outlets and special hobbies. Spiro, one of my neighbors and fellow students, purchased a mandolin and started learning how to play. I was fascinated by that instrument and spent a great deal of time in his house, where I was given the opportunity to learn and play the mandolin as well. Spiro was kind enough to share his mandolin with me, but after a few months, I sensed that his parents were getting a little annoyed with me for spending so much time in their house. So, I tried to find another way to continue learning to play the mandolin.

Stay Out of Father's Pockets!

When I was in the village during the Christmas break, the temptation of owning my own mandolin overtook my logical thinking and personal code of moral principles. I actually took seventy-five drachmas from my father's jacket pocket for the purpose of buying my own mandolin. Before I bought it, however, I told my mother what I had done and asked her not to say anything to my father. I told her that I would tell him myself a few months later and suffer the anticipated consequences.

I went ahead, bought the mandolin, and started practicing every free hour I had. When I went back to the village for Easter break, I enjoyed playing my mandolin around family and friends, who applauded my new-found musical skills.

One day, however, my mother pulled me aside and sadly informed me she had told my father I had taken the money from his pocket. I was not angry with my mother, because I was about ready to tell him the truth myself. My father took his belt off and started striking me. I did not mind the beating, because I was expecting such a reaction from my father when he found out. In the end, my father took my mandolin, locked it in a wooden box, and told me that I could not have it or play it until further notice.

A few years later, I learned how to play the guitar and also taught myself to play a real violin, as opposed to the homemade Lyra. After high school graduation, I managed to buy a guitar and, with two other people, I formed a band that played at small parties, christenings, weddings, and other special occasions. We established a good reputation that virtually guaranteed us a musical engagement almost every weekend.

Right after I was fired from my hotel position, these gigs began to amount to a regular weekend job that lasted up until the time I decided to leave the country. I don't remember why I did not take my guitar with me.

Chapter 13

Misadventures in Germany

uring my German adventure, I luckily had the foresight to record my observations and perceptions for posterity in a journal. As I look back on some of these entries with twenty-twenty hindsight, the scope of my naiveté, gullibility, and immaturity is embarrassingly evident—along with proof positive that I had a definite flair for blowing certain events all out of proportion. My readers will hopefully laugh along with me as my journal tattles on me for these and other youthful foibles.)

It was about 1:30 a.m. on Thursday, April 16, 1959. We were about an hour away from the Bonn station and I had already finished all the water I had in my aluminum canteen. The salty pretzel sticks I had wolfed down earlier had made me thirstier than a fish out of water. Fearing I was getting dehydrated, I made a beeline for the dining car with a yen for anything wet. To my dismay, I found it closed. I asked the conductor where I could find some water.

"Es gibt kein wasser," he answered me in German, which I understood to mean, "There is no water." There was nothing for me to do but endure my miserable situation until we arrived in Bonn, and so I suffered through one of the longest hours of my life. Desperately thirsty, I watched the barely perceptible progress of the clock's minute hand as it taunted me.

Outside, the train plowed through great billows of fog as a light rain pelted the windows. All of a sudden, the lumbering vehicle slowed down almost to a stop. Gazing out the window, I saw the horrific aftermath of a collision involving two trucks about 200 meters from the tracks.

As the flames from the resulting explosion lit up the night sky, the earsplitting shriek of fire trucks and ambulances rushing to the scene filled the air. The chaotic scene brought back dreadful wartime memories of bombing and destruction. In my fearful state, I considered it an omen, signifying my unpleasant welcome to a new country.

We finally arrived in Bonn at 2:34 a.m. I entered the station and hurriedly secured my suitcase in a locker. My first concern was finding some water to drink, so I followed the signs to the restroom, which guided me one flight downstairs. I rushed to turn on the faucet, but no water came out. My jaw dropped open and I shook my head in disbelief.

I desperately tried all the other faucets, only to see one or two puny droplets hitting the basin. I had no idea what was happening. *Didn't they have water in Germany?* I wondered incredulously. Desperate, my mouth dry as a desert, I skulked into the ladies restroom, only to find out that the faucets there were also dry.

Not knowing what to do next, I ran up the stairs and approached a gentleman wearing an official Bonn station hat and a gray uniform. *"Wasser, Wasser, bitte. Ich muss wasser haben!"* I pleaded—Water, water, please. I must have water! As an incentive, I offered him a pack of Greek cigarettes. Grinning from ear to ear, he took it and thanked me many times over.

"Es gibt kein wasser hier," he said matter-of-factly as he deftly extracted a cigarette, poked it between his full lips, and lit it.

There is no water here—almost the same response I had gotten from the train conductor! *This is crazy!* I thought. *Does this mean that there is no water in Germany, period?*

I asked the uniformed worker, *"Wasser in toilette?"* The only words of his response that I understood were "problem" and "station," so I left it at that.

"Bitte kommen sie mit mir"—"Please come with me"—the German said, exhaling luxuriously as he took my hand and led me outside the station. As he walked, he told me that his name was Hermann. We walked a few blocks and entered a building that seemed to be a newspaper printing shop. There was a vending machine where Hermann helped me purchase two bottles of soda, which I guzzled like there was no tomorrow as we walked back towards the station. I could not help releasing a long, satisfied belch, at which Hermann laughed heartily.

From the long strides he was taking, I gathered Hermann must have been in good physical shape. He was an average height, blue-eyed, blond-haired German with thick eyebrows, freckled cheeks, and a distinct, wide smile. When he realized my limited German vocabulary, he tried to converse with me by speaking slowly and separating each word and pronouncing it succinctly.

I asked my new friend if he knew of any hotels nearby, explaining as best I could that I was dead tired after three wide-eyed nights on the train. We checked four hotels, three of which had no vacancies. The fourth one was a four star hotel and thus too dear for my budget. Hermann realized I was looking for more reasonable accommodations when he saw my dumbfounded reaction to the astronomical nightly rate the desk clerk quoted.

As we strolled back toward the station where Hermann worked, he managed to convey to me that his shift would be over in a few hours and he would help me find a more reasonable hotel then. I thanked him for his kindness and for all the help he had given me so far.

At the station, I changed to my white summer shoes—aerated white oxfords—because my black shoes, being too tight, were pressing on the blisters that were developing on my big toes, making walking pure agony.

It was around 7:00 a.m. when I exited the station. I started walking along the wet streets of Bonn without an umbrella, trying to locate a hotel I could afford. Although the prices I encountered were again prohibitive, I reasoned that I should soon settle in one of them, even for one night, as I was almost to a point of collapsing from exhaustion on the street.

The light drizzle was penetrating the top of the white oxfords, which drew embarrassing stares from passersby. They obviously thought it was peculiar for anyone to have on this type of footwear on a cold, rainy day in the spring. Their gawking made me extremely uncomfortable.

When I came across a park, I hurried toward the entrance and began walking through the narrow, picturesque paths. Around 11:00 a.m., I began to feel dizzy and disoriented, so I slowed my pace until I was finally obliged to stop. When I saw a bench near a small pond, the memory of the park bench in Rhodes during my homeless year came to mind. Collapsing on the rain-soaked bench, I cried out wretchedly, "Oh no, not a park bench again!"

That was the last detail I remembered before I either fainted or fell asleep. I was hugging my knees to my chest when I felt someone gently nudging my legs. I awakened from my stupor to see someone standing in front of me, straddling a bicycle. The blurry figure shook me more insistently as I sat up, wiping the rain off my face.

"My God, it's Hermann!" I exclaimed, reaching out to shake his hand.

He smiled benevolently. "Yes, I was looking all over for you."

At least, that's what I understood him to say—but how in the world did he find me in that secluded part of park? The fact that he had been the first and only person I had met in Bonn made his finding me seem even more improbable. It seemed to me that on his way back to work, some inexplicable force had guided him to that nondescript bench by the pond, a few kilometers from the train station. Perhaps he was my guardian angel in the guise of an ordinary train station worker!

Hermann told me he had found a reasonably priced furnished room in a tenement near the station. After we fetched my suitcase from the locker, he took me to the tenement complex, where I completed all registration requirements and paid for four days in advance. The daily rate that Hermann negotiated with the desk clerk indeed seemed reasonable to me at the time. I vaguely remember it was between four and six marks per day, an amount equal to about one and a half dollars, based on the exchange rate at that time.

I didn't know how to thank Hermann for all he had done for me. I gave him another pack of cigarettes, thanking him over and over again as I pumped his hand like a madman.

"*Viel dank ... viel dank, Hermann!*" I said, choking with emotion.

"*Gar nichts, gar nichts. Auf wiedersehen, mein freund,*" he responded. ("It was nothing. Good-bye, my friend.")

With a wide smile on his friendly face, pleased at having helped his fellow man, Hermann took his leave. My last glimpse of him as he left the room became as perfect and everlasting in my memory as a snapshot, and it will always be precious to me. I wish I had been able to speak German fluently, so that I could express to Hermann my full gratitude. Nevertheless, I was blessed to have met this rare individual, who went out of his way to help a stranger without expecting anything in return.

I have often thought that, if society were blessed with more people like Hermann, we would all live in a world where peace, serenity, integrity, and prosperity would be the standard virtues in everyone's life.

It was 4:30 in the afternoon when I got ready for bed. I would finally get some quality sleep, after more than three sleepless nights. Before I closed my eyes, I mentally reviewed all the happenstances in which Hermann had figured. Since I could not explain his timely appearances in my times of need, I simply accepted them as providence and fell into a blissful sleep.

I awoke at 2:00 p.m. on Friday, having slept for more than twenty hours. I felt quite rested, but the rumbling sounds in my stomach reminded me that I was as hungry as a bear. After a quick shower, I had some bread and cheese to temporarily satisfy my stomach's urgent demands.

When I looked out the window, I noticed that the rain had stopped, which would make it easier to walk around the neighborhood as I looked for a deli or food store to replenish my food supply and other basic needs.

I located a small food store nearby and began searching for the most economical items I could afford. I ended up buying a variety of canned food (mainly tuna), a can opener, and two loaves of bread. If I were frugal, these provisions would surely last the rest of my three-day stay in the rented room.

After having a modest dinner, I planned my schedule for the next day and beyond. My first task was to find Niko, who lived somewhere outside Bonn. After studying the map, I charted the train route. I also made a short contingency plan, in case I couldn't locate Niko. Of equal urgency was the fact that my remaining funds, in a best-case scenario, would only last for a maximum fifteen-day stay in a hotel.

Part of my contingency plan was contacting Edith, my German buddy from the train, who was due to return to Bonn from Munich within ten days, or so. That thought made me breathe an encouraging sigh of hope and optimism, sort of a reminder that I possessed enough resiliency, determination, and creativity to survive under even the most challenging circumstances.

Although the specter of fear hung over my plans, I tried to convince myself that failure in my German sojourn was out of the question, utterly unacceptable. As in the past, where I had proved I was able to survive by overcoming much more difficult and dangerous conditions, I would scale the ladder to success in this exciting new country, one rung at a time.

My first task on Saturday morning was to go to Niko's house in Bornheim, which was ten kilometers north of Bonn. I walked to the train station and took a local train that stopped in his little town. When I arrived, I had a hard time finding Niko's home. I realized that must have misunderstood the directions, making a right instead of a left on the first street outside the station. I was told that I should keep walking until I passed a park, and then take the next left. Well, I walked several kilometers in the opposite direction before I asked a passerby for help, showing him Niko's address on a piece of paper. The kindly stranger put me on the right track, for which I thanked him effusively.

An hour later, I finally passed the park, took the next left, and located the house. I got to the house around eleven in the morning; unfortunately, his landlady told me Niko wasn't there. Noticing my dumbfounded expression, she said, "*Niko ist hier morgen.*" I understood that to mean, "Niko will be here tomorrow"—but just to be on the safe side, I wrote a little note in Greek, explaining that I had been to see him and would return on Sunday. I gave the note to the landlady and headed back to the train station.

When I arrived in Bonn, I tried to find Hermann to thank him one more time, but he was nowhere to be found, even after I had asked a few other uniformed workers. Unless he was off on Sundays, I would probably see him the next day, either in the morning on my way to see Niko, or when I returned from Bornheim. Before heading back to my hotel, I bought a detailed map of Bonn and the immediate surroundings. My first search on the map was Edith's home, which was a fifteen-minute walk from the train station.

Once again, on Sunday morning, I was disappointed not to find Hermann at the station before I took the train for Bornheim. However, unlike the day before, this time I knew how to get to Niko's house. Around ten that morning, he welcomed me with genuine warmth and friendliness, as if we were lifelong friends.

After serving me a cup of coffee, Niko began plying me with questions about my sister, Despina. He said that, according to the letters she had written to him, she seemed to be a nice person. He wanted to know more about her, as well as our entire family. We compared notes about our respective upbringings in Greece and the factors that had influenced us to come to Germany. As it turned out, his reasons were somewhat similar to mine. The small town where he grew up did not offer Niko any worthwhile opportunities to satisfy, as he put it, his "*ad-vend-urous inclinations.*"

During our conversation, I was conscious that my anxiety and nervousness were written all over my face. Niko, with his positive attitude and optimistic outlook, was as cool as a cucumber. Speaking with self-assured authority, he did his best to convince me that everything would fall into place and that he would take care of all work-related matters on my behalf.

He also said that he would help me find a room to rent, preferably in Brühl, a town between Bonn and Cologne, where several other Greeks lived and worked. Niko's reassurances made me feel much more at ease and helped me conquer my fears about the uncertainty of my situation. It was comforting to know I had someone to lean on in a country so far away from my homeland. My own optimism started to return.

Before I left Niko's house, we arranged to meet on Monday morning at the Bornheim station. My most pressing need now was to get a work visa that would allow me to work in West Germany for at least six to nine months; subsequently, everything else—such as finding work or renting an apartment—would fall into place.

Niko had suggested that we first apply in Cologne because, based on his past experiences in these matters, the Cologne immigration office was more lenient than those in other nearby cities. He also warned me that sometimes the administrators would red-stamp your passport, in which case you had to leave the country within a few weeks.

My worries started surfacing again when I met Niko at the station. Though Niko was in an upbeat mood, for some unexplainable reason, I was overtaken by thoughts of doubt. I kept asking myself a raft of "what if" questions: What if I don't get the visa? What if I don't find a room to rent soon?

After arriving in Cologne, we took the streetcar to the immigration office which was located a few stops down the road. Niko must have been there before, because he knew exactly where the visa administrator's office was. We walked one flight of stairs to the end of the hallway and then entered an office with its double doors wide open. We greeted the short, stocky man behind a large desk who, in turn, asked us to sit down and state our business.

Niko explained that my main objective for visiting Germany was to learn the language as a prerequisite to enroll in and attend university classes. Furthermore, he emphasized that my poor parents would not be able to support me; therefore, I needed to get a work visa to cover all related living expenses.

The officious clerk's stone-face expression made me quake with fear. The black, shifting eyes under his thick eyebrows were as mean and cold as Hitler's, and I feared he would throw us out on our duffs any second. I couldn't comprehend a word when he started shouting. He held my passport in one hand and, with the other, scavenged under the giant pile of papers on his messy desk. When he found what he was looking for—his inkpad—he grabbed a red stamp.

But while pushing some folders aside, he jostled his coffee cup, spilling the contents all over the papers. I seized the moment to snatch my passport from his trembling hands as I stormed out of his office. I could hear him shouting all the way to the end of the hallway. Niko was right behind me as we dashed, helter-skelter, for the exit.

"Good thing you took the passport away from him," Niko panted, his voice full of concern. "Otherwise, he would have red-stamped it. Let's get out of here double-quick, before he calls the police."

Not hesitating a moment, Niko dragged me into the first streetcar that stopped in front of the building. He said we would probably be riding away from the train station, but this convenient getaway would help us avoid possible police intervention. We exited after three or four stops, where we took another streetcar that was headed toward the train station.

On the train, I noticed that now even Niko seemed worried about my getting a work permit. I told him I didn't quite understand why the immigration man wanted to red-stamp my passport, not to mention what all the shouting had been about. Niko summed up what the "madman," as he called him, had said following our request: "All you foreigners use the same line, the same pitiful excuses to make the officials feel sorry for you. No, not this time! I don't buy it! We've had enough of you … foreigners! I will red-stamp your passport, so that you will never be allowed to reenter Germany again, *never!* Do you understand?"

Wow! Naturally, I knew from the clerk's tone and volume that I was being insulted, but had I understood what the blustery buffoon was saying at the time, I would have broken his nose and gladly suffered the consequences! I said as much to Niko in an angry tone, though I didn't know then whether my bark was worse than my bite.

Nevertheless, the problem at hand concerning my work visa remained unresolved. Once again, I put my trust in Niko. "I feel bad putting you through these tribulations," I said. "Thank you for everything you're doing for me—but what do you think our next plan of attack should be?"

"Don't worry, we will find another way somehow, in another city, to get you the work permit," Niko replied. I couldn't help noticing his conviction seemed a little shaken.

That week, Niko was working the night shift, so he suggested we should stop in Brühl to find a room for me to rent, because I had only one more prepaid night's stay in the hotel in Bonn. In Brühl, we went to a real estate rental agency to check on rooms to rent, preferably close to the train station. Niko knew the area well and suggested that we investigate a room in a private home on Neue Bohle Street, which was in a nice neighborhood.

We both liked the owner's family as well as the room, which appeared to have been professionally decorated. The rent was reasonable, so we closed the deal by paying for the last ten days of May, since I would move in on Tuesday, May 21, 1959.

After checking out of the hotel in Bonn, I moved to my new place on Tuesday afternoon. There was plenty of closet space, and I did not even fill one-third of the closet with the limited clothing I owned. I began reviewing my housing situation as well as all pending tasks.

Although the rental arrangements allowed me access to the bathroom and kitchen, I didn't quite feel comfortable sharing the facilities with a family of four. I wasn't sure whether I would be happy living in this house for a long time, but having no other choice, I decided I should stick it out until something better came along.

As for my work visa, Niko and I arranged to meet in Bornheim around 1:00 p.m. on Wednesday to discuss our remaining options. As I had promised my train-pal Edith from Bonn, I wrote a brief note to her, primarily to let her know my address in case she wanted to get in touch with me.

Chapter 14

Another Bench, Another Memory

The following day, I went to Niko's house a little before 1:00 p.m. His landlady told me he was still sleeping because he'd had to work more than three hours past his normal quitting time. Struggling with my limited German, I made her understand that I would come back in about two hours. It was a pleasant, sunny afternoon, so I headed for the park just a few blocks down the road. It seemed that the parks and I had formed some kind of affiliation; either I attracted them, or the parks' mysterious cosmic energies pulled me inside.

I started walking through the narrow, winding paths which were accentuated with flowering bushes on each side. *Here we go again!* I thought. An overpowering sensation of *déjà vu* came over me as I spotted a bench and dutifully sat down. A cinematic flood of all the park-related events of my life coursed through my mind. It was as if I were watching a film preview. I waited with bated breath, to see what would happen now, in a different park, on a different bench. With my eyes closed, I rested my head in my palms and reminisced.

Oh, I have forgotten to mention the very first "bench incident" that happened in our house in the village when I was eight years old. My younger sister, Mary, and I were sitting on each end of a small bench, two feet wide by one foot high, near a large pot of cooked spaghetti that my mother had just taken down to be strained. I stood up abruptly, causing the bench to tilt, which threw my sister forward into the boiling water.

The echoes of her screams as she jumped up and down from the excruciating pain on her burned forearm are forever etched on my psyche. Although my mother applied homemade remedies, Mary's arm ended up being badly scarred up to her elbow. Growing up together, she never blamed me for being the cause of the accident. But I never forgot that, because of me, my sister's arm would be scarred for the rest of her life.

As I thought about this ghastly incident, I rubbed my eyes and said aloud, "*I* caused that accident, *I'm* to blame, *I* did it!"

Just then, I saw two well-dressed men standing in front of me, asking me if there was anything wrong. I explained that I did not speak German very well, but one of the men asked me if I spoke English or French. I said that I spoke French better than German, so we started making some small talk about my home country of Greece. He asked what I was doing in Germany and other questions. After they introduced themselves, I could only retain the name of one gentleman, a Mr. Haas; the other man's name sounded like "*Schlossenbergender*"—too long and cumbersome for me to remember.

Anyway, Mr. Haas was pleasantly surprised to hear that I grew up on the island of Rhodes. He said that he had spent six months in Rhodes near the end of the war. He mentioned many familiar locations, including Atria, the original Italian military base three kilometers from the village, which was later taken over by the Germans. (I mentioned this place earlier; it was where a young man was killed while trying to dismantle a bomb.)

Having noticed my nervous demeanor, Mr. Haas asked me what was bothering me. If I were dealing with a problem or a crisis, he said, he could possibly be of assistance. Pausing for a few moments, I silently asked myself—or perhaps a higher authority—if the last two encounters with nice people near park benches had been mere coincidence or divine intervention. I managed to provide Mr. Hass with some details as to the reasons for my German visit, adding that, "I went to Cologne for the purpose of obtaining a work permit, but an angry clerk denied my request without giving me a good reason."

I almost fainted when Mr. Haas explained that he was the supervisor of the section that dealt with this type of immigration matter! He asked me to come see him the following day, saying he would personally furnish me with the necessary work permit documents. I looked at the business card he had given me and noticed, with great relief, that his office was in Bonn.

I gripped Mr. Haas' hand so tightly, I must have cut off his circulation. In my ecstasy, I exclaimed many thanks to him, to God, to all the German people, and to the whole world. I gushed in the few words I knew in German, "*Danke soviel, ich sieht sie morgen*"— Thank you so much, I will see you tomorrow.

"*Ja, werde ich sie morgen erwarten*"—Yes, I will be expecting you tomorrow— Mr. Haas replied. Then he bade me farewell. (Incidentally, I didn't know the meaning of the word "erwarten," so when they left, I looked it up in my little pocket dictionary.)

I was deliriously happy as well as flabbergasted. I couldn't believe what had just happened. How in the world did Mr. Haas appear in front of me? He was one of the few people in the Bonn/Cologne area who could approve my work permit. And what about Rhodes, our common link, which had fueled our conversation about Greece? Was that a coincidence once again?

I believe meeting him was most likely caused by the intervention of a universal, superior power at work, but more rationally minded readers are free to draw their own conclusions.

Shaking my head in astonishment, I slowly began walking toward the park exit, heading for Niko's house. I couldn't wait to tell him the good news about my encounter with Mr. Haas and his friend. Just before reaching the exit, I briefly gazed skyward and whispered an appreciative message to the man in charge: "Thank you, God, from the bottom of my heart for being here with me, for helping me reach my goal."

My deep philosophical ruminations were rudely interrupted when I arrived at Niko's place to find him standing on the front porch with a scowl of annoyance on his face. He scolded me for not waking him up and for walking around the neighborhood by myself like a little lost lamb.

"Niko, get a grip on yourself—are you ready for this?" I said as I enthusiastically described the fortuitous events in the park. He called me a lucky son of a gun—or words to that effect—and in his excitement, nearly smothered me in a bear hug.

"Oh, happy day! Our difficult task will be over tomorrow," he chortled. "But I want to come with you to Bonn, so when you get the work permit, we can have a few beers to celebrate."

"Sure thing, Niko, I would like that," I agreed.

Heaving a heavy sigh of relief, I left Niko's house and reflected on the extraordinary and wonderful events that had occurred during my short stay in Germany. It was uncanny, but again and again, exactly the right person for my need at hand had appeared—almost out of nowhere! My anguish, insecurities, and fears started to vanish.

I felt an emotional transformation taking place within me, a guiding force steering me toward accepting the admittedly paradoxical aspects of certain incidents that had no logical explanation. I simply removed the conventional blinders, which I had inherited from a society where tradition and blind faith—as well as the opinion of others—were the only guiding principles in most people's lives.

Not anymore! I thought. I would leap out of my comfort zone! I would thumb my nose at the notion of retreat and march on and on and on! As Robert Frost said in the last stanza of his poem, "Stopping by Woods on a Snowy Evening:"

> The woods are lovely, dark and deep.
> But I have promises to keep,
> And miles to go before I sleep,
> And miles to go before I sleep.

It is said that necessity is the mother of invention, but this truism can be taken one step further to include another life lesson: "Necessity is also the mother of success." Yes, I had promised my father, and I also had made a promise to myself, that I would prevail in my pursuit of a yet unknown success. I knew I would be braving perilous risks that most ordinary people would not dare face.

My quest for a better future was fueled by my belief that my own country, in some strange way, had exiled me. I felt that in my homeland, my opinion, ability, and creativity were neither recognized nor appreciated. Instead, I was labeled or stigmatized as a nonconformist due to my unconventional behavior.

Unlike the majority of my peers, I have to confess that I never accepted the status quo. I did not take the easy way out by always agreeing with someone who was in power or who had a higher economic status. I could not tolerate the selfish approach of many people who entertained the notion that their success would be above everything else—including the other person's misfortunes or even demise.

I believe my dissatisfaction was probably the main determining motivation that made me leave my country, family, and friends. I wanted to live in a society where compassion, truth, and ability were recognized as the most desirable qualities of individuality.

Although the Greeks have inherited the excellence, the creativity, and the philosophical mind of their ancestors, somehow these qualities could not surface and be expressed during the 400 years of the Ottoman occupation, where the struggle for survival was their main concern. However, the resilient Greek spirit could not be suppressed; it was largely this spirit that freed the country from "slavery" and consequently brought about the redevelopment of its new nation, culture, and traditional society.

The four centuries of Ottoman occupation had been an enormous set-back to a civilization that had spread the democratic ideology throughout the world. Nevertheless, I'm sure that someday, my country will again become an advanced nation of compassion, unselfishness, and concern for its fellow man. I believe Greece will again become a nation of substantial political classification among its European allies. I believe the homeland of Socrates and Plato will again influence the world, as it did in the Byzantine era.

The nation of Greece—including its families and individuals—needs to restore and live by the ethics inherited several eons ago. As Steven Covey wrote in *The Seven Habits of Highly Effective People,* paraphrasing or quoting Benjamin Franklin: "... the ethic is the yeast that raises a person."

The following day, Niko and I visited Mr. Haas in Bonn. It was an easy process—within ten minutes, Mr. Haas had arranged all the work permit documents I needed. Once more, I thanked him many times for his kindness and the help he had given me. I told him in all sincerity that he would be one of the few people in my life whom I would never forget.

"*Auf wiedersehen und viel glück, mein freund*"—Much luck, my friend—were Mr. Haas' last words as he told us good-bye.

Just as we had planned, Niko and I entered the first bar we came across to celebrate my first major accomplishment, the permit that would allow me to find a job and work legally anywhere in West Germany. As we tossed back a few beers, we played a slot machine, which, according to Niko, was a common fixture in almost every bar in Germany.

To be honest, I had never seen a slot machine up to that point. However, it was an interesting diversion for the customers to wile away their time and, more often than not, lose some money. Playing the slots for the first time in my life, I placed a *roschen* (one tenth of a mark) in the slot, for one in six chances to win five roschen. Well, I limited my losses to four tries and ended up losing one mark.

As we celebrated my new work status, Niko and I talked about our next strategy, which was to find me a job within a reasonable distance from my room. Kismet shined on me again: it turned out the firm Niko had once worked for was looking for new hires, and Niko said I could get the full details from a Greek fellow he had worked with in the past. The firm was called Heinrich Construction.

"His name is Theodore, and he lives with his wife," said Niko, giving me the gentleman's address. "Actually, you can see him as early as tonight. He gets home around five in the evening."

"Great! I will definitely go to Theodore's house tonight," I said, eager to take the next step that would guarantee me permanency in Germany, where I could work, master the challenging language, and cultivate for myself a diverse and culturally satisfying lifestyle.

I went to Theodore's house that evening at 6:00 p.m., explaining that Niko had sent me and I was looking for a job.

"I'm glad that Niko sent you here," said Theodore, bidding me to come inside. "I've known Niko for over a year. He is a good man."

Theodore was a typically hale and hearty Greek, full of life, with eyes that danced with warmth and good humor. His muscular physique, thick-skinned hands, and full, black mustache were some of the obvious signs that he had roughed it up for a good part of his life. Just being in the same room with him and soaking up his positive aura made me feel better about the Herculean challenges that lay before me.

After the introductions, his wife Irene served us some Greek ouzo as Theodore described the responsibilities of the open position at the place he worked, as well as the overall business model. Essentially, he said that his boss, Heinrich, owned a company specializing in the road construction sector where he was responsible for all facets of the project, from the job-bidding phase all the way to completion. He also owned all of the required heavy equipment, such as backhoes, bulldozers, stone stabilizers, and pavers.

"Listen, we are constructing a new road, located a few kilometers outside Brühl, about a ten- minute train ride," said Theodore, sipping the strong, anise-flavored liqueur. "In case Niko hasn't told you, we work outdoors using all sorts of construction equipment. But if you accept this job, you would mainly move road material from one spot to another, using a wheelbarrow. Basically, you would be helping the masons with the installation of curbs and sidewalks. How does that sound to you?"

"Sounds good," I said. "But what does the job pay, and is it per day or per hour?" "The pay is per hour," he replied. "The rate will be decided by the foreman when he meets with you. If you want, you can come with me tomorrow morning to see the site and meet some of the other workers."

I could barely contain my excitement. "Yes, tomorrow is fine," I said. "I will come to your house first so you can show me the entire route to the work site."

"I assume you have done manual labor in the past?" he asked. "Because the work at the construction site is not easy; you will be using muscles you did not even think you had. It is hard work, my friend, very hard work!" Theodore poked me good-naturedly in the arm to emphasize his point. I think he was also measuring the firmness of my bicep.

"Oh, sure, every summer I worked closely with my father, who is a farmer, doing almost every chore or task under the sun," I tried to reassure him, although I could almost feel my arms aching already.

We had another round of ouzo, and then Theodore and his wife clinked their glasses against mine and wished me good luck. I was cautiously optimistic about the following day's meeting with the construction foreman. When I thought of the type of work I'd be required to do at my potential new job, and its difficulty, it was a bit overwhelming. But I didn't show any negative emotions or reactions. Meanwhile, Theodore, the workhorse, was still talking about the job and bragging about the many overtime hours he could put in.

Chapter 15

A Bunch of Firsts

The following day, I rode the train with Theodore to the construction site, where I met Oskar, the group foreman. He was a busy, no-nonsense, wide-shouldered man. After a few terse questions, he offered me the job with the option of starting right away. I accepted his offer on the spot. It paid 2.8 marks an hour, which meant that I would be netting about eighty marks a week after the deductions.

After signing all the required paperwork, I was supplied with my primary tools—a hoe, shovel, and wheelbarrow—and started working that very day. As Theodore had warned me, the work was monotonous and backbreaking. At the end of the eight hour shift, my clothes were soaked in perspiration and every joint and muscle in my beleaguered body ached and throbbed. Nonetheless, I managed to complete all my assigned tasks fairly well, considering it was my first day on the job. As grueling as the work was, I took solace in the fact I had a job that would pay me five times as much as I would have earned in my home country—had I even been able to find a job.

After a few days, I got used to my daily schedule. The local train took me to work in the morning and brought me back to Brühl around 5:00 p.m. Then I had a half-hour walk to the house on Neue Bohle Street. Since my house was located on a small hill, the downhill walk to the train station in the morning was a little easier and took less than half an hour.

Our lunch break was only thirty minutes, giving me just enough time to have the sandwich and coffee that I had prepared the night before. Occasionally, on sweltering days, our foreman was kind enough to treat the crew members to a bottle of beer. Beer was a treat I couldn't yet afford on an everyday basis. I was also a smoker, which was an expensive habit in Germany, where the price of a pack of twelve cigarettes was one mark. The high cost persuaded some of us to buy tobacco and paper and roll our own cigarettes. I even tried smoking a pipe, but it was too much bother, so I gave it up soon after.

On the train to and from work, I often rode with the same female co-passengers, whose pulchritude I immortalized in my diary. My daily entries contained comments like, "Lucky me! Deep Blue Eyes sat next to me this morning," or "I'm sad, because Round- Face, who always smells so heavenly, did not get on the train today." The prettiest maiden of all was a blonde, green-eyed beauty with a long ponytail and bangs on her forehead. I called her *koukla*, which means "doll" in Greek. A typical diary entry might have read, "My heart rejoices because Koukla, the living doll, smiled coquettishly at me this evening!"

My number one priority after my first paycheck was to buy a guitar. I visited a music store and purchased an instrument of average quality. At the time, playing the guitar was perhaps my favorite leisure activity; I found it both relaxing and artistically stimulating.

Almost every weeknight, I studied German for about an hour, as I was determined to learn to speak the language fluently. My studiousness paid off; after about two weeks in Germany, my German had improved to the point that I was able to speak more comfortably and could understand the essence of others' conversation. For some strange reason, I was absorbing the language like a sponge, a welcome phenomenon that puzzled me for a while. It was as though I had known how to speak German before, perhaps in a previous life.

On Friday, May 1, 1959, I moved from Neue Bohle Street to a new housing tenement on Wilhelm Street, which was close to the center of town. It was a ground floor apartment with two bedrooms, a living area, and a kitchen. I shared it with two other people, which made the rent reasonable. We had our own kitchen with flatware, dinnerware, and cookware.

I thought it was a perfect setup, but I soon realized that it offered some extra benefits when Rita, the owner's daughter, came to my room holding sheets and blankets in one hand, and a cup of coffee in the other. I was playing the guitar at the time and she sat next to me, her eyes aglow with admiration as I ran through a series of fast arpeggios.

Rita started a flirtatious conversation, as if we had known one another for a long time. She was an attractive, playful, giggly, bouncy blonde whose main purpose in life, as I confirmed a few weeks later, was to tease men. Nevertheless, I truly liked this lively minx. She kept me on my toes and let her would-be suitors know, in no uncertain terms, that anything beyond a kiss—and any reaching below the neck—was *verboten*.

On weekends, she would often wake me up with a feathery, soft kiss while serving me coffee and cookies. However, when I tried to hug her and kiss her, she would run away from me like a playful kitten.

The Post, a cocktail lounge, was located in the center of Brühl, only one block from my apartment on Wilhelm Street. This was the main hang-out of all the people Niko introduced me to. I had a great time the first Saturday I went to the Post with two other guys. The place boasted an impressive bar and ample seating around the circular dance floor, which teemed with patrons kicking up their heels to traditional dance music— waltzes, tangos, and foxtrots—played by the house band, a crackerjack bunch of musicians.

That first night, I discovered that every fourth song the band played was a "Ladies Choice," where the *fräuleins* asked the gents if they would like to dance with them. Wow, I thought to myself, what a way to know where you rank among all the other men! There were many ladies who asked me to dance. In fact, one of them, whose name I unfortunately don't recall, asked me out that evening.

My journal entry from that day reads: "The fact that she had a few drinks, plus my limited German, made it difficult for me to understand what she was saying, so the silent universal language took over, thus ending the night with a pleasant finale."

I walked home that evening on cloud nine, thinking to myself: *I'm definitely going to like this town!*

Chapter 16

My Second Residence

From my journal: "Today is Sunday, May 3, 1959, Easter Sunday for all the Eastern Orthodox regions, where millions of faithful celebrate the resurrection of Christ after seven weeks of fasting. However, here in Germany, it's just another insignificant Sunday, since the date of the Catholic Easter does not usually coincide with the Greek Orthodox, which is still calculated based on the Julian calendar. Until 1054, the Eastern Orthodox and Roman Catholic churches were one body. Theological, political, and cultural differences split the church in two, and those differences were never completely reconciled."

While drinking my morning coffee, I couldn't resist recollecting the events that had taken place in the village during the previous Easter Holy Week and beyond, celebrating a combination of the religious resurrection and the rebirth of nature in all its springtime glory. At this time of year in my village, the countryside is crimson with fields of red poppies, the homes are freshly painted, and the people prepare in earnest for this important celebration.

The entire Holy Week, starting on Palm Sunday, is the most sacred period of the Greek Orthodox faith. In small towns like my village, the faithful observe a vegetarian diet for forty-plus days and attend church services every night. During Holy Week, the fasting becomes more rigorous for the faithful, so that they will be prepared spiritually and physically to experience Jesus' suffering, death, and the resurrection—called *Anastasis* in Greek.

I once asked a priest why olive oil is not allowed during the entire week, since oil is a pure vegetable. He explained that, in the early days of Christianity, olive oil was stored in sacks made out of goat or sheep's leather, thus contaminating the oil with the scent of the animal's skin. Although that type of oil storage is no longer customary, the church has kept the tradition intact— yet I still find it questionable that one can eat olives, but not consume olive oil.

The church services for Holy Thursday, Friday, and Saturday nights were the longest, lasting between four and five hours each. The church in my village had no pews except for a few tall, wooden stools with armrests that were secured against the sides of the walls to accommodate the old or disabled parishioners. Otherwise, everyone had to stand throughout the entire church service.

On Holy Thursday, the service of "twelve gospels" is a recollection of Jesus Christ's last days on earth, which ended with the last supper he shared with his disciples before he was crucified. On Good Friday, the faithful experience the culmination of Divine Drama through three services: morning, afternoon, and night. Good Friday is the holiest day of the year, a day of strict fasting and praying while spending many hours attending church services.

Holy Saturday features both morning and night services. Lasting about three hours, the night service begins at 11 p.m. At midnight, the priest, the cantors, and the faithful exit the church with lighted candles, emerging in the front yard where the Holy Gospel—essentially a description of Christ's resurrection—is read. At that time, while raising their glowing candles, everyone chants the words, "Christ Is Risen." Greek Χριστός ανέστη! (Christós Anésti!) and also "Truly He is Risen." Greek Αληθώς Ανέστη! (Alithós Anésti!) Then the liturgy follows, lasting a little more than an hour.

The service ends at about 1:30 a.m., at which time the priest doles out hard-boiled, red eggs to parishioners. The cracking of the eggs between family and friends marks the end of the fasting period and the beginning of the Easter Sunday celebration.

And so we have a brief description of the Holy Week highlights. But besides the religious aspect, there is another side of this holiday, a non-secular tradition that started many generations ago. The following is my recollection of an extraordinary experience during the 1958 Easter holiday:

Just before Palm Sunday, all single males from eighteen to fifty formed a group of about sixty strong and elected their own symbolic mayor. Last year, the group selected me to fill that role and assume the responsibilities thereof. As my first order of business, I had to select five people to serve as the "secret police," so to speak.

This delegation's duty was to observe the members of the young adult group, recording any unusual behavior or any inappropriateness, especially when nobody was looking. For example, if someone did not greet his fellow villager with a smile, or if one used curse words, or got to church late—these and other social misdemeanors were deemed worthy of notation.

As mayor, it was my duty to command every young adult to bring a two- to three- meter piece of firewood for the bonfire that blazed in the village square from 11:00 p.m. on Holy Saturday until the day after Easter. Everyone was supposed to be in church at the time the Holy Gospel of Resurrection was read at midnight. For those who were absent, the secret police placed a flag-like rag (*tsoukopana*) on a pole that was secured on the chimney of their house. This visible symbol was a humiliation for the adults in the marked household because everybody knew who had not been in church during the resurrection services.

Each recorded incident of bad behavior was given a point value, depending on its severity or importance. On Monday afternoon, the entire village gathered in one of the larger café halls. The young adults sat in a U-like table setting, with yours truly, the president, and my five secret policemen, reigning over all from a slightly raised wooden platform.

While the band played, drinks were served with a mouth-watering banquet of food and an assortment of homemade desserts, each more toothsome than the last. Then the announcement came, saying "the court was now in session." This meant that everyone who had done something of the "naughty variety" would be subject to a punishment or fine, depending on the severity of his misconduct.

The lesser punishments were along the lines of buying a bottle of wine for the person someone had wronged or apologizing to him or her publicly. But the most severe verdict involved carrying and throwing the accused into a shallow water reservoir without allowing him to take off any clothing.

A convoy of onlookers joined and followed the procession all the way to the reservoir, applauding and taking pictures of the wet, humiliated individual. The guilty person generally harbored no hard feelings and he ultimately rejoined the party at the café, after changing into dry clothes. The party went on until 3:00 a.m. while the court handed out fines throughout the night to those who had acted inappropriately.

I truly missed those moments of jubilation and traditional celebration together with friends, relatives, and my fellow townsfolk. I can only imagine all the festivities that occur today in the village: the abundance of food at all the Easter Sunday family dinner gatherings, the celebration with an all-night dancing party and all the delightful goodies they will enjoy after seven weeks of fasting.

Far away from home, I now realized the enormous importance of the Easter celebration. As I took another sip of my morning coffee, I whispered aloud: *"Thank You, Lord, for giving me the opportunity to have lived the Easter experience in the village, an event which enabled me to realize the symbolic meaning of sacrifice ... an event that revived my inner resurrection, fostering wonderful feelings of serenity. Thank You for bringing success into my life ... for opening the doors for me in a new country ... for being by my side, helping me overcome some difficult moments during the last two weeks."*

It almost seems like a miracle when I recount all the accomplishments I managed to complete in such a short period. I had obtained the work visa; learned to speak German competently; found a nice apartment; and secured a well-paying—if arduous— job. To say I was contented would have been a gross understatement!

Right after breakfast I went to my previous residence on Neue Bohle Street to check if I had any mail, as this was the first return address I'd used in my correspondence with friends and relatives. Awaiting me were four letters, one of which was from Edith, who invited me to visit her in Bonn on Thursday, May 7. I don't recall the reason why she chose a weekday to meet, instead of a weekend, but since I don't have a detailed explanation in my notebook, I assume that Thursday must have been a holiday.

Theodore had invited me for a traditional Easter dinner with him and his wife, Irene. At his home that evening, we had a few drinks, cracked red eggs, and enjoyed a delicious Easter meal prepared by Irene based on traditional recipes from her hometown in northern Greece.

Unfortunately, Niko, who had also been invited, was hospitalized in a nearby town for a minor surgery he was scheduled to have within a few days. So, while making a toast to his health, I let Theodore know that I planned to visit Niko at the hospital the coming Thursday. The three of us expatriate Greeks had a rousing good time, making the best of a mini-Easter celebration far away from home.

On Thursday, May 7, 1959, I woke up around 9:00 a.m., according to my journal. My schedule for that day was to visit Niko at the hospital and then proceed to Bonn to meet Edith. I took the bus to Wesseling, a town eight kilometers east of Brühl, then walked to the hospital. When I explained to a lady at the front desk that I had come to see my ailing friend Niko, she would not allow me into his room, saying the visiting hours were between two and four in the afternoon.

After much begging and pleading, and telling her that I had come from out of town by bus, she finally let me see Niko. He was so appreciative that I came to visit him and we exchanged a few hugs and kissed both cheeks, as is the customary European way.

We walked down to a reflective garden on the hospital grounds, where we spent almost an hour chatting about his condition and the fact that he had to spend Easter Sunday in the hospital. I promised him that, when he was released from the hospital, we would arrange a special event to celebrate his "getting back to normal" day. Then a nurse interrupted our conversation, informing us that Niko had to return to his room. After wishing him a speedy recovery, I left the hospital and headed for the train station.

I arrived in Bonn too early to meet Edith at her apartment, so I stopped at a bar on Krausfeld Street to have a beer and kill some time. Afterwards, I headed to Edith's one-bedroom efficiency apartment, which was in a brand new complex, and eagerly rang the doorbell.

"*Willkommen zu meinem haus!*" Edith exclaimed with a wide smile on her plain face.

She welcomed me to her house with a hug and a friendly kiss. She told me that she was impressed with the progress I'd made in learning German since we'd first met on the train, three weeks earlier. She also offered me a cup of coffee and some cookies—just in the nick of time, as I was famished.

As we sipped our coffee, she reminded me of the deal we had made on the train, which was teaching each other our native languages. Edith handed me a fourth grade German textbook and asked me to start reading it while she finished a letter on the typewriter. I spent about an hour reading the book she gave me. Although I used my little dictionary to look up unfamiliar words, I often asked her to use them in different sentences so I would be sure of their meanings. My inquisitiveness clearly pleased Edith and my questions bothered her not a whit.

We left her apartment early in the afternoon. She took me to a location adjacent to the Rhine River, a park-like setting with well-kept paths that meandered past a riot of flowering shrubs. We strolled along the river, savoring a blissful contentment in this Shangri-La where time seemed to stand still. Edith was in a cheerful mood that made me feel overjoyed to be with her. But even under these idyllic conditions, she tried indirectly to teach me new words in German. In fact, according to my journal, we laughed until our sides ached about the way we used the word *kwatz* (spelled phonetically kvatz)—a slang word for "foolish" or "silly"—in different sentences, each of us trying to outdo the other in terms of absurdity.

Author's note: The fact that I cannot find this word in the German dictionary means we might have made it up just for fun.

Before we returned to her apartment, we visited an old Catholic church with impressive murals and remarkable stained glass windows.

At her apartment, Edith prepared dinner for the two of us, mainly an assortment of light sandwiches, which is a typical dinner in most German households. As soon as Edith brought the platter with the sandwiches to the coffee table, a male friend of hers showed up. Without even being invited to join us, he just sat down and, as I described it in my notebook, started eating like a pig. I was not used to such uncouth behavior, but I saw Edith took it in stride, not minding his rudeness and gluttony at all.

I thought to myself that I still had a lot to learn about the everyday life of the German people and perhaps should learn to accept their sometimes brazen demeanor, as distasteful as it was to me. But I couldn't help being judgmental and annoyed with the boorish attitude Edith's friend demonstrated.

The experience put me in a bad mood, and I left Edith's place and headed for the train station. Although I tried not to show my disappointment while saying good-bye to both of them, Edith sensed what bothered me and escorted me to the staircase outside her apartment, where she tried to put my mind at ease. She told me that the man was just an old friend and nothing else, and that she would write to me soon for our next rendezvous.

Perhaps fate was punishing me for my negative attitude, but I missed the train to Brühl by less than a minute, so I had to wait for an hour to catch the next one. I treated myself to another beer at a nearby bar while waiting for my train. During the train ride, I had an unbearable headache, which continued to get worse even after I arrived in Brühl. On my way home, I made a brief stop at the Post bar, where I ran into my two Italian roommates. Since they were about ready to leave, all three of us walked home together.

Before I fell asleep, I pondered the events of the day, trying to understand the primary reason for my bad mood. It must have had a lot to do with Edith's friend, who had just dropped in unexpectedly and made himself at home. I probably wanted Edith's company exclusively for myself, in order to wrap up the wonderful day we'd had on a positive note. Instead, I'd had to share her with that pompous interloper.

Was it possible that I was envious of his apparent confidence, self-esteem, and cheery disposition? Maybe it was my penchant for exaggeration that had gotten me into this messy mind game.

Be that as it may, I was certain Edith had a great interest in me and a genuine concern for my well-being. I suspected she had slowly started molding my social education around a simple template, based on my limited cultural exposure. This was probably a good thing, I reasoned, and I should be grateful for having people care for me. This must have been the last thought I had before I faded off to sleep.

The following day, Friday, May 8, I felt tired while riding the train to work, because I'd had less than five hours of sleep. The sight of Koukla, the green-eyed goddess, would have perked me up–but she was not riding on the same train that morning. My eight-hour shift felt even more grueling than usual, because I was so tired.

After work, I went straight to Bornheim to get Niko's mail so that I could take it to the hospital the following day. Unfortunately, his landlady wasn't there; I waited for her for two hours, but she never showed. Niko had told me that she was always at home on Sunday, so I planned to return accordingly.

After dinner, back home in Brühl, I spent a few hours at the Post, enjoying a few beers with some friends and even found the energy to dance a little. But there was not what I would call a "good atmosphere" at the bar that night, so around midnight, I went home.

Rita woke me up on Saturday morning with her usual butterfly kisses, but for some mysterious reason, I tried to avoid her. After breakfast, I did my usual weekend food shopping, and then Rita was again in my room, wanting to know why I was giving her the cold shoulder. Well, I could not sustain my indifferent attitude any longer, nor could I resist her playful style. My smile was obviously the only signal she needed to run into my open arms.

Everything seemed to be back to normal with Rita after she realized I was not annoyed with her anymore. We enjoyed an afternoon walk in the park, holding hands and exchanging a quick kiss here and there. We sat on a bench, admiring the colorful scenery.

There was a long stretch of silence in which I seized the opportunity to ogle Rita's sensuous face and ripe, young body. She leaned back on the bench with her eyes closed and her pouting lips parted sultrily. Although I did not have any deep feelings for her, I admit I fantasized about her beyond a friendly or platonic encounter. But if I were to act on those impulses, what would be next? Would I just look for another outlet to satisfy my instincts?

As Plato wrote:

"As the supreme object of desire, the Good or the beautiful must be present in all phases of human life. It is what everyone seeks, that for the

sake of which everything is sought. But few people recognise it, for in the confusion of their lives, human beings know that they have desires, but they do not know what will satisfy them. When hungry, they eat, thinking that food is the object of their desire. But once they have eaten, they desire other things, and so on, till death (hopefully) puts an end to it."

At this stage of my life, at age twenty, I could not distinguish the difference between infatuation and love, nor between passion and lust. I thought I was falling in love with every woman I went out with. At that time, I didn't know that this sort of feeling was just a temporary attraction that faded away after my basic instincts had been satisfied. Nevertheless, every one of us needs a "Rita" once in a while to keep our hopes, dreams, and expectations alive—in other words, to enjoy the endless journey that offers us virtual gratification in the realm of our imagination.

On the way home, I told Rita that I truly enjoyed her company and her coquettish charms, and that I would never ask her to do anything she did not feel comfortable with. She seemed to appreciate my reassurance that I would never take advantage of her vulnerability in any situation.

Just before we entered the front door, she paused for a moment and stood there with a puzzled look. Then her face lost all expression. She stood motionless, just staring at me, her pretty brow furrowed and her lips forming a curious, Mona Lisa-like smile. It was as if she wanted to ask me many questions or reveal some profound truths, but she was not able to articulate a word.

I noticed that her eyes seemed about to shed tears, but she just kept on staring. Then, suddenly, she turned around and ran up the stairs to her room. I knew I was witnessing an unfamiliar part of her character for the first time, a side of her personality that was the antithesis of her bouncy, everyday manner. In vain, I wished I knew what had aroused these pensive emotions in her.

Back in my apartment, I was relieved to find that my two boisterous, Italian roommates were out. Taking advantage of the quiet, I spent a few hours studying German, using the books Edith had given me. I was proud of my growing mastery of this guttural language. I was also extremely happy with the progress I'd made in several other areas, such as my self-confidence, my sense of worth, and my sense of belonging.

For the first time, I realized that I was going through a phase of personal rediscovery, arousing attributes of my personality I didn't think I had—or perhaps those aspects of me had merely been suppressed by the limitations of my surroundings during my younger years.

In the evening, I walked to the Post, our usual weekend bar hangout. Salvatore, one of my roommates, was sitting at a table with a good looking-girl whom we all called *die hübsche blondine,* the pretty blonde. I was surprised when she introduced me to her father, who was sitting at the same table.

Salvatore whispered to me in Italian that he liked her a great deal and that he would do anything to go out with her. His nervousness, not to mention his poor command of German, became more obvious when he spilled his beer all over the table and exclaimed apologetically in Italian: "*O, lo perdona prego ... Madona, che cosa ho fatto? Stupido, stupido ... %#@$*"— Oh, please forgive me ...Madonna, what did I do? Stupid, stupid—capped by a few choice expletives of frustration. An Italian to the bone, Salvatore gestured maniacally with his hands as he continued to curse himself and the embarrassing situation.

When he calmed down a little, he bought a round of drinks for the four of us, although he was still mumbling to himself in a self-deprecating whisper. At one point, the band was playing a slow tune, which was also a Ladies Choice dance. The "pretty blonde" got up right away and asked me to dance with her.

I hesitated for a brief moment and glanced over at Salvatore, who seemed somewhat annoyed or disappointed that this bombshell had chosen me over him. Then I just I shrugged my shoulders and, taking the pretty blonde's hand, led her to the dance floor.

I felt a little uncomfortable, for Salvatore's sake, with the way she had glued her body against mine as we danced cheek-to-cheek. When I reminded her that Salvatore was attracted to her, she explained she considered him her "Italian drinking buddy" and nothing more. At one moment, I realized the true sensuality of the slow dance when her hair brushed my face ever so gently, spreading an enticing aroma that aroused my senses to a state of ecstasy.

I couldn't help but wonder what bliss awaited me when the night was done—would I see her again? Would I have the nerve to ask her out? She saved me the trouble by asking me if we could meet the following day in the park. I glanced guiltily at the brooding Salvatore, who had jealously watched our every sensuous movement on the dance floor. Not being able to resist her, I finally said, "Yes, I will see you tomorrow afternoon at one o'clock."

On Sunday morning, I took the train to Bornheim to pick up Niko's mail. Fortunately, this time his landlady was there. She gave me quite a few letters and insurance documents to take to the hospital. When I arrived there, Niko had good reason to be in high spirits: he told me he was looking forward to going home in two days.

I chatted with him for a while, bringing him up to date on all the latest news, including the date I had with the "pretty blonde." Niko commented that I was certainly taking the German girls by storm! I kind of shrugged my shoulders and accepted his compliment, which served as another block in the rebuilding of my self-confidence.

Niko was a good man who helped me a great deal in getting acclimated to a new country, a time-consuming task that only people who care deeply for their fellow man would seriously consider undertaking. I reminded him of my appreciation for what he had done for me and thanked him once more for being a good friend and an all-around good guy. Then, because I did not want to miss my date, I said good-bye to Niko and took the train to Brühl.

I arrived at the park, where I was supposed to meet the "pretty blonde" at 12:50 p.m., but she was nowhere to be seen. After pacing back and forth along the narrow paths, I spotted her sitting on a bench next to a little girl, whom she later introduced as her six-year-old sister. *Here we go again!* I thought to myself. The previous night, we'd had her father as a chaperone; today, she'd brought the little sis so she would not get herself into a compromising situation.

I bribed her little sister with a frozen Popsicle I bought from a nearby stand. That kept her busy for a while, thus giving us the opportunity to walk away toward a secluded area. We were necking and heavy petting in the bushes when the little girl discovered us, pointing at us and giggling to beat the band. Needless to say, her untimely arrival put the kibosh on our delicious intimacy, much to my frustration.

Although we had agreed to see one another that evening at seven thirty, she never showed up. That put an end to my brief affair with the "pretty blonde." According to the notes in my journal, I didn't mind the fact that I'd had my first and last date with the "pretty blonde" on that Sunday afternoon. My confidence in dealing with women was growing with every little experience like this that came my way.

On the whole, the week of May 11 was uneventful. I rode the train to and from work with the same passengers, including my fantasy girls—Koukla, Round Face, and Deep Blue Eyes. It was fun exchanging quick, penetrating glances with these beautiful ladies, the underlying message of which all parties mutually understood—or so I surmised.

On Wednesday night, I visited Rita in her room, where we spent several rapturous hours of passionate foreplay without "going all the way." At one point, I noticed Rita was getting tired; she leaned over towards me and let herself flop onto my lap, where she slept for more than half an hour.

When it was time for me to leave, I told her, in somewhat garbled German, *"Ich möchte nicht gehen warum morgen ich werde sein allein."* It should have been, *"Ich möchte nicht gehen, weil morgen ich wieder allein bin,"* which means, "I would not like to leave, because tomorrow I will be alone again."

Rita did not have any problem understanding my incorrect language syntax. *"Ich auch"*— Me too—she answered. But it was getting late, and both of us had to work the next day.

So, I reluctantly left around eleven, having enjoyed a lovely evening with Rita, whose presence always filled me with delight—despite the fact that our relationship remained at the 'hugs and kisses" stage. Of course, I wanted her to surrender, to give me her body, her heart, and every part of her existence. But as I mentioned earlier, I respected her and would not ask her to engage in any act that would compromise her principles.

Thursday, May 14, is the day we celebrate my village's patron, Saint Isidore. Back home, there were many festivities to honor this annual event. In Germany, however, I simply marked the occasion by purchasing a grey blazer with a pair of black pants for eighty-seven marks, which exceeded my weekly paycheck of eighty marks. The clothing store manager accepted an arrangement of forty marks down payment and ten marks per week until the balance was paid in full. I looked forward to wearing my new outfit that coming weekend.

Chapter 17
Seconds with Edith

From my journal:

After completing my food shopping on Saturday morning, I went to see Edith in Bonn, who was expecting me in the early afternoon. When I arrived at a quarter to three, I found Edith in a jolly mood—but, as on my previous visit, she was typing a paper while referring to an open book next to the typewriter. According to the notes in my journal, when I asked her why she worked on weekends, she used the term *"Ich bin fleissig,"* which means, "I am industrious" or "I have diligence."

While I waited for her to finish her paper, I studied another German textbook that Edith had ready for me, opened to a specific lesson she had highlighted. Edith did not seem to be bothered by my incessant requests for a definition or usage of a word in a different phrase. Similarly, Edith demanded that I translate the same phrase to Greek. She repeated it several times until I nodded my acceptance of the correct pronunciation.

After our mutual language lesson, Edith brought out two cold beers, and then she placed a few LP records on the turntable. I asked her to dance with me when the last song played a slow Argentinean tango. Overall, I felt pretty comfortable about my dancing skills. But when she embraced me closely, my legs started taking slower steps and my heart pounded like a jackhammer. This was an even more pleasurable experience than the one I had had the previous week with the "pretty blonde!"

All sorts of strange emotions were crowding my mind as I danced with Edith, a genuine lady with high standards and superior social status. At that moment, I found myself in a confused state of mind, not being able to distinguish the difference between friendship, lust, and passion. And then there was that "mystery connection," when we both slowed down before coming to a full stop while the music was still playing, staring at each other with a purposeful intensity.

I didn't realize that the romantic conquest I subconsciously wanted was gliding toward me on gossamer wings, completely taking me—perhaps both of us—by surprise. Our lips met passionately and we plunged into a kissing marathon that ended up in a silent staring contest, as if we were questioning whether two friends should be engaging in that sort of activity.

While gathering our thoughts, trying to decide what should come next—after a prelude to what usually comes naturally—we were literally "saved by the bell" as someone rang the front door bell. I was not surprised to see Edith's German friend, the same man I had met during my last visit. Perhaps this was an omen meant to signify that Edith and I should preserve our relationship at the friendship level.

Anyway, after a light dinner, I left for the train station. However, this time I was not as angry over the intrusion of Edith's friend as I had been on my previous visit, when I characterized him as a pig.

On the train ride back to Brühl, I reviewed the day's events, specifically how Edith would compare me against her friend, who was also an established educator with several other notable qualities. According to Edith, he had written a few short stories and had published newspaper and magazine articles. Overall, he was well-known within the circle of intellectuals. This was a level of knowledge and status I had yet to acquire.

I could not control her other suitors, but if I tried to develop my own strength of character, knowledge, and insight, I could perhaps build some sort of competitive advantage. I knew I had made great progress in many areas of self-development in a relatively short period, but there were still many underdeveloped aspects of my individuality that only time, focus, and experience would define and solidify.

Chapter 18

The Other Women

A s I came to synthesize everything I knew or had accomplished up
to that point in my life, I realized I had no clear idea where I was
headed. I didn't have any defined short- or long-term goals except
for the determination to elevate my life to a higher social and economic
level. My self-esteem was flourishing as the small successes kept piling
up, which encouraged me to remain motivated and basically maintain an
overall positive outlook.

I thought about the road construction work I was engaged in. It was a
job that, on one hand, I needed to survive. But on the other hand, instead
of leaving it up to chance, I decided I should develop a plan defining the
steps necessary to ascend to the top of the pyramid. I was starting from the
lowest point of survival, but I wanted to reach the highest level of "self-
actualization," a term coined by Dr. Abraham Maslow.

As I rode the train alone, I used the time as a mind exercise, analyzing
thoughts or dreaming of future successes, leaving no room for boredom.
Although I knew quite well that I had to set my priorities in order, my
thoughts and desires helplessly gravitated towards—you guessed it, dear
reader—girls! Perhaps my limited exposure to girls during my teenage
years brought out unfulfilled desires and ranked them at the top of my
emotional priority list.

All of a sudden, women to me were just like magnets, pulling me in
every which way, offering me an abundance of choices to satisfy my basic
instincts. Essentially, I felt like a mosquito in a nudist camp! Like any hot-
blooded Greek male worth his salt, I took advantage of every opportunity

for physical pleasure without allowing any emotional attachments to get in the way.

While I couldn't resist the temptations—who am kidding? I thoroughly enjoyed them!—I halfheartedly hoped my "weakness" was a passing fad that would fade in the near future so that I could concentrate on the more substantial matters of my self-development.

When I next arrived in Brühl, I made my usual stop at the Post Lounge. My Italian and Greek friends were all there, having a good time. The "pretty blonde" was there with her father—but this time, I ignored her completely. Another lady, named Maria, asked me to dance with her during the ladies choice numbers.

For the most part, I spent the entire evening dancing with Maria, who was an attractive and cheerful woman, perhaps six or seven years older than I was. Her age didn't bother me at all. I stayed at the bar until closing, relishing Maria's company. She made sure I knew she would be back the following night and that she would like to see me again.

While drinking my late morning coffee on Sunday, May 17, I suddenly realized I'd been in Germany for one month. During that relatively short period, I had made tremendous progress, both in terms of my accomplishments and my lifestyle. These developments had exceeded my wildest expectations. I was looking forward to my rendezvous with Maria at the Post that night.

When I got there, around seven, I was a little disappointed that Maria and her friend were not sitting at their usual table. I joined Salvatore at the bar, ordered a glass of beer, and lit a cigarette as I waited impatiently for Maria to show up. The band was playing a lively dance song when I spotted Maria entering the front door with a wide smile on her face. Right away, she greeted me with a kiss on the cheek and invited me to sit with her group at their usual corner table.

She danced with me all night while drinking quite heavily, mixing beer with schnapps and other hard liquor varieties. All night she kept calling me "*mein lieber jung*," which means "my dear young," a phrase that has a more sensuous or affectionate connotation in German than the English translation. By the end of the night, her friend asked me if I would take Maria home, because she was drunk.

When I took her outside, she told me that, before I took her home, she wanted to go for a little walk with me on a quiet dirt road across from the train tracks. She repeatedly cried out in German, "You should have stopped me, why did you let me drink so much?" and "I will never drink again!" and so on.

Well, I did not want to take advantage of her vulnerable condition, but the sensation of the alcohol and cigarette smoke combined with her kisses was like an aphrodisiac, which ultimately made me succumb to her amorous advances. What a night! We enjoyed a lustful interlude under the starry sky, with the chirping of the crickets providing the background music for that incredible experience, which modesty prevents me from describing in too much detail.

We stayed in that quiet place for a long time. As we scaled the heights of passion, Maria expressed words of concern, such as "You will probably forget me soon," and "You will find another girl younger than me," and so on. I tried to reassure her that I liked her a great deal. In fact, I told her, "I love you and I would never forget you or leave you."

Author's note: Earlier in the book, when I wrote about my arrival in Germany, I noted that there were many occasions when I exaggerated unintentionally. Well, this night was one of these occasions, when I overstated an emotion by telling someone that I was in love with her without even knowing much about the person. Unfortunately, while I'm writing this book, I have to reference my journal with a mature criticism, using today's mindset.

All the way to her house, she kept telling me, "Life without you would be so empty! Don't ever leave me!" Again, I tried to reassure her that I would definitely be with her as long as she needed me or cared for me. However, I questioned whether her lovesick declarations were the result of her intoxicated condition. I also wondered how she would feel the next day, after the hangover, when she would be forced to view the situation with a clear, logical mind.

Monday, May 18, was either a federal or a religious holiday, so I took this opportunity to sleep in late to make up for the previous night's escapade. I had promised Edith that I would visit her that day, so I took the train for Bonn in the early afternoon. While on the train, I must have been daydreaming, because I exited the train in Bonn West, one stop before my usual destination.

I walked for more than an hour before I arrived at Edith's apartment. As always, she was in a jolly mood, welcoming me with open arms, hugging me and expressing a sincere "nice to see you" attitude. What a pleasant and genuine person she was! She always had a positive outlook. She was always finding the goodness in people, often emphasizing that "you will always find what you're looking for, so you might as well let your search yield positive things."

Edith couldn't wait to show me the letter she had written in Greek, which I actually found to be very well written. It was amazing that she had reached this level of familiarity with Greek in just a month or so. (The expression, "That's Greek to me"—which means, "that something is incomprehensible"—surely came from someone attempting to learn this most difficult language!) I complimented her for her accomplishment and we both agreed that her *fleissig*—diligent or industrious— studying, along with the little help I was giving her, had yielded better results than expected.

We continued going over her Greek document and I made a few corrections. During the lesson, we had a few laughs when she tried to translate a colloquial German expression, "*zuckerpuppe*" (sugar doll), into Greek. Of course, the translation sounded funny, as every language has its own unique idiomatic usage of phrases that were made up and passed on from generation to generation.

After an hour of studying, Edith prepared dinner for us as a "form of reciprocation for the great lesson we had today," she said laughingly. We also finished a bottle of Portuguese wine, which was indeed good. When it was time for me to go, I don't know what triggered my emotional outbreak.

The wine must have had a lot to do with my mood, but perhaps I was also homesick. I took a picture of my sister, Despina, from my wallet and stared at it intensely with, I'm sure, the most woebegone look on my face.

Edith seemed understanding of what I was going through; she put her arms around me and tried to console me by patting my back ever so gently. She walked with me to the train station, but before I boarded the train, she gave me a little note indicating that she wanted to meet me next weekend at 5:00 p.m. outside the museum in Cologne. I nodded my assent and said goodnight with a soft kiss on her cheek.

A few minutes into my trip, I realized that I had taken the wrong train, so I got off on Bonn West, waiting for the next train to return to the central station in Bonn. The entire process, including the time it took me to ride to Brühl, delayed me by more than an hour and a half. It was too bad that an evening which had started so well had to include my emotional outburst and end with this senseless blunder.

As the hurtling train jostled my innards, I realized the wine must have not agreed with me at all. My vision was blurry and my head throbbed with an unbearable headache. Fortunately, I took a little nap on the train before we arrived in Brühl, which made me feel a lot better.

It was ten minutes past midnight when I found myself outside the Post Lounge on my way home. Well, you guessed right! I went in to see what the action was, who was there, and so on. An acquaintance named George pulled me aside and told me that Maria had been searching for me all night.

"She asked me to check if you were home, to make sure you were not sick or something," said George, shouting a little to be heard over the music. "In fact, I went to your apartment twice, looking for you."

Just then, I saw Maria approaching me with a Cheshire cat grin on her face, a sure sign she was glad to see me. After explaining my whereabouts, a man came over and introduced himself as Maria's ex-husband—or perhaps he meant they were just separated. Regardless, they remained on good terms and enjoyed a friendly relationship. The situation was a bit confusing, to say the least. And to top it all off, they matter-of-factly said that they had a six-year-old son!

"I will explain it to you another time," Maria called over her shoulder as the two of them walked toward the exit. I trudged home feeling dog-tired, thinking that I was going to face a difficult day at work in the morning.

As expected, the following day (Tuesday), I did not have the energy to get up and go to work. Although Rita woke me up a few times, I decided to stay in bed so as to get enough sleep to face the day. I arose around two in the afternoon and had brunch. Afterwards, I wrote a letter to my sister and then went to Maria's house, where I met her son, Rolf, for the first time.

I was probably somewhat emotionally attached to her already, because I didn't seem to mind that she had a handsome little boy. His grandmother took care of him while Maria was at work. I joined them for dinner and left around 9:30 p.m., after Maria gave me a picture of herself, which I had requested a few days before.

The rest of the week at work was more or less the same routine at the road construction site. One notable observation I would like to mention was the fact that both the workmanship and the material used to build a neighborhood secondary road were of excellent quality. In addition, the Germans' diligence, punctuality, and deferment of instant gratification are some of the individual attributes that have earned them the reputation of excellence in almost all the products and services they build or provide. They take pride in their work, a key factor that starts at the individual level and subsequently expands throughout the entire nation. It's no wonder, then, that nations like Germany have enjoyed well-earned success academically, socially, and economically.

Indeed, the individual work ethic of the German people is impeccable, but the most important description I can apply to them is: *The Germans enjoy their free time!* They pay attention to the people they are with, and they *do things* with their free time. They spend lots of time with their friends and family, and they pursue hobbies much more complex than just watching television. They visit museums, read complex books, drink a whole lot, and go to parties, fairs, and circuses. They also take lots of vacations.

The German people don't fall into the trap so eloquently described by Edmund Burke: *"The only thing necessary for the triumph of evil is for good men to do nothing."*

I admired the Germans' overall attitude and performance at work. You cannot differentiate the boss from the peons if you observe the type of chores they perform during the workday. In fact, when I asked my supervisor why he had to work even harder than his crew did, his answer was, "When I go home at night, I look in the mirror and ask myself, 'Hans, how was your day? What did you accomplish today?' If I'm satisfied with the answer, I ride my bike to the neighborhood bar and enjoy a few beers with my friends."

And then he followed with an important clarification. "The reason I ride my bike instead of driving my car is because, if I have a few extra drinks, I don't want to lose my license for driving drunk, since the penalty for DWI in Germany is harsh—you can lose your license for a year."

This was good advice, but I was not even dreaming of getting a car any time soon—although I had begun to think I should consider buying a used bike.

On Saturday afternoon, May 23, I was scheduled to meet Edith in Cologne. I arrived at a quarter to three, but I had a hard time finding the museum where we were supposed to meet at three. Fortunately, an older fellow showed me the way and I arrived there a few minutes before the appointed time. Edith showed up precisely on time. Again, I had to admire the Germans' punctuality, an inherent quality of their culture.

Edith looked stunningly beautiful, wearing a colorful spring outfit and a tight, wide belt around her small waist that accentuated her tall, slender figure perfectly. We stopped at an outdoor café for a beer that was served in a tall glass. Well, it seemed that I was talking with my hands, like Salvatore at the Post. You guessed it—I knocked my glass over and spilled the beer all over Edith's lovely outfit!

94

Edith just laughed, but I felt absolutely terrible for being such a clumsy oaf. She assured me that everything was fine after the waiter brought some paper towels and another beer.

Next, we walked along the banks of the Rhine River and sat on a bench where we spent some time reading and enjoying the view as well as the relaxing sound of the whispering water. The best feature of that locale was a spectacular restaurant complex inside a park with an indoor/outdoor dance floor. The park was surrounded by water and all sorts of flowering shrubs.

It was a picturesque setting, something I had previously seen only at the movies. This was truly an unforgettable experience. In that place, I found true serenity, which offered me genuine food for the soul.

"Thank you, Edith, for exposing me to this majestic spectacle," I said in the best German I could muster. I didn't use exactly these words, but I meant the gist of the thought wholeheartedly. We then headed for the train station, having agreed that Edith would visit me in Brühl the next day around 11:00 a.m.

When I arrived in Brühl at ten minutes of ten, I made a brief stop at my apartment to have a quick bite. Then I hurried to the Post Lounge, arriving a quarter after ten. As I had expected, Maria was waiting for me impatiently. She launched into an interrogation as to my whereabouts that evening, since we had agreed to meet two hours earlier.

I managed to come up with a convincing excuse, saying that I had fallen asleep on the train, missing the Brühl station. I told her I'd had to ride all the way to Bonn, and from there I had taken the next train back to Brühl.

We drank quite a bit and danced for more than three hours. This expensive revelry marked the first time I had spent much more than my allowed budget for a single night at the lounge.

After the bar closed, we ended up at our usual location near the train tracks, basking in a few hours of passionate intimacy. This long, long day finally came to an end at 4:00 a.m. when I arrived home. I believed I would sleep for less than six hours, since I had a date with Edith on Sunday morning, only seven hours later.

I woke up at 10:35 on Sunday morning, took a quick shower, had a bite on the run, and rushed for the train station. Fortunately for me, the train was about an hour late, so Edith did not have to wait for me.

The program for that day was to continue our respective language tutorials, so we walked to the park, where we found a quiet place that was ideal for studying. Having spent two productive hours in the park, we were both pleased with the fruits of our labor. I don't recall why we made this type of arrangement—why Edith came to Brühl, that is—since early that afternoon we took the train to Bonn and headed straight to her apartment. We both took a shower—separately, of course—and then enjoyed a delicious dinner that Edith prepared.

Author's Note: I hate to reveal some truths, but up to this point in this writing, I was patiently referencing my daily journal without criticizing that self-centered, one-track-minded, twenty-year-old "me." However, I have exhausted my patience and realize that I am embarrassed—or rather, very upset—as I read the detailed description of the events that took place in Edith's apartment the afternoon of May 24.

Compared with my current way of thinking, I can honestly say that my interaction with women after I arrived in Germany was kind of childish and undoubtedly immature in terms of the words I used to describe my feelings. That approach can be chalked up to the universal awkwardness of intimate communication. How did I dare tell Edith, "I love you and would like you to be my wife ..." along with other words of intimacy?

But I did so. And as a logical person, Edith responded, "I'm old enough to be your mother. You don't really love me; at this moment you only love my body."

I completely disregarded the fact that my uncontrollable desire jeopardized our priceless "just friends" relationship. Instead, my expectations were audacious and animal-like. I kept insisting that we should enjoy the moment and that I would never forget her; even her crying plea did not stop me from the uncontrollable desire of achieving instant gratification.

Even when Edith said, "Another man also promised that he would never forget me, but I was left with a broken heart," *I would not back down. Even after all these emotional pleas, I had the nerve to tell her that I was different.*

Yeah, right! I was different; I was as different as a vulture in disguise, ready to attack his prey, ready to take advantage of a vulnerable soul.

Edith finally gave up when I told her that I was totally defenseless when dealing with women and that I could not resist the temptation of a beautiful body next to mine. She gave in to weakness momentarily, lying in bed next to me, after taking her clothes off, piece by piece. Fortunately, she was the stronger person for not letting the situation get out of hand. When she realized what my intentions were, she insisted that we stop.

I'll never forget her sage words: "If we continue this way, we will both regret it, so let's leave it at that." She drew a sigh of relief as I nodded in agreement, though my face registered my supreme disappointment.

(Well, describing all of the above was a release of frustration, and I'm glad I've gotten it off my chest!)

Despite the unseemly turn of events, Edith's indomitable cheerfulness was still in evidence as she walked with me to the train station. In fact, she asked me to see her again the following Thursday!

Chapter 19

Looking for Hans Janssen

Over the next several weeks, I saw Maria regularly on the weekends and occasionally got together with Edith. During this same period, I also began looking for another job in an unlikely sphere of business.

Before I left Greece, my friend, George, had given me the address of a German gentleman named Hans Janssen who had visited George's delicatessen while on vacation with his wife. Hans told George that if he or any of his friends were ever in Germany, he was willing to help in any way. George also told me that Hans owned a chain of grocery stores in the metropolitan Bonn area. I kept this gentleman's address in my "to do" folder.

Excited by the prospect of becoming involved in one of Mr. Janssen's enterprises, I decided to take a day off from my manual labor job. I rode the train to Bonn for the purpose of looking up this successful entrepreneur. I felt a little apprehensive, because I was going to meet someone for the first time without an appointment.

At the Bonn station, I tried to access the street locator apparatus, a map-like board where you punch in the name of the street and a glowing red dot indicates the location you are searching for. There was another gentleman in front of me who, coincidentally, punched in the exact same street I wanted. The red-dotted street on the map seemed to be far away from the station, in a section of the city that required one to take either a bus or the inner-city tram.

When the gentleman asked me if I wanted to go with him, since we were both going to the same location, I thought to myself that he was God-sent—just as Hermann had been. I couldn't help but wonder if this encounter were further proof that my guardian angel in Bonn took the guise of good Samaritans in the train stations, who seemed always on duty to put me on the right track, as it were.

I put my trust in my fellow German—by now, you see, I was starting to consider myself a countryman—who knew exactly where to get off the tram. I simply followed him when we got off. But his puzzled expression clearly showed that this was not the street we were looking for. The area seemed almost entirely barren and in the middle of nowhere.

We walked a few blocks down the road to a gas station, where my German guide asked someone for additional directions. Then he explained to me that the same street began at another location, a few kilometers away. There were plans to connect the two parts of the road at some time in the future—but apparently, no one had told the makers of the street locator apparatus that the connecting road hadn't been built yet.

I sighed with relief, thinking that, if not for my nice German guide, I would have never found Mr. Janssen's store on my own. I have to admit, I didn't even ask him his name. But in all honesty, I wouldn't have been surprised if he were another version of "Hermann," a supernatural being impersonating an ordinary mortal.

We finally located Mr. Janssen's store. The number "46" was emblazoned on the awning that traversed the entire storefront. After thanking my German guide, I entered the store, introduced myself and told one of the clerks that I would like to see Mr. Janssen. The clerk informed me he was not there, but he called his boss on the telephone and explained who I was, where I came from, and so on. When the clerk hung up the phone, he told me that someone would take me to see Mr. Janssen at another store.

At this new location, I first met his wife, who greeted me cordially. She asked me to tell her the reason for my visit as well as why I had come to Germany and other relevant details about my situation.

In my journal, I noted that Hans Janssen arrived at 12:10 p.m. My first impression of him was positive, in that he seemed to be a nice person. He was a handsome man, about thirty-five years old, six feet tall, with light brown hair and blue eyes. His dimpled face reminded me of the actor Paul Newman, especially when he cracked a smile, which made his dimples more pronounced.

Hans Janssen was a businessman, so he immediately began explaining the nature of his business operation. Then he began talking about a hypothetical job offer for me, should I decide to join his company. He gave me some details of the potential job, indicating that, for the next three to four months, I would ride with one of his drivers to purchase and distribute various vegetables to his stores around the metro Bonn area. When I had become more fluent in German, he said, I would be promoted to the selling sector.

Well, I understood everything he said except for the selling part; I had no idea what type of selling I would be involved with, and I didn't inquire. He then invited me to join him for lunch at his home.

After driving for about ten minutes, he stopped in the driveway of an exquisite mansion. The place was palace-like in its grandeur. It was surrounded by trees and manicured shrubbery. As I had expected, the interior of the house was, without a doubt, the most luxurious dwelling I had ever seen.

We sat down for lunch with his wife and two teenaged daughters. I felt like a fish out of water when the maid started serving what turned out to be the first course of a multi-course meal. Having only enjoyed informal dinners with Edith, I was not used to such regal dining. I realized that this family no doubt expected proper table etiquette from their guests. I carefully observed my hosts with regard to how they placed their napkins, used their utensils, and their overall approach, desperately mimicking their movements.

At one point during the meal's second course, the two daughters, who were sitting across from me, started laughing and whispering to one another, but Hans told them their behavior was inappropriate in front of a guest and made them stop. I assumed I must have done something improper that the girls found either amusing or totally deplorable within their high society circle, prompting them to make fun of me. I suspect it was the way I ate the soup—perhaps I made a distinct slurping sound as I sipped the hot broth.

As I struggled not to make a fool of myself in front of this upper-crust family, I suddenly felt insignificant and humiliated. I resolved, then and there, to improve my social etiquette and also promised myself I would learn to speak and understand German as fluently as a true native, so I would never have to face another similarly embarrassing situation.

After lunch, I rode with one of Mr. Janssen's drivers, who gave me a firsthand look at my potential job by completing the pick-up and distribution of vegetables to several grocery stores in the suburbs of Bonn. The driver was a pleasant fellow who patiently explained to me all aspects of the job. I have to admit that, as we rode along, I became somewhat apprehensive about the job. I was overtaken by uncertainty, a familiar feeling that, once again, started undermining my self-confidence.

When we finished the distribution route, we went back to the central store, where Hans spent most of his time. Hans explained that, if I accepted the job, I would have to find a room or apartment in Bonn. I told him that

I would start looking for a new residence and that my friend Edith, who lived in Bonn, would help me in my search. Hans asked his driver to take me to Brühl, saving me the expense and bother of taking the train. On the way, the driver told me that he also would help me find a room.

We drove past Edith's apartment, but unfortunately, she was not there. I left a brief note in her mailbox making her aware that I would like to see her soon because I was considering a job offer in Bonn. I thanked the driver when he dropped me off in front of my apartment. However, instead of *me* giving *him* a gift for all he had done for me, he gave me two packs of cigarettes! *What a nice person*, I thought to myself, as his car disappeared around the corner.

In fact, all the people I had met in Germany so far were "salts of the earth" who had been willing to help their fellow man without blinking an eye. It was as though they were trying to compensate for all the pain and suffering their country had inflicted on the whole world during the war years. (Speaking of the war, every time I brought up the subject in casual conversation, everyone avoided discussing or commenting about it. They just wanted to forget!)

In my apartment, I found two letters. One was from Edith, who wrote that I should visit her on the following Wednesday if I were not working that day. I went to bed at ten after a long, adventurous day. My adventure had been fraught with embarrassment, but also had presented me with opportunities that required tough decisions on my part.

I had to decide whether to stay in Brühl or move to Bonn and start all over again in a completely new line of work. This dilemma reminded me of an old saying: "Luck is what happens when preparation and courage meet opportunity." However, I had a strange feeling that the job in Bonn was not the right one for me.

When I went to work the following day, the foreman noticed I had a problem with my right arm—I was in agonizing pain each time I tried to lift even the lightest object. The foreman sent me to the doctor, who ordered me to stay home for a week to give the muscle inflammation in my forearm a chance to heal.

Because I was off that week, I visited Edith in Bonn on Wednesday. As always, she seemed happy to see me, welcoming me with a big smile and a hug. I told her all about the new job possibility and said that I would have to find a room or an apartment in Bonn, should I decide to accept Mr. Janssen's offer.

After discussing all the pros and cons, Edith left it up to me to decide, suggesting that the best way to find an apartment in Bonn was to search through the Saturday newspaper want ads. I had hoped Edith would advise me one way or another, to accept or not accept the job, but she indirectly told me that the choice was only mine to make.

I also told Edith that I was determined to accelerate my German language studies. She was pleased by my commitment and promised me she would try to help me become fluent. Not wasting any time, we hit the books, spending two to three hours of intense studying. She gave me a good deal of work to complete at home, asking me to return the results to her either by mail or in person, the next time I saw her.

Chapter 20

The Missing Notes from My Journal

F or some unknown reason, the pages in my journal between July 8, 1959, and April 30, 1960, are missing. I will do my best to describe the most vivid events from memory.

I continued my German studies by allocating an average of two hours every day, either at home or in the park. I preferred the park on weekends when the weather was favorable. I visited Edith every chance I had, but for the most part, I spent my weekends with Maria, whom I had considered my steady girlfriend for at least two months.

After rejecting Mr. Janssen's job offer in Bonn, Maria influenced me to seek employment in Cologne, where she worked in a textile factory. I took that job, but I resigned after two weeks because the environment was dangerous and unhealthy. An unbearable smell, similar to that of rotten eggs, permeated the work area. The air quality was so poor that the work schedule required a shift to be exposed to those noxious chemicals for only ten minutes, and then to take a ten-minute break outside the smelly area.

Fortunately, right after I resigned, I found another job. This one was in Brühl, within a ten-minute bike ride from my apartment. There was no public transportation to my new place of work and it was a bit too far to walk, so I bought a used bike for twenty-five marks.

My new job was almost as hard as the road construction had been. It entailed unloading raw material and loading trucks with finished liquid products in 200-kilo drums. I worked with a bunch of nice guys in a relatively small firm. That's where I met Richard, a warmhearted, outstanding individual who ultimately became my best friend in Germany. Richard introduced me to Charlie, who ended up being a good friend as well. The three of us formed a tight bond that was destined to last for a long, long time.

Richard was about my height, five feet ten, though a little bit heavier than me. He had a round face with puffed cheeks and well-trimmed blonde hair and mustache. Richard (who liked to be called Teddy) was a happy man who always concentrated on the positive aspects of an individual. He accepted others just the way they were. He was a rare find, a true friend!

Charlie, on the other hand, was more than six feet, four inches tall. He was a strong man with curly brown hair and brown eyes. Although people who met Charlie for the first time often formed the opinion that he was a mean, selfish, and stern individual, behind that façade was a child-like personality that emerged after a few minutes of casual conversation.

A few weeks after starting the new job, I broke up with Maria. She was becoming "too demanding and dangerously jealous"—that was the phrase that Richard and his girlfriend, Carmen, used to describe Maria one night when we were out at a nightclub in Cologne. (Carmen was a beautiful lady, a bit older than Richard was, but she possessed an unusual, exotic Spanish exquisiteness. Richard was utterly crazy about her.)

During this period, I moved to another two-story house, where I rented a room right above a delicatessen, a family-owned business that took up the entire first floor. The family of three consisted of the mother, who had a full-time job, and her two young daughters, who took turns managing the store seven days a week. It was a convenient arrangement for me in terms of food shopping, because I just had to go down the stairway to buy the items I needed for the day, and never needed to store any food in my room. I used a portable electric cook-top to prepare simple meals, mostly omelets, pasta, and rice dishes.

Next to the delicatessen was a small, one-story house occupied by a retired psychologist named Friedrich Wagner. He often invited me to have a beer with him and discuss Greek philosophers. When I told him I wanted to enhance my language skills, he gladly offered to help me, but he only demanded that we converse in "*hochdeutsch*," the "High German" language intellectuals use.

High German is a form of the language with a succinct pronunciation of the words, without any trace of dialectic or slangy connotations. Of course, I took Dr. Wagner up on his offer, and he turned out to be one of my best German tutors. He also became my mentor regarding the true joy of life, the meaning of self-confidence, how to get the things you want, and other self-developmental pursuits.

I remember once asking him why some people are born more intelligent than others. Without missing a beat, he answered, "*Faulheit ist dummheit des körpers und dummheit is faulheit des geistes,*" which closely translates to: Laziness is stupidity of the body, and stupidity is laziness of the mind.

And then he uttered loudly (in German): "So keep on studying, keep on learning, keep your mind busy. Don't let your mind get stale! Do you understand?"

"*Ja,* Herr Wagner, I understand," I politely responded.

Up to this point, I had been exceedingly satisfied with the tremendous progress I'd made in mastering the German language. I was more or less fluent now and could truly converse with ease on any subject, but I did not stop studying. I continually expanded my vocabulary.

One Saturday night, I went to the Post Lounge and sat at the furthest table from the band. Not being in a good mood, I wanted to be alone, drink my beer, listen to the music, and just watch the others dance. Some girls asked me to dance with them, but I politely refused. When the place became crowded, a beautiful lady approached me and asked if I would share the table with her because there were no other seats available. "Of course!" I exclaimed as I pulled out the chair for her to sit down.

Her name was Heidi. As we talked, drank, and danced all night, my melancholic mood transformed into a state of euphoria. She was about 5'7" tall and slender, with light brown hair and green eyes. When we first hit the dance floor, I realized she was a good dancer; her body in my arms felt and moved like a feather. Her posture showed a confident, pretty lady. I hoped her inner world would be as beautiful as her looks.

Dancing with Heidi was a unique experience—that is to say, she was not like any other girl I had danced with before. In her eyes, I saw the elegance, the charisma, and basically most of the attributes I was looking for in a woman. I found her simply irresistible. I hoped and prayed she felt the same way about me.

Fate smiled on me once again. Heidi and I developed a close relationship, seeing each other almost every day. On weekends, we went out with Richard, Carmen, and Charlie, forming an inseparable group that stayed together for a long time.

(Incidentally, Charlie was not committed to any particular girl—unlike Richard, who was madly in love with Carmen—for more than a few weeks. Every so often, he brought a new date along on our weekend outings. Charlie was witty, good-natured, a quick thinker, and a funny guy overall, able to hold his own on any subject. He always found humor, kindness, and positive aspects in everything and everyone. Bottom line, Charlie was a fun guy to be with!)

Chapter 21

My Father in Germany

I corresponded with all my friends and family on a regular basis, especially with my father, who expressed an interest in coming to Germany for a visit. I wrote a letter encouraging him to join me for a few months to see and experience an urban lifestyle that was completely different from our pastoral village. I also sent the money for his train ticket, which was really a repayment for my one-way fare to Germany.

My father wrote back that he had decided to accept my invitation; he also outlined his itinerary, starting from the village to the city of Rhodes, taking the boat to Athens, and finally the train from Athens to Bonn.

On the day of his arrival, a Friday night— September 4, 1959—I waited in the Bonn station. The train was right on time. I watched the passengers exit the train platform and enter the main building, where I stood waiting, but I did not see my father anywhere. I waited another ten minutes; when I saw the last passenger exit, I decided to leave, thinking that he must have missed the train and that he would probably take the next one the following day.

I got home around 2:30 a.m. and went straight to bed because I was scheduled to work half a day on Saturday. When the doorbell rang at half past three, I ran downstairs and saw my father standing there. He asked me why I had not been at the train station to pick him up, which had forced him to take a taxi.

Finally, we unraveled the misunderstanding. We had missed one another because, as soon as my father got off the train, he stood waiting for me on the platform outside the station. In the meantime, I was inside the main building, expecting him to show up like all other passengers. It never occurred to me that he would stay on the platform. After chatting for a while, we both went to bed—but an hour later, I had to wake up and go to work.

About a month before my father's arrival, I had helped two friends, Emanuel and Giacomi from Rhodes, come to Germany. I had helped them secure jobs and I'd found a place for them to stay—a small apartment only a few blocks from the delicatessen. They both worked in a factory called Sekova, which was within walking distance from the street where we lived.

Emmanuel and Giacomi offered to help my father get at job at Sekova, where he was hired. He began working just a few days after he arrived in Germany.

All of sudden, I realized I had a big problem: I did not know how to entertain my father on the weekends. How in the world would my father, a man accustomed to working like a dog all his life, spend his free time in a single room?

I weighed the pros and cons of my father living with me and concluded that his coming to Germany had not been a good idea after all. I had acted impulsively, without considering the consequences or the impact his constant presence would have on my life.

For several weeks, I was in complete turmoil. My father was cramping my style, as the saying goes, particularly when it came to my friends and Heidi. I actually regretted the fact that my dad had joined me in Germany, and I was mad at myself for making it happen.

After a while, I discussed my problem with Emanuel and Giacomi, who offered to take my father with them on weekends to some clubs and other places suitable for his age group. My father accepted their suggestion, and life became a little more balanced for all of us.

There were many occasions when my father and I spent time together, either walking in the park or having a few beers at a bar. Most of our discussions had to do with our family back home. I could sense how homesick he was, being away from my mother and the seven other children. He often said that, although Germany offered great job opportunities, there was nothing like being together with the entire family in your own country, in your own house.

I truly did my best to keep my father happy, despite the adjustments I had to make to allocate time for him. However, at the end of three months, he decided to return to Greece. I did not try to convince him otherwise, for he was lonely and miserable away from the bosom of his family. So one day we took the train to Bonn and off he went back home.

When my father had finally made it home safely, I tried to understand my primary motives for inviting him to Germany. I felt somewhat guilty for having to put him through an unnecessary inconvenience. In retrospect, I realize it had been selfish of me. I believed I wanted someone close to me, like my father, to see me in action and to witness how much I had accomplished. I wanted him to see my successes firsthand. I wanted to convince him that I could scale the heights when someone gave me a chance, so that he could act as a messenger and invalidate the ne'er-do-well reputation I'd left behind and reverse the negative opinion others had of me.

I had counted the days until his arrival, but after only a few days, the novelty had worn off and the roles had been reversed. That is to say, the son had to take care of his healthy, forty-three year old father instead of the other way around. Perhaps I needed to go through this period with my father for my own good. The experience taught me a valuable lesson in terms of being responsible for another person. I learned about sacrifices, adjustments, and how to make decisions that affected someone other than me. I wholeheartedly believe the experience made me a better and more responsible person.

I wrote a letter to my father apologizing for not spending enough time with him and begged him not to be disappointed in me. He wrote back indicating that, during the three months he lived with me, he had marveled at the tremendous progress I had made in so many areas. He added that, ultimately, he had simply realized he could not stay away from the family that still needed him. He went on to say he was proud of me and that I owed him no apologies. And with that, I went back to my old routine.

Chapter 22

The Cold Months

M r. Haas, our foreman at work, was a standout individual who treated all of us with fairness and respect, an approach that promoted camaraderie among the workers. The entire plant was like a family—we "had each other's backs" on both job-related and personal matters. Our bosses, the father and his two sons, addressed everyone by their last name and talked to us as if we were equals. They were fair-minded employers with impeccable work ethics, which they never compromised. Needless to say, I liked the place a lot.

I had grown accustomed to the arduous work conditions, but I will admit there were some occasions, such as when we had to work outside on cold days in late autumn, that I wished I had a cushy office job. The two other workers in my age group were my friend, Richard, and Rolf, who was married with a young child.

All three of us hung out together during lunch and coffee breaks, having a great time and lots of laughs. I truly felt contented with everything that was happening in my life. Time seemed to stand still as I was living in the "now," savoring every moment at work and with my friends. Life was good!

I saw Heidi quite frequently. The two of us would go out alone or double date with Richard and Carmen. Charlie came along, too, when he had a date. Heidi and I enjoyed each other's company so much that we decided to "go steady." Coincidentally, Richard had also made the same arrangement with Carmen, so every time we got together, we were like four peas in a pod, united in our mutual friendship and our love for our respective significant others. Instead of the Post Lounge, we spent most weekend nights at the Fischer Lounge, five blocks from my previous apartment on Wilhelm Street. Our new place catered to a slightly more sophisticated crowd of young people, mainly in their early twenties.

I was saddened, though, when Heidi told me that she planned to spend Christmas with her mother in a small town near Wiesbaden. She was leaving the next day, Christmas Eve, which fell on a Thursday in 1959. Heidi said she would return on the day after Christmas, which meant I would be all by myself over the holiday. Even Richard would be with his parents. Also, Niko had moved to another town in northern Germany near Hamburg.

The following day, on my way to work, I escorted Heidi to the train station and wished her a Merry Christmas as she got aboard. She blew me a kiss from her window and I waved sadly until the train disappeared down the long railway.

Because it was Christmas Eve, we worked only half a day. Our foreman did not assign any real work. Instead, there was plenty of food and drinks for everyone to celebrate the holiday at the workplace with all our associates, supervisors, and big bosses. We all gathered outside Mr. Haas' office in a long hallway where the caterers set up a few tables with German delicacies. The variety of treats satisfied everyone's taste.

At the end of the party, just before noon—out of the blue—the son of one of the big bosses invited me to come to his house that afternoon, much to my surprise. He gave me directions, but I already had a good idea that the house was located near a park, about a ten-minute bike ride from my house.

It was a cloudy, misty afternoon when I arrived at the house. Although I could only see the front part of the house, I surmised that the structure was a real mansion, surrounded by well-positioned pine trees that concealed the side and rear view of the white brick house. The immaculately trimmed evergreen bushes in the front yard were festooned with lighted garlands, which lent the place a certain charm. It looked both festive and homey.

Before I rang the bell, I stood there for a minute or two, reminiscing about the Christmas holidays in the village, thinking of my friends and family and the preparations that were underway for their Christmas Day celebration. The boss' son opened the door and wished me "*Frohe Weihnachten*"—Merry Christmas—and addressed me by my last name, as was customary among my bosses.

He said he understood that I was alone in a new country during the holidays and that he wanted to give me something extra besides the Christmas bonus everyone received at work. So he gave me a sealed envelope, a box of fine German chocolates, and a new, double-breasted, brown suit. I thanked him over and over again for this generous and compassionate gesture, which showed that the wealthy are perhaps not so different from the rest of us. I told him he was the best boss I'd ever had and that I felt lucky to know him and work for him.

As I was leaving, we shook hands warmly and wished each other "*Frohe Weihnachten.*" On the way home, I became somewhat emotional, reflecting on what had just happened. The envelope contained a hundred marks, an amount I normally would earn in a little more than a week. And how about the suit, and the box of chocolates? These were definitely the best gifts I had ever received in my whole life!

When I was younger, once in a while at Christmas, my father would buy me a pair of new shoes, which I valued and enjoyed a great deal. But these presents surpassed anything Kris Kringle himself could have given me!

When I woke up on Christmas Day, I rubbed my eyes and smiled at my splendid new suit, which I planned to wear when I went out that evening, even though I would be celebrating alone—perhaps feeling miserable and sorry for myself at some bar or restaurant.

Late in the afternoon, I took a long walk on Main Street, which, unlike every other day, was rather deserted. A few people were just passing through, probably heading for a friend's or loved one's home. I wandered aimlessly, gazing idly at the window displays in the closed stores. A few bars and restaurants were open, however, and as I was getting a little hungry, I ended up in a tavern a few blocks from the Post Lounge that our little group had frequented so many times in the past.

Helga, the barmaid, knew me well and greeted me with a hug and the usual holiday wishes. I decided to have my Christmas dinner there, so when I asked Helga to bring me a beer and a knackwurst with sauerkraut, she offered a crooked smile and told me that the first beer—plus the food—would be on the house today.

Standing there silently for a moment, lost for words, I hugged Helga and thanked her profusely for this wonderful gesture, which made my Christmas away from home a little more bearable and a little more meaningful. And then, averting her eyes from meeting mine, she wiped a tear from my cheek.

During the previous two days, I had experienced the true meaning of kindness, compassion, and giving. I reflected on my boss's largesse the day before. Now Helga, who owed me nothing, had rescued me from my doldrums. Seeing me alone, she had sensed I needed someone to lift my spirits—and she came through with flying colors. I thanked God, when I finished my dinner, for the opportunities He had given me to meet such nice people, knowing that He was always next to me, protecting me and granting me the emotional strength I needed to go on in a foreign country.

My best Christmas gift that night was not the free beer or the meal I enjoyed. No, it was the act of giving, the true holiday spirit I felt when Helga said, "It's on the house today." Her kindness warmed the cockles of my heart and made me feel less alone.

I asked Helga to keep a tab when I ordered another beer, because I intended to stay for a while, since I had nothing better to do. A few more couples came in, but understandably, it was a slow night. Nursing my beer mug with both hands, with my elbows propped up on the table, my mind took me back to the events that took place in the village during the Christmas holidays.

One traditional event in the village was that every household slaughtered a pig on Christmas Eve. This pig was fed and cared for from the time it was a little piglet and was kept in a pigsty close to the family's property. It took almost a full year for a pig to grow close to one hundred kilos.

Every year, I looked forward to the day when my father and my uncle, after tying the swine's legs, would slaughter the pig in the front yard of our house. My mother would pour hot water on its skin to loosen the bristle, which was then easily removed with a rigid steel brush. Next, my father started the butchering process by cutting off different pieces of meat to be used for specific purposes. A small portion would be cooked and eaten during the holidays, but most of it would be prepared and preserved so that it could be used during the upcoming winter months.

We had a number of delectable meat dishes on Christmas Day and several days after. However, the day after Christmas, my mother and grandmother were busy all day cooking the various butchered pig parts in a large kettle. The cooked product was then separated and stored in different vats.

First, the pure fat was taken from the top of the kettle, and then the remaining meat was covered with enough fat so that it could be preserved without any refrigeration. They also prepared pork sausages, using the pig's intestines as the outer layer. For breakfast, we used the pork fat in place of butter by spreading it on a thick slice of homemade bread and then topping it with either sugar or honey.

The preserved meat was mostly used as a main course for either lunch or dinner, by just reheating it for a few minutes. As I was told, this preservative technique had been used and passed on from many previous generations, when refrigerators were not available.

Christmas Eve was a special day for the younger people. In groups of five or six, we visited neighbors singing the only Christmas carol we knew at that time, a hymn called "Kalanta" which had more than twenty stanzas describing, in detail, the birth of Christ and other sacred events and figures, such as the three Magi, King Herod, and so forth. At the end of our rendition, each family rewarded us with a small amount of money, which ultimately was divided among the group members. The evening before Christmas was always memorable; it was an unforgettable experience that I truly enjoyed.

On Christmas Day, the entire family got together for the rich holiday supper, splurging on all the meat dishes and all the other goodies, after forty days of fasting.

Those were the good old days, I thought to myself, taking a deep breath and sighing nostalgically. I thought of the letter my father had sent me a few days earlier. He had written that, this year, they would not have a pig to slaughter. A few weeks earlier, some people with a pickup truck— probably from another village or the city — had stolen the pig that my mother and sisters had cared for the entire year.

How could anyone commit such a hideous act? How could the thief's conscience allow him to enjoy either a meal prepared with the stolen animal, or the money he received if he sold it to a butcher?

Judging from the tone of my father's letter, he was not angry with the perpetrators and did not want to take revenge. Instead, he was certain that God would smite them with the appropriate punishment when they least expected it. My father was convinced that, sooner or later, everyone paid for their sins.

I felt saddened by this incident, yet somewhat comforted by the thought that relatives, friends, and neighbors would most certainly pitch in to provide my family with enough meat to last them for the duration of the holidays and beyond.

While taking another sip from my tall beer glass, I saw a man in a wheelchair approaching the table next to me. He greeted me with a big smile and I responded with a hearty "*Frohe Weihnachten*." I asked him if he was alone. When he nodded, I invited him to join me, if he wished. He gladly accepted my offer and, with a swift motion, turned his wheelchair around toward my table.

"Thank you for the invitation," he said. "I assume you're also spending Christmas alone?"

"Yes, all my friends are with their families," I sighed.

As I asked Helga to bring us two beers, the man shook my hand and introduced himself as Fritz. When the beers came, he spoke of the car

113

accident that had left him paralyzed from the waist down. He had been traveling with his wife and five-year-old daughter when a truck hit them broadside, killing his family instantly and leaving him handicapped for life. I expressed my sincere condolences.

"What's your story?" he asked abruptly. "Why are you alone?"

I gave him a brief overview as to when, how, and why I came to Germany. I told him that, especially on Christmas Day, I felt lonely being away from my family in a foreign country. Fritz shook his head a few times, looked me in the eye, and spoke with a trembling voice.

"Listen, you are alone in a foreign country, but you still have a family you can go to anytime you want. On the other hand, I am alone, like a prisoner in my own country, with no family to go to—ever again! Do you understand that? How do I go on living? Should I hope for a miracle so that I can walk again and have my family back? No, no, my friend. I drink every day to ease the pain, to forget for a few moments, to numb my senses and create my own reality."

I'd thought I had problems until I realized what Fritz was going through. "A lonely prisoner in his own country"—what a profound statement! He felt he had nothing to live for. He was one of those people who was not willing to give himself a second chance. He actually had given up and resigned himself to being a pathetic cripple. I tried to cheer him up, to convince him that he could rebuild his life if he put his mind to it, but he did not want to accept any suggestions or advice.

All of a sudden, I saw Fritz staring at something or somebody behind me. Then I felt a pat on my shoulder that made me turn around. It was Heidi! Oh, my God, had Heidi returned earlier than her scheduled date, leaving her family's holiday gathering, just to see me? I didn't believe it! I hugged her, kissed her, and thanked her again and again.

After introducing Heidi to Fritz, I asked Helga for another round of drinks, for I knew that the night and the celebration were just getting started. I can honestly assert that Heidi's unexpected return was one of the most enjoyable surprises and pleasant experiences of my life. I still remember the overwhelming sensation that washed over me, a feeling I would classify as euphoria more potent than winning a multimillion-dollar lottery.

Heidi and I stayed with Fritz for more than an hour, listening as he chokingly described how he had spent the previous Christmas holiday, when his wife and daughter were still alive. As Fritz spoke, Heidi and I occasionally wiped away a few tears of empathy. We understood the emotional pain he must have felt.

After we said goodnight to Fritz, I asked Helga to combine my tab with my guest's, but Helga refused to take any money from either of us.

"Alles, was heute abend ist frei. Frohe Weihnachten," she said–Everything is on the house (free) tonight. Merry Christmas.

I didn't know whether Helga was part owner of the establishment or just worked there as a manager, but while she was serving another customer, I decided to leave a ten mark bill on the counter for her as a tip.

Heidi and I spent the rest of the weekend together, and I can state unequivocally that absence truly does make the heart grow fonder. We also met with Richard and Charlie at the Fischer Lounge on Sunday night, where we spent a few hours taking it kind of easy with our drinking in order to recuperate from the too-much-of-a-good-thing aspect of the holidays.

The following weekend, we celebrated New Year's Eve at Charlie's house. About eight couples were present, some of whom I was meeting for the first time. We stayed until the wee hours of the morning, having a great time with lots of drinking and dancing, as well as being entertained by the talented Charlie's witty joke-telling and marvelous celebrity impressions.

Everyone wanted to be among Charlie's circle of friends because he could transform even the most depressing situation into carnival of fun. (His real name was Karl, but he liked to be called Charlie, and everyone obliged him.) Charlie had the talents of an actor, impersonator, and singer. His favorite impersonations were Katerina Valente's "Tipi Tipi Tipso," a Calypso song; Lauren Hardy's gaffes; and Charlie Chaplin's walk. Charlie was everyone's entertainer, amusing both friends and strangers.

After the holidays, everyone experienced a letdown as winter literally took over "by storm." We had to cope with snow blizzards and cold temperatures. One unforgettably frigid day, we had to work outside in minus 20-degree Celsius weather. I was getting used to the cold climate as I rode my bike to and from work, although a few times, I lost control of my bike on the icy roads and fell on my *arsch* (behind)!

Most of the time, after work, Heidi would be waiting for me outside the plant. We went together either directly to my room or to the park, weather permitting. I thought I was falling in love with Heidi. I began to get jealous every time she talked to another man, or if another man paid her a compliment. I knew I was torturing myself, but I could not control those feelings, which manifested another aspect of my insecurity.

One night, I had a disturbing dream that was so intense, I woke up wondering what the meaning was. This is how the dream unfolded:

"I was lying in bed in my apartment in Rhodes, trying to take an afternoon nap. All of a sudden, I heard footsteps and a conversation, as though some people were coming up the stairs toward the front door. Then the door opened and a little person with a hairy, gorilla-like face entered the room and signaled with a hand gesture for an unseen third party to stay

outside. This beastly kid stood there in front of me, crying out, 'It's not my fault that I look like this!'" That was the scene that made me jump off the bed. I stayed motionless for some time, shivering.

Because it was already early morning when the dream awakened me, I did not bother to go back to sleep. Over breakfast, I tried to puzzle out the reason I'd had this particular dream. All day at work, I couldn't get that awful scene off my mind. As I had often done in the past, I struggled to come up with an interpretation of the dream and tie it in with something relevant to the reality of my waking life. Toward the end of the day, I had a vague idea about the dream's meaning, the validation of which I intended to pursue.

Right after work, Heidi was waiting for me by the plant gate. It was a sunny, comfortable day, so we decided to ride our bikes to a nearby park. We sat down on our usual bench, where I silently stared off into space, virtually reliving the dream as if that hairy-faced kid were in front of me.

"Was ist los?"—What's the matter?—Heidi asked me, her face puzzled.

"I hope you don't get offended, but I would like to ask you a personal question," I said with a trembling voice.

"Yes, go ahead! Ask me anything you want," she confidently replied, as if she had nothing whatsoever to hide.

"Please answer me 'yes' or 'no,'" I said, pointing my finger at her.

"I will," she promised, but now I sensed a little concern in her voice.

Somehow, I found the courage to ask the disturbing question that had troubled me all day long, an assumption I could not get off my mind.

"Again, please answer 'yes' or 'no'!" I barked. "Do you have a child—and if so, is there anything wrong with that child?"

Heidi remained silent for a few seconds as she wrestled with the answer. Then she buried her face in her hands and shook her head to and fro. When she looked up, I saw her eyes were wet with tears. The color had drained from her face, which now had a ghastly aspect, like a dead person.

She ran her trembling fingers through her hair and finally blurted out, "Yes, I have a child. But I wonder how you found out, since only my parents and I know about this! No one else knows the existence of this child!" She began crying hysterically as I put my arm around her shoulders to comfort her.

"One more thing," I said calmly, doing my best to keep my cool in the aftermath of this bombshell. "You haven't told me everything. What's wrong with the child?"

She hesitated a moment, sniffling. "Well, I don't know how to tell you this, but the father of the child is my own father! Yes, my own father!"

"Oh, my God, how did that happen?" I asked, utterly bewildered.

Heidi drew a heavy sigh. "When I was fifteen years old, my father, who was a bus driver, occasionally took me with him when he drove to other countries, such as Belgium or Holland. We stayed overnight in the same hotel room, where he took advantage of the opportunity and forced me into the hideous act. The rest is obvious."

I was truly stunned by this awful revelation. My head was spinning. I didn't know how to react, what to say, or what the consequences would be in terms of our relationship. I wanted to know a few more details about the child and asked gently, "Where is the child now, Heidi? Is it a boy or a girl, and how old is it?"

"It's a boy, three years old. He's staying with my mother back home. As far as all relatives and friends are concerned, they assume Wilhelm—that's his name—is my mother's son."

"Wow, what a mess we're in!" I said. It was a selfish comment, but unfortunately, I could think of nothing more meaningful to say at the moment.

Then Heidi said, *"Ich erklärte alles, ich sagte dir die wahrheit"*—I explained everything, I told you the truth.

At that moment, I didn't know whether I was in a dreamlike state or if everything I had just heard truly was grounded in reality. I didn't know how to react, nor did I have the emotional strength to either express resentment or give her a compassionate hug. In order to get out of the predicament, I simply told her I wanted to be alone to mull over the day's revelations. Without further discussion, we got on our bikes and pedaled homeward along separate paths.

It took me a few days to comprehend the seriousness of the secret Heidi had hidden from me all the time we had known each other. I was considering a long-term commitment to someone whom I loved and cared for, and now this! I found myself at a major crossroads where I had to decide which path to take and which decision would be the right one for both of us.

I started putting the entire situation into logical perspective by analyzing the sequence of events from Heidi's point of view. She had been only fifteen years old. Her father, who was an adult, should have known better. He should have realized the emotional damage he was inflicting on his own daughter. He should have thought of the consequences, the guilt, and the shame to which his entire family would be subjected.

Heidi had been forced to engage in an unwanted sexual act, and in her immature state of mind, she had not been able to resist this premeditated exploitation by her so-called mature father—whom I considered an inhuman monster.

But what was I to do? Leave her, or stand by her and love her even more, with all my heart? I asked myself whether I was mature enough to make a logical decision without having emotion play a major role in my assessment. I pondered the fact that I did not have the courage to share this secret with anyone, not even my best friend Richard. And I knew the magnitude of the situation would significantly impact my relationship with Heidi, should I decide to pursue it more seriously.

I had not seen Heidi since our conversation in the park that Monday afternoon. On Friday, however, she was waiting for me outside the plant gate, just as usual. She asked me if we could talk for a while, to decide the next step for both of us. We went back to the park, where we spent more than an hour trying to find a satisfactory solution to our dilemma. Heidi defended her position, emphasizing the fact that she had not been fully aware of what was about to happen until it was too late. She added that her parents were now divorced and she did not know the whereabouts of her father.

"I don't want to lose you—you are the best thing that ever happened to me," she told me with conviction as she begged me to forgive her for withholding the truth from me.

Suddenly, I had the urge to hug her, to hold her in my arms and kiss her over and over! I could not just leave her, not when she needed me more than ever. So I hugged her, kissed away her salty tears, and held her in my arms as if there were no tomorrow. We both became very emotional, expressing sweet nothings of love, regret, and forgiveness. Our relationship showed a renewed spark of survival, so we decided to spend the weekend together.

It was a sunny March day when we arrived at a nearby lake. It was a quiet place at this time of the year, unlike the summer months, when the entire area was crowded with people of all ages, swimming, playing, and having cookouts with friends and family. The place was deserted now; only the two of us enjoying the serene privacy inside a crude straw hut, which resembled a child's playhouse. We made ourselves comfortable in that cozy hut, spending many pleasurable hours in the realm of ecstasy, experiencing the ultimate intimacy. The pictures we took on that day, in and around the hut, are among my fondest possessions.

Judging by the loving way we treated one another that day, I would say our relationship had survived a major storm. We had overcome a crisis that ultimately made our bond even stronger. We began seeing each other almost every day. However, my jealous tendencies started becoming more pronounced, causing me to instigate unnecessary scenes and unwarranted arguments.

I suppose all these emotions resulted from my being in love, as well as lacking confidence in myself and mistrusting others. The fact that I couldn't control this green-eyed monster became detrimental to our relationship, as it ate away at the one thing that held us together: trust. My jealousy also took away from our quality time together, leading to numerous arguments in which I focused on Heidi's negative qualities.

Furthermore, I ended up spending the bulk of my time foolishly thinking up scenarios in which she might cheat on me. Within a period of a few months, I began to dwell on what *could* be happening rather than what really *was* happening.

In the grip of this unhealthy obsession, I questioned myself as to why my jealousy had intensified ever since Heidi had revealed her secret to me. Did I now believe she had probably not made an attempt to defend herself against her father's sexual depravity? If that were the case, I conveniently reasoned, she would likely be prone to succumbing to any temptation that came her way. Although I loved her with all my heart, deep down, I no longer trusted her as I had before.

Despite my jealous tendencies, Heidi and I were having a good time for the most part during the early days of spring, taking leisurely walks in the parks and getting together on weekends with our usual circle of friends.

One Sunday afternoon, Heidi and I were walking in the center of the city—just window-shopping, because most stores were closed. A man holding a light, carry-on bag stopped to ask us if we knew of a reasonable hotel in the immediate area. His German was not very good, but we understood what he was trying to say. When I told him my nationality was Greek, a cheerful smile bloomed upon his swarthy face. When he explained that his funds were limited and that he had neither a job nor a place to stay, I invited him to stay with me for the night. I also offered to take him with me to work the next morning and said I would ask my boss to interview him for possible employment. He accepted my offers enthusiastically and kept shaking my hand, thanking me many times in both Greek and German.

All three of us went to a nearby restaurant, where we had dinner and a few beers. After dinner, Heidi walked home and I took Yanni, as he was called, to my place. He spent the night in the spare bed my father had used.

In the morning, we arrived at the plant earlier than my regular starting time, which gave me a chance to speak with my boss about interviewing Yanni. My boss agreed he would talk to him in about half an hour and asked me to tell Yanni to wait in our lunchroom. I gave Yanni a cup of coffee and asked him to wait until someone guided him to my boss's office.

An hour later, my boss tactfully informed me that there was no one waiting in the lunchroom. He said that I should not have wasted his time and that he had rearranged his schedule for a phantom interview. Despite by boss's reaction, I didn't think much about the incident, as I thought Yanni had simply changed his mind about the job.

At the end of the day, however, when everyone opened their lockers, we discovered that all the money we'd had in our wallets was missing! Immediately, everybody assumed that the Greek guy, Yanni, who had been left alone in the lunchroom, was the culprit. I couldn't agree with them more. I even offered to repay everyone, since I was the one who had brought the wolf into the fold, as it were.

Although they refused to accept any money from me, I felt terribly ashamed that my countryman was a thief in a country where honesty and integrity were sacred principles. I couldn't look anyone in the eye, knowing that this scumbag thief came from the same country as me. I was more than just embarrassed—I was concerned about the negative image of Greeks my coworkers would undoubtedly form after this incident.

It was ironic that I had to go through this type of experience, to face a mentality similar to the ones that I left behind—wise guys like Yanni who discovered it was easier to snatch all the money from our lockers than to work like everybody else. In my lifetime, I've come to the sad realization there are many people like Yanni who truly belong in an institution or who should be made to perform hard labor in prison, so they'll understand there really is no such thing as a "free lunch." You have to work for it!

A few days later, I went to Cologne for the purpose of renewing my passport, which was about to expire. At the Greek consulate, I was told that they could not renew my passport in Germany and that I should go back to Greece for a few days to receive the required approvals. Despite my pleading for a possible exception, they were not willing to compromise their initial decision, which left me with only one choice: I would have to go back to Greece.

Since I was at the consulate, I seized the opportunity to report Yanni's crime at my workplace. They took all the pertinent information and promised me that they would send a telegram to the Greek/Yugoslavian border checkpoint, where the bastard stood a good chance of being arrested the next time he tried to travel to Greece.

When I got back home, I met with Heidi to discuss my imminent need to travel to Greece. I told her there was no other way to renew my passport, adding that I would use this opportunity to spend a few weeks with the family and friends I had left behind.

Friday, April 29, was my last day at work. I made all necessary arrangements with my landlady, such as paying the rent for April and leaving instructions regarding my incoming mail. Over the weekend, I saw most of my friends before departing for Greece, but I spent most of Sunday night carousing with Richard and Charlie.

Chapter 23

Home Sweet Home

O n May 1, I boarded the train in Bonn for a three-day ride back to Greece. Fluent now in German, I carried on freewheeling conversations with my fellow passengers, especially the German vacationers, who picked my brain about the interesting things to see and do in Greece.

This time, the train trip was completely different from the year before, when the prospect of traveling to a foreign country had so unnerved me. My train ride this time was a wholly pleasant experience. I had three days to sit back, relax, and review my "conquest of Germany," as it were.

Edith had told me, when I'd seen her over the weekend, "You've come a long way within a year, Mike, and you've matured. You have made huge strides in your personal development, but you still need to climb many steps before you can accept yourself as the individual you have imagined yourself to be. Don't worry, though. In time, you will get there. I'm sure of that!"

Coming from a person I thought highly of, I cherished these words of goodwill. I'm sure Edith's intention was not to flatter me. On the contrary, her remarks were essentially constructive criticism that I gladly welcomed, as they came from a person who was honest and caring to a fault with people close to her.

Edith had become my mentor, a stabilizing force in my life. She was an intellectual and a highly principled, original thinker; I always looked up to her. Together, we explored a wealth of exciting ideas on a wide range of subjects, allowing our imaginations to soar free of earthly limitations.

Despite my limited German vocabulary, I was able to keep up with her keen intellect most of the time.

On the other hand, Heidi was not as educated as Edith, but her un-inhibited nature—she was a true free spirit—made me feel relaxed and contented when I was with her. Although the two women had little in common, each of them offered me what I essentially needed to satisfy my emotional yearnings and help me further my societal ambitions.

Despite Heidi's past, she made me feel that love was a sweet mystery I could never comprehend, and that's what kept me vital, excited, and forever exploring. In some ways, she constantly baffled me. Yet I saw that aspect of mystery as a bittersweet gift.

The train trip was rather uneventful. However, one troubling aspect was the fact that the 500 marks I had with me would not be enough for a two- to three-week stay. I wished I had planned the jaunt as a true vacation to Greece and had saved enough money to enjoy my stay in Rhodes without having to worry about being strapped for cash. I knew that I should have been putting aside more money, but during the year, I had been peri-odically sending money home to help my family, a household of eleven, to defray everyday expenses.

Concerned about how long my money would last, I asked a Greek fellow in my compartment about the current cost of living in Greece. I inquired how much someone would need for a three-week stay there. Judging from the way he described his lavish lifestyle and the fact that he had traveled to Germany to purchase a brand new Mercedes-Benz, he impressed me as a well-to-do individual.

Cocking one eyebrow, he regarded my neat but hardly fashionable outfit and said with an air of insouciance, "I would probably need 1200 to 1500 marks if I planned to go out often with friends and relatives."

That answer left me speechless, as I also had to consider my expenses for returning to Germany, which I would have to set aside, thus giving me a balance of 300 marks spending money. Well, I thought, I would just have to get by with what I had.

As bothersome as my financial worries were, I still felt a sense of contentment. I was visualizing myself as a more advanced, emotionally and socially richer person than I had been a year ago.

I arrived in Athens on May 4 and took the boat to Rhodes, an eighteen-hour voyage. After visiting with some friends and my two sisters, Despina and Mary, in the city, my first order of business was the renewal of my passport. I went to the appropriate service bureau and stumbled across a huge problem. The gentleman who reviewed my records informed me that they could not renew my passport because there was an outstanding military obligation that I had to clear up with the army recruiting office.

At the recruiting office, I told the clerks that I had fulfilled my military obligation before I traveled to Germany. I showed them the signed papers, which indicated I was to be excluded from serving in the military since I was the firstborn male in a family of eight children. I also presented a receipt showing the amount of money my father had paid to obtain the signed exclusion document, which I had needed to travel outside the country.

I was then informed that an amendment was currently in effect that superseded the previous year's ruling, which had granted exclusion to the firstborn male from military obligation. Moreover, I would have to serve in the army for one year! As for the money my father had paid, the clerks stated it would be returned within a few weeks.

In the meantime, I was given a document indicating I had to report for basic training at the base in Tripoli, a city near Sparta, on July 13, 1960. I pleaded my case, explaining I had left all my belongings in the apartment in Germany, but there was nothing they could do, even after I offered to pay a significant amount of money—a sort of indirect bribe.

I felt as if the roof of the building had fallen on top of me. I refused to accept what had just happened to me. This cruel and totally unexpected turn of events threatened to disrupt my life, my plans, and my dreams. Only God knows how I had achieved a high level of success by vaulting over the many hurdles that had come my way, by taking excessive risks and by plunging into situations without a safety net. Yes, only God knows how I survived, because He was by my side, all the time!

I spent the evening with my friend, Dimitri, who took me to one of the most famous nightclubs in Rhodes. Over a few drinks, Dimitri tried to pacify my anger by downplaying the significance of spending one year in the military. Others, he said, had to serve two years. But I could not be reasoned with. I just could not accept the fact that I would not be allowed to return to Germany, to get back to the lifestyle I had cultivated. Now, thanks to idiotic army red tape, everything I had built so far had come crashing down, like a house of cards.

For all I knew, perhaps next year I would have to start all over again. As a result, I would lose my momentum, an inspirational advantage that had enabled me to keep reaching for heights I had never thought possible.

I told Dimitri how I envisioned this cruel reality, but I knew that I had to face it, whether I liked it or not. The next day, I took the bus to the village, where I planned to spend most of my stay before reporting to the military base. I received a warm welcome from the rest of the family, who still lived in the same house in which I was born. The house had changed little since I had seen it last—but for some reason, it seemed smaller now.

The simple life in the village bored me to tears, so one day in June, I convinced one of my old schoolmates—a young man named Apostolos (nicknamed Postoli)—to go on a "survival trip" for a week. My plan was to settle on a remote, rather deserted beach locale called Kerameni, about ten kilometers from the village. It was too far to walk all the way to our destination, so we took the bus up to the seventh kilometer and then trudged across the rugged terrain to our remote, seaside location.

My original purpose for this expedition was built around the concept of survival. In other words, we would survive on food that was available to us, either on land or in the sea. We had fishing knives and our homemade fishing gear, which was a long, rigid bamboo cane instead of a commercial fishing rod. The fishing line at the end of the cane was of fixed length, because we didn't have the reel that usually is attached to an actual fishing rod.

We also brought a cooking pot and only one loaf of bread, which we would ration during the week in case of emergency. Since we were both smokers, we brought along a good supply of cigarettes. It was the beginning of summer and the weather was balmy, so we felt there would be no need for blankets, even though we planned to sleep out in the open.

We started a fire and kept it going with gnarled pieces of driftwood we collected on the beach and fallen tree branches we gathered from the surrounding area. Our fishing expedition was less than stellar; the puny fish we caught made for a most unsatisfying dinner, and our stomachs growled for more filling fare.

Sitting by the fire, Postoli bombarded me with questions about my life in Germany. We talked for a long time, enjoying the serenity of the night, where the ominous cry of an owl and the soft swishing sound of the tiny waves breaking on the pebbles along the shoreline were the only noises that pierced the gloom. We cut an old, discarded tire into quarters, covered it with a towel, and used it as pillow. When we lay down on the soft, pebbly beach in complete darkness, I felt so close to nature and so connected with God and His creations. Watching the millions of stars flickering in the cosmos above us, my spirit soared in amazement. What a sight!

Our careful planning had not taken into consideration the early morning dew that shrouded the area in a misty fog. We awakened in the wet chill to discover that our clothes were drenched, as if we had sleepwalked into the sea! We immediately restarted the fire and began drying out our clothes. Even when they were dry, we did not try to go back to sleep, because the grounds around us were all wet and sloppy.

Since we had so much free time, I suggested we record some of the highlights of our survival expedition in a journal. So, early in morning, I started writing a satirical rhyming poem using a dialect of the language spoken in the surrounding villages, including our own Agios Isidoros. The inspiration for the poem came about while we were holding our wet clothes at the tip of a long stick over the flames as we sat around the fire in our underwear, laughing hysterically.

"Can you imagine if someone showed up and saw us in this condition, in the wee hours of the morning?" I chuckled. "He would think that we were some kind of ghosts or had escaped from a nut house." I thought it was a funny scene, and thus it became the first stanza of the poem before it was edited into its final form.

When the morning sun had burned off the dew, we took a little nap to make up for the sleep we had lost. Later on that morning, we went fishing at a rocky location around an inlet, about half a kilometer from our campsite. We caught only a few small fish, but on the way back, we spotted a donkey sticking his long nose into our bags, obviously looking for food. After we chased him away, we discovered we had arrived a little too late, because the donkey had eaten the loaf of bread we had kept as our contingency food supply.

We then realized that the only source of food for the rest of our stay was the sea. Because our fishing expedition that afternoon had not been particularly fruitful, we decided to do some night fishing. We cut the rest of the tire into long strips and used the slow-burning pieces of rubber as crude torches. They provided enough light for us to spot any sea creature resting or feeding along the shore. We actually caught five crabs that evening and charred them in an open fire that night. One of the crafty crustaceans must have escaped through the flames, so Postoli and I each had two crabs for dinner.

I suppose it is the human instinct for survival that inspires us to be creative and forces us to find some means for staying alive. The next day, we discovered another source we could use to satisfy our hunger. There were many mollusk-like little creatures affixed on the seashore rocks with only their hard shells visible. They were firmly stuck on the wet rocks, but using our sharp knives, we were able to remove them and eat them like clams on the half shell. The mollusks were our last resort when the few fish we caught failed to quell our grumbling bellies.

We also had to deal with the relentless mosquitoes in the early evenings, since we did not have any sort of protection for our bare skin. The exposed parts of our bodies were covered with angry red bumps that itched like the devil. There were times when we jumped into the sea just to avoid the unbearable mosquito attacks.

Early one evening, as Postoli and I took our ease by the fireside, two fishermen approached us in a small boat and invited us to join them for a short boat ride. We had a grand time on their boat, drifting along in the calm water under a clear, starry sky. The only sound around us was the soft humming of the motor. We observed the fishermen using a long stretch of nets, catching all kinds of fish and sea creatures, including squid and octopus. When the fishermen took us ashore, they gave us a small part of their catch, which turned out to be the most substantial dinner we had during our stay in Kerameni.

On the last day of our expedition, we reviewed all the major events of the trip and also completed the poem saga, which ended up being fifty rhyming stanzas of four verses each. Those who read it and understood the dialectic idioms enjoyed it, laughing uproariously at its satirical nature and showering me with plaudits. This poem became part of my collection, which I came to call "My Artistic Corner."

When we got back to the village, we were reminded by our friends that we had lost some weight, a fact we were fully aware of, given our meager rations.

The remaining three-plus weeks before I was due to report to the military base, I spent mostly in the village, although I did travel to the city for several short stays. During this period, I had a brief, innocent affair with a teacher that never developed into anything serious. She was a bright lady with a personality similar to Rita's in Germany. Our favorite pastime was solving crossword puzzles together, an activity we both enjoyed.

I also went out with my friend Dimitri several times, either to a beach during the day or a nightclub after hours. Dimitri said I should enjoy myself to the hilt because life in the army would be just like "hell." And so we did! We drank like fish, tripped the light fantastic with the ladies until our legs were like spaghetti, and sowed our wild oats in general. It was much like enjoying the calm before the storm.

In the meantime, I wrote several letters to all my contacts in Germany informing them of the unexpected turn of events with the army. I told them that I would soon send them my military address.

Chapter 24

The Army Service

U
nfortunately, all good things must come to an end, and so did my life as a civilian. On July 13, I boarded the train in Athens, along with many other recruits. We arrived in Tripoli early that afternoon.

As the first order of business, we were guided into a large room where several barbers were cutting the new recruits' hair down to the scalp with electric razors that buzzed like a hive of angry hornets. My turn came too soon. The barber did his job with alarming efficiency, finishing me in just a couple of minutes. I got up from the chair, rubbing my nearly bald head in bewilderment and staring down in dismay at the pile of shorn locks on the floor that had once been my enviable head of hair!

I remembered the remark my barber had made the last time I'd had a real haircut, when he was combing my slightly wavy, thick hair: "Any lady would be thrilled if she had this thick and healthy hair!" What a shocking experience my new haircut was—and I knew this was just a small sample of the many rude awakenings in store for us in the days to come.

The base housed more than a thousand rookies in four, two-story buildings. As in other army units, our sleeping quarters had two rows of bunk beds from one end of the hall to the other. Right from the start, our sergeant seemed to take a liking to me. I had brought my guitar with me, which obviously intrigued him. He wanted to know a lot of details about me, such as what type of music I liked to play and other personal information. He assigned me a bed near the window so I could jokingly say I had a bedroom with a view. I decided to take the upper bunk so that I would have a better view of the entire sleeping hall as well as the few trees through the window.

A significant portion of our eight weeks of army basic training was taken up with marching, drill, ceremonies, and hour upon hour of standing in formation. Sounds easy, dear reader? Well, try standing in one place, ramrod straight and perfectly still. If a mosquito bites you, don't slap it. If sweat rolls into your eye, don't wipe it away. And if you scratch your thigh, do twenty push-ups and jump back into position.

We also learned how to make our bunk with hospital corners. This is a good time to practice sleeping on top of the covers to save time because, as in all military boot camps, there are never enough minutes in the morning—between the time you're awakened and the time you have to fall in—to get everything done that's supposed to be done. Not having to remake your bed each morning can save a soldier ten minutes of valuable time.

Another humiliating chore we had to endure was the cleaning of the grounds around the barracks. This assignment was mainly supervised by a rather sadistic corporal who demanded that we pick up every cigarette butt off the ground. In fact, one day he threw his cigarette on the ground, ground it into the dirt, and ordered me to pick it up. My first reaction was to punch him in the face and tell him to get lost, but I somehow restrained my anger and politely refused to obey his order. My refusal outraged the corporal, who took me to the lieutenant and demanded that I be punished for insubordination.

When the lieutenant and I were alone, he explained to me that demeaning tasks, such as the one the corporal had tried to subject me to, were necessary to transform the civilian mindset to the more rigid way of military thinking.

(It bears mentioning here that the lieutenant knew me personally because I had written a marching song specifically for my unit or company (λόχος) of forty draftees. During our marching exercises, our sergeant insisted that we sing my song because somewhere in the lyrics, his name was "unintentionally" mentioned as the rhyming word of the last verse. Flattery never killed anyone. Subsequently, the sergeant introduced me to the lieutenant as a soldier who took the initiative to do something creative and inspirational for his company.)

Back to my conversation with the lieutenant, he asked me to be patient and said he would talk to the drill instructors, asking them to be a little more selective when imposing humiliating tasks on certain men who had a higher education than the average soldier.

Breakfast, served at 6:00 a.m., consisted of one bowl of tea and two slices of bread. Right after breakfast, we jogged for two hours, going up-hill on rugged terrain. It was a strenuous exercise that would exhaust a mountain goat. Lunch was more substantial in quality and quantity. It included a protein base of either beans or meat, but dessert was definitely out of the question, except on special occasions.

After lunch, we had to take the traditional Greek afternoon nap in our barracks, where the supervising sergeant demanded absolute quiet. If anyone made the slightest noise or whispered something to his bunkmate, the sergeant ordered everyone to get up and run three kilometers up the mountain under the blazing midday sun. As crazy as it sounds, they didn't just punish the fool who couldn't keep his mouth shut during siesta time—the *entire company* had to suffer the consequences. As it was explained to me later, they wanted to instill in every soldier the notion that the entire company has to function as a synchronized unit, without any deviations or compromises, because during an actual battle, it takes only one person not following the rules to cause a major catastrophe. In a way, I had to agree with that rationale, but I hated being punished for something for which someone else was responsible.

Our dinner was similar to lunch, with a little more variety of meat or fish. After dinner, we had some free time to socialize. I often played my guitar during our sing-along sessions. As I recall, one of the most popular songs at the time was "Marina," an Italian love song written and sung by Rocco Granata. This polka tune, which featured a frisky accordion solo, had taken Europe by storm. We must have sung it hundreds of times in Italian. Well, just for old time's sake, here are the lyrics of "Marina," one more time:

The Italian version
Mi sono innamorato di Marina
una ragazza mora ma carina
ma lei non vuol saperne del mio amore
cosa faro' per conquistarle il cuor.
Un girono l'ho incontrata sola sola,
il cuore mi batteva mille all'ora.
Quando le dissi che la volevo amare
mi diede un bacio e l'amor sboccio'...

Marina, Marina, Marina
Ti voglio al piu' presto sposar
Marina, Marina, Marina

Ti voglio al piu'presto sposar
O mia bella mora
no non mi lasciare
non mi devi rovinare
oh, no, no, no, no, no...
Marina, Marina, Marina
Ti voglio al piu'presto sposar
Marina, Marina, Marina
Ti voglio al piu'presto sposar
O mia bella mora
no non mi lasciare
non mi devi rovinare
oh, no, no, no, no, no...

The English version
Rocco Granata / English Lyrics: Ray Maxwell) Dean Martin – 1962
The whole wide world is wild about Marina
In Italy they call her La Carina.
If you see her you never will forget her
And you can tell the world I'm gonna get her.

Marina, Marina, Marina
You're lovely, you're sweet, you're divine,
Marina, Marina, Marina
I won't rest until you are mine.
All my love is for you
How I do adore you
Oh my darling, I implore you
Please listen to my plea.
When we go out dancin'
You are so entrancin'
You've got all the others glancin'
I'm filled with jealousy.
(The whole wide world is wild about Marina
In Italy they call her La Carina
If you see her you never will forget her
And you can tell the world I'm gonna get her)
Marina, Marina, Marina
You're lovely, you're sweet, you're divine
Marina, Marina, Marina
I won't rest until you are mine

(All my love is for you
How I do adore you
Oh my darling, I implore you
Please listen to my plea.)
My heart caught on fire
You filled me with desire
Now there's one thing I aspire
To hear you say, "Si, Si"
(Transcribed by Monique Adriaansen & Mel Priddle—February 2004)

After four weeks in basic training, we were allowed to visit the town of Tripoli one Sunday afternoon. We had six wonderful hours to do whatever we pleased—within military guidelines, of course.

The most crowded spots were the "pleasure houses," where long lines of desperate soldiers, their hormones in overdrive, were willing to pay to for the female companionship they had been deprived of for so long. That Sunday afternoon, those obliging ladies operated like an assembly line. What a racket!

Toward the end of basic training, I was given an opportunity to compete for a United Nations service position in a foreign country. I had to take a written test, which involved translating a block of text from Greek to my language of preference, which, in my case, was German. The ten applicants, including myself, took a two-hour train ride to a military base in Corinth, where we met other candidates from different basic training sites.

All together, there must have been more than forty soldiers ready to take the test. The seating arrangement placed me next to someone who was taking the Italian translation, to prevent us from copying or helping one another. When I read the text, which pertained to the economic and political differences between Europe and America, I knew my chances were slim. There were some Greek words I couldn't understand, let alone translate into German. Needless to say, I did not pass the test—but I was able to help the person next to me with some Italian words he did not know.

After basic training, I was given a choice to either serve one year with the possibility of being promoted to sergeant, or two years with the potential to make lieutenant. Without even giving it a second thought, I took the one-year option, because I was not planning a career in the military. After the aptitude test results, I was placed in the specialized branch of telecommunications, which meant I would spend about three months in Athens in a school-like setting.

Life on the base in Athens was almost like going to school every day from 8:00 a.m. to 3:30 p.m. The rest of the afternoon, we did all sorts of physical exercises, as well as applying the theory we had learned in the classroom to hands-on experience with actual wireless equipment.

In the meantime, my sister, Vasilia, was about to get married in the village. At this point of my armed service, I was not yet eligible for a short leave, so I couldn't attend the ceremony. When the appeals to my sergeant failed, a scheme occurred to me.

I approached the lieutenant colonel in charge of the entire base. I told him I needed a few days' leave to attend my sister's wedding, and in turn, I would bring him a few umbrellas from Rhodes. Umbrellas were one of the most well-known items imported from Italy, yet a rare bargain in Rhodes for those on the mainland. The umbrellas would be inexpensive, because all items bought in Rhodes were duty-free, which made them less than half the price they would be if purchased in Athens. My idea won over the lieutenant colonel, who immediately approved my request and granted me a five-day pass.

I arrived in Rhodes on Saturday morning, planning to take the afternoon bus to the village. When I passed through my old neighborhood, I was told that two German fellows were looking for me. I assumed that only Richard and Charlie would have made the trip, because I had previously written to them about the wedding and indicated I would try my best to be there. Excited, I started checking at every cheap, "no star" hotel in the city that I thought they could afford.

A few hours later, I located them in a hotel in the old city of Rhodes. It was one of the happiest moments of my life, meeting my two best German friends in my hometown. The reunion made me cry tears of joy.

Although we had missed the afternoon bus, a truck driver heading toward the village gave us a ride on the open bed of his truck. We got off in front of the café, where the pre-wedding party was already in full swing. Our surprise entrance caught everyone off guard, but my bride-to-be sister told me that my presence was the greatest wedding present I could ever give her.

Chapter 25

The Village Wedding

A wedding in the village is a unique experience for both the bride and the groom. Preparations begin a week prior to the wedding day, which is always on Sunday. This important event is intense—not only for the married couple and their family members, but also for the entire community.

The most significant pre-wedding events begin on Thursday, when the female relatives and friends bake the bread and prepare the home-made pasta. They also make the couple's new bed and decorate their new house. When the bed is made and the bedroom is decorated with various knick-knacks, they toss a little boy onto the bed for good luck, so that the couple's first born is a boy.

On Saturday morning, the male relatives slaughter several sheep or goats and they begin preparing the various meat dishes to feed the guests on the following three days. On Saturday night, there is a pre-wedding party that lasts until a few hours past midnight. The bride usually wears a new dress in the color of her choice with a semi-circle of white flowers as a tiara on her hair.

That's how I remember my sister, Vasilia, when I joined the party and saw her in her blue dress with the fresh, white flowers on her head.

On Sunday, the female relatives and friends help dress the bride in her wedding gown while singing traditional wedding tunes, accompanied by musicians playing a violin and a lute. The groom is accompanied by male friends, including the best man (*koumbaro*), to the center of the village where most people—almost the entire village—are waiting to walk toward the church.

The bride and her female companions join the procession about fifty meters behind the groom. Meanwhile, as everyone is slowly walking and occasionally stopping in front of the cafes, the musicians play traditional wedding tunes while a few relatives refill everyone's empty glasses with drinks (wine or ouzo).

The groom arrives at the front yard of the church and the bride joins him a few minutes later. While the band is playing folk songs, the bride and groom lead the first dance. Joined by close relatives first, they form a circle and dance around several times. Then other people join in and continue dancing for about half an hour, before everyone enters the church for the religious ceremony.

After the ceremony, the main wedding feast takes place at the couple's new home, where several banquet-like tables are set inside and outside the house. In order to feed everyone, there are probably three to four sittings within a period of about three hours. At about 8:00 p.m., the celebration moves to a large café.

In our case, the party adjourned to the same café we had been in on Saturday night. This time, Vasilia was wearing her wedding gown and her husband Emmanuel had on his dark suit. The celebration at the café lasted until three in the morning, at which time the couple headed for their new home.

On Monday at noon, the relatives and friends, along with the musicians, walk toward the couple's house singing and drinking until they stop in front of their house. The songs have the connotation of, "Hey guys, you've slept enough, and you've enjoyed one another, now it's time to get up." After dinner, the party continues at the café until about midnight.

During those three days, my two German friends and I were swept up in the never-ending eating, drinking, and dancing. The wedding was a merrymaking marathon that mercifully ended Monday night. With an unbearable hangover on Tuesday morning, the three of us took the bus to the city. After buying the two umbrellas I'd promised the lieutenant colonel, Richard and Charlie accompanied me to the harbor, where I was to take the boat to Athens.

Dressed in my army uniform, I boarded the ship, after exchanging emotional good-byes with all my friends and relatives. When I got to the base in Athens, my sergeant gave me a hard time for the preferential treatment I'd received by going directly to his superiors, an act he considered blatant insubordination. I apologized to him, and a few weeks later, the matter was forgotten.

(As of this stage of writing this book, I had managed to locate a possible address for my friend Richard in Germany. I wrote a letter to him

*in the hope he was the same person I had been friends with so many years
ago. Surprisingly, he responded a few days later, indicating he was indeed
that person and that we should keep the communication lines open from
now on. Sadly, he informed me that our jovial friend Charlie had passed
away at the age of forty-five.)*

On the Athens base, I bonded with a soldier from Crete named Paul
(Pavlos was the exact Greek pronunciation) with whom I remained friends
up until the last few weeks of my service. (I will explain later in the book
as to why I'm using the term "up until the last few weeks.")

Paul was a good-looking man with light brown hair and green eyes,
about my height, 5' 10." Though selfish at times, he was a confident, sincere, and proud individual who would never settle for anything other than
the best, as he came from a well-to-do family. As most people from Crete,
keeping his promise was one of the most principled traits he possessed.

Paul told me he had begun his studies in Italy, following in the footsteps of his brother, who had graduated from an Italian medical school and
was already a doctor. He also told me about his fiancée, Stella, a young
lady with whom he was madly in love. As he proudly showed me photo
after photo of her, he was convinced Stella had to be the best-looking girl
in the world.

"Look at how beautiful she is, just look at her!" he chirped, admiring
her picture with awe.

Paul's constant chattering about Stella inspired me to write a poem
that I would later turn into a love song—called "Stella," appropriately
enough. Paul and I sang the sentimental ballad many times on and outside
the base when we had a chance to have a few drinks. Paul and I became
bosom buddies, sharing many details of our personal lives.

Around the middle of September, right after our wireless-radio school
session at the Athens army base, there was an incident that shook me up.
On that sunny afternoon, we were playing volleyball near the fence at the
far end of the base. Two specialized electricians were preparing a broken
wire outside the fence. One of them climbed the pole while the other was
controlling the power flow at the switching station, which was located
about a hundred meters away.

The man on the pole shouted loudly, "Turn the power off, now!"

The other electrician yelled back, "Okay, I turned it off."

When the man on the pole grabbed the two ends of the severed, high-
voltage wire, sparks of electricity shot in all directions. The current forced
the helpless soldier to bend backwards so far that he broke his spine. His
face turned completely black. The other electrician realized he had inad-

vertently turned the switch on, because someone had already placed it in the off position.

When they brought the soldier's charred body down from the pole, he was pronounced dead at the scene. Many of us stood there, speechless, wondering how a tragic accident like this could have happened. Due to a careless error, a young soldier I personally knew had just lost his life. His grisly, senseless death would haunt me all my days.

An interesting event from my army stint in Athens involves Spyros, a sensitive, well-educated individual who feared the rigors and monotonous routine of army life. His tour of duty was driving him toward a nervous breakdown. As friends and confidantes, we had our share of intellectually stimulating conversations, but his main goal was to find a way to get out of the army immediately. Otherwise, he would go crazy, as he plainly put it.

Spyros asked me, his most trusted friend, to help him achieve his goal by playing along with a scheme he was about to put into action. His plan was to convince the muckety-mucks in charge that he was mentally ill. Let me tell you, he was a convincing actor! For example, he would get up in the middle of the night and, completely naked, run down the hallway screaming at the top of his lungs, "The ghosts stole my clothes!" Other times, they found him on the roof of the building in his underwear.

Spyros' deranged behavior went on for several weeks, at which time the doctors began to take him seriously and keep a close watch on his actions. One of the doctors asked me a bunch of questions about my relationship with Spyros and whether I had noticed the sudden change in his personality. Knowing Spyros' goal, I emphasized that he had lately become an irrational, unreasonable person. I said he'd become impossible to deal with and suggested his personality had taken a 180-degree turn for the worse. In other words, I said, he was a nut!

Finally, Spyros was discharged from the army as mentally unfit to serve the rest of his two-year obligation. In appreciation, Spyros took me out one Sunday evening for dinner in a classy restaurant and we ended the night with a visit to a house of pleasure "of the better quality," if the cost (which Spyros took care of) was any indication.

Unfortunately, the following day I experienced a bothersome itching sensation around my family jewels, especially during the morning marching exercises. The sergeant noticed my unbearable discomfort, pulled me aside, and sent me to the doctor.

The doctor explained to me that the lady I had been with the previous night had given me a nasty case of "the crabs," which meant parasitic lice were having a party in my pubic hair. The itching was making me crazier than Spyros! The method of treatment was a simple application of medicated powder three times a day. To my great relief, the problem went away in a few days.

While in Athens, I wrote many letters to Heidi without receiving a single response. I didn't know what to think. Had she forgotten me? Had she found someone else as soon as I left Germany? Perhaps she felt a year was too long to wait for me to return to Germany, and she had shifted her priorities elsewhere—to a more sure relationship.

Edith and my other contacts in Germany promptly wrote back as soon as they received letters from me. Even my friend, Arne Pedersen, the dentist from Denmark, was corresponding with me on a regular basis. I had met Arne a few weeks before I joined the army in Rhodes, where he had taken a short summer vacation. We spent time together at the beach, restaurants, and night clubs. We conversed in German, as Arne was fluent in four different languages.

Arne was a typical blonde, blue-eyed Scandinavian with an even-tempered personality. Overall, he was a low-key, down-to-earth individual. In fact, when he again vacationed in Greece in October, he stopped by the base in Athens to see me. I immediately rushed to the gate, where my friend greeted me with a hug and a big smile. We reminisced about the old times and he listened with a sympathetic ear to my miserable stories of army life.

After completing three months of schooling in Athens, some of us transferred to a heavy artillery base in Thessaloniki to be part of the communication unit. Fortunately, Paul was part of the same unit, which handled both land and wireless communication processes.

Our extremely strict lieutenant there expected all of us to be neat and to have all our belongings in perfect order. A few weeks after we arrived at the base, I had a confrontation with the lieutenant when he demanded to know why some of my clothes were unwashed. When I told him I had no money to buy soap, his face turned fire engine red and he hauled off and slapped my face so hard, the blow sounded like a gunshot.

The embarrassment and humiliation I felt were far more painful than the stinging sensation I felt on my cheek, because this strutting little bantam had hit me right in front of my fellow soldiers. I was confused and bewildered by the lieutenant's harsh reaction. For one brief moment, I thought about taking a gun and blowing his brains out. Fortunately, my cooler side prevailed and I took no action—but man, was I tempted!

(Just to put the record straight, we were responsible for all personal expenses including cigarettes, shaving stuff, soap, and so forth, while our monthly allowance was forty-two drachmas, an amount equivalent to

$1.35. Although my father frequently sent me money, I often ran out by the middle of the month.)

Some of us, including my friend, Paul, were selected to participate in additional training programs for a potential advancement to either corporal or sergeant. We were sent to Kilkis, a town seventy kilometers north of Thessaloniki. This area of Greece is known for its bitterly cold climate and snow-covered grounds for the better part of the winter.

When we arrived at the base, it felt as if we were starting basic training all over again. The drill instructors demanded that we perform unreasonable, demoralizing, childish acts. For example, a sergeant ordered someone to express his deep feelings of love by imagining that the light bulb hanging over a table was Sophia Loren.

"Let me show you," the sergeant said. "Oh, Sophia ... my beautiful treasure! Mia bella, bellisisma ... I love you so much, I want you so much ... ti voglio bene...!" I have to admit, the sergeant displayed a convincing impression of an intimate vow of love. However, some of the soldiers who had to simulate the sergeant's performance were awkward, shy, and intimidated. I watched with disgust as several newcomers were ordered to take a turn with the light bulb.

When my turn came to perform this foolish act, I politely refused, explaining that this practice was not part of the military training guidelines. The furious sergeant pulled me aside, promising that I would pay dearly for being a wise guy in the presence of the rank and file.

It didn't take long, however, for the sergeant and me to become friends after he heard me playing the guitar. I suppose it's true: music hath charms to soothe the savage beast! I could always count on my guitar to help me win friends and influence people. The sergeant and I spent a lot of our free time together, just hanging out or taking part in sing-alongs with other soldiers and officers.

The real test of the upcoming training became evident a few days later when we had to walk an uphill route on a small mountain covered with snow. Some of the snow drifts reached my waist. Many of us had a hard time keeping up with the veterans, who were used to these adverse conditions, but the drill instructors mercilessly pushed us to pick up the pace. This exercise went on for several hours—but as the instructors slyly informed us, that day was only a taste of what was to come.

The next day, a heavy snowfall started as we set out on the same route up the mountain. We were carrying all our gear this time, which made the hike more arduous, and the wind blew snow in our face. It was an exhausting, almost unbearable experience. I felt lucky to have survived.

One Friday afternoon during the strenuous uphill walk, I kept thinking of the "mentally unfit" trick my friend Spyros in Athens had played so well to obtain his civilian status. Spyros' crafty example must have triggered a creative nerve, and I came up with an idea that had a good chance to get me out of this barbaric exercise.

The following day, I approached the lieutenant in charge and made a proposal, a small change that would significantly improve the image of the entire base. I pointed out the sorry condition of the faded signs on the doors of every office. I suggested that we replace these signs with new ones and said that I would personally take on the responsibility.

He was skeptical at first, but I reminded him that he didn't need to make a decision before I had prepared a sample sign, which he and his fellow officers would have to approve unanimously before I began the project.

It took me two days to paint a beautiful door sign with three-dimensional, shadowed lettering. The lieutenant and the other officers were impressed with the sample and gave me permission to replace all the signs, most of which displayed the officers' names and ranks. Others were for the shared places, such as Mess Hall, Library, Game Room, Officer's Club, Latrine, and so forth.

I set up a makeshift studio in a large, heated room on the second floor and began working in a comfortable setting near a cozy, wood-burning stove. The weather outside was brutal. The fields where my fellow soldiers had to suffer through the torturous uphill walk were packed with more snow, while I basked in the warmth of my art studio, out of the elements.

I didn't feel guilty for getting this preferential treatment, nor did I think I had taken advantage of the system. Instead, I felt justified because the military had disrupted my life and the promising future I had started to build in Germany. I was simply getting even with the powers that be, who had changed the rules in the middle of the game, forcing me to serve for a year even after I had been officially excused from my military obligation.

Based on my calculations, if I were to paint one sign per day, completing the project would take me close to the end of our training in Kilkis and I might never have to participate in the field exercises again! It sounded good to me, but just to be on the safe side—in case anyone resented my cushy arrangement—I started writing a satirical military revue to be performed by the soldiers and presented to all personnel as a good-bye gesture at the end of our training. I selected the most qualified actors and started rehearsals three weeks before day of the performance.

I also had to study for the final test, the passing grade of which would determine who would earn the rank of sergeant; those who scored below the passing grade would be ranked as corporals. Just before the show, we all took the two-hour test. When the results came back, I was pleasantly surprised to learn I had received the highest grade, an achievement that earned me special recognition in the form of a letter of commendation addressed to the commander of the Thessaloniki base. I'm proud to say my friend, Paul, also achieved the rank of sergeant.

The large theater hall was full when we gave the two-act performance on the last day of our stay in Kilkis. First, I went onstage to say a few words about the content of the parody, whose first act was actually a spoof that mocked characteristics and behavior of the officers.

When I started delivering my opening monologue, I suddenly froze in place; deep in the grip of paralyzing stage fright, I forgot everything I had memorized! I stood with my mouth agape for a few terrifying moments, staring helplessly out at the expectant audience. Then I regained my composure and ad-libbed my way through the introductory part. *Whew!*

Ten men had parts in the play, including eight in the first act who did mocking impersonations of targeted officers. The second act was a two-man, twenty-minute slapstick comedy sketch. The performance was a big success, earning me kudos from my fellow sergeants as well as the officers. As the saying goes, the show had everybody—grunts, noncoms, officers—rolling in the aisles!

I felt great for having accomplished such a feat. Writing and presenting a show for the first time in my life helped me discover a talent for theatrics I hadn't known I had. At the same time, by undertaking the sign-painting project, my budding artistic skills had improved a great deal. I had previously exercised my artistic talent in Rhodes when I was in high school by completing several watercolor and charcoal paintings.

Overall, the three months I spent in Kilkis were a great experience that would have a positive impact on my future endeavors.

As sergeants, Paul and I triumphantly returned to the base in Thessaloniki as trainers in the communication section. My direct responsibilities were training and supervising a unit of twelve or so soldiers on wireless equipment in both voice and Morse code transmission.

During my three remaining months in the army, I tried to be a patient instructor, using kindness and understanding to get my point across. Unlike the instructors I'd had, I found it unnecessary to use drills as a form of punishment. Because I used kindness instead of fear, no one in my unit gave me a reason to resort to these inhumane practices. I truly enjoyed our daily outdoor practice after each classroom session, out in the flowering fields during the spring and early summer season.

After a long period of silence, I received a letter from Heidi in which she shared a few new revelations. She wrote that she had gotten engaged after I left Germany, but things had not worked out and she had ended that relationship. She also claimed she had never received all the letters I "supposedly" sent to her. The most shocking news was her casual mention of a second child she'd given birth to—also fathered by her own father.

The way she wrote about this subject so matter-of-factly suggested she thought I had known all along about the existence of a second child. Obviously, she was under the misguided impression that she had told me everything concerning her two children.

My readers will recall the terrible dream I had about the gorilla-faced boy before I confronted Heidi about my suspicion of her having a child. Now the interpretation of the dream made sense! As I described the dream in an earlier chapter, "I was lying in bed in my apartment in Rhodes when a hairy, beast-like kid showed up in the front door, motioning for someone else to wait outside." That unseen person was probably the second child I was not supposed to know about at the time.

I could not believe what I had just read! I had understood her one and only sexual encounter with her father, but having a second child with him—the thought was mind-boggling! Who knows how long they had an intimate relationship? With a groan of disgust, I tried to dismiss what I had learned about Heidi's escapades. Utterly lost for words, I didn't respond to her letter. I wondered if it would be wise ever to see her again.

Just before Easter, I slightly modified the parody I had written in Kilkis for the purpose of presenting it on Easter Sunday, right after the Easter meal, late in the afternoon. Some of the actors, including my friend Paul, had been in the original cast, and I had no problem finding new talent for the remaining roles. We set up a stage in an outdoor area and gave a performance that everyone probably is still talking about!

Right after the Easter holiday, Paul began to see a girl named Eleni who lived with her parents in a small house just beyond the fence that surrounded the base. They first started to chat near the fence, but as time went by, they went on dates, most of which were fairly innocent. We teased Paul by nicknaming her "the fence girl."

I talked to Paul a few times, reminding him he should not forget he was still engaged to Stella, that he was playing with fire, and so on. He told me that this is just an insignificant relationship and that he would soon see Stella in Crete when he got his one-month leave in June. Paul had a two-year hitch in the army, whereas I had to serve for only one year.

Toward the end of June, when Paul got his leave, we exchanged our last good-byes because I was scheduled to be discharged on July 13. When

Paul left, I was not able to dismiss the thought that Eleni, with whom Paul had started what he called a platonic relationship, was madly in love with him. She told me about her feelings for Paul one day when I spotted her standing near the fence, as if she were waiting for him to show up.

She also claimed that Paul had promised her the world and told her that she should wait for his return from leave, when they would embark on a more serious relationship. That poor girl was suffering as she counted the days until his return.

The thought that Paul was playing this game with these two women troubled me; I was especially concerned about Eleni, who was banking her future on an empty promise. At least, that was how I evaluated the situation when I decided to speak to Eleni about Paul's "other woman" in Crete.

She would not stop crying when I made her aware of everything I knew about Paul's engagement to Stella. A few days later, Paul must have found out about my conversation with Eleni, because he asked one of his compatriots to deliver a message to me that said "he never wanted to see me or speak to me, ever again."

In retrospect, I have tried to analyze the motives that prompted my decision to speak with Eleni, questioning whether I had acted out of genuine concern. Had I been bitter because Paul—instead of me—had built a relationship with a beautiful girl? Was I jealous? In any case, my attempts during the next few years to communicate with Paul were unsuccessful. Most of the letters I sent to him were returned without any explanation. I surmised he did not want to forgive me for what I had done. How the triangle of Paul, Stella, and Eleni turned out, I have never learned.

Chapter 26

Mission Accomplished

On July 13, 1961, I was discharged from the army, after a year of what I called "lost time." Although the military had made me a little more resilient, I believed the army had stolen a part of my life I could never get back and had put a monumental crimp in the purposeful plan I had started building in Germany. While on the ship heading for Rhodes, I decided to chalk up my military stint, for all its negative aspects, as a good learning experience.

I remembered what Dr. Wagner, my neighbor in Germany, had said: "You are always learning something new when you go through an experience for the first time, even if it yields unexpectedly negative results."

I convinced myself I should pick up the pieces and start over—or rather, start right where I had left off by returning to my original plan with renewed vigor.

One evening, I was relaxing in a comfortable chair on the deck under a canopy of twinkling stars as the ship glided silently along the smooth waters of the Aegean Sea. I was traveling with a married woman and her young child who also were going to Rhodes, where she was to join her husband, a policeman. I had met her outside the base in Thessaloniki a few weeks before my discharge. Eleni had introduced her as her next-door neighbor and said she was also scheduled to travel to Rhodes about the same time I was, so we decided to make the same travel arrangements.

I was having a glass of red wine when my lady companion joined me on the deck. I ordered a drink for her as well and started a conversation about the island of Rhodes: what to expect, the cost of living, and many other topics of interest to newcomers. We abruptly stopped our casual conversation and began looking into each other's eyes to read the unspoken words, as if we both were hypnotized by the romance of the winking stars and the swishing sound of the water breaking off the ship's bow.

We were about to exchange a kiss when the cabin steward arrived, informing the lady that her son was crying. I drew a sigh of relief and silently blessed this timely intervention, which saved us from something neither of us wanted to happen: a forbidden—she was married, after all—act of intimacy. I was thankful that our lips had stopped an inch apart, so that we each could go our own way without having a guilty conscience.

And so we did. We went our separate ways when we said good-bye and good luck as we disembarked from the ship. Her husband was there, eagerly waiting to reunite with his family.

When I went to my old neighborhood in Rhodes, I was informed of the birth of my nephew, Takis, born July 16, 1961, who was my parents' first grandchild. Then I was told of the tragic death of my ex-landlady's only son, a sixteen-year-old who had been killed in a motorcycle accident. I recalled a prophetic dream I'd had before I left for Germany:

There was a black cross with red blood dripping from it on the outside part of my landlady's window; the phrase, BEWARE OF VEHICLES was written under the cross in red letters.

A cold shiver ran down my spine as I thought about the dream. It was as if a mysterious force had been trying to warn me that something terrible was to happen. I had forgotten all about the dream until I learned of the teenager's accident.

This incident became more upsetting when I visited my landlady to express my condolences. I saw a woman dressed in black staring with unseeing eyes into the nothingness of her shattered world, not hearing my words and probably unaware I was even there. The only thing I felt at that moment was the pain of a mother who had lost the most precious part of her existence, her only son.

After I saw my newborn nephew at the hospital, I went to the village, where the rest of the family was spending the summer. Fresh out of the army, I was understandably broke, so I had to borrow some money from my father. I promised I would repay him once I was situated in Switzerland, where I intended to go next.

I enjoyed my short stay in the village, knowing that I was now free to travel anywhere I wanted. I remember the frequent, one-hour walks I took with friends in the early evening, during which the soothing, westerly breeze called *exo-kairos*—meaning "out-wind"—gently kissed our faces and filled the air with an intoxicating, flowery scent. This unusual phenomenon often prompted us to comment, "Ah, you can feel *and* smell the breeze!"

One evening, I sensed that a beautiful young lady named Seva, who had joined our walk, was showing an interest in me. Towards the end of our walk, she gave me a yellow wildflower she had picked from the side of the road and said, "Please take this flower so that you remember this moment; someday, I will explain what I mean."

Seva was a village girl who had recently moved and now worked in the city of Rhodes. I had become acquainted with her prior to my trip to Germany and had viewed her as a typical teenager who wanted to grow up fast. That evening, however, walking close to her, I'd noticed that her full lips, high cheek bones, almond-shaped eyes, and tanned complexion comprised a young lady with many enticing qualities.

As we strolled side by side, I could smell her pleasant perfume as the light breeze played in her long, raven-black hair. At that moment, I realized I liked her. I wondered why I hadn't noticed such an exotic beauty before.

Seva and I started a brief, innocent affair that threatened to become a full-blown romance. I was still preparing for my trip to Switzerland, where I had decided to sojourn before I went back to Germany. During the last two weeks before my departure, I spent a lot of time with Seva in the city. I realized I had an emotional attachment to this gorgeous creature, who admitted she was in love with me on our last night together.

Although I had strong feelings for Seva, I don't remember telling her "I love you," even during the kissing and necking marathon, the last intimate moments we'd spend together.

Chapter 27
Off to Switzerland

When I arrived in Athens, I decided to change my Switzerland itinerary by traveling through Italy instead of Yugoslavia. While getting the appropriate tourist visas for the countries I planned to visit, I was allowed to take a maximum of $100, supposedly for a one-month stay outside Greece. The limited amount of money a tourist was allowed to take outside Greece was a bureaucratic way of ensuring that the person would return to Greece on or before the visa expiration date.

I took a ship to Brindisi, Italy, which sailed through the postcard-pretty Isthmus of Corinth, which connects central Greece with the Peloponnesus, my home country's mountainous southern peninsula. It was an overnight trip, so I had a chance to sleep for several hours. From Brindisi, I took the local train to Bari, where I spent about six hours roaming the streets before boarding the train to Milan, another overnight ride.

When the train arrived at the station, a big crowd stormed through the doors and commandeered all the seats. I ended up in a space next to a door between the cars, where I sat on my suitcase for the next twelve hours. I got a few hours of sleep on the floor, using my suitcase as a cushion, but the entire trip was a painful experience.

The train from Milan to Zurich left around noon. In less than two hours, we stopped at the border, where the Swiss officials checked our passports and other traveling papers. One of the officials asked everyone in our car to take our suitcases and exit the train.

When we stepped outside, we were ordered to enter a bus; after a twenty-minute ride, the bus stopped in front of an isolated office building. I tried in vain to get an explanation for this inexplicable diversion, but the authorities brusquely advised me to follow their instructions. I was trying to communicate in Italian, but the dialect of the northern region was such that I could not understand a word they said.

When we entered the building, I located someone who spoke German. He explained there was a group on the train that was commissioned to work in Switzerland for a given period and they had to undergo a medical evaluation first. When I told him I was not part of the group, that I was just a tourist traveling to Zurich on my own, he immediately apologized for the misunderstanding and offered to drive me back to the train station.

On the way there, he told me I would have to wait for the next train, which was scheduled to arrive in about three hours. I had left my jacket on the train, thinking we would return to our seats, but I was sadly mistaken. The man who drove me back called the lost-and-found section of the transit authority in Zurich, asking them to locate and hold my jacket.

I had plenty of time before the train arrived, so I sat down and wrote a letter to Seva. Being alone in a strange region, away from all the people I knew, my emotions got the better of me, I suppose. I wrote how much I already missed her and said that I truly felt a void without her next to me at that moment. I also wrote a letter to my father describing the day's unfortunate turn of events. After mailing the letters, I tried to take a nap by lying down on three wooden chairs I pulled together, but sleep just wouldn't come.

The ride to Zurich was about two hours; I arrived a little after 8:00 p.m. At the lost-and-found section of the station, I found my jacket—but everything I'd had in the pockets—cigarettes, candy, and the like—was missing. My next main concern was to find a reasonable hotel to spend the night, because I hadn't had a good night's sleep for two days. There were not many vacancies in the immediate area, so I ended up sharing a room with a chance acquaintance in a seedy hotel near the train station.

The following day, I visited an employment office, where I was given a choice of locations for possible employment. On my application, I indicated I was not too particular as to the type of available jobs or their location. Someone from the office suggested that, until I found a job, I could stay in the boy's section of Zurich University (*Universität Zürich)* dormitories, which were vacant during the summer months.

The price was right, and I stayed there for two weeks, paying three Swiss francs a day, which included a continental breakfast—a good deal! During this period, the employment office sent me to a few nearby towns for possible work, but nothing materialized—the interviews ended with the usual, "We will let you know in a few days," which really meant, "Don't call us, we'll call you."

After an interview at a chocolate factory thirty kilometers outside Zurich, I went to the only restaurant in the area for lunch. A quick glance at the menu let me know the place was a little pricey for my budget. I was not too familiar with the Swiss cuisine, so I decided to order one of the low-priced items on the menu—what seemed to be a cold salad—along with beer.

I was at a loss when the food arrived on two different platters covered with cellophane. An empty plate was placed in front of me along with two service spoons, as if two people were sitting at the table, not just one. I sat dumbfounded, staring at the food, not knowing how I was supposed to start eating! Should I just take one of the platters and place it in front of me, or use the large spoon and transfer the salad from one platter to the empty plate in front of me? And why had they brought two separate platters of food?

When the waitress came over to ask me if there was anything wrong with the food, I simply told her everything was fine and ordered another beer. Anyway, I chose the logical approach. I transferred the salad from one platter to the empty plate, finished eating, and left the second platter untouched.

Having enjoyed the tasty salad dish, I was tempted to attack the second platter, but I took the safe choice and left it alone in case they'd made a mistake and brought lunch for two, in which case I would have to pay double. I was embarrassed to ask for an explanation of that perplexing setup, and I never found out what approach I should have used in that particular restaurant to simply have lunch.

The employment agency finally found a job for me in an alpine resort town called Andermatt. When I checked the map, I saw the town was situated 67 kilometers southeast of Lucerne and 140 kilometers from Zurich, near the junction of four alpine passes: St. Gotthard, Grimsel, Susten, and Oberalp. I spoke with my potential boss, a Mr. Wenger, on the phone, and he cordially offered me a position in one of the two hotels he owned. I made an appointment to meet him the next day.

On my last day in Zurich, I did quite a bit of walking through the city, enjoying a comfortable summer evening and admiring the quaint little bridges over small ponds and creeks. The tranquility of the scene, coupled with the fact I had a job and looked forward to meeting my new boss, put my mind at ease as twilight settled on this sylvan paradise. To cap off the evening, I went to a theater where I saw the movie "A View from the Bridge" with Raf Vallone and Maureen Stapleton. The film was either dubbed or subtitled in German—I forget which. Many years later, when I saw the same film after I had learned to speak English, it reminded me of that lovely night in Zurich.

Early the next afternoon, I arrived in Andermatt after taking a train to Lugano and then a smaller trolley up the mountain to my destination. The area was breathtaking! The town was nestled in the lowest part of the valley and surrounded by majestic, snowcapped mountains. A stream, flowing adjacent to the main road, wended its gentle way through the center of the town where the Hotel Löwen, my new place of employment, was located.

I met with Mr. Wenger, a nice man, who explained my responsibilities and my compensation, which included a base salary plus commission. The commission was based on the number of tourists I influenced to select our hotel. To accomplish this, I would go to the train station twice a day, welcome the tourists, and try to woo them to stay at the luxurious Hotel Löwen.

At the train station, I was competing with two older fellows who represented different hotels. But being the youngest and wearing a Hotel Löwen uniform, I had no problem convincing tourists to select our hotel— especially the ladies who were traveling without a male companion

I also had to work at the front desk when Mr. Wenger was not available. In addition, in between the train arrivals, while the guests were out skiing, I had to wax the hardwood floors of all their rooms after removing any water stains caused by the skiers' wet clothes. I hated this chore, because Mr. Wegner's wife always found a few stains I had missed during her afternoon inspection. We also had two maids who only spoke Italian, thus giving me an opportunity to practice the language of love, as I was the only employee who would play interpreter between Mr. Wegner and the Italian staff.

Below is a picture of the Hotel Löwen as it appeared on a 1961 postcard.

HOTEL LÖWEN ANDERMATT

My work day was an average of ten hours, from 7:00 a.m. till 7:00 p.m., with a two-hour break in the afternoon. There was no day off for me, but even if I'd had a day off during the week, I wouldn't have known what to do. The town had only a small number of entertainment venues. Although our hotel had a nice bar in a lounge setting, once in a while we would go out to a nearby club for a change of scenery.

Caterine, the Hotel Löwen's barmaid, made my daily routine more tolerable. After we'd realized we liked one another, we began spending our afternoon breaks together. We enjoyed strolling alongside the burbling creek, which was swollen with the chilly water from the melting mountain snow. Caterine was one of the nicest girls I had ever met. She was honest and upfront with me, asking me to respect certain limits of our relationship, which she had defined. I was happy with this arrangement and enjoyed the company of this Swiss miss immensely.

I communicated with my family and friends back home, including Seva. Her letter surprised me; she wrote that she was cancelling her scheduled immigration to Australia because she wanted to be closer to me. She planned to move to Germany by signing a one-year work agreement with a company in Wiesbaden.

My sister, Despina, informed me that she was considering getting married to a Greek-American man. He had been born in our same village but had moved to America when he was a teenager. She explained he was much older, but she was willing to go ahead with the wedding so the entire family could immigrate to America at a later date.

My sister's underlying message was, "Although I don't love him, I'm sacrificing myself for the purpose of ensuring a better life for everyone else in the family." Although my response to her was somewhat vague, I tried to point out the folly of her spending the rest of her life with someone she might never come to love. Alas, when I received her next letter, she had already married Peter.

My good friend, Arne, the dentist, drove all the way from Denmark and came to see me one weekend. My boss kindly gave me half a day off, and I spent the afternoon and evening with my friend. While taking a long walk through Andermatt's main street, Arne wanted to stop at the general store (the only one in town) to buy a toothbrush.

When we entered the store, I noticed that the storekeeper, a jovial lady who was always behind the counter, was not there. Instead, there was a handwritten note on the counter that read, "I will be back shortly. Please take what you need and leave the money in the basket. Thank you very much." This didn't seem to surprise Arne, but to me it was an amazing phenomenon that the storekeeper would trust everyone to do the right thing and not take advantage of the situation.

When I asked Arne why he didn't find this unusual, he remarked that he also had seen this level of good faith in smaller towns throughout the Scandinavian countries. The self-respect of their people was in concert with what the American social writer and philosopher Eric Hoffer had written: "The capacity for getting along with our neighbor depends to a large extent on the capacity for getting along with ourselves. The self-respecting individual will try to be as tolerant of his neighbor's shortcomings as he is of his own."

No wonder these countries are far more socially and economically advanced than the southern part of Europe, I thought.

We had a nice conversation over dinner about my hometown of Rhodes, a place Arne visited almost every year for his summer vacation. He was seriously considering buying some property there so he would have a place of his own, instead of having to stay in a hotel room for almost a month every year.

THREE GRAINS OF WHEAT

After staying overnight at the Hotel Löwen, Arne left for Denmark early Sunday morning. As we said good-bye, I thanked him many times for going out of his way and driving all that distance just to brighten my day. I considered that selfless gesture the mark of true friendship, and I never forgot it.

The following week, Caterine told me she was leaving the hotel for another position near her hometown in the suburbs of Bern. I was devastated by this new development, because Caterine was the motivational force that kept me going in Andermatt. What would I do without her reassuring presence, her innocent sweetness, her kind nature? With only three precious days left to us, we spent every possible moment together after our shift ended. Her departure day arrived all too soon, and we promised one another we would definitely stay in touch.

A few days later, I received a letter from Caterine in which she expressed deep feelings she hadn't been able to bring herself to say to me in person. That letter made me feel even more disconsolate. I was mired in a miserable state of abject loneliness, and the picture postcard setting of Andermatt no longer held any allure for me.

At one point, I considered moving back to Germany. I felt I would go crazy if I stayed in the hotel any longer. Out of desperation, I suppose, I wrote a letter to Heidi, informing her of the possibility of my returning to Germany. She responded with an enthusiastic two-page letter, absolutely thrilled that I hadn't forgotten her. She said she could not wait to see me again.

The letter was sprinkled with sweet nothings along the lines of "I have always loved you," "You're the only one for me," and so forth. I wasn't sure if I believed everything Heidi wrote, yet a little voice inside me kept reminding me of the good times we'd had together. I still have that letter, which I kept for a reason to be explained in a later chapter.

I remember one sunny afternoon, during my time off, I was lying on a grassy knoll, gazing at the natural beauty of the mountains all around me, when I spied a group of skiers swooshing down the steep slopes in the far distance. The sublime beauty of the moment made me realize how much I had missed Caterine—yet at the same time, I was thinking of Heidi, who was a motivating factor in my decision to go back to Germany.

When I went back to work, I met with my boss and told him that I wanted to resign immediately. I expected Mr. Wenger to start hollering at me and demanding I stay until he could find a replacement, but he calmly said he respected my decision, as he knew it was not easy for a young person like me to be subjected to a seven-day work week for so long. He said others who had held the same position typically lasted about three months. Well, I kept pace with the averages because I also lasted almost three months.

Mr. Wenger said that, in the morning, he would have all the necessary documents ready for me, including my passport and a letter of recommendation, plus my pending salary. Mr. Wegner was a good businessman, to be sure. Above all, I considered him a true gentleman.

The next day I boarded the train to Bonn. However, when we arrived at the German border, I was a little concerned about whether I would be allowed to reenter the country. I maintained a nonchalant attitude when the inspector asked for my passport, keeping up a conversation with a Swiss passenger while the inspector reviewed the previously stamped visas in my passport. Fortunately, he granted me the required entry permit without asking any questions.

It was already dark outside when we crossed the border, which once again meant I would arrive in Bonn around midnight. Heidi had promised, when we'd spoken on the phone earlier that day, to be at the station waiting when I arrived. But she was nowhere to be seen.

Crestfallen, I looked all over for her, and assumed she had a good excuse for not showing up. At least this time, I had made reservations at a hotel that was only a five-minute taxi ride away.

When I got to the hotel, the desk clerk gave me a note from Heidi that explained why she could not be at the station and said she would see me tomorrow afternoon. Heidi was working as a nanny and had been asked by her boss to stay with the children that night because of an emergency.

Around one o'clock the next day, I met Heidi in the hotel lobby. Although I was not totally convinced by her excuse for failing to meet me at the train station, I could not be angry with her as we hugged and kissed passionately after eighteen months of separation. We spent the rest of the day together, catching up on all the major events each of us had experienced.

I was not sure if I felt the same way about Heidi then as I had before I'd left Germany in May of 1960. It seemed as though something were missing this time from our relationship, almost as if the "broken vase" had more cracks now than the one we had glued back together the previous year, when it broke for the first time—after the revelation of her child. As I wondered if there were more skeletons in her closet, I decided to give her one more chance and try to rebuild our relationship on a more solid foundation.

The following day, I went to Bonn city hall to obtain my work visa, only to find that getting the permit was even more difficult than it had been the last time. I was told the only way to get a work permit was if an employer sponsored me, in which case I would have to sign a one-year work agreement with him. I was aware of this type of work arrangement, which usually involved employing a group of relatively unskilled and undereducated people from another country.

These people were provided food and board in tenements within the company's compounds. Their compensation was much lower than that of a typical German worker or anyone else who did not fall within such groups. In the early 1960s, Germany had a shortage of low-skilled workers. Many countries from southern Europe and the Middle East had made available a pool of workers who were contracted and subsequently distributed to various factories throughout West Germany.

Under no circumstances would I accept this type of work arrangement, as I was a much more qualified individual than the bulk of the menial laborers that had flooded Germany during the previous two years. I was determined to make it on my own. After all, I had enough money to stay for a few more weeks at the hotel in Bonn. I also tried to get a work permit in Cologne, as well as in some of the surrounding towns, but I was left in a more desperate frame of mind each time my application was rejected.

A week later, Heidi and I visited Brühl where I also tried to get a work permit. Unfortunately, the immigration official there denied my request, citing the same reason as all the other bureaucrats. While in Brühl, we visited some of our favorite clubs, including the Post, the place we had met for the first time.

The atmosphere at the Post had certainly changed over those two years. The foreign customers (mainly Greeks and Italians) outnumbered the locals by at least three to one. Back in 1959, there were only eight Greeks in the entire city. Now, two years later, the number had grown to 2500, representing a staggering proliferation of foreign workers from just one country.

We spent a night at Rita's Guesthouse (Pansion) on Wilhelm Street, a place that brought back fond memories of my "rookie days" in Germany. Although I wanted to see Rita one more time, her mother told me she was visiting relatives in Munich and would be back in a week or so.

As time went on, with no luck regarding my work papers, I started to get more concerned. My funds had depleted to the point that I had to economize, even for basic needs such as food and transportation. Computing my budget one Sunday afternoon, I reckoned I had enough money to last me for about one more week. After I paid the hotel my agreed-upon weekly rental (Monday through Sunday), I barely had enough money left for food and other necessities.

During the week, I made a few more attempts to secure my work papers in different towns, but to no avail. I couldn't even get in touch with Heidi, who was visiting her mother and was scheduled to return on Monday.

On Thursday night, I went to a bar to have a beer, feeling desperately squeezed between a rock and a hard place. A bitter truth hit me: I simply could not survive in a foreign country without money. As I contemplated calling Arne in Denmark, a gentleman sat down on the bar stool next to me and ordered a beer. I detected a familiar accent and asked him where he came from. I was delighted to learn he was Greek and that he lived nearby.

As we chatted, I explained my situation with the work permit and the fact that I was at my wit's end about what to do next. He suggested I try to get the permit in Bergheim, a town about two hours by bus from Bonn. He said he'd had the same difficulty getting his permit, and that this was the only place he knew of where the officials could be counted on to be lenient.

After all the rejections I had received, this sounded simply too good to be true. I was just about to pay for my beer and call my friend Arne, but this kind stranger wouldn't hear of it. He paid for my first beer and bought two more rounds! As we were leaving the bar, he emphasized again that I should try Bergheim before I did another thing.

Chapter 28

One-Way Ticket

I woke up Friday morning in a state of panic, realizing I was in big trouble as I was down to my last four marks, which would only buy me food for the day. I sat at the foot of the bed, head in hands, reviewing my options one more time, but I could not come up with a reasonable way out of this personal hell.

I took a long walk toward the bus station to check on the cost of a bus ticket to Bergheim, should I decide to make the trip. Unfortunately, my four marks would only buy a one-way ticket, which cost 2.65 marks. That meant I would not have enough for a return ticket.

Here we go again! I thought to myself. *What the hell do I do now?* I could stay put and spend my piddling cash on food, but where did I go from there, flat broke? Would I be reduced to begging on a street corner?

I decided to call Arne in Denmark collect, but the telephone operator said no one was answering the phone. *Well, that tears it,* I sighed. I had no recourse but to buy the one-way ticket to Bergheim and pray to God to help me one more time, as I needed Him now more than ever. Knowing God was on my side gave me a renewed sense of optimism, and a comforting feeling that I would not be alone on the bus to Bergheim.

And so, I bought my ticket and boarded the bus around 1:00 p.m. A traffic jam caused by an accident turned the two-hour trip into a three-hour one. Then it took me almost an hour to walk from the bus station to city hall, where I ran up two flights of stairs to reach the office of Mr. Otto Schenck, who was my last hope. It was a little before five when I saw Mr. Schenck jingling his keys, ready to lock the office door. Taking long strides, I dashed down the hallway and stopped in front of him, almost out of breath.

"Mr. Schenck, I have to speak with you for a few minutes," I said, huffing and puffing.

"The office is closed now, come back on Monday," he replied nonchalantly.

"Please, please, hear me out!" I begged, sinking to my knees. "I have to speak to you today—*pant!*—please give me one minute to explain—*pant!*—it's a serious matter!"

Mr. Schenck sighed and shook his head. "All right, young man, come in. I will give you five minutes, but you'd better have a very good explanation for insisting to see me today instead of Monday."

Once inside his office, I described my travails in trying to get the work permit, the fact that I was down to almost nothing after spending most of my last four marks on a one-way ticket in Bonn—the whole nine yards. From his facial expression, I gathered he was stunned by my tale of woe.

"Do you mean that you don't have a return ticket to Bonn?" he asked.

"Yes, sir, I'm ashamed to admit that's true," I said, shrugging my shoulders.

"Hold on one minute, I have to make a call," he said. He excused himself as he dialed the phone and spoke to someone; I gathered it was his wife.

"Darling, I will be home a little late tonight because I have to take care of an urgent matter that just came up unexpectedly. Oh, and another thing—I have a very interesting story to tell you!"

As he hung up the phone, I was puzzled by the curious smile on his face. He then asked me how I would get back to Bonn if he gave me a work permit. I told him that, as long as I had my work permit, I would *walk* to Bonn, even if it took me a full day to get there.

Pursing his lips and nodding his head, he grabbed the phone again.

"Good evening, Dr. Blassberg, this is Otto Schenck," he said into the receiver. "I have an interesting proposition for you." There was a little pause while the other party spoke. "I'm sitting here with an interesting individual who, besides needing a job, speaks fluent German as well as Italian." Another pause. "That's fine, Dr. Blassberg, I will see you in twenty minutes." With that, he hung up the phone.

At the time, I didn't know what was happening. Mr. Schenck put my mind at ease by telling me I was a lucky man, because all the pieces had just fallen into place. He said things would be fine for me from that point on.

First, he stamped my passport with a one-year work permit. Then he told me that the owner of a brick factory was waiting to meet me in a little town called Manheim, where I might get a job. As we rode in his car, Mr. Schenck explained that several Greek and Italian workers in the factory didn't speak German. He said I would be a great asset to Dr. Blasberg, because I could bridge the communication gap between the Germans and the foreigners.

I thought I was dreaming! I couldn't believe what had just happened—getting my permit plus securing a job was the stuff of miracles. If I had gotten to Mr. Schenck's office just five minutes later, the entire sequence of events would have been completely different.

Had luck—or was it fate?—not shined on me, I might have ended up wandering the streets of Bergheim, searching for the all-too-familiar park bench to spend the night, or begging like a common panhandler for money to buy a bus ticket to Bonn. I could only conclude that, once again, God had indeed heard my prayers and had dispatched my guardian angel once again to rescue me by the proverbial seat of my pants, at the last possible second.

When we arrived in Manheim, Dr. Blasberg was waiting for us in his office. Welcoming me with great enthusiasm, he immediately offered me a job to start as early as the following Monday. When he realized I did not have a place to stay, we walked over to an adjacent building, where most of the foreign workers were housed. It resembled the army barracks, although each apartment accommodated four to five people. At that moment, I impulsively hugged Mr. Schenck, who was ready to go home. I thanked him many times for his help, telling him that he was truly my God-sent guardian angel.

As Dr. Blasberg and I walked into the section where the Greeks were housed, everyone in the room jumped to their feet, because a visit from the boss man was a rare event. After he introduced me, I started speaking to my new coworkers in Greek, explaining that I had been hired as an interpreter of sorts because of my facility in German and Italian. I told them that I would be working with them starting the following Monday. I was perplexed when everyone applauded, as if I had won a gold medal.

Just then, a man named Kostas introduced himself. Judging from the way he confidently dominated the conversation, he seemed to be the group spokesman. After Dr. Blasberg left, Kostas brought out a bottle of ouzo and filled glasses for everyone in the room. "Let's drink to the person that God sent to help us with all the language problems!" he cried.

"*Yassou!*" everybody cheered in unison, raising their glasses.

When I told them I'd had had nothing to eat all day, they offered me a large bowl of *fasolada* (a Greek bean soup) with half a loaf of Italian bread, some feta cheese, and Greek olives. I savored every tasty bite of that homemade dinner, a meal which is considered the traditional "poor man's feast."

I explained to everyone what I had been through trying to get my work permit, that my suitcase was still in the hotel in Bonn, and that I had no money for the train ticket. They offered to chip in for the fare and other expenses, as well as allowing me to stay in their quarters until I got situated elsewhere— if I chose to live in town instead of the factory dormitories.

I felt great to be among such a friendly crowd of people who genuinely appreciated me, viewing me as a future leader who would help them solve their job- and language-related problems.

Chapter 29

Don't Take the "Man" Out of Manheim

O ver the weekend, I went to the hotel in Bonn to get my few belongings, a suitcase and a guitar. I started work on Monday morning,
which was in essence a training period that would last for three
days. The work entailed the removal of the wet-formed, seven-kilo bricks
from a rotating cylinder. We picked them up with the leather-covered, outer part of a pointer pressed against the rest of the fingers.

In other words, you couldn't just pick the soft, wet brick with your
hands; you had to gently lift it with the fingers. Otherwise, it would crum-
ble in midair into a sandy mess. Then, turning around 180-degrees, we
placed the bricks onto carts that traveled slowly along a railway into a
continuously fired tunnel, or kiln, where the bricks would harden to the
required consistency. This was the final phase before distribution.

The lifting and placing of the bricks from the cylinder to the wagon
was a cumbersome activity that would quickly wear one out if certain arm
muscles were not accustomed to the repetitive motion. I remember that,
on my first try, my arms dropped limply to my sides after ten or so bricks.
It took me almost an entire week to gain the required arm strength to complete the five-minute shift for the 300-brick cart load.

The five-minute shift was served by a two-man team, one on each side
of the cart. When the cart was completely loaded, we rested for five minutes while another team took over the same process. That's how the entire
eight-hour day went.

It was amazing to me how some of the experienced workers, like
Kostas, were able to place the soft bricks on the cart in perfect alignment
without breaking a sweat. After that first day, I held out little hope I would

ever be able to perform as well as my comrades, but everyone assured me that soon I would be able to work with my eyes closed.

In the meantime, Yanni, one of the workers who lived in town, helped me find a place to rent on Buirer Street, a few houses down from where he lived. I made arrangements for room and board with a nice, older, retired couple, Mr. & Mrs. Floss, whose children were grown and had moved out of the house. Mrs. Floss was so nice to me, making certain I always had nutritious meals and treating me as if I were her own child.

The main street of Manheim was only one block away, putting all the shops and clubs within walking distance. My workplace was a ten-minute bike ride away. The town was so small that everyone pretty much knew each other, a setting that reminded me of my village in Rhodes. Hanes Lounge, our favorite bar/lounge, was located at the far end of town. It was owned and operated by a nice, young married couple, Hanes and Helga. The train station was a little more than three kilometers away, a distance we usually walked each time we wanted to travel to Cologne or some other city in the main rail corridor.

I got in touch with Heidi, who had already returned from visiting her mother's place, where her younger brother and her two children lived. Heidi came to Manheim almost every other weekend; we would go out to my favorite lounge and then she would spend the night with me.

Although she made every effort to demonstrate how much she cared for me, I subconsciously doubted her intentions. Eventually, the deep feelings I had once had for her regressed to plain fondness. However, I hoped our relationship would again regain the spark of uncontrollable desire that had made me want to be with her every minute of the day.

One weekend, I reluctantly accepted Heidi's request to visit her mother and the rest of the family. I met her in Bonn, where we took the train to a town in the Black Forest. It was a homey hamlet about the same size as Andermatt in Switzerland.

I met her mother, who appeared to be a nice lady, although I detected an underlying agony expressed by her pale, careworn face. As Heidi introduced us, I could only imagine what was going through her mind, as she was fully aware that I knew the truth about Heidi's two children. She stared at me in silence, yet the intensity of her expression revealed her despondency, as if she desperately desired the power to go back in time and change or eliminate those terrible events between Heidi and her father.

I met Heidi's two young children, who had grown up believing Mrs. Kroscher was their natural mother and Heidi was their sister. I went outside on the front porch where I saw the two little boys, too busy playing with some worn-out, wooden toys to notice me standing nearby. I reflected sadly on the tragic situation. Here were two innocent human beings who, through no choice of their own, had come into this world under the most abnormal of circumstances.

Eventually, a friend or relative would tell them the cruel truth, or they would stumble upon it accidentally; either way, the awful stigma would shatter their lives and normalcy would be forever denied to them. It's truly a damned shame the way things were destined to turn out for these two children.

I just couldn't understand why Heidi continued the incestuous relationship with her father. Why didn't she just walk away? I conjectured her father's love for his daughter was a substitute for friends or his own wife. He had forced his teenage girl to submit to his sexual depravity, a situation in which he could exercise total control over her. But that did not explain Heidi's apparent willingness. There was no reasonable explanation for how she could engage in the act of incest, probably multiple times, resulting in a second child being borne.

Would Heidi be able to maintain a stable relationship with me, or would she view me as a substitute for her father? Would she end up having psychological problems a few years later, especially when her children found out the sordid truth? As disturbing as these thoughts were, I could not change the current reality—I just had to accept the situation and move on.

Early that evening, right after dinner, Heidi and I borrowed her brother Werner's motorcycle and went to see a movie in a nearby city, about six or seven kilometers away. On the way back, the motorcycle suddenly stalled in the middle of the road. I assumed we had run out of gas, but when I checked the gas tank, it was not empty. After many unsuccessful attempts to restart the engine, I presumed there was a mechanical difficulty I could neither diagnose nor fix. We pushed the motorcycle back to the house, which was only a couple of kilometers away.

When we got there, Werner noticed that the gas cut-off valve was in the off position, thus shutting off the flow of gasoline to the engine. As he explained, I must have accidentally hit the valve with my knee. Anyway, live and learn! The rest of my overnight stay was rather uneventful.

When I got back to Manheim on Sunday afternoon, I ruminated on the previous day's events, specifically how blithely Heidi accepted that her children were being raised by her mother under such blatantly false pretenses. It seemed as though she had erased her teenage years from her memory and had decided to live and enjoy the "now," since the past was immutable. This might be the ideal approach to life for some; but those of us who consider ourselves rational thinkers cannot ignore what we've learned and we refuse to sacrifice our principles and morals for instant gratification.

After a month or so at the brick factory, I had gained enough strength and dexterity to carry out my five-minute shift with relative ease. I was in such good physical shape that I seriously considered working nonstop on both sides of the cart, which would earn me twice the daily pay, since my wages were calculated based on the number of completed carts.

Kostas, who was left-handed, and I thought about trying this approach. The only obstacle was the training of our respective weaker hands, the left for me and the right for Kostas. It only took us a week to master this difficult task, and we were able to double our daily income, though we had to work for two straight hours before taking our first ten-minute break.

However, as it has often been said, "Every good thing comes with a price." I discovered this adage applied to me when I found out a year later that the use—or rather abuse—I had subjected my weaker left hand to had resulted in nerve damage to my wrist, necessitating surgery. I will elaborate on this later, as the surgery triggered other events whose outcome was somewhat part of my destiny.

During this period, I also kept in touch with my friend Richard, who now worked for the Ford Motor Company in Cologne. Heidi and I got together a few times with Richard and his longtime girlfriend, Carmen. In the meantime, another friend from the village, Elias, invited me to his wedding to Georgia, another village girl, in Wiesbaden. Seva, who had come to Germany when I was in Switzerland, was also in Wiesbaden and would be part of the wedding party. According to her last letter, she couldn't wait to see me after all this time.

Richard had gotten a huge kick out of my sister's wedding in the village, so he and Carmen were eager to attend another Greek celebration. I invited them to Elias and Georgia's wedding, and they picked me up in Manheim in Richard's car. The relatively low-key wedding celebration in Wiesbaden paled in comparison to the wingdings in my village, yet we still had plenty of Greek food and drink, especially ouzo, which some of us indulged in a little too much.

Seva got rather tipsy and would not let me leave her sight. She was practically glued to my side, holding my hand or dancing with me cheek to cheek, telling me how much she loved me, and saying that she wanted to come with me to Manheim.

As the party wound down, Richard, Carmen, and I extended our best wishes to Elias and Georgia for a long and happy marriage. Then I hugged and kissed Seva good-bye and started heading for the car. Seva clung desperately onto my arm, crying hysterically, letting her limp body be dragged behind me as I tried to get away. She continued screaming, begging me to take her with me. She was completely uncontrollable and at one point she threw herself in front of Richard's car crying out, "If you don't take me with you, you will have to drive over my body!"

Fortunately, Elias and some other men pulled her away from the car, enabling us to escape. Richard and Carmen were stunned, describing that episode with Seva as another Greek tragedy—because she was willing to die for me.

Chapter 30

Seva's Visit

A few weeks after Elias' wedding, Heidi and I were having a drink in a lounge near my house. All of a sudden, the customers sitting at the bar exclaimed, "*Ach du lieber Got, wer ist diese zuckerpuppe?*" which means, "Oh, dear God, who is this sugar doll?"

I turned around and whom did I see? Seva was standing there, looking stunning in a tight-fitting, light yellow dress that perfectly complemented her olive complexion. No wonder the Germans were salivating over this ravishing, dark-haired temptress!

I was speechless for a minute, but when I approached her, she said she absolutely had to see me so that we could settle some things once and for all. Heidi was utterly confused, unsure whether to leave the place or confront her provocatively dressed rival.

I asked Heidi to wait for me in the lounge while escorting Seva outside, where I realized she had taken a taxi from Wiesbaden all the way to Manheim—a 200-kilometer ride that would probably set her back more than a week's wages. She told me she was certain I was going out with other girls, but she didn't mind because I couldn't possibly have the same deep-rooted feelings for the German blondes as she thought I had for her.

She told the taxi driver to wait while we went to my room. First, she apologized for her behavior in Wiesbaden, blaming her emotional outburst on too many drinks. She went on to say I was the reason she had chosen to come to Germany instead of immigrating to Australia, where she had relatives and friends waiting for her.

I couldn't believe my ears when she blurted out, "I am still a virgin, but I don't want to stay that way anymore. I know the reason why you go out with German girls— because they give you *everything*—so I have decided to offer you my most valuable possession: my virginity."

I sat in awestruck silence as she started taking off her clothes until she was completely naked. Leaning awkwardly on the edge of the bed, she crossed her legs at the ankles and stretched them out, and then she laid her palms down flat on either side of her hips, slightly thrusting out her full, round breasts. Suddenly, she rocked forward and extended her tanned arms toward me, signaling me closer. I stood frozen in my stance.

"I'm all yours," she said. "Come and get me! I want you to be the first one …"

I could tell her sexual bravado was merely an act, as her eyes were glistening and her voice broke as she uttered these hollow-sounding words. Under most circumstances, I would have reacted as any other young man alone with a beautiful, naked woman would have. But instead, I wiped the tear off her cheek and then I hugged her protectively, holding her tightly as she sobbed with her head resting on my shoulder.

There was nothing titillating in this; it felt as if I were comforting my own daughter. I held her camisole out to her and begged, "Please put this on. I don't want it to be this way—I don't want to take advantage of the vulnerability you are experiencing right now. Save this once-in-a-lifetime experience for the right moment."

Still sobbing, Seva clutched the camisole to her chest as I went on. "Listen, even if we were to get married in a month or two from now, I would still have asked you to wait for that special moment of shared ecstasy you have been waiting for. It should be the night you reward your partner with your most valuable possession, when you cuddle together in your love nest after taking off your white wedding gown. If this were to happen today, dear Seva, you would be losing your purity with tears in your eyes, as opposed to gifting it to your new husband with a smile on your face."

My words must have convinced her, because she hurriedly put on her camisole and the rest of her clothes. She then hugged me, thanking me for not taking advantage of her bold offer and agreeing with me that we should wait for the right moment.

She was sniffling and trying to put on a brave face as I took her back to the taxi and we said our good-byes. The wind tossed her long black hair as she stuck her head through the open window and said, "Don't forget me, Mike, I love you!" as the taxi sped away.

When I went back to the lounge, where Heidi was still waiting for me, some of the lounge customers who knew me made humorous remarks about my having to choose between two beautiful girls. Although I had been gone for almost two hours, Heidi understood. I explained to her that, all that time, I had been trying to convince Seva to go back to Wiesbaden. I promised her that we had not had an intimate encounter.

I spent the rest of the day with Heidi, mostly at Hanes's lounge, where we ate a light dinner and danced a little. She then stayed with me overnight, thus ending a day full of unexpected events that had indeed tested my manly mettle. It was truly miraculous that I had been able to control myself and not give into my desires with one of the most enticing temptations God ever placed on this earth lying right there in front of me!

When I was alone on Sunday afternoon, I kept thinking of Seva and what she meant to me. I asked myself if I cared enough to move on to the next phase of our relationship. I concluded that what she had done the previous day was not rational behavior on her part; she had acted irresponsibly and purely on impulse.

I asked myself many times if she were the type of woman I would spend the rest of my life with. After all, her recent behavior—her outburst at the wedding, her impromptu appearance at the lounge, her ill-advised seduction—indicated she was, at the very least, flighty, and at the very most, possibly mentally unbalanced. She was a lovely, desirable girl, but in the end, the cons outweighed the pros with regard to a serious relationship with her.

The following week, Elias sent me a letter telling me that Seva was getting out of control and that he was afraid she might try something stupid. He begged me to consider her feelings as true love and he emphasized his belief that her emotional intentions seemed so strongly rooted that she would definitely make the perfect wife for me.

Although I appreciated my friend's concern, in my response to Elias' letter, I was rather vague so that I wouldn't give any false hopes or promises. Seva also wrote to me that she regretted the way she had behaved during her visit to Manheim. In fact, she had realized her actions had done more damage than good to our relationship.

Chapter 31

Spring Fling

One sunny Saturday afternoon, Heidi and I took a long walk through the main drag of the town. We were both in a good mood. At one point, after a short silence, she asked me what my intentions were regarding our relationship. I hadn't expected such a direct question, but I calmly responded with what I thought was not only a convincing answer, but also a true one.

"As you know, a few weeks ago I went through a peculiar experience with Seva, who also demanded a sort of commitment from me," I began. "Although I don't think my relationship with Seva has a promising future, I am not in the proper emotional state of mind to give you an answer right now. I'm still shaken over that episode."

Heidi apologized for posing such a question as we went inside Hanes Lounge for a bite to eat. We stayed there for a few hours, had a few beers, and danced to the never-ending flow of contemporary hits on the jukebox. I recall that the most-played song that night was "The Twist" by Chubby Checker, which was an international hit in 1962.

After we left the lounge and headed to my place, we met some friends outside another lounge who insisted that we stop for a drink. The six of us, including Kostas from work, sat at a round table in the middle of the room. When we were about to finish the first round of drinks, I noticed Heidi was making frequent eye contact with someone at the next table.

I pretended not to notice her blatant flirting until she excused herself to go to the restroom, which was literally an outhouse located in the back of the lounge. When the man she was flirting with followed her half a minute later, I ran outside to see if my suspicion was justified. To my amazement,

I saw them standing in the shadows, kissing passionately as if they were lovers who hadn't seen one another for a long time.

I could not believe what I was seeing! My vision became blurry, my blood felt as if it were boiling inside my veins, and my body literally shook with rage. I rushed toward them, first pulling Heidi away and telling her I would deal with her later. Heedless of my opponent's larger size, adrenaline took over and I started hitting the guy with all my might, striking his face repeatedly with my fists until he fell on the ground in a bloody mess.

I had some bloodstains on my shirt when I walked inside, a telltale sign that everyone took to mean I had gotten into a fight. But when they saw the other guy walking in slowly and drenched in blood, Kostas and the bartender marveled that I could have beaten a big guy like that. They made comparisons to David and Goliath.

I then dragged Heidi out the front door and, holding her flailing arms, pushed her hard against the wall and screamed in her face, "How could you do this to me? Didn't you do enough already? Didn't I forget or forgive all your past wrongdoings? Why, why did you do this?"

"I am so sorry, he just grabbed me when I went outside," she sobbed.

"No, I don't believe you! I saw you were not making any effort to get away from him, so no more lies! I don't know what else to say. Let's go home now."

The following morning, after Heidi left, I realized that this incident could very well have been the straw that broke the camel's back. What happened was probably a blessing in disguise; far from being trustworthy, she had revealed herself to be a weak, self-centered person who gave in to temptation at the drop of a hat when she presumed nobody was watching.

Perhaps it was this part of her personality during her teenage years that triggered her irrepressible desire to have multiple intimate encounters with her father. A few days later, she wrote me a long letter apologizing for what happened, painting herself as the victim of circumstances over which she had no control. This time, I didn't swallow her assertions; I just could not trust her anymore.

At the same nightclub, there was another incident. I was sitting on a bar stool next to a good-looking woman. On the other side of her sat a man I assumed was her boyfriend. Kostas and some other Greek fellows were sitting at a table not too far from me.

The woman was a little drunk and started flirting with me openly. All of a sudden, I received a blow with brass knuckles, just above my right eyebrow. I was knocked unconscious for a while, but when I came to, I saw my friends pushing the guy who hit me against the wall.

When I staggered back to my stool, the lady next to me started calling her boyfriend a "coward" for hitting me from behind with brass knuckles, as I'd had no way to defend myself. "You could have killed him, you cowardly bastard!" she hissed at him as he returned to his stool with an evil scowl on his face.

At that moment, I jumped on the stool and, standing up, I raised my right fist as high as my coiled upper body would go and struck his face with all my might, knocking him on the floor. "That was to get even, you coward!" I crowed. "But the difference is that I hit you face-to-face, like a man!"

As her boyfriend lay bleeding on the floor, the girlfriend stood over him, arms akimbo, and applauded. "You definitely deserved it, you rat!" she spat venomously. "And by the way, I don't want to see you again— we're finished!"

I will never forget that incident because the steel knuckle punch left a permanent scar just above my right eye.

During my second round in Germany, I saw Edith four times, including an occasion when she invited Heidi and me over for dinner. Another time, I spent the day with her, visiting several interesting places in Bonn, mostly walking from one location to another. At day's end, we had dinner in her apartment. Afterwards, I was too tired to go home, so we both agreed I should stay for the night. And so I did, enjoying her closeness and her candid views on a plethora of intellectual subjects.

That evening, I told Edith about the recent episode with Heidi and the man at the lounge. I asked her opinion. Without any hesitation, Edith advised me to keep my distance from Heidi on account of her instability, her obvious low self-esteem, and her lack of self-control.

Given the circumstances, Edith's final assessment of the situation was that Heidi and I had a slim possibility of sustaining a meaningful and healthy relationship. I had needed some sort of affirmation, but I had to agree with Edith's judgment and her opinion of Heidi.

Chapter 32
Anni from Ichendorf

After the incident with Heidi, I did not make any effort to get in touch with her. Instead, I began spending my weekends in Manheim at the local establishments. On Thursday, March 1, while having a beer at Hanes Lounge, I spotted an attractive *fraülein* who was giving me the eye. She was sitting at a table with two other, older ladies, whereas I was all by myself, sitting on the corner barstool.

I thought she must be an out-of-towner because this was the first time I had seen this girl in the lounge. She was completely unlike the German women of my experience, who were mostly willowy blondes. Standing about five feet six, she had green eyes and a fair complexion that contrasted strikingly with the dark brown hair that grazed her shoulders. She mesmerized me, as my first impression led me to believe she had to belong to a much higher social class than all the other women I had met so far.

While a French song, *"C'est La Vie, Chérie"*—"That's Life, Darling"— played on the jukebox, I went over and asked her if she wanted to dance with me. She gladly accepted, thus making me a happy person as I held this beautiful lady so close to me, dancing to a slow, waltz-like tune.

"My name is Anni and the two ladies I'm with are my aunts," she said with a wide smile.

"What brings you here to this small town?" I asked.

"We were on our way home to Ichendorf, a town twenty kilometers from Manheim. One of my aunts, who knows the owner, suggested that we stop here for a drink."

"I am so glad you stopped here. Otherwise I would not have met you!" I said as I softly squeezed her hand, which, like mine, was wet with nervous perspiration.

We stayed on the dance floor, just holding one another, even after the song had ended. Then we continued dancing to the next few songs in the jukebox's vast library.

Later, she joined me at a separate table, away from her aunts, and we practically spent the entire evening together. We both were convinced there was an undeniable mutual attraction.

I asked her, "Where were you hiding all this time?"

"Waiting for you to come along," she whispered with her lips ever so close to mine. I felt her teasing breath caressing my face, delicate and sweet as a spring breeze, and it heightened my senses and made me desire her even more. When I told her that I definitely wanted to see her again, she wrote her address on the only piece of paper we had available: a paper beer coaster, which I have treasured all these years.

Here is a scanned copy of that coaster on which Anni wrote her aunt's address and signed it *Chérie*, which was the French word she remembered and kept repeating all evening as a memorable symbol of the song that was playing for our first dance.

I also gave her my address. The night ended with a goodnight kiss and plans to meet the following weekend.

A few days later, I was pleasantly surprised to receive a letter from Anni. She wrote how much she missed me already and also confirmed our weekend date. The three remaining days until Saturday seemed like an eternity; I couldn't wait until Anni and I could spend some quality time together, just the two of us.

The joyous day finally came and we met at a restaurant situated along the scenic riverbank, an achingly romantic setting, appropriate for our first date. We were probably the only restaurant customers at that hour of the day (three in the afternoon), having a rather late lunch over a bottle of red wine.

Later, we walked along the riverbank, holding hands and exchanging a kiss here and there. Being in that jovial mood, a state of mind that I had not frequently experienced, I wondered if it might be possible to capture these blissful moments and relive them each time I would get depressed. I remember many details so clearly from that walk, especially when Anni was happily singing a few lines of what I thought was a Russian song, the first two words of which were: "Ivan, Ivanovicz ♫.♪.♫ ..."

Her smiling face was like a painting by a Renaissance master, her musical laugh was a symphony, and the brush of her lips against mine was sweet ambrosia of the gods. The positive energy of her aura was intoxicating; I did not want the day to end; this was the epitome of those rare occasions when we wish time would freeze.

When we arrived at the train station, we had agreed to see each other the following day as well. On Sunday, we met at a place in Bergheim, where we spent a wonderful day walking through the quiet streets, talking and dreaming about our burgeoning romance.

Over the next few weeks, we saw each other every weekend. I was eager to show Anni off to Richard and his girlfriend Carmen, so I made arrangements for the four of us to get together at Carmen's apartment in Cologne one Saturday afternoon. Both Carmen and Richard were impressed with Anni's beauty, her impeccable good taste, her poise, and her air of sophistication. (At least that's what Carmen told me when Anni went to the powder room.)

We enjoyed a few drinks and the delicious hors d'oeuvres Carmen had prepared. We were having a great time, and it seemed Anni felt comfortable with my friends. She told me over and over how happy she was that I had come into her life.

After several fun-filled hours, we went out to Carmen's favorite restaurant, where we had a delicious dinner and two bottles of white Rhine wine. At around nine, a band arrived and started playing hit songs from all over the world. The intoxicating ambience of the place, as well as the great company I was in, lent the night a dreamlike quality; I pinched myself to confirm it was all really happening.

It was close to 1:00 a.m. when we realized we had already missed the last train. Being that Carmen did not have enough space in her studio apartment to accommodate us, Anni and I decided to spend the night in a nearby hotel.

The hotel room had a queen-size bed, a serendipitous convenience for consummating our relationship as the crowning event of an already delightful night. When Anni came out of the shower with a towel wrapped around her luscious body, I joined her under the covers, eager to get down to what comes naturally.

To my dismay, when I tried to make the first move, she stopped me with a pleading request: "Please, not tonight, not like this. If you love me, I'm begging you, let's wait."

Of course, I froze in silence for a minute or two, not knowing how to react to this new and unusual predicament of being asked to restrain myself from the tortuous temptation of the beautiful, naked goddess lying next to me. It was torture indeed, from a man's point of view—a cruel night I had to tolerate, thus respecting the wishes of a lady I sincerely respected. The only thing left to do was to get up and take another shower—a long, cold one this time!

It was so ironic because, not too long ago, I'd had a similar naked encounter with Seva. But that time, I did not succumb to the temptation at hand and take advantage of her vulnerable position. This time, the proverbial shoe was on the other foot, and I had to control my urges for an entirely different reason. I don't know how much sleep I had that night, but I felt fine in the morning. During breakfast, Anni thanked me for being so understanding when she poured saltpeter on my ardor, as it were. She said that she would make it up to me ten-fold when the time was right.

On weekends, I spent at least one day with Anni, either going to our local haunts or venturing to larger cities nearby that offered better entertainment choices. One Sunday night, we went to an upscale nightclub in Cologne, where we were seated at a cozy, semi-circular corner table. The band was from Yugoslavia and played mostly Latin-style music. Anni and I cuddled into our corner love seat, drinking our cocktails, enjoying ourselves and soaking up the good vibrations all around us.

Time flew by and we realized we had to catch the last train. After paying the bill, we rushed to the train station, running as fast as we could to reach the platform before midnight. The big clock on the Cologne cathedral was tolling twelve times as we vaulted up the stairs two at a time, only to see the train pulling away.

We stood on the platform in silent disbelief, having missed the train by no more than twenty seconds. I told Anni that our only option was to stay in Cologne again, since she had to come back to work there at nine o'clock the next morning anyway.

Her emphatic response surprised me. "I'm sorry, but I absolutely, positively must go home tonight!"

"How are we going to do that?" I asked.

"Let's take a taxi!" she suggested.

I did a quick calculation and determined that the taxi fare would come in the neighborhood of seventy to eighty marks—close to a week's salary! I told Anni this was out of the question and that she should reconsider spending the night in a hotel. After going back and forth, I made up the story that I had to be in Cologne at 5:00 a.m. for a reason I supposedly could not disclose.

"I will take a taxi myself!" she sobbed, her voice trembling with anger and sorrow. "Tonight you showed me your true character. I never want to see you again … good-bye!" She then ran down the stairway and exited the station, where I assumed she would take a taxi home.

I immediately realized what I had done. It was a huge blunder on my part for not using sound judgment, for refusing to offer whatever help Anni needed—especially tonight, as she was depending on me to provide the necessary support. She had desperately begged me for help at this difficult moment.

In my defense, I had assumed the only other reason she wanted to go home was to change clothes before going to work. I even suggested that she call her parents or her aunt to explain the situation, but she did not want to bother anyone at that late hour.

In the end, I spent a little more than five hours in the station before I took the first train home Monday morning. During this time, I came to the realization that I had lost Anni, a beautiful lady inside and out, a person with self-worth and sound principles. If I didn't find a way to regain her trust, I wondered, how long would it take me to come across another person like Anni?

Only time would tell if this was a once-in-a-lifetime opportunity that had knocked on my heart's door. And fool that I was, I had failed to invite her in.

Chapter 33

Quick Recovery

Prior to my last encounter with Anni, I had begun corresponding with Margareta, a Swedish lady I'd met in Rhodes where she was vacationing the previous summer, just before I left for Switzerland. I had promised I would get in touch with her when I settled down somewhere in Europe. We exchanged several letters within a month or so, during which I was seriously thinking of moving to Stockholm, where she lived. When I wrote to her of my intentions, she liked the idea.

Margareta started sending me instruction manuals of the Swedish language tailored for German-speaking individuals. So I began learning Swedish while Margareta was trying to find an apartment and possibly a job for me, though I informed her I needed a few months before I could make a move to Sweden.

After failed attempts to reestablish my relationship with Anni, I decided to pursue the Sweden option as the best choice for me overall. I could not get Anni's image off my mind, and I felt it was an unhealthy obsession that only a change of scene would remedy.

I had tentatively decided on the approximate date I would leave Germany, so I began taking my Swedish studies more seriously. I knew I had to get a visa from the Swedish embassy; to do so, I took one day off from work and took the train to Cologne.

On the train, I saw Vasili, an old coworker, sitting just across from me. After exchanging pleasantries, I asked him to sit beside me. When I told him I was going to the Swedish embassy, his face lit up with pleasure.

"What a coincidence!" he exclaimed. "I am also on my way to the Canadian embassy to get the necessary visa approvals for migrating to Canada."

I was intrigued. "What made you choose Canada? Can you tell me a little more about it?"

"Here, I have some brochures—you can read for yourself," he said, handing me two or three folded pamphlets.

By the time we arrived at the station in Cologne, I was enthralled with the positive benefits of the Canadian lifestyle and the unlimited opportunities that awaited new immigrants. I also knew that if I immigrated to Canada, I would be closer to my sister, Despina, who was already in America, somewhere near New York City. Then and there, I made up my mind to change boats mid-stream.

Sending Sweden my mental regrets, I followed Vasili to the Canadian embassy instead of going to the Swedish one. Unlike my friend, I did not have an appointment, so I filled out the necessary paperwork and waited for someone to tell me what the next step was. To my surprise and delight, I was informed there was plenty of time for the initial interview with an embassy executive to determine if I had "the right stuff" for assimilating into the Canadian culture.

When they called me into an office for the interview, I saw a distinguished-looking gentleman with a neatly clipped mustache and thick, dark hair graying at the temples sitting behind a massive mahogany desk. He politely asked me to sit down and, while thumbing through my passport pages, asked me the reason I wanted to go to Canada. Without missing a beat, I answered in perfect German, "I know a country like Canada would afford me the opportunity to expand my knowledge in linguistics, an area in which I happen to have a natural inclination."

"I see," he said, looking at me with interest over the top of his bifocals. "How many languages do you speak?"

"Well, besides German and Greek, I also speak Italian and French," I responded with conviction.

"Yes, I see you speak German well," he replied, nodding and knitting his fingers together. "Do you know any English?"

The question threw me for a loop. He had posed this last question in English, a language I was not conversant with whatsoever. "Just a little bit," I responded tentatively as he continued using English for the next question.

"And where did you learn English, Mr. Papasavas?"

Thankfully, I recognized the word "learn" and answered brightly, "In school." He seemed satisfied with my answer and commented, "*Sehr gut,* very good," using both languages.

After leaving that office, the clerk at the front desk told me that, within a week or so, they would inform me of the next step in the process. He also ensured me that the interview must have gone well, because otherwise they wouldn't have called me for a follow-up.

I was pleased with the outcome at the Canadian embassy, thinking to myself how one's life could change from one day to another! Was meeting Vasili on the train mere happenstance, or was it evidence of a higher power preventing me from going to Sweden? We mortals are not privy to this divine knowledge; we can only take one route of the forked road presented to us, and we'll never know what would have happened if we had taken the other one.

When I got home, I was racked with mixed emotions about my latest undertaking: a fresh start in a new country with practically no knowledge of the English language. My other concern was Margareta in Sweden, who had everything almost ready for my arrival. What sort of excuse or explanation would be convincing enough to justify my change of plans? I couldn't just tell her I was influenced by someone on the train to go to the Canadian embassy instead of the Swedish one, although that *is* what actually happened.

I knew she would deem such an explanation far-fetched or even foolish. Well, I sighed, I would just have to wait until my visa was approved and then write a letter to Margareta notifying her of my decision.

The following weekend, I met with Richard and Carmen and told them I was almost certain that I would get the required approvals for my upcoming journey to Canada. I hadn't seen Heidi for more than two months, though in her last letter, she had written that I should visit her in her newly rented apartment on the outskirts of Bonn.

Before responding to Heidi, I was waiting for the notification from the Canadian embassy for my second interview, which would determine the final phase of the visa approval.

Exactly one week later, I received the notice to meet with another executive at the Canadian embassy. I took another day off from work and, one Tuesday morning, I took the train to Cologne. When I arrived at the embassy, after taking a streetcar from the main Cologne station, I noticed the waiting room was overflowing with people, probably potential Canadian immigrants.

As I waited to be called, I sat across from a stunning lady with long, red hair. Now, I have never particularly liked redheads—it is one of my more curious peccadilloes, I suppose—but this beauty's statuesque figure and sparkling green eyes more than made up for this "shortcoming." I assumed she was also going to Canada and thought it would be nice if we could make arrangements to travel together. Wow, what a great idea!

But how could I approach her to find out what her plans were? I didn't think it would be proper to approach her directly in this crowded room to ask her personal questions.

At that moment, my name was called and I was escorted to an office all the way at the end of the hallway. The interview turned out to be a litany of the dos and don'ts Canadian immigrants were expected to abide by. For all intents and purposes, my visa had already been approved. The only remaining detail was to stamp my passport and off I went! Canada, here I come!

On my way out, I did not see the redhead in the waiting room. I cleared my throat and asked the receptionist a little hesitantly, "Excuse me, Miss, do you by any chance know if the tall, red-haired lady is still inside the embassy? Or has she perhaps left already?"

"She is still being interviewed," the receptionist replied with a subtle smirk. "She just went in a few minutes ago."

The only thing to do was wait for her outside, so I walked down the stairway and out to the street, where I leaned against a wall and kept my eyes on the embassy's exit door. When I saw her coming out, I approached her and asked her politely if she was also traveling to Canada. She totally ignored me and started walking toward the streetcar that had just arrived, the same one I was supposed to take.

In the crowded streetcar, I stood right behind her, holding onto a bar. But despite my repeated attempts to start a conversation, she gave me the silent treatment. Her rude behavior baffled me until I saw her meeting a man at the train station. I understood this was no doubt her boyfriend and she simply hadn't wanted to egg me on.

Just before disappearing into the teeming crowd, she turned around, shrugged her shoulders, and gave me a deliberate stare that spoke volumes about her own regret. I immediately felt better about her snub and wrote the incident off as something that just was not meant to be.

My visa secured, my next order of business was to write a letter to Margareta informing her of the change in my traveling plans. I explained that my decision to go to Canada had to do with my sister, who was already in America. She wanted me to be as close as a seven-hour car drive from her house, I said, with the possibility of joining her permanently in the future.

Margareta responded that she understood my position and said that I should do whatever I thought would be best for me. I also wrote a letter to Caterine, who was one of the sweetest girls I had ever met, sending my regrets that I would not be returning to Switzerland and saying I was planning to go to Canada instead.

Since I was leaving the country for good, I was entitled to collect any accumulated pension benefits for all the time I worked in Germany. I went to the appropriate regional agency, where they prorated my pension benefits and gave me a bank check for an amount much greater than I had expected. I also found out that my total earnings in Germany were 12,157.34 Deutschmarks. Given the exchange rate of four marks to a dollar, it would have been equivalent to $3,039.33.

Another pressing matter was Heidi, who was making every effort to regain my trust. In her last letter, she had invited me to spend a weekend in her new apartment in suburban Bonn. It was a private oasis, she said, where we would not have to be concerned with neighbors or landlords.

After completing my travel arrangements to Canada, I arranged to visit Heidi on the following Saturday. I was not sure how to handle the situation with Heidi and didn't know whether to tell her about my Canada decision. On one hand, she deserved to know; on the other hand, if I told her, she would think my decision to leave Germany was a devious scheme on my part to get even with her. In any case, I would let things run their own course.

Arriving at Heidi's apartment on Saturday afternoon, I was instantly impressed with her aesthetic sensibilities. She had decorated the place beautifully, although I wondered how she could possibly afford this spacious place, given the fact she was just an average working stiff.

She prepared a luncheon of sandwiches, which we ate at the kitchen table. Despite my efforts to cheer her up, she was quiet and pensive, a far cry from the happy-go-lucky spirit I had come to know. She barely cracked a smile at my jests.

Early that evening, we went out to see a movie and then we had dinner in a nice restaurant, where she became a little more talkative. Her overall attitude since I had arrived in her apartment indicated that she sensed I was planning to leave her forever. Although I tried to test myself in terms of how I felt about her, I couldn't forget the last incident, which had diminished my warm, loving feelings for her.

During dinner, I almost told her about my upcoming Canada plans, but I decided it was not the right time or place. When we got back to her place,

I thought I would tell her after we finished a bottle of wine—but even then, I didn't have the heart to disappoint her. After spending the night in Heidi's apartment, I left late Sunday morning, assuming this might be the last time I saw her.

When I got home on Sunday afternoon, I wrote a letter to Edith, who was now teaching English in Istanbul, letting her know of my new adventure and thanking her for everything she had done for me. The following day, I picked up my two tickets, one for the train from Cologne to Amsterdam, the other for the ship from Amsterdam to Montreal.

Although I didn't keep any notes in my journal during the last month, I have a clear mental recollection of the trip to Canada. On August 7, 1962, the taxi I had reserved the night before arrived at 5:30 a.m. After saying good-bye to my landlords, who were two wonderful people, the taxi driver dropped me off at the train station, where I took the next train to Cologne.

I still had about forty-five minutes to spare before the next leg of my trip to Amsterdam. While waiting for the train on the platform, I decided to call Heidi to tell her all about my trip, to let her know I was angry with her, and to get some other things off my chest. It was around 6:30 a.m. when I started dialing her number on the rotary pay phone, thinking she had probably just awakened to get ready for work.

When I was about to release the last digit of her phone number, I held the dial in place for a few seconds, trying to decide whether I should remove my finger from the hole and let the call go through. Perhaps my logical mind overrode my emotions, because I hung up the receiver before completing the call.

I had wanted badly to talk to Heidi that morning, to tell her this was "even the score" time. However, had I vented my anger on her, what would I have gained besides the emotional pain I would have caused her? My decision not to speak with her would at least leave a ray of hope that someday I might resurface in her life one more time.

I finally realized I was not really angry with Heidi; I held no grudges, nor did I want to exact revenge for all her wrongdoings. Isn't it ridiculous that, in supposedly getting even with other people, the only ones we hurt are ourselves—physically, spiritually, and emotionally? As a famous Chinese proverb states: "Whoever opts for revenge should dig two graves." Dear reader, the second grave is *your own.*

In essence, my decision to forgive and forget helped me realize that getting ahead in life would always be more important to me than getting even.

Chapter 34

Transatlantic Voyage

I was in a good mood when I boarded the train to Amsterdam, from which I would sail aboard the Arcadia, a transatlantic ocean liner that was scheduled to depart around 1:00 p.m. It was a cloudy, misty late morning when we arrived in Amsterdam. It was so refreshing to see the ocean again after spending a year in a landlocked region in central and northern Europe. The Amsterdam terminal building by the pier was crowded with passengers milling about as they waited to board the ship.

After going through the official process of ticketing and passport verification, I checked my one bag but kept my guitar, in its brown case, with me as I joined the rest of the crowd. That scene reminded me of the first time I had taken the train from Athens to Germany. I recalled the emotions I had felt while standing on the train platform: the fear of the unknown, my limited social exposure, and my lack of self-confidence. The only positive quality I had going for me then was the desire to succeed; it had been distinctly to my advantage that I was unaware of just how much I didn't know about getting along in the wide, wide world.

This time, however, I considered myself socially and economically on par with the other passengers. Over the previous three years I had attended the most challenging reality academy in the world—the school of hard knocks—and had gained the knowledge and wisdom to hold my head high and face whatever the future threw at me with courage and aplomb. I now had a definite plan, a definite destination, and healthy self-confidence— and I could communicate with almost anyone in several languages.

A gentleman who also was holding a guitar approached me and introduced himself as George. It turned out he was also Greek and was traveling to Canada for the purpose of finding a way to reunite with his sweetheart in Mexico, a girl he had met while serving in a NATO military unit.

As George showed me a picture of his girlfriend, he was almost in tears. He broke down about how much he missed her and all the trouble he had gone through to engineer a plan to be close to her. I guess love can give us all the energy we need to achieve a goal, no matter how difficult or unreachable it seems. George introduced me to Niko, another Greek fellow who also was traveling to Canada. The three of us agreed to hang out on the ship for the next nine or so days.

When we boarded the ship, I realized, much to my dismay, that I would be sailing in a cabin with five other fellows. The cabin reminded me of the army barracks beds with lower and upper bunks—such were the Spartan accommodations my third-class ticket bought me. But I was sure I would enjoy the rest of the amenities, as described on the ship's daily event calendar.

I didn't mind the crowded cabin because, besides sleeping and showering, I would be spending the rest of my time elsewhere on the ship. Before departure, I took a quick tour and realized that this ship was at least three times larger than the ones on which I had previously traveled in the Mediterranean Sea. I had chosen sea travel over flying simply because it was cheaper, but I was happily looking forward to what amounted to a worry-free, nine-day vacation aboard a luxurious cruise ship.

As the ship set sail around 1:00 p.m., I was on the upper deck gazing at the Amsterdam pier line we were leaving behind. I remember how contented I felt at that moment as I exhaled a deep sigh of satisfaction—my private thanks to God for once again shedding His grace upon me. I stayed on the upper deck until the European coastline disappeared on the far horizon. The next port of call was London, where we were scheduled to arrive sometime in the evening.

George, Niko, and I made arrangements to be seated at the same table in the dining room for the entire trip. In the meantime, all three of us enjoyed the buffet lunch that was offered in a casual dining area on an upper deck. During lunch, we talked quite a bit about each other's plans, aspirations, and past experiences. When I mentioned I was headed to Toronto, Niko agreed to join me, because he hadn't made any plans about settling in a specific city. It was comforting to know I had a teammate to help me brave the challenges ahead, starting afresh in a new country with a new language to learn.

As we approached London, the weather took a turn for the worse. The light drizzle that had been falling gave way to a steady rain and fog by the time we made port.

The ship was scheduled to stay in the harbor for only one hour or less, allowing just enough time for the new passengers to board. We were having dinner when the vessel left London, heading toward the open waters of the Atlantic Ocean. Through the portholes in the dining room, we could see that the rain and the wind had intensified, causing the choppy waves to rock the vessel as if it were a toy boat in a bathtub.

Many seasick passengers ran up to an open deck, skipping dinner altogether. Niko turned the most peculiar shade of green and stumbled away from the table with his hand over his mouth. Interestingly, George and I were only slightly affected by the motion and managed to finish our dinner.

As we walked up the stairway, I observed a handful of nauseated passengers helplessly throwing up while holding onto the side railing. When I reached a higher level, I could see the huge waves splashing over the deck while the violently swirling wind howled like a banshee. As I approached a door that led to an outside deck, I saw a young lady pacing nervously back and forth as if she were trying to decide whether she should try to open the door in the gale. I asked her if everything was okay and she said, "I was supposed to meet a lady in the library so we could go to the dance hall together. However, the only access to the library is through the outside deck."

Looking at the puzzled expression on her beautiful face, I reassured her, "Don't worry. I will go to see if she's there—but who should I say is waiting for her?"

"Doris. Doris is my name, but you don't have to do that for me," she said as she slightly pulled my arm toward her, to stop me from braving the thunderstorm. I gently broke away from her, forcibly opened the door and ran outside.

By holding onto the inner railing of the deck, I was able to reach the door to the library—but not before I was soaked by the rain and splashing waves. I spotted a lady on the inside, through the side glass of the door, but I did not bother to go in. When I got back, I told Doris that no one was there, but I would be honored to accompany her to the dance hall.

"I will meet you in an hour, right here, on this spot," I said. To my delight, she accepted my offer with a smile.

After going to my cabin to shower and change my wet clothes, I quickly ran to the dance floor deck, where the nauseating seesawing of the storm-tossed ship was more bearable. I had time to spare when I arrived at the spot where I was to meet Doris, and so I watched in awe as Mother Nature vented her wrath. Colossal waves crashed on the deck as jagged lightning bolts skittered across the sinister-looking, cobalt sky. All the while, the thunder boomed, the wind screamed, and the mighty ship pitched and rolled.

Logically, I should have been afraid, but not even for a moment did I feel any danger. On the contrary, I was looking forward to getting together with Doris, the tall, slender lady with a movie star's perfectly proportioned, hourglass figure. Her curly brown hair, her green eyes, and the rest of her face and figure seemed as if she were Ava Gardner's twin sister.

I wondered, though, if I had done the right thing by not telling Doris that her friend had indeed been waiting in the library. On the other hand, here was a rare opportunity to kindle a shipboard romance, and I wasn't about to let it pass by! I resolved to tell Doris the truth, either that night or at another opportune moment.

Doris showed up on time, looking stunning in a light blue sundress that showed off her long legs and perky bosom. Neither of us minded that the vessel was swaying even more noticeably than an hour earlier. Holding Doris' arm close to me to steady her, we entered the showroom lounge, wobbling a little as we took our seats. The showroom had an elevated stage, a circular wooden dance floor, and a bandstand next to the stage.

We were not surprised to see there were only two other couples on the other side of the dance floor. Our drinks were placed in recessed coasters; otherwise they would have immediately slid across the table.

Doris and I bonded well, I thought, over the usual getting-to-know-you chitchat, especially considering the fact we had known each other less than two hours. We attempted to dance a few times, but we ended up sliding from one end of the dance floor to the other!

After I gave her a brief overview of my life story, Doris told me she was going to Saskatoon, where some of her relatives had resided for the last three or four years. She also told me she was in the process of getting a divorce from her husband. When she finished talking, she grabbed my hand and kept looking at me so intensely. While shaking her head in disbelief, she slowly poured out her heart to me.

"I'm so glad I met you tonight, so happy you came my way near that door," she said, her eyes sparkling. "And, to be honest with you, I'm also glad that the other lady was not waiting for me in the library. Otherwise, I wouldn't be here with you tonight."

I kept quiet for a moment, but then I told her the truth. "Doris ... please forgive me, but ... I lied to you! The lady was there waiting for you, but when I first saw you, I was so fascinated with your appearance, I just had to find a way to get to know you!"

She started laughing, covering her mouth with her hands. "You mean to tell me she was there waiting for me?"

"Yes, but you see ... this was my only opportunity to take her place. I hope you don't regret it—do you?"

"No, not at all! I'm glad, in fact. After all, I had just met the lady as we were boarding. She is also traveling alone and needed some company, but she's probably found somebody else by now. As you can see, I would rather be with *you*."

With that, she squeezed my hand and gave me a soft kiss. We were having a great time, but as the ship was tossing like a cork, we decided to call it a night. Before she entered her cabin, we both agreed to meet for breakfast in the buffet area.

All night the tempest raged, but in the morning, the ship was sailing in calm, sunlit waters under a clear sky. What a difference from the night before! Doris showed up on the breakfast deck, wearing a big smile; she was a knockout in her tight jeans and a flimsy blouse with the front shirt-tails tied in a knot to expose her delectable belly button.

When we sat down for breakfast, the captain announced on the loud-speaker that good weather was predicted for the rest of the eight days. Everyone on the deck applauded, though Doris and I questioned the accuracy of this extended forecast.

A short distance away, I saw George and Niko sharing a round table with some other passengers and I invited them to join us. Introductions out of the way, George informed me there would be a talent show in a few days, with contestants competing onstage in front of an audience. He suggested the two of us should form a guitar duo and perform a Greek song, an idea Doris and Niko heartily encouraged.

We decided to participate and chose to play "Never on Sunday" from the 1960 film of the same name. Popular all over the world, the song had won the Oscar for Best Original Song.

While Doris and I strolled around the deck, the early morning sunshine was dancing over the ripples as the ship swished through the calm ocean waters, generating an enjoyable, soothing breeze with the briny tang of the sea. At that moment, I felt a sense of belonging for having come together with Doris, a wonderful lady, and George and Niko, two nice gentlemen. I can recall how happy I was during those moments as if that carefree vacation had just ended yesterday. I can still feel the deliciously agonizing anticipation of looking forward to dancing with Doris that night. I couldn't have asked for anything more.

What a difference from my first train trip to Germany, three years earlier. My mind drifted back to the happy couple—honeymooners or vacationers, I surmised—I had observed on the train platform in Athens, and how I had wondered if I would ever know their bliss. Well, here I was now, walking next to Doris and realizing that my wish, however serendipitous, had come true.

When my friends left me alone to enjoy a cup of coffee on the upper deck, I began thinking of all the people I'd left behind in Germany— especially Anni, who was one of the most sophisticated people I had ever met. I kept wondering what would have happened had I agreed to hire a taxi after missing the last train in Cologne. Would we still be together today? Did my relationship with Anni have to end in order for me to go to Canada? These were big questions, and perhaps I would never know the answers to them.

As for Heidi, I believe I gave her enough chances to prove she was trustworthy and she had botched them all. I thought about Caterine from Switzerland, who was one of the sweetest, purest, and most innocent human beings I knew. I suppose we didn't have enough time together for any type of relationship to mature, despite the fact that she'd sent me more letters than anybody else, always expressing the deep feelings she had for me. Seva, on the other hand, by begging, crying, and being willing to give everything, demeaned herself to a point that my once deep feelings for her had shriveled up and died.

I honestly wanted to define the feelings I had with all these ladies, to determine if they were worthy of being called "true love." Although I used the phrase "I love you" many times—perhaps too cavalierly, I admit—I had not felt the bonding of two souls without boundaries or restrictions. Perhaps I had never accepted or loved myself, owing to the fact my parents and siblings never used the word "love" for anybody in our household. I had never really known how it felt to be loved.

Perhaps the immensity of our twelve-member family had something to do with our inability to express our innermost feelings and affection for one another. Instead, we were more practical, responding to everyday realities and external needs, forgetting that there was also an "inner self" needing the food of love.

It was probably the view of the ocean, so tranquil yet so overpoweringly vast, that brought about these reflective thoughts. However, as hard as I was on myself, I had to at least define my expectations and hope someday I would find that elusive devotion, called *agape* (a Greek word that means spiritual, emotional, and physical love).

In the early evening, George and I spent a little more than an hour rehearsing "Never on Sunday" on our guitars for the talent competition, which was scheduled in two days. Right off the bat, we sounded great, as if we had been playing together all our lives. We were confident enough to take the stage then and there. With two more days to practice, we were almost certain we would take first place.

After rehearsal, we went to dinner, where Niko and Doris were waiting for us. The dinner theme was Italian, so all of us had a pasta dish followed by chicken cacciatore. I remember we also had a bottle of Chianti that night. Otherwise, notwithstanding the abundance of food, I cannot recall any other standout meals for the rest of the trip. Unlike many people, I was never a connoisseur of food. Instead, I consider eating as a basic necessity to live, instead of living to eat.

Right after dinner, we all went straight to the ballroom, where the band carried forth the Italian theme night with popular tunes by the well-known Italian songwriter and bandleader Renato Carosone, such as: *"Tu Vuo 'Fa L'americano," "Maruzzella," "Torero o 'Sarracino,"* and other tunes with a Neapolitan flavor. George and Niko left after a few hours, but Doris and I danced all night, enjoying each other's company more and more as time went on. At one point, she asked me if I wanted to finish the rest of our wine in her cabin. Of course, I had no objections—in fact, I had been waiting for an invitation like this. In her private cabin, we had an extraordinarily wonderful time—a truly amazing experience!

I won't elaborate on the details of the private moments I spent with Doris. Suffice to say my cabin mates saw me only on the first night and at the time of disembarkation. Doris was an unusual specimen: a wholesome beauty you'd be proud to take home to mother, but behind closed doors, she turned into a sexual dynamo who would flat-out knock your socks off. In scientific terms, she might even have been labeled a nymphomaniac, which most men would definitely consider a positive female attribute! Doris was the unexpected exotic spice of my unforgettable trip to Canada, a joyous nine-day experience I wish had lasted forever.

We took a few pictures, some of which I still have. There's one of me sitting in a beach lounger wearing a navy blue sweater I bought in Bergheim a few days before I left Germany. Another picture shows Doris, looking tall and elegant in white slacks, wearing a quizzical expression as the gentle ocean breeze pushes back her brown hair. (Thank goodness for my notes and photographic memorabilia, which have been such useful tools for helping me remember the details of yesteryear!)

George and I were ready to knock 'em dead on the night of the talent competition. However, I had a strange feeling of nervousness similar to the anxiety I had experienced in the Kilkis army theater when I presented the play I wrote. This time, I should have known better—I should have had a few drinks before going onstage, because when I touched the guitar strings, I realized my fingers were trembling. George noticed my condition while waiting backstage and tried to help me alleviate my stage fright. My main concern was Doris, who was eagerly waiting in the audience to hear me perform. I had to live up to her expectations and not disappoint her!

When the little Dutch girl ahead of us finished her song, the announcer introduced us as "two Greek guitarists." When we started the introductory part of the song I fumbled the chords and paused for a few seconds, and then asked George if we could start over. The second time it went fairly well, but after the first verse, a heckler in the audience yelled, "Hey, this is a Greek song! Why don't you sing along while you play?"

The announcer seemed to agree. "Yes, we'd all like to hear you sing it in Greek!" he egged us on.

George and I looked at each other and shrugged our shoulders as if to say, why not? "Okay, you asked for it," I announced. "We didn't rehearse the song with the lyrics, but we'll give it a shot—but don't judge our singing talent!"

The audience applauded my candor, and George and I got down to business.

We played the introduction again and then we harmonized on the two verses, sounding in pretty good voice for two fellows who had never sung together before. In fact, this impromptu performance turned out to be better than the instrumental interpretation, judging from the audience's ovation. We were not surprised, though, that we finished behind the little Dutch girl, who sang superbly and won first place.

In retrospect, the person from the audience who yelled out for us to sing the Greek version of "Never on Sunday" was a blessing in disguise, because after that little interruption, I felt great and finished the song without any nervousness or inhibition. Bad start, great finish—and we were awarded a bottle of wine for winning second place.

Doris and Niko were pleased with the outcome and raised their wine glasses to us in congratulations. Just before we finished the bottle of wine, the emcee announced that a panel of judges was about to choose the best-looking girl on the ship and crown her as "Miss Arcadia." I immediately nudged Doris, trying to convince her to join the line of about twenty girls forming in front of the stage.

"Go ahead—I know you are the most beautiful lady on this ship!" I said with absolute certainty.

The judges reduced the field to just three contestants, including Doris. Sizing up the competition, I knew she deserved to win. The emcee kept the audience in suspense for several minutes and then he announced the winner. I leapt to my feet, whistling and cheering as Doris was crowned the ship's queen, Miss Arcadia! She pranced over to our table wearing a tiara in her hair and holding a bottle of champagne.

What a night! It was truly an unforgettable part of the trip, an evening filled with so many happy events. My friends had the time of their lives and Doris looked so beautiful, like the queen she was.

At one point, she whispered into my ear, "I'm all yours ... you can have me tonight, tomorrow, and forever!" That was probably the most memorable night of the entire trip; it was as if my guardian angel had sprinkled fairy dust over the ship and everything had just fallen into place.

After six-plus days on the Atlantic Ocean, we could see the hazy bluish outline of the North American continent on the horizon. The captain announced that in a few hours, we would reach Newfoundland, an island off the eastern coast of Canada.

In the early afternoon on the following day, the ship docked in Quebec City, where we were permitted to go ashore after completing the entry process for immigrants. I was impressed with this bustling city that sprawled along both sides of the St. Laurence River. The captain informed us this was the capital city of the Quebec province, with a population of 380,000. The official language was French, whereas English was spoken in all other Canadian provinces.

As I enjoyed the panoramic view from the ship's upper deck, I promised myself I would visit this city again in the future, when I had gotten settled on this new continent.

When we got off the ship, George, Niko, Doris, and I wanted to have our first Canadian beer, so we entered the only bar we found near the pier. To our surprise, however, we were told that ladies were not allowed in that establishment. So I bought two beers and joined Doris, who was waiting outside. We sat near the water, where we drank our beers while enjoying the view of the harbor and the surroundings. After a few minutes, Doris' face clouded over with sadness as if she were about to start crying.

"What's the matter?" I asked as I grabbed her hands.

"I feel sort of depressed, because we will only be together for one more night, and then I will not see you anymore," she whispered as a tear trickled down her cheek.

"Come on, don't do this to yourself," I said, squeezing her hands. "I thought we had an understanding that we'd enjoy being together for the duration of the trip without any strings attached, and then we'd go our separate ways—you to Saskatoon and me to Toronto. You knew that all along, didn't you?"

Doris dabbed her eyes with a tissue. "Yes, but I didn't expect to have such strong feelings for you. My body aches for you, my lips want to kiss you all over. I have no willpower left, my mind cries out your name, my heart beats for you and you alone. I can't help it, I just want to be with you, *all the time!*"

I tried to tell her that, after a month or so, when she was among family members in Saskatoon, she would feel differently. Time was the great equalizer, putting all things—including an unforgettable shipboard romance like ours—into perspective.

Holding hands, we walked along the pier, and I could tell she was still preoccupied with the subject of "us." She tried to talk me into going with her to Saskatoon, or as an alternative, she was willing to go to Toronto with me. I finally convinced her otherwise.

After spending a wonderful evening with Doris, we arrived at last at Montreal. Together with Niko and George, we headed for the train station to continue onward to our respective destinations. Before boarding the train, Doris had tears in her eyes as we hugged and said our last good-byes. However, we made a promise to one another that we would definitely stay in touch.

Niko and I had to wait a few hours for our train to Toronto, so we tagged along with George, who was looking for a public telephone to call his sweetheart in Mexico. We stood next to him while he talked to her in Spanish. Although we didn't understand a word of the entire conversation, George seemed to be in seventh heaven. He explained to us that he told his girlfriend he would stay in Montreal until he finalized his permanent status, and then he would go to Mexico, where they would get married, after which both of them could reside in Canada legally.

I was impressed with the ease with which George handled this situation. Another reason George decided to stay in Montreal was because he spoke French fluently, thus making it easier for him to acclimate to the new country. Wishing George good luck, Niko and I headed for the train platform to Toronto.

On the train, Niko fell asleep a few minutes after we sat down, whereas I was wide awake, contemplating the dilemmas we'd have to face in Toronto—specifically, the fact that neither of us spoke English. I didn't know what type of work we would get, not to mention how we would find an apartment for both of us. Then I thought about Doris, no doubt pining for me on the long, long train ride to Saskatoon. Selfishly, I put her out of my mind and wondered what adventures lay before me in the Great White North.

Chapter 35

American Invasion

It was early evening on Friday, August 17, 1962, when Niko and I arrived in Toronto. Our first concern was to find a hotel with relatively reasonable rates. Luckily, we found a nice one within walking distance from the train station. We booked a room for three days with an option to extend our stay until we found a permanent residence.

As we walked up Yonge Street, one of the main thoroughfares downtown, I was impressed with the clean sidewalks and artfully decorated store windows. Dundas Square, at the heart of the city, was alive with hustle and bustle. Maple Leaf Gardens—home to the Toronto's fabled hockey team—was on the right, and a three-block shopping mall on the left. On every corner, it seemed, we met friendly people who were willing to go out of their way to help us, the wide-eyed immigrants. They were of every race and color, a testament to Toronto's reputation as an international city shaped by the blood, sweat, and tears of immigrants from all over the world.

When Niko and I went to dinner for the first time at a Canadian restaurant, we had a hard time understanding the menu and communicating with the waitress. We finally ordered spaghetti with meatballs, as we were both sure about the "spaghetti" part of the phrase. When we finished our meal, Niko wanted to have ice cream, a word he thought would be the same as in German: *eis*, pronounced as "ice." Well, you guessed it: The waitress served Niko a glass filled with ice!

The next morning, we decided to have breakfast at a coffeehouse across from the hotel. Because it was Saturday morning, the streets were far less crowded than the day before, as most businesses were closed for the weekend. As we walked toward the coffee shop, my optimism about settling in this invigorating city had put me in a good mood, whereas Niko felt just the opposite. He had admitted a few times that he was totally depending on me to find a place to rent, as well as jobs for us both.

Although I had my own concerns about the imminent responsibilities in the new country, I didn't mind that Niko expected me to take care of him, as if I were his guardian. In fact, I felt flattered that he had entrusted me with all the major tasks necessary to get situated within the Canadian society.

A handful of customers sat at the counter, chatting amiably, as we slid into a booth and began studying the small menu, which was wedged between bottles of ketchup and mustard. The menu's cover depicted the Acropolis, a good sign that Greeks probably owned the coffeehouse. Sure enough, a tall, husky fellow sporting a thick, push-broom mustache and a tousled mop of curly black hair ambled over to take our order and introduced himself as Vasili, the proprietor. Vasili—a Greek name if ever there was one! Niko and I introduced ourselves and the three of us Greeks established an instant rapport.

Not being very busy, when Vasili brought our breakfast, he sat in our booth and wanted to know how we ended up in Canada. After giving him a brief description of our journey from Germany to Canada, he volunteered to help us get situated in our new country.

"After all, as compatriots, we should help one another the best way we can," he said. "So, instead of paying through the nose for a hotel room, I will offer you a room in my house, which you can rent at a low rate and stay until you find an apartment to your liking."

Vasili went on to explain how he had first come to Canada and started working as a dishwasher, twenty years earlier. After ten years of learning the restaurant business working as a short order cook, he had managed to save enough money for the down payment to buy his own coffee shop. He emphasized how grateful he was to those who had helped him start his business. For this reason, he wanted to express his gratitude by helping us land on our feet in this new country.

We couldn't have asked for a better opportunity! We gladly accepted Vasili's offer, as staying with a Greek family was an ideal arrangement for two newcomers who didn't speak English. Vasili also gave us the name and address of an employment agency where one of the managers was Greek, another happy coincidence that would serve to mitigate the language barrier.

While we were drinking our second cup of coffee, we overheard Vasili talking to his wife on the phone, asking her to prepare the second floor room and commenting that he would bring the new tenants by later on. After Vasili closed the store at noon, as he did every Saturday, we took the streetcar for a ten-minute ride to his house on Boon Street. Vasili's wife, a nice lady, showed us a large room on the second floor. Vasili told us the room would be ready the following day, because they had to move some furniture (two single beds and two dressers) from his brother's house, a few blocks away.

After checking out of the hotel the following day, we got comfortable in our new digs at Vasili's house. Our beds were against one of the larger walls with the dressers on the opposite wall. The room also was furnished with a coffee table, a couch, and twin end tables with matching lamps.

Above my bed, I hung a framed portrait of Anni that I had drawn with charcoal pencils, using for reference a small picture she had given me on our first date. It was a striking likeness, if I do say so myself: Anni looked so alive and vibrant, as if she were ready to jump out of the frame. This memento lent the room considerable cheer. It also would serve as a constant reminder that, by acting immaturely, I had let this sublime creature slip through my fingers on that fateful night, on the train platform in Cologne. I smiled ruefully at that painful memory and girded my loins for the challenges ahead.

On Monday morning, Niko and I went to the employment agency. I was not optimistic as to the choice of available jobs, considering my knowledge of English was next to nothing. However, I would try anything for a while, just as I had in Germany, where my first job was in road construction.

At the employment agency, we met with the Greek recruiter, who told us about available positions in two different factories—but the hourly pay was low. Many more low-level positions were available in the restaurant business, none of which sounded interesting to me. Niko, however, decided to take a position at a factory, despite the low pay.

The rest of the week, I tried different agencies, but again I was offered only the drudgery of factory work or bottom-of-the-barrel restaurant jobs, just because I did not speak English. Utterly discouraged, I wondered if I had made the right decision to leave Germany, where I had made much more money than they were offering me in Canada.

In the middle of the second week, I went to see Vasili at his coffee shop to ask him for guidance with regard to my limited employment choices. Over a cup of coffee, he told me I should take one of the factory or restaurant jobs I'd been offered, just so I'd get to know the Canadian work ethic.

"Listen, we all had to go through this process by starting at the bottom and slowly moving up the ladder," he said, stroking his massive mustache with conviction. "I know you are a bright individual, so it won't be difficult for you to improve your employment situation sooner than most people. But you shouldn't try reaching for the brass ring too quickly. You are a newcomer in a foreign country, so be patient and you'll see that things will fall into place."

The following day, I accepted a job at a restaurant on Yonge Street. Washing dishes was my main responsibility from Tuesday to Sunday on a ten-hour shift. During the afternoon hours, when there were no dishes to wash, I peeled potatoes as well as cleaning or washing other vegetables. In other words, unlike the waiters or the short-order cooks, I had no free time at all during the ten-hour shift, except the time when I gobbled down a quick lunch or dinner.

At the end of the first week, when I received my first paycheck, I was crestfallen to see that my net pay for six days work was $26.00, which was much less than Niko was making for five days at the factory. Furthermore, it was about half of what I had been earning in Germany. And not only were the long hours and the low pay discouraging, but the prospect of finding something better seemed unlikely.

The following Monday, my day off, I spotted some flashing neon signs displaying German words while walking outside the Franz Joseph hotel. Out of curiosity, I stopped to read the hotel restaurant's menu, which was enclosed in a glass case on the building's facade. When I saw the two-page menu was written in both German and English, I thought this might be a good opportunity for me to get a job, if the management of the hotel was of German origin.

Without a second thought, I went inside, where a gentleman asked if he could help me. Detecting an accent, I responded to him in German that I wanted to see the restaurant manager for possible employment. He first complimented me for my fluency in German and then he escorted me to the manager's office.

The manager, a Mr. Schneider, also spoke German. He told me that the restaurant was ranked among the highest in Toronto, and he was therefore selective about his new hires. Due to the fact I spoke German fluently but did not speak English well, he could only offer me a busboy position, which entailed helping a team of three waiters during dinner hours, between 5:00 and 11:00 p.m.

Mr. Schneider recommended I attend classes tailored for foreign students at an extension of the University of Toronto, in order to improve my English skills. He gave me the school administrator's business card, telling me that he had also attended classes there when he first came to Canada.

Mr. Schneider went on to explain that my average weekly compensation would range between $70.00 and $80.00. I gladly accepted the offer, which seemed too good to be true. After I filled out the necessary paperwork, I was told that I could start as early as the next day, to which I had no objection. I immediately quit the dishwasher job at the other restaurant, where I had worked for less than ten days.

Before I started working at Franz Joseph's restaurant, I went to see the administrator at the English school, where my enrollment paperwork was handled with dispatch. Classes would start the first week in September. I would attend from 8:30 a.m. to 2:30 p.m. Monday through Friday, a schedule that was convenient for me, since I didn't have to be at work before five in the evening.

Later that day, I started working at the restaurant. I was assigned to assist two waiters. Serenaded by strolling gypsy violinists and the exotic voice of Miss Lena, a singer who crooned torch songs in the soft glow of a spotlight, young couples fell in love for the first time and older couples fell in love all over again amidst the ritzy establishment's romantic ambience.

Although my first day at work was hectic, getting paid for my work and being entertained at the same time was a hard combination to beat. I had no trouble carrying out my assigned tasks, and the waiters were pleased with my performance.

It gave me great pleasure to meet my first relatives on the new continent when my newly married sister, Despina, and her husband, Peter, visited me in Toronto. She looked as beautiful as ever and spoke animatedly about her new home in New Jersey, where she seemed to be quite happy. Despina's long-range goal was to bring the entire family over to America. This had been her primary motivating factor for marrying an American citizen, although she had hoped that love and a stronger marriage bond would follow.

We had lunch at a restaurant near my apartment on Boon Street, where I ordered liver and onions, my usual, inexpensive dish. Peter tried to convince me to order a steak, but he was paying for lunch and I did not want to take advantage of the opportunity by ordering an entrée that was twice as expensive. After so long apart, I enjoyed the quality time with my warmhearted sister, reminiscing about the good old times back in the village.

After they left, a comfortable feeling overtook me, a sort of "peace of mind" sensation, knowing that my sister lived in relatively close proximity, about an eight-hour drive from Toronto.

After a week or two, the work became routine, and school became my number one priority. I liked the teachers as well as the students of various nationalities. In the classroom, I sat next to a French-Canadian lady named Colette who had come to Toronto from Quebec City to learn English.

As time went on, Colette and I became good friends; together, we took many walks in almost every park in Toronto, visiting museums and often attended classical music concerts, as she was a devotee of "longhair" music.

In the meantime, Niko and I found another apartment off Dundas Avenue, a much more convenient location to downtown. The major streetcar crossroads and the shopping malls were only a few blocks away from our apartment. A Greek fellow named Tasso, who coincidentally had been one of my high school classmates back in Rhodes, owned the house.

Tasso was married with two young children, and his brother, Kostas, lived with him as well. I liked our new living quarters much better than the previous ones, simply because both Tasso and Kostas were around my age, but most of all because their hospitality made me feel as if I were "home" with my own family.

When I had settled in our new apartment, I started concentrating on my English studies, which I took seriously. I convinced myself I would learn the language in a short period—after all, I had learned a new language in Germany, where the conditions for a newcomer were more challenging, and I had to deal with a language much more difficult than English.

My weekday routine began with school from 8:30 a.m. until 2:30 p.m., leaving me a few hours to do my homework before I started work at five. The curriculum pace was rather accelerated. Our goal was to complete the course in three months, and we were expected to speak, write, and understand the language at close to the fluency level. Our professor emphasized that *only* those students who truly wanted to learn by doing more than their work assignments would reach that goal. I took the professor at his word and resolved to be one of the few who would reach that level of proficiency. I never missed a day of school and neither did I neglect to do the optional extra homework, which earned me extra credits and, more importantly, broadened my knowledge base.

A few weeks into the course, I felt proud of the progress I was making in the area of comprehension when I actually understood the first joke our professor told us. He asked some of us to repeat the joke in our own words. It went like this:

199

A mother who had a young boy invited the bishop to her house for afternoon tea and cookies. However, she was concerned that her son might say something about the bishop's nose, which was large indeed, so she cautioned him to be on his best behavior. When the bishop arrived and the mother began serving the tea, she took a quick look at her boy and asked the bishop, "Your Eminence, would you like some sugar in your nose?"

Those of us who understood the joke laughed aloud, but when we attempted to repeat it in our own words, it didn't come out so funny.

Through a classmate, I was introduced to a circle of young Greek immigrants, some of whom had a variety of artistic talents. The group consisted of two girls and three other guys. We began hanging out together every chance we had. Over time, I became good friends with Paul Thimou, who happened to have an excellent singing voice between the baritone and bass range. Paul and I spent many hours playing and singing various contemporary Greek tunes such as "Never on Sunday" and most of the newer songs by Mikis Theodorakis, the composer who wrote the "Zorba the Greek" soundtrack.

We often got together with the rest of the group for spur-of-the-moment sing-alongs at Sotiris' spacious apartment. Sotiris was the funny man of the group whose talent for ad-libbed one-liners made us laugh with almost every sentence that came out of his mouth. He was a happy individual with an indomitable lust for life, and there was nothing or nobody in the world that could make him feel sad.

It was Sotiris' positive outlook that gave me the idea for another play. His optimism refueled my creative abilities and gave me the inspiration to start writing again. The play, which was a comedy, revolved around Sotiris getting into a prearranged engagement to a Greek girl from the old country.

After finishing the first draft in a little more than a week, I met with the group and suggested that we create a theatrical company, using my play as our launching pad and targeting Toronto's Greek community as our audience. Encouraged by my fellow thespians' hearty approval, I used all my free time to work on the play, which was turning into a funny scenario.

Every Saturday and Sunday afternoon, there was a three-hour Greek program on the radio hosted and produced by a lady named Elena. While listening to the radio program one Sunday afternoon, I thought it would be a good idea if I were to meet this lady to discuss my aspirations with her and perhaps get some ideas about how to promote and advertise our budding theatrical plans.

I called the radio station office and managed to set up an appointment with Elena for the following Saturday, right after her program went off the air. Sotiris was acquainted with Elena, so he told me what to expect. She was a successful and beautiful lady, he said, still single and selective of the people she would go out or associate with. Since my meeting with Elena would be strictly professional, I was not expecting anything more than some business guidance.

I thought I was mentally prepared to meet Elena when I entered her office at the radio station's building, but the stunning beauty of the woman sitting behind the desk froze me in my tracks. She had wavy, chestnut, shoulder-length hair, with hazel eyes and refined facial features that depicted her as a distinguished lady. Her approximately 5' 6" figure was well proportioned and her overall appearance was striking.

When my eyes retreated back into their sockets, I somehow introduced myself gracefully and took her outstretched hand, which was as fine and delicate as a queen's.

"Please, sit down and tell me all about yourself," she said pleasantly as she shook my hand—which, to my chagrin, was as wet as a fish.

I gave her a brief overview of my past travels, emphasizing my achievements and successes as well as the hardships and homesickness I had faced during my time away from the homeland. I then explained my aspirations for establishing a theatrical company to perform plays for the Greek community in Toronto and beyond. She remained silent for a few seconds, and I thought my cause was lost. But suddenly she leaned forward in her chair, smiling broadly and shaking her head enthusiastically.

"You are an unusual person and I would like to know more about you and your plans," she said, "but unfortunately I don't have much time today." Her tone was apologetic.

"Thank you so much, Elena, for your valuable time—you are so kind!" I said, my voice dripping with sincerity as I rose from my chair.

"Oh, no, you misunderstand," she said, motioning me to sit back down. "I would like to see you again—we'll take up where we left off and decide what to do next to bring your idea to fruition. I want to help, really! So, what would you say if we meet this coming Monday for a drink?"

My voice nearly caught in my throat. "Sure, I would love to!" I said.

Sotiris could not believe I actually had a so-called date with Elena and repeatedly reminded me that, according to the gossip he had heard about her, she was unapproachable beyond a professional level.

Elena had a full-time job at a downtown bank where I was supposed to meet her on Monday a little after 5:00 p.m. I was waiting outside the bank when I saw Elena coming toward me, primly dressed in an unflattering business suit. She shook my hand and suggested we go for a drink at a nearby cocktail lounge.

We sat down at a corner table. Her tight-lipped, business-like demeanor was intimidating, and I felt a little uncomfortable being with her. When the waiter came over, Elena knew exactly what she wanted—a mixed drink with some cold appetizers—so I ordered the same thing. Elena remarked that one order of appetizers should be enough for both of us, to which the waiter agreed as he walked away. I was thinking, however, that the appetizers would be my only dinner for the evening. But I dared not say a word along those lines.

We continued our conversation where we had left off a few days earlier at her office. Our meeting that night had all the trappings of an interview, as if she were trying to evaluate my social skills in an upscale, public place. I felt like a schoolboy talking to my teacher, my unsure words and actions betraying my inferiority as she fed off my uneasiness.

Oh, how I hated the way she indirectly tried to put herself on a pedestal, repeatedly wanting me to acknowledge the fact she was one of the most prominent personalities within Toronto's Greek community. The more time I spent with her, the more it seemed her snobbish attitude was slowly diminishing her physical beauty. I couldn't help but think how quickly we can change our opinion about people based on a few inadvertent hints they reveal during a conversation. Pretty is as pretty does, indeed!

Right after I picked up the check, I thought how impossible it would be to live with an insufferable snob like Elena. I'm sure she must have felt the same way about me, based on the way the evening ended up. Needless to say, my fledgling theatrical outfit would not be benefiting from Miss High-and-Mighty's input, which was fine by me.

We took the streetcar and I politely offered to escort her all the way to her destination, but she asked me to get off one stop before hers so that we would not be seen together by her neighbors. If there hadn't been people around us, I would have told her what I thought about her in no uncertain terms, but I kept my cool and exited on the next stop without saying a word to her. At the exit, I paused to fix her in an angry, venomous stare that said all the nasty things I was too much of a gentleman to say aloud.

When I moved to the new house, I sent a short letter to Doris in Saskatoon letting her know of my situation in the new country. After all, I had promised her I would get in touch with her once I established a permanent address in Toronto. She responded immediately, but the content of her letter was surprising, if not downright shocking.

She wrote that she was still very much in love with me and that she wanted to come to Toronto to stay with me. Furthermore, she explained that, although she had gotten back together with her ex-husband, her only desire was to spend the rest of her life with me!

In my response, I emphasized the fact that we sometimes get enticed by a fleeting passion or obsession, which fades away as time goes on. In her next letter she said she rejected my take on the situation, however poetically I had expressed it. Instead, she was convinced I was her soul mate and she was experiencing true love for the first time in her life—with me! She also wrote that she and her husband had a young boy, and that her husband knew how she felt about me.

Her willingness to give up everything in Saskatoon just to be with me was appalling, to say the least. After my response, in which I tried to convince her to stay put with her family and friends, I received a letter from her husband. Here's what he wrote, translated from German:

"I have a big favor to ask you! I would appreciate if you don't write to my wife anymore. Our marriage is in danger and perhaps you could help. I love my wife and my son and I don't want to lose them. As an unattached young man, you'll have the opportunity to find so many other girls who are not married or have a child! You would truly help me if you stop writing to my wife; otherwise I would be an unhappy man who would not know what to do next. I hope you understand and you see my point. I would be grateful to you for a hopefully positive outcome."

I was shaken by this unexpected letter, which I answered by promising that I would write to Doris one last time to let her know that I was involved in a serious relationship, which I did. That was the end of Doris's story.

As the Christmas holidays were approaching, our English teacher began teaching us a selection of Christmas carols we were supposed to sing at a holiday celebration scheduled a few days before Christmas. I was familiar with the German lyrics for some of the songs, such as "Silent Night" and "O Christmas Tree," two enduringly popular Christmas carols that had originated in Germany.

I had a great time at the Christmas party, which took place at the school's cafeteria on Friday, December 21, 1962, as this was the last day of school before the holiday recess. I felt blessed, experiencing such a joyous celebration. Even though I was away from my real home, I was in the warm company of my extended family: my dedicated teachers, who wanted me to succeed almost as much as I did myself, and my wonderful classmates, whose voices lifted high on the timeless carols, blending perfectly with mine.

In addition, I was happy with the progress I'd made in learning to speak and write English. I was able to carry on simple conversations with my new Canadian acquaintances and could understand most of the dialogue on television.

On my way home from school, I was conscious of a problem I was experiencing with my left wrist, a nagging pain that got worse every time I had to carry a heavy tray full of plates and drinks at the restaurant. I attributed the problem to the stress I had subjected my wrist to when I worked at the brick factory. I didn't mind working through the holidays, but the thought that doing so would further aggravate my condition was vexing.

I had already seen a doctor, who had made it clear that the only solution was for me to have outpatient surgery. My boss, who was fully aware of the problem, had repeatedly suggested that I go to the hospital to have the procedure done. I knew I couldn't continue working in this condition, so when I got home, I decided to call the doctor. He scheduled the surgery for around the middle of January.

On Christmas Day, I woke up with the dismal thought that I would spend another holiday alone. My landlord, Tasso, invited Niko and me to have dinner with his family, but unfortunately, I had to work that night. Most everyone else I knew planned to get together with family and friends to celebrate Christmas over a traditional dinner, whereas I had to settle for a late lunch at a fish and chips-style fast-food restaurant.

I remember how lonely I felt that afternoon, sitting on a stool at the counter, eating the tasteless, greasy food. Yet I remained hopeful that better days would come and I might again enjoy a real holiday dinner with family, as I had back in the village.

I planned to visit Despina, my closest relative in North America, in New Jersey during the recovery period after my wrist surgery. About four months had already gone by since Despina and Peter had visited me in Toronto, and I was looking forward to seeing them again. This time, fortunately, I would have the opportunity to stay with them for a while.

In reward for working during the Christmas holidays, including the following weekend, my boss gave me New Year's Eve off. This came as a pleasant surprise because Sotiris was throwing a big party at his place with a huge guest list. Paul Thimou and the rest of our circle of friends were already there when I arrived, wearing silly party hats and whooping it up with noisy party favors. I knew I was going to have a great time ringing in 1963 in madcap fashion! Sotiris outdid himself decorating his apartment with bouquets of colorful balloons and streamers. He also had prepared a buffet of various Greek delicacies, as well as a cart filled with bottles of wine, beer, and other spirits.

By eleven o'clock, more revelers showed up, some of whom I hadn't met before. After the introductions, everyone acted as if they'd known one another for ages. As we gathered around the TV to watch the traditional heralding of the New Year—the dropping of the time ball in New York's Time Square—the party was at its peak. Everyone had a champagne glass in hand. We were careful not to spill a drop as we swayed to and sang along with the melancholy strains of "Auld Lang Syne" as performed on the tube by Guy Lombardo and his Royal Canadians band.

We counted down the seconds—ten! ... nine! ... eight! ... until the ball reached the street at One Times Square, whereupon we sent up a collective cheer—*Happy 1963!*—that rattled the windows in Sotiris' little apartment!

Right after midnight, a good-looking brunette came over and sat next to me and wished me "Happy New Year" with a kiss on the cheek. "I was expecting you to ask me to dance, but as I have noticed, you probably have other preferences—isn't that true?" she whispered teasingly. I smelled the tantalizing scent of her perfume and gulped.

"Oh, no, I haven't been ignoring you," I apologized. "Please forgive me if I gave you that impression, but you are such a beautiful creature, a woman who could have any man you want. Let me make amends. May I please have this dance?"

As we danced to a slow, romantic tune, she whispered in my ear, "Are you playing with me, or do you really not remember me? I'm Sylvia!"

"Should I remember you?" I asked with astonishment.

"I daresay you should, because once in the past, I got the definite impression you were *very* interested in me."

"I'm still drawing a blank. Honestly, Sylvia, I don't believe we have ever met. But if we have, please don't torture me any longer—just tell me who you are!" I pleaded.

"Well, okay, then. Think back to the Canadian embassy in Germany. Do you remember the redheaded girl whom you followed all the way to the Cologne train station?"

The revelation stopped me cold in the middle of the floor. "Oh ... my ... God! What a small world! Are you really that beautiful redhead who refused to talk to me? You gave me the royal cold shoulder!"

She smiled ruefully. "Yes, I am that girl! I wanted so much to talk to you, as I suspected that you were also going to Canada. Plus, I liked you a lot—but as you saw, my jealous boyfriend was waiting for me at the station, and I couldn't take the chance appearing to be friendly with you."

"Yes, I gathered that was the case," I said as we resumed our slow dancing. "And then, as you were walking away from me, you turned your head toward me, shrugging your shoulders as if you wanted to tell me, 'I'm sorry, but under the circumstances I couldn't do anything different.' "

"That was exactly the message I wanted to send to you, because I didn't dare give my jealous boyfriend a reason for another argument. Fortunately, I left him behind in Germany, and here I am now in Canada, as free as a bird!"

"Well, it seems that destiny has given us a second chance," I remarked, taking advantage of the opening. "What would you think about getting to know one another a little better?"

Without missing a beat, she responded as if she had prepared her speech ahead of time. "Of course, I would like to see you again! In fact, I hope you don't think I'm coming on to you or being too forward, but if you have no objections, we could go over to my place after the party."

Of course I agreed, but in light of the fact that we had "officially" known one another for only a few hours, I found her proposal a mite aggressive. Arriving later at her apartment, I waited on tenterhooks to see what would happen next.

Sylvia poured two drinks and sat next to me on the couch. She clinked her glass to mine, took a sip, and sat the glass on the coffee table. "We have to make up for all the lost time between Germany and Canada," she purred in my ear. "This is our night—let's enjoy it." Suddenly, she put her arms around my neck and attacked me like a wild woman, rubbing her body all over me wantonly, shamelessly, as her carnal desires ran amuck.

I have always believed that men should initiate everything, from the first contact, to sex, to proposing marriage. Guys are the ones who have to do all the hard work while women sit around and wait for wonderful things to happen. But Sylvia wanted to be the aggressor, which greatly diminished her femininity—and desirability—in my eyes.

For a little more than an hour, I was a reluctant participant in the brand of rough sex that was obviously commonplace for her, but repellant to me. I thought to myself, *Whatever happened to that beautiful redhead at the Canadian embassy in Germany?* I realized then that we form a different opinion of someone when we begin to interact with that person, especially when they behave like a common tart, as Sylvia did. She asked me several times to stay with her overnight, but I honestly couldn't wait to get out of there.

During the following week, Sylvia tried to get in touch with me, either through my friends or by leaving messages with my landlord, but I managed to avoid all her attempts. My friends told me she became angry with me and demanded to see me so that we could discuss our alleged "relationship." Did she really consider the one-night stand she had forced upon me a relationship? Indeed!

When I finally met her at Sotiris' place, I tried to make her understand that absolutely nothing romantic existed between the two of us. She dismissed my notions out of hand, however, and questioned the interest I had shown her in Germany, as well as the time I spent at her apartment, supposedly taking advantage of her.

Seething with rage, I let her have it with both barrels. "Listen, lady!" I roared. "Leave. Me. *Alone!* Get the hell out of my life *for good!* I never want to see you again! *Never!*"

She gave vent to a hair-raising scream, bolted from the couch, and unleashed a torrent of invective at me while wagging her finger in my face.

"Oh, no!" she said threateningly, her green eyes flashing. "You are going to pay for this, you bastard. I will tell all your friends what a terrible person you are. I'll show you the other side of me. I'll show you!"

She peppered her threats with quite a few spiteful, filthy epithets not fit for publication, which sank my opinion of her to sub-animal status. "Hell hath no fury like a woman scorned," as they say. Sylvia embodied the adage and perfectly fit the description of venomous, borderline psychotic people who become dangerously unforgiving if things don't go their way.

A week or so later, Sotiri told me that Sylvia was going out with an Italian immigrant with whom she claimed she was in love, saying that they would get engaged soon. "Poor guy," I thought, for *encaged* would have been a more appropriate description than *engaged*.

I finally was admitted to the hospital to have surgery on my left wrist to correct the aching tendons and ligaments that controlled the thumb movement. I was told this should be a simple procedure entailing an overnight hospital stay and then I would go home the following day. I remember there were several interns observing the operation as the surgeon explained every step of the process.

When I came out of anesthesia, my bandaged wrist began to ache a little, but the pain became more bearable as the day went on. Before I left the hospital late the next morning, a nurse changed the dressing and taped it quite tightly.

When I arrived home, I noticed that my left hand was starting to swell and my arm ached with a painful throb. Without waiting for these symptoms to subside, I took a taxi and went straight to the hospital's emergency room. The attending physician immediately determined that the overly tight taping of my wrist, which restricted the blood flow to my hand, had caused the problem. After he replaced the dressing and re-taped the wound with a little slack, everything went back to normal.

Through my doctor, I had already made arrangements with my employer to stay out of work for two or three weeks or until I felt completely capable to carry on my duties at the restaurant. My convalescence afforded me a great opportunity to visit my sister, Despina, in America. So, after I secured my visa from the American embassy in Toronto, I called my sister to inform her of my exact arrival in New York City. I couldn't wait to spend some quality time with relatives, a luxury I hadn't experienced since I'd left my hometown, more than two years earlier.

Chapter 36

Reunion

The delicious anticipation of seeing my sister again—not to mention the other relatives who had emigrated from the village to New Jersey right after the war and throughout the 1950s—made the seven-hour bus trip to New York not only bearable but actually enjoyable. It was early evening when I caught my first glimpse of New York's amazing skyline, just before the bus entered the Lincoln tunnel. The skyscrapers were all lit up and rose to impossible heights toward the heavens, like mysterious monoliths built by an advanced, alien race. I sighed in satisfaction, feeling as small as a bug in the midst of this awesome cityscape, and I thanked God for the privilege of beholding it.

When the bus pulled into the New York Port Authority terminal, my sister and my brother-in-law, Peter, were waiting for me at the bottom of the platform stairway. I bit my lip to keep from crying because I was so happy to see them again, and we hugged and kissed with abandon. When we were in Peter's car driving toward New Jersey, Despina said our first stop would be Peter's uncle's house in Union City, where we were expected for dinner.

As we entered the house, the décor, the unique smell of ouzo, and the heavenly aroma of Greek goodies cooking in the kitchen made me feel as if I had just entered a house in the village. Peter's two nephews and his niece joined us for a few drinks before we sat down in the dining room, where a convivial atmosphere prevailed. Looking at the long, oval table filled with Greek delicacies, my mouth watered at the thought of the feast in store for me, something I hadn't had in a long time.

The entire evening was a wonderful experience. Being among close relatives with whom I felt completely at home bolstered my confidence and made the future look bright.

Although my exposure to this new country was still rather limited, my first impression of New York and the warm welcome I received at Peter's uncle's house comforted me to the point that I knew I wouldn't mind living in America instead of Canada.

When we left the house, Peter began driving toward upstate New York to a small town called Garrison, where he and Despina lived and worked. Peter was the chef at St. Basil's Academy, a two-year school that provided room and board to young ladies seeking their teaching diplomas in the Greek language. The graduates were then assigned to teach Greek in parochial schools throughout America. My sister, who had already received her teaching diploma from a Greek college, also worked there as a teacher.

As we drove along the unlit country roads, three hitchhikers suddenly appeared in the middle of the street, trying to make us stop. As Peter swerved around them, he explained that, although these people might legitimately need help, he would not take a chance on picking up anyone in the boondocks.

We arrived at their apartment on the academy compound around midnight, after a little more than an hour's ride. I made myself familiar with the layout of the apartment, and then took the spare bedroom, where I slept quite soundly after a long, wearying day of traveling. I must have been very tired indeed, because the following morning I didn't wake up until around 9:00 a.m.

Peter had already left to assume his kitchen duties at the cafeteria, but my sister was waiting for me in the kitchen, where she had prepared a hearty breakfast. I sat at the kitchen table next to a window, enjoying my breakfast and gazing out at the snow-covered winter wonderland through the frosty glass. It was freezing cold outside, so we stayed in the warm and comfortable apartment. My sister spent the entire Sunday morning with me, bringing me up to date on all sort of subjects, but the conversation inevitably gravitated to the family we had left behind in Rhodes.

Around noon, Despina took me to the cafeteria for lunch, where she introduced me to the other teachers as well as the many uniformed female students who came over to our table, supposedly to extend me a "get well" wish regarding my bandaged wrist. At that moment, I wondered what all those girls were thinking, as I was the only eligible bachelor in the entire academy compound! It felt marvelous to be the only rooster in the henhouse, so to speak, and the girls' flirtatious comments did wonders for my male ego as they flocked around, vying for my attention.

For a moment, I closed my eyes and pictured myself as a sultan in a harem, lolling lazily on a mountain of pillows as these charming school girls danced around me in their silky, colorful lingerie. (Well, I had the right to dream, didn't I?)

I was going to stay in the compound for about a week, so I decided to keep myself occupied with something that required only my right arm. When my sister told me there was a case of oil paints in the apartment, I jumped at the opportunity to resume my painting hobby, although I hadn't previously worked in oils, only watercolors, charcoal, and pastels. However, since I had some painting talent, I thought I would give it a try. This was a great opportunity for me to learn how to paint with a new medium.

As the subject of my painting, I chose a little Scandinavian town center depicted on a postcard that Margareta had sent me when I was planning to emigrate from Germany to Sweden. I had purposely kept that postcard to remember Margareta, a person who went out of her way to make all of the arrangements for my smooth transition to a new country—a trip than never materialized. When I had written to Margareta explaining the reason and my motive for switching my destination to Canada instead of Sweden, she had understood and had wished me luck in my new endeavors.

It took me a few days to finish the painting, working on it about six hours every day while Despina and Peter were at work.

I remember that one night during the week, I was tossing and turning in bed, unable to fall asleep, despite the fact that I had awakened early that morning. All of a sudden, I felt the urge to take a walk outside along the snow-covered paths of the compound. Donning several layers of clothing, as well as insulated gloves and a furry hat that was hanging behind the front door, I ventured outside.

I walked toward a wooded area at the end of the moonlit path. I was completely in awe of the wondrous phenomenon of both the evergreen and barren trees, standing tall, holding their ground, enduring the cold weather as if they were hibernating. Only the repeated howling of wolves broke the silence of the quiet night.

The setting reminded me of my forlorn situation back in Rhodes when, on one brutally cold night, sleep would not come as I hunkered down in my nest-like refuge behind a park bench, feeling sorry for myself and praying I had a warm, comfortable bed to go to. Thankfully, this time the situation was reversed, in that I had made the conscious decision to leave my warm bed for a short walk among Mother Nature's wintry splendor.

Despina and Peter were invited to a wedding that was scheduled to take place over the weekend in northern New Jersey. I was told that a

Greek lady was marrying a Jewish man, but the entire ceremony would be performed according to the Greek tradition. They asked me to go along with them and said they had already made arrangements to include me as a guest at the reception hall.

The church ceremony was exactly the same as all those I had attended in Greece. However, the reception setting was something else: a huge hall with many tables decorated artistically with flowers, ribbons, and ivy-like greenery placed as a centerpiece on each table. The leaves encircled dry twig and stretched all the way to the ceiling, augmented by intertwined, flickering little lights. This was the first time I had experienced such a spectacular event, and I was awestruck by the frilly ornamentation.

After we had cocktails and hors d'oeuvres at an adjacent lounge, we sat down in the main hall, where the bride and groom entrance ceremony was another new experience for me. During dinner, the band played soft tunes of all kinds, including contemporary Greek music. I sat next to my sister, who had already introduced me to many people, some of whom were first-generation immigrants from our village.

Among those I met during the cocktail hour was a good-looking girl named Eve, who happened to be sitting across from our table on the other side of the dance floor. I suspected my sister was playing matchmaker as she kept encouraging me to ask Eve to dance. I finally went over to her table and invited her out onto the dance floor while the band was playing a slow tune.

After some small talk about my bandaged wrist, Eve asked me if I knew the name of the song the band was playing. I said that I'd heard the tune before but didn't know the title. She then told me it was called "Moon River" and was a song from the film "Breakfast at Tiffany's." She said composer Henry Mancini had written the music. "He's from Aliquippa, Pennsylvania, a town close to the place where I grew up," said Eve, who went on to explain the song had won the Oscar for Best Original Song in 1961.

Toward the end of the song, I sensed Eve felt the same chemistry I did, as her body was getting closer to mine and her hand was squeezing my hand intensely. I didn't know what had just happened, but when I escorted her over to her table, I told her how much I enjoyed dancing with her.

"The night is still young," she said, smiling broadly and giving me an enticing look. "We can dance as many times as you like!"

I took this to mean she liked me as much as I liked her. Eve and I danced several more times as the celebration continued, and each time our emotional connection was twice as strong as the last. It was as if the planets had aligned in a once-in-a-lifetime configuration favorable for the development of a serious relationship, and had concentrated their cosmic power on the two of us.

I just could not believe the intensity of the emotions I went through in such a short period! My sister, who had noticed my strong interest in Eve, suggested I ask her out for a date where the two of us could get to know one another in a more private setting. When I said I thought that was a good idea, Despina promised me she would try to set it up.

True to her word, my sister made all the arrangements for my date with Eve. First, she suggested that I spend a few days in New Jersey, staying with relatives who lived close to where Eve lived and worked. Our first date was on a cold evening at a nearby diner. Luckily, it was within walking distance, since neither of us owned—or knew how to drive—a car.

We spent more than an hour at the diner, which admittedly wasn't the most romantic place for a first date. Nevertheless, we enjoyed each other's company and chatted on every subject under the sun, conversing in both Greek and English. (Although Eve was fully Americanized, she spoke Greek quite well because her parents did.)

Despite the cold night, we stopped along an unlit side street on the way home, and that's where I kissed her for the first time. This was, without a doubt, one of the most memorable moments of my young life. Even as it was happening, I knew I would never forget it. I asked myself what in the world I had done to deserve this sublime experience, being together with Eve, holding her in my arms, and telling her I wanted to be with her forever.

She told me she hoped our relationship would develop into something of substance. I was a happy person and felt lucky to have met Eve, an encounter that only the hand of destiny could have orchestrated.

When I went back to my relatives' place after escorting Eve to the house where she was renting a room, I began examining the chain of events that had led up to my fateful meeting with this earthbound angel. First, I had injured my wrist at the brick factory in Germany; I had forsaken Sweden and followed my nose to Canada, where a flare-up of the ailment forced me to have surgery; during my recuperation I visited my sister, went to the wedding, and *voilà!* I met Eve.

Call me a hopeless mystic if you want, but I believe a force we cannot understand ordained these events so that I might ultimately meet this enchanting creature. To put it more succinctly, "It was meant to be!"

The next morning, right after breakfast, I met Eve's father, George. He had come to the house where I was staying, probably to get to know me better, since he knew I had gone out on a date with his daughter. As a first generation Greek, he was protective of Eve.

George wanted to be certain that my intentions were serious, so he came right to the point and asked me what my plans were regarding my relationship with his daughter. I was surprised by his directness; nevertheless, I had no problem giving him a direct answer as well. I told him I liked Eve very much and that I had no doubts about taking the next step.

George seemed overjoyed with the possibility that I might take his daughter's hand in marriage. A tear of happiness rolled down his cheek as his broad face erupted in a huge smile. Lumbering toward me, he seized me in a bear hug, chortling like the proud papa he was.

I had been planning to return to Canada the following day, but he begged me to go with him to Pennsylvania instead to visit Eve's hometown and meet her mother. Before I gave him an answer, I called my boss in Canada to ask him for a few more days off, to which he had no objection. An hour or so later, I was riding in George's car, heading toward Pittsburgh—about an eight-hour drive.

We made one stop for lunch at one of the fast food places on the Pennsylvania Turnpike. Overall, the trip was pleasant, as George was in a good mood and rather talkative, and the time passed quickly. I remember that, at one point, he made a comment about how smoothly his blue Chevy Impala rode and said that the small European cars couldn't compare with this American vehicle as far as comfort was concerned.

When we entered Eve's house, George said to his wife, "Look, Ellie, I brought the groom home!"

With tears running down her cheeks, Ellie came over and gave me a big hug. A few minutes later, another lady came to the house and hugged me with warm familiarity, as if she had known me for years. In fact, she happened to be a great aunt I had never met because she left Greece before I was born. She stood back for a minute, staring at me and crying out that I looked exactly like her brother—my grandfather, that is, who had died in 1918 when he was only twenty-one years old during the Spanish influenza pandemic.

Right after dinner, Ellie took me upstairs to my room where I was to spend two nights before departing for Canada. When she showed me Eve's room which was completely decorated in pink, I noticed an almost-life-size poster on the wall of a handsome young man with dark skin and full, sensuous lips. While staring at the poster, I asked Ellie who the young fellow was—I assumed he was probably Eve's ex- or current-boyfriend. I felt a pang of jealousy, imagining Eve involved with another man, and Ellie must have noticed my pained expression.

"That's Johnny Mathis, Eve's favorite entertainer," she said, laughing. "He's one of the most famous singers in the world. Don't tell me you've never heard of him!" I had to admit I hadn't, as another pang of jealousy stung my psyche.

When I analyzed my feelings for Eve, I concluded that I really, really liked her "a whole lot" and that I would do everything possible to advance our relationship to the next level. The thought of being together with Eve forever gave me great pleasure, a sensation of security and comfort that was missing in my young life.

As I was lying in bed, I felt Eve's presence; I visualized her beautiful face flashing in front of my eyes and wished she were there with me. I knew that better days were ahead of us, as the future looked brighter and brighter with Eve in my life. When I had been in Eve's room, earlier that evening, her mother had given me a framed picture of her, which I liked very much. I put that picture next to the night table and stared lovingly at it until I fell asleep.

The next day, I had breakfast with Ellie, who told me all about Eve (no pun intended!) including her past, her friends, her achievements, and her aspirations. It was a pleasant conversation because the subject matter meant everything to me, despite the fact I had only known Eve for a few days. I realized this was a rather quick turn of events, but something inside me just kept telling me this was the right road to take.

In the late afternoon, I was introduced to many other Greek families whose houses were on the same block. The first-generation immigrants, most of whom were already retired, had come to America at the turn of the nineteenth century and worked in various railroad construction jobs. They all had one goal in life: that their children would have the opportunity to get a better education than they had received to build a brighter future.

I was surprised to see that everyone, including the young children, spoke Greek and kept most of the traditions of their homeland throughout their well-organized, religious community.

Right after dinner, I called Eve and told her how wonderful her mother was and that I was also so happy to meet all the nice people in the neighborhood.

The bus ride back to Toronto was one of the most pleasant trips I had ever taken, as my mind was totally occupied with thoughts of Eve, remembering the few tender moments we had spent together on that cold, fateful night. Every so often, I looked at the picture her mother had given me, admiring Eve's smiling face as though, in my eyes, she were the most beautiful girl in the world—which she was!

I didn't know how long I would stay in Canada before moving permanently to New Jersey to be with Eve in our own house. I was almost certain that, in a month or so, I would make the next move—provided that Eve was in agreement with my plans.

Back in Canada, my landlady and Niko were happy for me when I told them about all the events that occurred during my visit to America. They both commented that the wedding bells were about to ring, sooner rather than later! Back in my room, before going to bed, I placed Eve's picture on my nightstand, facing my pillow.

I remember the exact thought I had and the emotions I experienced when I awoke the next morning and gazed longingly at Eve's picture for a good five minutes. I wondered whether I was already in love, because I could not get her off my mind. Even when I went back to work, I couldn't think of anything else but Eve's face flashing in front me.

A few days after my return to Toronto, I wrote my first letter to Eve, in less than perfect English. I somehow got hold of it later on and have kept it all these years as a reminder of the feelings I had at that time. Without making any corrections whatsoever, it reads exactly like this:

Toronto 13. 2. 1963
My Dear Eve!
The time is now two o'clock after midnight and I'm still writing. I wrote to Mama (her mother) before and now I've got to write you before I go to bed. I missed you to much today and that's why I phoned you to night. I just wanted to hear your voice. I can't believe it how fast happened it! But I am happy when I know that you love me and you will be my wife. Do you remember what I said you?
"In our house, you, me and the love." Oh darling it will be so nice, I shall try to make you very, very happy. I found you, and you found me, that's enough for us and don't be afraid, I go away, no darling, I'll stay with you for ever because you already became my sweet and great love. I didn't want to write you before you write me first as I told you, but my heart said to me: "you must write her if you love her" and I did. So, sweetheart I have to leave you now because I'm going to bed, and don't you forget to write me soon. Say hello to (a list of friends and relatives).
With thousand kisses forever yours

(Well, since I had not read the original, handwritten letter in all these years, I find it much better than I had thought—if I do say so! I notice that, from the way I expressed some of my thoughts, I was still simulating German sentence structure and language rules. But the writing "ain't too shabby" for someone who had only been exposed to English for six months!)

As soon as Eve received my letter, she called my landlord's phone, but unfortunately, I was not there. She left a message for me to phone her, no matter how late it got, and said she would wait up for my call before she went to bed.

Eve was almost in tears of joy when I talked to her, a little before midnight. She told me that she had also missed me and that I should do my best to try to join her as soon as possible. I promised her it wouldn't be long before we were permanently united in New Jersey as a happy couple.

I went to bed that night holding her picture under the bed covers. Looking at her picture was my first activity in the morning and the last one at night.

As the days dragged by, I was getting more impatient being away from Eve. Every day was a struggle for me. I decided to leave Canada, which I did on February 22, 1963. My passport, stamped by the Buffalo authorities, permitted me to enter the United States as a tourist, although my intention was to stay permanently if I got married to Eve.

My mind was a restless beehive, racing with mixed emotions, all during the bus trip to New York City. But all of my uncertainties and fears vanished when I saw Eve again. I was certain I had made the right decision to join my beloved, who reassured me that, no matter what difficulties came our way, we would face them together as long as love, respect, and caring for one another were the common denominators in our relationship.

Eve and I made a to-do list of all the matters that needed immediate attention. The number one item was to resolve my visa status, a subject with only one solution: to get married! So, on March 11, 1963, we went to the city hall in Union, New Jersey and had a civil marriage ceremony with only a few relatives present. Of course, once the tedious immigration process was out of the way, we planned to follow the civil ceremony up with a religious ceremony as soon as possible.

A few days later, we went to the immigration office, where we filed the required forms for my permanent resident status, which would be followed by the issuance of my "green card." Eve helped me fill out the forms, as she was more knowledgeable with the terminology than I was. Although my first name is Emanuel (in Germany, they called me Manuel), Eve wrote "Michael"—the name by which I was known to most of my friends—on the forms. That ultimately became my official name, as shown on the green card and later on my passport when I became an American citizen.

Later on, I found out why Eve used the name "Michael" while filling out the official papers. Her brother also had been baptized as Emanuel (his grandfather's name), but his official name was Michael, so she assumed the translation was correct. Although my immediate family still called me by my original name, I hadn't made any attempts to change it back to Emanuel, because this was an opportunity to forget the "old me" and start a new chapter in my life as Michael (or my nickname, Mike), a name I've kept all these years.

While in New Jersey, I kept in touch with my friend Paul in Toronto, who always wanted to come to America to launch a singing career. He finally came to New Jersey as a tourist, but Paul had the same intention as me: to stay here for good! I helped him find a place to stay as well as a job at a relative's restaurant, where he started working as a waiter.

I had asked Paul to be my *koumbaro* (best man) at the wedding, which was scheduled for May 5, 1963, at a Greek Orthodox Church in a suburb outside Pittsburgh. In the meantime, Eve and I started looking for an apartment as well as a job for me near the town where she worked in northern New Jersey. After finding a one-bedroom apartment on the second floor of a two-family house for $75.00 a month, we began shopping for furniture—the cheapest available, since my savings were pitiful.

Someone informed me that the custom in America was to buy a diamond engagement ring for the blushing bride. Bless their hearts, Eve's parents, who were aware of my financial situation, bought the ring and asked me to give it to her as if I had bought it myself. Since I had no other choice, I reluctantly accepted their offer, promising I would pay them back after I had taken care of the essential house furnishings. I was paying monthly payments on a two-year installment schedule.

As time went on, I was spending more and more time with Eve, especially when we started painting our apartment, a task that took us three or four days. During that time, I began noticing Eve was given to unusual mood swings, which often escalated into loud outbursts.

As I observed this part of her character more closely, I recalled my great aunt's comments when we'd had a short conversation in her house in Pennsylvania. She had said to me, "Don't you think you should wait for a while to get to know her better before throwing yourself into a lifetime commitment which you may later regret?"

My aunt didn't want to elaborate on her comments, but I began to understand Eve might have an underlying problem I hadn't been made aware of.

Before Eve put her wedding gown on, we had a terrible fight at her mother's house. She went berserk, breaking everything within her reach.

I walked out of the house with Paul, to whom I sadly confided that I just wanted to run away from this mess I had gotten myself into. Paul told me to be patient, because Eve's outburst that morning was likely just wedding-day jitters.

And so, early that afternoon, we went to a crowded church where the religious ceremony took place, followed by the reception at a nearby catering establishment. I should have been happy that day, but I truly felt as if I were imprisoned for a crime I had not committed by rushing into this so quickly. I don't remember any details of the reception, as I was in a world of my own in which I was doomed to carry the heavy burden of a marriage that had started on shaky ground and only promised to get worse.

Whatever had happened to that beautiful girl I kissed on our first date? Eve was definitely not the same person who had stolen my heart when we danced to "Moon River." She had either transformed into another personality, or else I was seeing the manifestation of her true character and her real image—and God help me, it was ugly.

Back in New Jersey, our number one concern was our dire financial straits, since I did not have a job as of yet. What a way to start a marriage! As my job search continued with no prospects, there was one occasion during the first two weeks that we did not even have enough money to buy a loaf of bread.

Although I was going through a stressful period in terms of the fast pace at which everything in my life was developing, after I found a job as a shipping clerk at a chemical factory, I felt much better. Our combined salaries would definitely fatten up our tight budget.

Incidentally, I attempted to resume my journal after a three-year hiatus, but the logging only lasted for two months, covering June and July of 1963. Reading some of the details in my journal, I've noticed that most of my arguments with my new wife were triggered by insignificant matters that we both magnified to a point where we thought they were insurmountable.

The most frequent and most heated disputes stemmed from our limited financial means. Eve simply could not understand that I could not buy something she wanted with money we didn't have, since everything we bought we had to pay for in cash. In addition to these ongoing problems, I had developed my own jealousy issue, something that was damaging our relationship. All too frequently, I unjustifiably questioned Eve when she came home a little later than her regular schedule. A telling entry in my journal on Thursday, June 13, 1963, bears inclusion here: "Despite all the difficulties we're going through, my jealous propensity indicates that I still love my wife."

On Friday, I was paid $53 for four days work. When I got home, our usual argument started over the money situation: after paying the required expenses, we had only $3.00 left to last us for the entire week. I knew I could not make it through the week, so I had to borrow money from someone. Another entry in my journal on that day reads: "I'm just asking myself if that's how my married life would be from now on. If that is the case, then I would not call it life, to find myself in a situation where I couldn't even afford buying a loaf of bread."

As difficult as it was for me to disclose my pathetic financial condition, I finally broke down and borrowed $50 from my sister, explaining that the money would go mainly for food. She could not believe I was going through such hard times.

While reading my journal with a mature and more critical eye, I can say that I was not helping the situation. Each time I faced little problems or inconveniences, I made no effort to help her see or understand my point of view. Now I understand that it was selfish on my part, and all too convenient, to blame Eve for everything I did not agree with. Each time I thought she had done something wrong, I was reconfirming my argument and refueling my belief that I should not have married her in the first place. Bottom line, we were operating as enemies instead of friends.

As our arguments became more frequently violent, Eve began to throw household items at me. There was one time where, at the peak of her rage, she threw a heavy crystal ashtray at me, missing my face by only a few inches. I remember that I left the house that afternoon and ended up in a bar, where I stayed for more than three hours, drinking beer. I thought the alcohol would diminish the misery I was going through at the time.

Another detail in my journal regarding the time I spent in that bar was the blond girl who sat next to me at the counter and tried to initiate a flirtatious conversation. Being preoccupied with my personal marriage troubles at home, I completely ignored her come-ons.

I developed a rather close friendship with an elderly couple, Elias and Eugenia Callas, who lived almost across from our apartment. Since they gave us permission to drop in at any time without calling in advance, we visited them almost every day, especially when a professional wrestling match was on television. Years later, I discovered that this type of wrestling is just a show—but at the time, I certainly believed these brutal contests were real.

Bruno Sammartino was our favorite wrestler, a real hero who was able to overpower most of his opponents—especially when he defeated Buddy Rogers in less than a minute. Elias was first-generation Greek, Eugenia second generation, and they were one of the nicest couples I had ever met.

Every time Eve and I had an argument, one of us ran over to the refuge of the Callas house, where we were welcomed, any time of the day or night. Everyone should have neighbors like Elias and Eugenia, a rare breed of people whose home was our safe haven when we needed a shoulder to lean on. Moreover, they were our life mentors in many difficult moments of our marriage.

Elias was an inherently happy person who owned and operated a hot dog stand. He prepared all the toppings himself. Every day, he wheeled his stand to a little strip shopping center, where he sold his hot dogs until sundown. Regardless of whether his day was profitable or not, he always came home with a smile on his face, thanking God for enabling him to do what he loved: selling hot dogs!

Because our own parents weren't close by, Eve and I considered this harmonious couple our surrogate "mom and pop." Unfortunately, toward the end of the summer, we decided to move to another apartment about five miles away. After that, our visits to the Callas home were not as frequent as when we had lived across the street.

Chapter 37

Behind the Wheel

The new place was in a two-story building that had been converted from a school to an apartment complex. My commute to work was completely different, as I had to walk about a mile to the bus station and then walk another mile to work after I got off the bus. At this time, the only person I was hanging around with from my own age group was my friend Steve, who had a car and was kind enough to drive me to destinations where there was no public transportation.

Steve Kontos was also a product of Agios Isidoros. He had started his career as a sailor on a merchant vessel. When the ship docked in New York City in 1962, Steve decided to abandon the vessel and try to start anew in America. Of course, he began working in Greek restaurants, where he progressed from the dishwasher position to a short-order cook to owning his own restaurant in Linden, New Jersey, which he called "Linden House." Despite his sixth grade formal education level, after he became an American citizen—through marriage—he built a successful construction business.

Steve volunteered to teach me how to drive after I got my driving permit. One evening, he took me to a quiet street to show me how to make a U-turn. When I finished the second part of the turn, I did not straighten the steering wheel and, while stepping on the gas pedal, I slammed into a brand new Cadillac that an elderly lady had just parked!

I was petrified when the police arrived at the scene to assess the accident. They took Steve and me down to the station, where we were asked all sorts of questions while they filled out an accident report. Then they let us go home, but I was still shaken. I told Steve I wasn't sure if I ever wanted to drive a car again!

But after a few weeks, my fear subsided, so I went to a professional driving school. I felt more comfortable having another steering wheel on the passenger side, where my patient and experienced instructor sat. Within a week or so, I was ready to take the road test, which I passed with flying colors.

I went to a nearby bar to have a beer to celebrate getting my first driver's license, which I proudly kept in my wallet. Next to me at the bar was a gentleman who started talking to me about the fact he had lost his license due to his many traffic violations. He said he needed to hire someone to drive him around, as his job involved the distribution of products in several locations throughout northern New Jersey. He asked me if I was interested, but I declined. The irony of being offered a delivery position just one hour after getting my driver's license wasn't lost on me, and I assumed there must be a catch.

My first car was a used 1957 American Motors Rambler I bought at a gas station for $300. It didn't even have a radio, but there was a hole on the floor next to the driver's seat that served as a natural air conditioner! Overall, it was not in good shape, but it enabled me to drive the five miles to work, which was a little more convenient than taking the bus.

During this period, I attended night classes at Columbia University, mainly taking English courses three times a week. Right after work, I would take the bus to New York City, have a quick bite, and then take the subway to the 116th Street Station. Classes lasted from six until a little after ten. Then it took me another hour and a half to get home. It was a grueling schedule, but I gradually adapted after a few weeks of riding the bus and subway.

My humdrum job at the chemical plant revolved around the difficult routine of loading trucks with heavy containers of lacquer, the base compound used in oil paints. I clearly remember the afternoon of November 22, when all of a sudden I started shaking like a leaf for no apparent reason. My coworkers were understandably concerned and suggested I should see a doctor or go to the hospital, but the trembling curiously stopped when we found out that President John F. Kennedy had been assassinated in Dallas, Texas. Again, this incident got me wondering whether my subconscious mind foretold the assassination before it became public knowledge.

I also remember a cold day in February of 1964 when the Beatles were visiting New York for the first time. All the radio station deejays were talking about the pandemonium surrounding their arrival (which was dubbed "Beatlemania") and the band's concert schedule, which included their American television debut on *The Ed Sullivan Show*. I had been a huge Beatles fan ever since I'd known about them and their music. I vividly remember their first performance on Ed Sullivan's show, especially when they sang "I Want to Hold your Hand."

I knew that the four boys from Liverpool would change history in the realm of music, because they used an unorthodox composing methodology. Their clever hairdos and the chord transitions of their songs were revolutionary at the time. Many times, I caught myself humming "All My Loving" or "Yesterday," two of my favorites.

Toward the end of spring, I quit my job at the factory and accepted a position at my cousin Louis' restaurant, working behind the ice cream counter. I had to learn all the abbreviations the waiters used to order a specific ice cream dish. Factoring in all the flavors and different toppings, there were more than a hundred combinations! For example, "black & white on" was vanilla and chocolate ice cream with hot fudge topping.

Within a week or so, I had memorized the abbreviated names and I was able to take three or four orders at a time, especially on weekends, when all of the teenagers in town had to have their ice cream treat. On Fridays, the place was mobbed, with lines forming outside along the sidewalk. I was making more money than in my previous job, but I also worked longer hours, six days a week.

I was still driving my decrepit Rambler back and forth to work. The aging heap was just about on its last legs and one evening, I found I could not control the steering wheel. Ever so slowly, I drove the Rambler to a car dealership, where I bought a 1964 Dodge Dart. I did not get any trade-in credit for the Rambler; the dealer said he was going to transport it to a junk yard. Although used, my new compact car was in excellent condition with only 12,000 miles on the engine, and it had a radio to boot. I loved driving that car—I really did!

When our apartment lease was about to expire, we decided to find a place closer to the restaurant where I worked. The new place was the typical garden apartment with four large rooms, and it was only a few miles from the restaurant.

Around this period, my sister, Despina, and I began filling out the necessary paperwork to bring the rest of the family over to America. This process would take more than a year, because everyone needed to get their immigrant status visas. Stacy, one of my other sisters, was working in Germany as a seamstress. Her wish was to come to America as soon as possible, so I decided to find a way to invite her over as a tourist. To accomplish this, it would be necessary to put an elaborate plan in motion, because the tourist visa was difficult to get.

First, I called upon Stacy to suffer an injury by letting the needle of a sewing machine pierce through her finger. I then wrote a letter to her in English, inviting her to stay in my house until she was well enough to go back to work. I also emphasized that it would be a good opportunity for her to visit the World's Fair in New York City and that I would be responsible for all her expenses, including airfare. She took this letter, along with the disability form, to the American consulate in Frankfurt, where she got her visa without a hitch. My plan had worked flawlessly!

On Christmas Eve, 1964, she boarded the plane in Frankfurt, which was scheduled to arrive at JFK International Airport at 3:00 p.m. However, due to a blizzard, her flight was diverted to Montreal, where the plane landed and the passengers were taken to nearby hotel. My friend, Paul, and I were still waiting at the airport, but when we were informed that no flights would be allowed to land until the next day, we slowly drove home along the snow-covered roads.

When I got home, I made some calls and managed to locate the hotel where the stranded passengers were staying. I asked one of the airline spokespersons if I could possibly speak with my sister. When she came to the phone, she asked me why I hadn't picked her up from the airport, as she presumed the plane had landed in New York! I guess she didn't understand the announcement or no one had explained to her why they had to land in Montreal. Anyway, I put her mind at ease when I told her that I would pick her up at JFK around mid-morning the next day.

Christmas Day dawned, cold but sunny, with the blizzard all but forgotten. Paul and I picked up Stacy from the airport and we drove to my apartment, where Eve, Despina, and Peter had already prepared the holiday dinner. It was truly a happy occasion having Stacy with us to celebrate Christmas together. Paul also dined with us because, having been *koumbaro* (best man) at our wedding, he was like a member of the family.

During dinner, I gazed lovingly at Stacy, who seemed so happy to be with us. Over dessert, she suddenly cried out loud, "I don't want to go back to Germany! I want to stay here with my family!" Tears trickled down her cheeks. Greatly moved, I tried to reassure her that we would do everything within our power to find a way to keep her in America permanently.

Stacy was staying with Despina and Peter in an apartment they were renting in Union City, New Jersey. The easiest way for Stacy to get her permanent visa status would be to marry someone who was either an American citizen or an immigrant who already had become a permanent resident. Accordingly, we started the search for a beau good enough to take my beloved sister's hand!

Chapter 38

For the Love of Music

During the summer of 1965, my friend, Paul, and I decided to explore the opportunities for our musical talents and find out if we were good enough to record some of the songs I had written. Among my original compositions, Paul's favorite was the one whose lyrics I wrote when I was having lunch in a coffee shop and spied a one-dollar bill on the floor next to my chair. I kept staring at it and, when no one claimed it, I finally picked it up.

It occurred to me that the main reason many of us immigrants left our home countries was the pursuit of the almighty dollar. And thus was born "The Dollar," a song I wrote in Greek, as a cautionary tale targeted at the Greek audience. Here are the lyrics in the original form, as well as the closest English translation:

THREE GRAINS OF WHEAT

Το Δολλάριο

The Dollar

Είναι ένα πράσινο χαρτί
χωρίς καρδιά χωρίς ψυχή
το προκυνούν σαν άγιο.

It is a green paper
Without heart, without soul
They worship it as a saint.

Πιστεύουν πλούσιοι και φτωχοί
σ΄αυτό το πράσινο χαρτί
πού λέγεται δολλάριο.

Rich and poor believe
In this green paper
That is called dollar.

Δολλάριο πράσινο, δολλάριο
πού'χεις πάρει
τον γυρισμό γιά την πατρίδα τη
γλυκειά
του μετανάστη τού 'χεις βάλει
χαλινάρι
τον βασανίζεις μεσ' τη μαύρη
ξενιτειά.

Green dollar, dollar that you have
taken away
The return to the sweet homeland
You have chained the immigrant
And you torture him in a foreign
land

Όλους μας ξώρισες
και μάς εδώρισες
της ξενιτειάς το πικραμμένο το
ψωμί
όλα τα χάσαμε
κι΄ όλοι ξεχάσαμε
τη φτωχική και τιμημένη μας
δραχμή

You have exiled all of us
And you rewarded us
Your land's bitter bread
We lost everything
And everyone forgot
Our poor but precious drachma

After writing the music for "The Dollar," we began to think seriously about making a record. For the flip side, we selected "Stella," the song I had written when I was in the army in Thessaloniki. (Stella was the fiancée of my friend Pablo, who never stopped talking about her.)

Paul and I spent many hours practicing the two songs, but we needed a few more instruments, in addition to my guitar, to produce a commercially viable recording. I located two ladies who called themselves The Duo Happy Angels, and they turned out to be just what we needed. One played the guitar and the other played the bouzouki (a long-necked, Greek instrument akin to the mandolin), so we would have three string instruments and a drummer we hired through the recording studio. Even better, the ladies were excellent vocalists and would be perfect as our background singers.

The four of us practiced for three days, averaging twelve hours each day. Since our funds were limited, we only rehearsed the two songs with the drummer at the studio for about an hour.

My funds were severely limited, but I booked a recording session in a shabby, no frills studio in Elizabeth, New Jersey. Paul sang both songs while the two ladies and I harmonized in the background as well as playing our instruments. We taped three versions of each song and ultimately selected the best takes for our debut single.

Now we just needed to locate a record production facility. To my dismay, Paul mysteriously disappeared somewhere in New York City at a crucial time when I needed his help to finalize what we had started. First, I designed the labels that showed the song on the first line, then "written by M. Papasavas" on the second line and then, in bold letters, "Paul Thimou" on the third line "with the Duo Happy Angels" on the last line.

I managed to find a place in NYC to print the round labels and a plant in Kearney, New Jersey, that would conduct the electroplating prototype process, from the silver, grooved disc all the way to the mass production of the 45-rpm vinyl disks. The master disc was made of black lacquer, so it could be etched with grooves to carry the sound. Then it was coated with either aluminum or chromium-plated nickel. The finished master disc was used to press the vinyl records.

The pressing of a few thousand records cost me a substantial amount of money, but I was so happy and proud of my accomplishment in a field in which I had no prior knowledge.

After loading all the boxes of records into the trunk of my car, I raced home, eager for Eve to hear the record. We called the Callas family, our ex-neighbors, and played both sides of the record while holding the phone close to the speakers. George and Eugenia were elated with the songs, especially the "Dollar," according to the comments they made.

A few days later, Paul reappeared and apologized for his disappearance. He explained that the grueling practice sessions must have gotten the best of him. He could not muster the emotional strength to follow through with the record production process.

"In other words, I panicked," he said. Paul promised he would try to share the production expenses, but his funds were limited. He ended up giving me an expensive accordion in lieu of his share of the expense.

Faced with the task of promoting and selling the record, I visited a number of Greek stores in New York City and supplied them with enough records to be sold for a price of their discretion. I also approached a few radio hosts who agreed to play the record during their weekend Greek programs—but there was a cost associated with each time the disc jockey played one of our recorded songs on the air, for which I had to pay in advance.

In the end, I gave most of the records away to friends and family members, as the money I collected from the stores was a small fraction of the entire production expense I had incurred.

I switched my job responsibilities from dispensing ice cream orders behind the counter to the more profitable position of waiter. However, the twelve- to fourteen-hour shift, six days a week, was an exhausting schedule with no free time to do anything besides work. I truly enjoyed working as a waiter, dealing with all kinds of people. Some were nice—overall, most customers fit into this category—but others were rude and insulting.

One early afternoon, about a month after the completion of the recording process, the lunch crowd at the restaurant had just thinned out when I noticed a good-looking lady sitting at a booth, shuffling through a sheaf of papers on the table. Wearing my red waiter's vest, I approached her, greeted her with a smile, and took her order for a cup of coffee. She mentioned that she liked my accent and wanted to know where I was from.

When I served her coffee, she asked me if I had a few minutes to sit down for a brief interview. She introduced herself as Ellen De Rogatis, a reporter for the *Union Leader* newspaper, and explained she was on assignment to locate interesting or unusual individuals and write short articles about them. She said that she found me interesting and thought I would make an excellent subject for one of her profiles.

I was flattered and gladly consented to the interview. She took out her legal pad and jotted down notes on my artistic endeavors, starting with the two plays I had written in Greece and up through the record we had just completed. When I told her I also wrote poetry, she asked me if I would write a verse to be used as an introduction to my story. I wrote the following, which appeared directly after the article's headline in the October 28, 1965 edition of the *Union Leader*:

He Left Rhodes To Seek His Fortune—Mike Papasavas Is Still Searching For It
"With fear and hope on a stormy night
I'm running after little candle's light
In the deepest darkness I reach the flame
I have the picture but I need the frame"

The story was a bit exaggerated in terms of my accomplishments up to that point of my life. For instance, in my zeal to build myself up as a worthy subject, I had given her the idea that 5,000 people had attended my play, "The Army Life," instead of 500, the actual number. I was a little embarrassed when this "white lie" appeared in print. It was nice, however, to be a local celebrity for a while, especially since the article included a nice photo of me.

Her closing comments in the article were: *"I have the picture," he said, referring to his poem, "but I need the frame." The picture is the talent, and the frame is the break."*

I still have a clipping of the original newspaper article, but after forty-odd years, the once bright white newsprint has faded to yellow.

Chapter 39

Workin' for a Living

I stayed at my cousin's Louis' restaurant for another seven months or so, at which time I began to explore other possibilities in higher-class restaurants. I took a job in a hotel's restaurant where, in addition to food, I had to serve cocktails. In a few weeks, I became an expert on garnishes and how to distinguish a whisky sour from a gimlet. After a few short job hops, I settled down in a high-class French restaurant, where I made good money and only worked during dinner hours.

Around this same time, several significant events occurred. Stacy met a Greek gentleman named Demetrius (we called him Demo) and began a serious relationship that finally ended up in a happy marriage. As for Eve and me, we bought a one-family house after borrowing some money for the down payment.

Then my parents, my brother, George, and my sisters, Katina and Anna, finally came to America! It was an overwhelming experience when they got off the ship in New York City, especially for George, Katina, and Anna, who had not previously traveled beyond the borders of Greece. They were happy to be reunited with Despina and me, and they also were looking forward to meeting relatives they hadn't seen in a long time.

However, the fear of the unknown, the immensity of the new world, and the large crowds of the city painted a silent uncertainty in their faces. It was a trying period, because my parents and my sister, Katina, stayed with us for a few months. The atmosphere in the house grew so tense that I had to find other living arrangements for them.

Although my parents and siblings initially liked Eve, it didn't take long for them to realize she had frequent mood swings and unprovoked outbursts of anger. During these moments, I didn't have to ask my father how he felt; he would shake his head, clearly expressing his disapproval of Eve's behavior. On the other hand, my mother was playing the role of a mediator by trying to calm things down as if she were feeling the anguish Eve was going through.

Even when it was finally just Eve and me in the house, our relationship was deteriorating drastically. I believe I was going through the lowest point of our marriage, being depressed most of the time and having arguments with Eve. I also argued with the rest of her family, as they were advising Eve about what to do and how to treat me as a husband. Specifically, they were telling her to "put her foot down" and not let me have the upper hand.

Within a period of three months, I went to several specialists to find out what was wrong with me, because after a few hours at work, I would get dizzy to the point that I had to go home. One particular afternoon, I went home early and completely blacked out, unable to see anything for a few minutes. At that moment, I thought I had gone blind.

Fortunately, it was a temporary condition. However, the next day, I followed the suggestion of a coworker named Barbara and saw her family doctor, who had a reputation as one of the best physicians in the state. She was certain Dr. Bloink would diagnose the problem and set me on the road to recovery.

I went to see Dr. Bloink, whose waiting room was crowded with about fifteen patients squeezed shoulder-to-shoulder in closely arranged chairs. After an hour or so, I was called to the examination room, but the waiting room was still full, as more patients kept coming in. The crowd gave me confidence that Dr. Bloink was indeed as good as his reputation suggested.

After I described my symptoms, Dr. Bloink started asking me many personal questions, especially about my relationship with Eve. I expressed my concern over all the patients who were waiting to see him, because he had spent almost an hour with me. However, he emphasized that his concern at that point was *me* and he would not brush me off just because his waiting room was full. I was so impressed with his attitude and the caring he had shown me. He was probably the best doctor I had seen in my entire life. He was a rare specimen who hadn't just taken the Hippocratic Oath, but lived and breathed it.

Dr. Bloink was absolutely certain my problems were psychosomatic, caused by the stresses and strains of my marriage. He referred me to a psychologist, whom I saw a few days later. He spent an hour listening to my life story, prompting me to concentrate on details within the period I had been together with Eve, before and after our marriage.

When I left his office I felt great, even though the doctor hadn't done anything but listen to me while occasionally taking notes on a yellow pad. It was as if a thick, black veil had been lifted from my eyes, and I went from a state of hopeless depression to a normal, happy state. I concluded that by talking to someone about the problems we experience, we relieve a heavy burden on our inner selves; by doing so, we can either diminish the degree of our struggles or completely eliminate them.

Some days later, I wanted to test my theory that talking to others about our problems is therapeutic. So instead of keeping all my frustrations bottled up inside, I started sharing everything with my friend, Paul, who was indeed a good listener—and a lot cheaper than a psychologist!

Unfortunately, my relationship with Eve was spiraling out of control, with little hope of recovery. One evening when I got home, I noticed that a good many household items were missing, as if our house had been burglarized. It didn't take me long to realize that Eve had chosen to terminate our marriage by leaving the house and taking with her the household items she considered hers.

After surveying the entire house, I noticed that the bedroom and living room furniture were still there, as there were quite a few loan payments remaining before they were completely paid off. In the kitchen, I found a few plates and glasses, a handful of utensils, and a frying pan. The family room was empty except for the old blue couch, which stood out starkly in the large space.

A sudden feeling of emptiness overtook me. I could not believe Eve had found the courage by herself to make the difficult decision to opt for separation. Surely she had been influenced—or more probably, *ordered*—by her family to leave the house. In any case, we both knew our marriage was falling apart, despite several visits to the marriage counselor we had consulted as a last resort.

Could it have been the marriage counselor who influenced Eve to take the drastic step of separation? At that point, it didn't matter who or what was behind her decision. The deed was done, and I would have to suffer the consequences.

I was going through one of the lowest periods of my life, both socially and job-wise. My unfocused career was headed into the abyss of uncertainty. My last job as a waiter was at a restaurant that was famous as a Mafia meeting place. I served these "wise guys" at their usual, round table and learned I could not approach them to ask if everything was all right or if they needed anything else, unless they gestured to me with a snap of their fingers to come hither. This was the demeaning etiquette I had to follow, but I must say, they were the greatest tippers! I made more money from the wise guys in one night than from all the other customers I served, combined!

I worked at that restaurant for about six months, making good money from a circle of repeat customers who specifically asked the hostess to be seated in my section. There were some evenings, especially during the week, that half the restaurant was empty— except for my section, which had three or four tables occupied by customers who had asked for me.

As time went on, the other waiters complained to the manager, because there were days when they were not making any money from tips. So the manager issued a directive that we should all pool our tips and, at the end of the night, each of us would get an equal share of the proceeds. I knew it wasn't fair to me, because I had worked hard to build my own clientele by providing the best service anyone could possibly receive, no matter how difficult or fussy the customers were. My patience and diplomacy had earned me the reputation of being the best waiter in the restaurant, so the new rule of sharing the tips did not sit well with me.

One day, I was reading the help-wanted section in the newspaper when I came across an ad that caught my attention: *"I'm an unusual person and I'm looking for a unique individual who is not willing to settle for a secure, hourly job. I can offer you unlimited income possibilities, provided you are the unusual person I'm looking for."*

Without a second thought, I called the number and, although the person I spoke to would not provide a job description, I made an appointment for the following day. As I rode the elevator to the tenth floor of the building in Newark, New Jersey, I knew I was the unusual person they were looking for, the risk-taker who had always overcome whatever obstacles stood in my way.

The receptionist took me to the office of a gentleman named Joe, who greeted me with a firm handshake. When I sat down, Joe went over the job description as well as the company's products. He further explained this was a sales position, selling the Encyclopedia Americana plus other sets of art and classic books. The salary was based strictly on commission, which came to an average of 20 percent of the gross sales amount.

Should I accept, Joe said, there would be a three-day training session for the presentation of the products, followed by on-the-job training, which entailed going out with an experienced salesman to observe the live presentation and the various methods used to close a sale.

I accepted the position. As part of the training, I had to make phone calls using a prepared sales pitch to set up appointments with prospective customers. I was told that, using the law of averages, if you called a hundred people a day, you would make three appointments, out of which you would end up making one sale, which translated to a $75 to $125 commission.

"It's that simple, boys!" our trainer emphasized with conviction.

Highly motivated to make a hundred phone calls a day, I spent three or four hours in the office with my face stuck to the receiver. Referring to the telephone book, I selected Greek-sounding names and concentrated on that group of potential buyers. Using this method, I was doing better than the "one hundred to three to one" statistical formula. In the first three or four months, I was one of the top salesmen, averaging two to three sales a week, which resulted in some serious money!

During this period, I tried to make an in-person sale to a single mother named Sheila. She was a keypunch operator with limited income and heavy expenses, including the support of her five-year old, mentally disabled son. I stopped in the middle of my presentation because I knew she didn't need encyclopedias and she couldn't afford them anyway.

I felt sorry for Sheila as I listened to her life story over a glass of wine she offered me. Sheila was appreciative of my interest and my listening to the problems she'd had to face. Her husband had left her when he found out his son was not a normal boy.

I left that evening promising her I would call her again for a date, if she were agreeable. As I was going down the outside stairway, Sheila nodded affirmatively and then said she would definitely like to go out with me.

The following weekend, Sheila and her son came to my house, where I had been living alone for more than a year, since Eve left. We spent the evening having a few drinks and some stale snacks I found in the kitchen. Considering this was our first date, our intimacy went much further than I had hoped.

After our first date, I saw Sheila quite regularly, because she was always available every time I needed a companion. Neither of us had made any long-term commitments, nor did we promise one another that we would not see others. In other words, our relationship was rather free and easy, without any restrictions or emotional attachments. Bless her heart, Sheila was there for me almost every time I needed her.

One evening, when I attended a company function at the Playboy Club in New York City, Sheila could not go with me. I asked Joan, an ex-co-worker and casual friend, to accompany me instead. She gladly accepted, drove to NYC, and parked the car a few blocks away from the club.

Right after dinner, Joan and I separated, as both of us found interesting drinking companions with whom we spent the rest of the evening in different areas of the club. The club closed around 2:00 a.m. and I appeared to be the only soul around. I looked all over to find Joan, but she was not inside. Venturing outside, I observed a handful of straggling patrons getting into a taxi, but Joan was not among them. I assumed she must have found someone with whom she had decided to spend the night. Otherwise, she would have waited for me.

I started walking toward the street where I had parked my car, but the many drinks I'd had made my head spin, and I couldn't even tell which direction I was going. I just stood on a street corner, hugging a lamppost and hoping I would soon remember where I'd parked the car. When a young lady stopped to ask me if I was okay, I told her about my dilemma and she offered to help me, but only after I had a drink with her at a bar just down the street.

Later, we finally located the car, after searching every adjacent block near the Playboy Club. I was not in a position to drive, so she offered to take the wheel—but before she got to the end of the block, I realized that she didn't know how to drive! I roughly took the wheel, asked her to get out, and started driving toward the Lincoln Tunnel.

I must have been drunk, because only when I was going through the tunnel did I notice she was still sitting next to me! Anyway, after opening all the windows so that I'd stay alert, I finally made it home—God only knows how, as I was seeing double during the entire trip. In the meantime, I didn't know what to do with the "lady," whose name I don't remember, who wanted to go to bed with me for a "price."

"You mush be out of your mind!" I stormed, slurring my words. "Do you mean you expect me to get involved in some sexual act with you? Haven't you noticed I'm drunk as a skunk? Plus you want me to pay you for shumthing I never asked for in the first place?"

She sidled up to me and groped me in a way that made my skin crawl. "Yes, you brought me here from New York to spend the rest of the night with me," she said throatily, "and you promised you would pay me well after I made you feel really, really good."

I did my best to focus my eyes on her. My stomach turned as I finally realized she was an unattractive prostitute with stiff, cotton candy hair and a heavily made-up face from which a long nose stood out like a vulture's beak.

"Lishen, lady, I'm going to bed alone, do you undershtand? Alone! As for you, you shlut, get out of here before I call the police!"

My little tirade exhausted me and I lay down in bed. I heard her talking to someone on the phone, but then I dozed off for a while. Later, the hooker came to the bedroom, demanding that I wake up to take her to New

York. When I told her that I was in no position to drive, she started cursing and screaming out loud while stalking around the house.

Desperate and not knowing what else to do, I picked up the phone and called Sheila at 4:30 in the morning, begging her to come over to get me out of the mess I was in. Sheila arrived within forty-five minutes and took my unwelcome houseguest to a bus station near her house, which was only seven or eight miles from New York.

The next day, on my way to work, I stopped to get a cup of coffee. When I took out my wallet to pay, I discovered all my money was missing. Shaking my head in disgust, I realized my lady of the night had wiped me out before Sheila took her away.

When I arrived at the office, I called Joan to find out what had happened the night before. She was furious with me for leaving her stranded in the city, forcing her to take a taxi home. Even after I explained that I looked all over for her, she was still angry with me. But a few days later, we were friends again, as she'd gotten a big kick out of my tale about the hooker episode.

Speaking of the "lady," I later discovered she had taken some other valuable items—small enough to fit in her purse—from my house. Well, at least that episode taught me a lesson about depending on the kindness of strangers—especially when you're three sheets to the wind!

Chapter 40

Could It Be True Love?

O ne day, while making my daily phone calls using the Jersey City phone book, I came across another Greek name and called, using the Greek version of my telephone pitch. The elderly lady who answered wasn't interested—but she indicated her tenant, a teacher, probably would be. She gave me the teacher's phone number and suggested I call her after 6:00 p.m. Before I left the office for my next appointment, I called and talked with Angela Miliaresis, who told me she was an art teacher.

Originally from Athens, Angela had joined her relatives (her brother, Bob, and sisters, Katie and Nina) in America to pursue her college studies in fine arts with the intent to then return to Greece. Her interest in the art books was evident right off the bat, and I promised her I would come by her house to show them to her around 8:30 that evening.

I was familiar with almost every neighborhood in Jersey City, as I had made many sales there, especially to Greek families. After I closed the sale on my first appointment, I went to see Angela, who was renting an apartment in a two-story house. Looking dapper, I thought, in my black suit with a white pinstripe, I breezed confidently into the house. There I saw a good-looking young lady in a light green dress standing at the top of the stairs, beckoning me to come up to the second floor.

I remember I paused for a few moments, staring at the winsome "lady in green" as all sorts of wild thoughts whizzed through my mind, including the overconfident and fantastical notion that she could someday become my wife!

After the introductions, I made myself comfortable on the couch and began my presentation while Angela sat in a chair across from me. She was not interested in the encyclopedias, but she adored the set of art books and agreed to buy them on the spot. As I completed the sales contract, I was helpless to stop my gaze from drifting to her petite figure; it was as if a mysterious aura surrounded her, mesmerizing me.

I felt a peculiar sensation being close to Angela, but I could not define what it was. Looking directly into her eyes, I smiled as I thought to myself, *I like what I see.* Her long black hair, majestic brown eyes, and her luminous, flawless skin highlighted the "angelic" face of "my" lady in green. Her unforced composure convinced me she definitely had something special: a childlike innocence, the sincerity of her words, and the kindness behind her big, liquid eyes. Before I left, I assured her that I would call in a few days to let her know of the exact delivery date of the books.

As I had promised, I called Angela one evening and, after I gave her the status of her book order, we talked on the phone for almost half an hour. I told her I was impressed with her and asked if she would like to go out to dinner with me. She accepted and we set up a date for the following Sunday.

That same Sunday, our boss had invited all the sales associates to his house in Connecticut, where we had a nice lobster dinner in his park-like backyard. I had driven to Connecticut with another associate, so I had to take him home first before I met Angela. However, on the way back, we encountered a huge traffic jam, which made me almost two hours late for my date.

When I finally picked her up, I apologized profusely for my tardiness, the reasons for which I explained in detail. I was making a lousy impression on our first date and I knew it, especially when we went to a restaurant and I could only eat a shrimp cocktail because I was still stuffed with all the lobsters we had devoured in Connecticut! The rest of the evening was uneventful as we carried out what I would call a "forced conversation" just to be polite to one another. I knew it was all my fault for scheduling two events on the same day, especially when I was taking out Angela for the first time.

After I dropped Angela off outside her house, I doubted she'd ever want to see me again. But a few weeks later, my friend, Paul, who had moved to New York City, was having a party at his apartment with all sorts of artists invited. Since Angela was an art teacher, I thought she would fit in with this Bohemian crowd, so I asked her to accompany me. She gladly accepted.

Joan, who was a mutual friend of Paul's and mine had also been invited to Paul's party, and asked me if she could ride with me to Paul's place, since she lived only a few miles from my house. I agreed to pick her up from her house and, on that Sunday afternoon, with Joan in the back seat, I went to pick up Angela. She seemed shocked to see another girl in the car. Even after I explained my relationship with Joan, I could sense that Angela was annoyed that I would bring another woman along on our date. *Mike, old man*, I said to myself, *you've blown it again!*

We had a great time at Paul's party. However, at one point, Angela kept asking me if we could leave soon, as she had to get up early the next morning to go to work. I shrugged her off because the night was young and I was having too much fun. It was close to midnight when we finally left, and Angela made it clear that it had been inconsiderate of me to disregard her request to take her home earlier. She was fuming on the way to Jersey City, whereas Joan was quiet as a mouse in the back seat.

All of a sudden, I felt incredibly thirsty, so I stopped at a vending machine to get a quart of milk. Disgust was written all over Angela's face as she observed me guzzling the milk directly from the carton. When I finally took her home, she rushed out of the car and slammed the door behind her.

"Well, I guess I won't ever see her again," I said sheepishly to Joan as she moved into the front passenger seat. We drove the rest of the way home in silence.

I didn't expect to have any more dates with Angela, despite calling her a few times, so I continued going out with Sheila—a casual relationship based on having fun, pure and simple. In the meantime, Eve wouldn't agree with the sale of our house; she was refusing to sign the necessary paperwork, just to punish me.

Finally, her relatives convinced her to go along, and we sold the house to my sister, Despina. She took over the balance of the mortgage after paying off the money we had borrowed for the down payment and another $2,000 to Eve. Although I did not make any profit out of this transaction, I was happy that I did not have to worry about the house's upkeep and its related expenses.

Our divorce was uncontested, because Eve did not show up for the court proceedings.

After this whirlwind of draining events, I found myself in a melancholic state, which adversely affected my initiative to work. I had no drive to go out on appointments, and suddenly everything I wanted to do was a huge effort on my part; it was as if I had a colossal boulder on my shoulders, weighing me down, making every movement agony.

I remember one evening, sitting at a bar drinking a beer, when I realized the only way I'd get out of my rut was by going on vacation, perhaps going back to Greece that coming summer. However, in order to afford a trip like that, I would have to save a few thousand dollars in only three months. That evening, I convinced myself to put my nose to the grindstone. I intended to earn enough money for the trip, because I seriously needed to recharge my batteries by seeing all my friends and relatives once again.

My newfound energy and purpose fueled my willpower to work almost seven days a week for two straight months. Between March and June, I earned enough money to allow me to live for two months in Greece quite comfortably, considering the strong dollar exchange rate.

Toward the end of June in 1968, I was going through a brand new experience: traveling to Europe by plane for the first time in my life! I didn't sleep a wink during the entire trip, as the ten-hour flight was an enjoyable prelude to my vacation. I was stunned when the sun came out around 1:00 a.m. (New York time) as we soared over the Atlantic Ocean. Close to the Irish coastline, I beheld the European continent spread out below me, looking like a perfectly stitched crazy quilt. A beautiful sight!

I stayed on the island of Rhodes almost two months, having the greatest time of my life. I hooked up with some friends and we spent most evenings at an outdoor nightclub called Rhodes By Night. Everyone knew us there, including the members of the band, who joined us after closing, and all of us stayed up until the wee hours of the morning.

I remember one morning, I was having breakfast with Yanni and Minos. Minos was an acquaintance I had met when I was working at my Cousin Louis' restaurant; he just happened to be vacationing at the same time that I was. Yanni, who was working as a waiter at Rhodes by Night, was our exclusive server most of the nights we were there. He was a funny guy with a good sense of humor, but his dream to go to America was never fulfilled, despite the promises many tourists had made to help him immigrate to America.

When I told him I would try my best to make it possible for him to go to America, his answer was, "I know you mean well, Mike, but when you go back, you will forget all about me."

"Yanni, I know I can't convince you that I will do more than all the others promised you," I replied. "But I believe actions speak louder than words." I winked and added mysteriously, "So, just wait and see, my friend, just wait and see!"

That morning, we had *patsas*, a traditional Greek breakfast, which is a type of soup made out of the intestines and stomach of a lamb after they are boiled clean to use as the soup base. This dish is also reputed to be an excellent antidote for a hangover, so we usually had it for breakfast as our epilogue to an all-nighter.

After returning my rented car, I decided to take the bus the first time I went to the village. I intended to stay there for three or four days in my sister Mary's vacant village house. As I sat on the left side of the bus a few rows from the back, I spotted a lady a few seats in front of me on the opposite side who looked familiar. When she turned around, it didn't take me long to realize it was Seva, who looked more beautiful than the last time I had seen her, six years earlier in Germany.

Although I was sure she had noticed me, when we got off the bus in the village, Seva and I went our separate ways without saying even a simple hello to one another, despite all the good and bad times we had gone through in both Greece and Germany.

I was bothered of the fact that she didn't even try to approach me. She got off the bus before me and immediately ran off to meet her family or friends who were waiting for her without making an effort to turn around to see if I got off the bus. I knew that during my stay in the village, as small as it was, I was sure to run into her and satisfy my urge to see her up close.

A few days later, we met at a mutual friend's house, where we spent a few hours reviewing our past experiences together. We both realized how immaturely we had handled a relationship that was shaky from the onset. I could see how much she had matured and wished that the girl I knew then had the serenity, wisdom, and logical mind she possessed today. Alas, she was a married woman now. I had had my chance with her and now I would have to stay away from her once and for all, as I respected the sanctity of marriage.

That same evening, we got together with a few people I knew at a café, enjoying drinks and hot and cold delicacies, an assortment of feta cheese, olives, souvlaki (a kebab variety), Greek salad, fried smelts, and cod fish with garlic sauce. A dog belonging to a member of our party lay next to my chair, thumping his tail and begging for food. Everyone at the table was stunned when I asked the waiter to grill a big steak for the dog!

Since I was picking up the tab for the night, no one gave me a hard time, but I'm sure they thought this was a crazy extravagance on my part. Anyway, after the waiter brought the steak to the table, I cut it up into bite-sized pieces and began feeding the adorable pooch the best meal of his life.

After we all left the café, the dog followed me to my sister Mary's house, instead of going with his owner. I sat outside and petted the dog as he lay next to me, contentedly wagging his tail and smiling his drooling dog smile. It was as if he wanted to tell me "thank you" for the delicious dinner and for the attention I had shown him. Holding a drink in my hand, I let myself become one with the dark stillness of the night. The countless stars flickering across the cloudless sky were the only light for miles and miles around.

It was a perfect moment for reflecting on my recent past. Here I was, alone again, having failed to develop a bond with Seva before I met Eve. More recently, I had met Angela, who had given me a few chances to court her in a manner suitable to her expectations.

Feeling sad, I sighed deeply. Suddenly I felt a warm, pleasant sensation on my hand. I smiled as the dog began fondly licking me, as if he sensed the emotional turmoil I was experiencing.

Soon afterwards, I went to bed. I left the dog outside, assuming he would eventually go home to his master. However, when I woke up later in the morning, I found the dog still waiting for me outside. At that moment, I understood the degree of appreciation the dog had for me. It was because I had shown him genuine affection and an unconditional compassion I had never felt for or shared with any human being.

For the first time in my life, I understood the meaning of devotion and true love. Only a dog had been able to teach me that valuable lesson.

The rest of my vacation in Rhodes became a routine of spending my time between Rhodes by Night at night and the beaches during the day. By the last week of my stay, I wanted to go back to America. I had partied quite enough, thank you, for seven weeks. Before I left Rhodes, I sent postcards to many friends, including Sheila and Angela, to whom I wrote a brief note highlighting some of the memorable moments I had experienced on the beautiful island.

Back in the States in late August of 1968, my family addressed all the preparations for my sister Katina's upcoming wedding to Emmanuel, who was also a product of the Agios Isidoros village. Both the religious and reception ceremonies were similar to those of a typical Greek wedding.

My brother, George, Despina, and I were responsible for all the reception expenses, but because I came back from vacation a few weeks before the wedding, I was completely broke. I asked George to cover my share, and instead of a repayment, he accepted the accordion my friend Paul had given me.

George was happy with that arrangement and started learning how to play the accordion immediately, eventually becoming quite a virtuoso. In fact, he still owns the instrument and plays it during special or traditional occasions, such as the serenading that goes on during the "gown dressing" of the bride prior to the religious wedding ceremony.

During baseball's World Series in October of 1968—which pitted the defending champion St. Louis Cardinals against the Detroit Tigers—my friend, Minos, told me he was in big, BIG trouble. The mob was after him to repay some bets he had lost in the underworld sports betting ring. He begged me to lend him $500, because if he didn't pay them within a day or so, he might be "sleeping with the fishes," in the vernacular of the Mafia. Not having any money, I took a loan from my bank and gave Minos the half a grand with the understanding that he would pay me back in monthly installments.

At the same time, I was corresponding with my friend Yanni in Greece, who wrote me that he was having difficulties getting a tourist visa from the American consulate. He said he planned to fly to Algiers, where others of his acquaintance had been successful in getting their papers. When he called from Algiers to report that he had received the visa, I told him I would buy his plane ticket, which he could pick up at the airport in Algiers.

I borrowed another $500 from my bank and bought the ticket for Yanni, who finally arrived in America in October of 1968. He recalled my cryptic "Just wait and see!" comment back in Rhodes and was so appreciative that I was a man of my word. He promised he would repay me tenfold as soon as he got on his feet financially in America.

Within a week, I found a place for Yanni to stay as well as job at a Greek restaurant in New York City. Yanni, Minos, and I were hanging around all the time, mostly in Big Apple nightclubs after Yanni finished his shift at the restaurant.

In November of 1968, I learned that Minos had disappeared. The most likely scenario was that he had fled to Greece. I found out he had gambled and lost the money I had given him—not to mention the tidy sums he had bummed from many other people—instead of repaying the mob for his outstanding debts. Then he had quickly fled the country because, this time, his life really was in jeopardy. The Mafia had no sympathy for welchers who skipped out on a debt.

When I approached his brother to tell him that Minos still owed me $400, he humbly apologized and pointed out that I was not the only one he had taken money from; he had borrowed from all his family and friends to satisfy his gambling addiction. Now he was running for his life, hoping the mobsters would never find him. But he would always live in fear, no matter how far away he went or how cleverly he hid himself.

I was still seeing Sheila once in a while, but nothing serious seemed to be developing. The weekend before Thanksgiving, I was planning on going out with Sheila until I received an unexpected phone call from Angela, who thanked me for the postcard I had sent her. She asked if I wanted to accompany her to an affair in New York being held at one of the university club facilities in Manhattan (I can't recall which one).

The event had been organized by the Hellenic University Club, a cultural and educational organization whose members are college graduates of Greek descent. The club members represent a wide range of professions. Angela also asked me if I knew someone else— male, of course—who might join us, since her friend Rena was also planning to attend the affair. Angela told me she had been in Athens exactly the same two months I was in Rhodes and had found my postcard when she returned.

I certainly had thought that Angela had forgotten all about me, due to my awkward behavior on our last two dates. Now I was curious about why she had taken the initiative to invite me to the Greek soirée, which was scheduled for Saturday night.

My friend, Steve Kontos, who accepted the invitation to join us, drove together with me to Jersey City to pick up our dates at Angela's apartment. There I supposedly met Rena for the first time—but as we shook hands, she insisted we had first met about six months earlier in her sister's house, when I tried to sell them a set of books. I then remembered her as the quiet girl who had sat in a corner during my presentation. As a newcomer from Greece attending college in America, she had probably been either homesick or lonely in a country where the lifestyle is a race in the fast lane with no end in sight.

At the affair in New York, Angela and I got along well. We began getting to know one another better over dancing and stimulating conversation, but Steve and Rena didn't seem to be clicking. In fact, Angela and I thought they were bored to tears and couldn't wait to get out of there!

As Steve drove us home, Angela and I held hands in the back seat, telling one another what a wonderful time we'd had and how much we'd enjoyed each other's company. At that moment, I asked her if she wanted to go out the following weekend to a restaurant I knew in Sayreville, New Jersey, where they had a great variety show during and after dinner. Because it would be Thanksgiving weekend, Angela was not sure if she could make it, but she promised to let me know.

Chapter 41

Can't Get Her Out of My Head

Over the next few days, I could not get Angela off my mind. It seemed as if she were a completely different person than the one I had met so many months earlier. The day before Thanksgiving, I sent her a dozen red roses with a note saying I couldn't wait to see her beautiful face again. The day after Thanksgiving, Angela called me, thanking me for the beautiful roses as well as the flattering note. Most of all, she wanted me to know she couldn't wait to go out with me on Saturday night.

Wearing a simple but elegant red-orange silk dress and a stylish black coat, Angela looked beautiful and was in a jolly mood as we drove over the Bayonne Bridge en route to the Madison Restaurant. Both of us sang along with a song on the radio, the bittersweet ballad "Those Were the Days" by Apple songstress Mary Hopkin. It was a song that, in years to come, would always remind us of the happy moments we experienced as we traversed the scenic, steel arch bridge that connects Bayonne, New Jersey with Staten Island, New York.

Neither of us could explain why we were in such good spirits. It was as if we were without a care in the world for the duration of that unforgettable song, which seemed to last for a whole hour.

At the restaurant, we enjoyed the dinner and the first-class variety show, which featured a cavalcade of comedians, dancers, and other performers. On the way home, Angela said she'd had a great time.

It was only when we were at her apartment that she let me kiss her for the first time. It was a kiss that she shared with me wholeheartedly, a kiss that showed me how we had suddenly bonded; a kiss with a definite promise that the best was yet to come. I was spending the most wonderful evening with the most precious lady, whom I utterly adored and also greatly respected.

After that evening, we talked on the phone three or four times a day and went out almost every other day. It appeared that our relationship started going through the all-important nurturing stage, when we were both like tender young seedlings whose relationship needed patience, sweet talk, and tender loving care in order to thrive and weather the cruel elements life can throw at you.

During the first three months, we became more aware and tolerant of one another's idiosyncrasies. Sure, we had some ups and downs—often having little arguments or disagreements—but we both felt certain that, in time, we would get used to one another.

On my birthday—Tuesday, December 10, 1968—I bought a bottle of red wine and went to Angela's apartment to have a toast to celebrate the occasion. I don't remember the reason why, but we had an argument that resulted in me having to drink the whole bottle of wine, all by myself! Then, as I was leaving her apartment, instead of saying good night I said sarcastically, "Thanks a lot for the birthday present!"

It didn't take us long after my birthday incident to get back to normalcy, enjoying each other's company as well as having long phone conversations when we were home at night. During the holidays, we had attended a few house parties, including the one on New Year's Eve. It was there that I found out Angela didn't particularly like to dance, except for the slow, traditional tunes. I pretty much wanted to kick up my heels to whatever the band was playing, but I respected Angela's limitations in that area and compromised.

Everything was going well until the middle of February 1969, when some argument or disagreement (the reasons for which, forty years later, totally escape me) caused us to break up. Myopically, we viewed this setback as the end of our relationship, but I had forgotten we had already agreed to attend my company's annual, black-tie dinner at the Waldorf Astoria. So, four days before the dinner, Angela told me it was over between us and she would not go with me that Saturday night. I begged her to reconsider, but she told me her mind was already made up and she thought it would be better for both of us if we didn't drag it out any longer.

When I realized I was losing her, I recognized how important she was to me, because of the degree of hurt I was experiencing. On Tuesday, February 18, I got home late, grabbed a bottle of Scotch, and made an earnest effort to wash my problems away. I just couldn't digest the fact that our relationship was over, just as I was beginning to fall in love with her.

Taking another sip of whisky, I cried out, "No, no, it's not over! Oh, God, I love her so much and I won't give up so easily." Around four in the morning, drowsy from the liquor and my lovelorn feelings, I finally fell asleep on the couch. During this period, I started writing a poem about Angela, which I finished many months later.

But now I had to address my immediate problem of finding someone else to go to the company dinner with me. Unfortunately, Sheila was out of town at that time; that meant I had three days to choose another lady friend from among my past acquaintances. So, I opened my little black book and started calling them, one by one, in alphabetical order.

One of the most peculiar phone calls was when Shelly's mother answered and told me Shelly couldn't come to the phone at that moment because, in ten minutes, she was going to the church to get married! I thought this was the most ironic incident, as my timing had been impeccable!

The only one who accepted my invitation was Karen, whom I had met at my friend Steve's Linden House restaurant. She was a beautiful young lady, but she lamented she didn't have anything to wear to such a ritzy affair. I told her not to worry, because I was willing to buy her a dress. That made her happy, so we agreed to meet the following day (Friday) outside the building where she worked, around her quitting time, which was five o'clock.

That Macy's store—in those years, it was called Bamberger's before they merged with Macy's—was just across the street, so we could just walk over and pick out whatever dress struck her fancy. I waited for an hour, but Karen never came out of the front door, through which a steady stream of "thank God it's Friday" workers were emerging. Since I had no way to get in touch with her, and she was likewise unable to communicate with me if some urgent matter had held her up, I decided to leave and activate what I called my emergency plan.

I drove to Greenwich Village in New York City where I located an artist who agreed to paint Angela's portrait from a picture I had with me. I could have painted the portrait myself, but it would have taken me at least two or three days. I knew that having someone else paint the portrait and present it to her as if I had done it was blatantly deceptive, but I logically thought that sometimes the end justifies the means. I was so desperate to get Angela back. Breathlessly, I explained the situation to the artist, who promised he would have the portrait ready in about two hours.

I then drove to Paul's apartment, where we spent some time analyzing all the unpleasant events I had been going through of late. Paul's advice was that everything happens for a reason and in the end, things fall into place.

After I left Paul's place, I picked up the portrait from the Village and drove back to New Jersey. It was almost 10:00 p.m. when I called Angela on that Friday night. She answered the phone with a surprised tone in her voice, questioning why I was still calling her, since she had decided to call it quits.

"Listen to what I have to say," I said calmly in a near-whisper. "It will only take a few minutes."

"Okay, go ahead," she said brusquely, as if she wanted to get it over with.

I took a deep breath and spoke from the heart. "I know what we thought we had is over, but I am going to ask you one more favor before we go our separate ways. I would like to see you one more time. Please go to tomorrow's affair with me and let's view this as a separation celebration. Let's spend our last good-bye in style, and I will promise you I won't bother you again. After all, we are civilized adults. By the way, I also have a gift for you so that you'll remember me as a friend, if nothing else."

After a long silence, she finally spoke. "I'm not sure if this is a good idea, but let me think about it and I will call you in the morning."

"Okay, that's fair," I said. "We'll talk tomorrow. Good night!"

When Angela called me the next day, I couldn't predict what she had finally decided, but she said she would go with me. I thanked her for the understanding she had shown me and told her that I would be at her place around four that afternoon.

On my way to her apartment, I stopped at a flower shop and picked up a dozen red roses. I was dressed in a tuxedo, holding the roses in one hand and the wrapped portrait in the other, when Angela opened the door for me.

"Wow, you look so handsome!" she said, rather amazed at how well I was turned out.

"Thank you, and YOU look as beautiful as ever," I said as I gave her a soft kiss on the cheek. She loved the fragrant roses, which she placed in a vase, but the flattering portrait was totally unexpected and knocked her off her feet. The black and white portrait was painted from a small picture Angela had given me, the same one she used for her college yearbook, highlighting her long black hair and her "Mona Lisa" smile.

We were both in a good mood when we sat down for dinner at the Waldorf Astoria and had a glass of wine. We felt as though we were spending our last night together, so we "let it all hang out," as we said back then, tossing our inhibitions to the wind. We danced more that evening than all the other times combined since I've known Angela.

Right after dinner, the guest of honor, Hubert Humphrey, who was associated with our company, gave a speech during which he poked fun at himself for losing his presidential bid to Richard Nixon. Angela and I commented on the fact that we were dancing next to a humble man who almost became the president of United States!

After coffee and dessert, neither of us was ready to go home, so we decided to go to see our friend Yanni at the restaurant where he worked. It was almost closing time when we got there, and Yanni was about to give the check to his last customers. We took Yanni to a nearby Greek nightclub called Mykonos, which had a cozy décor highlighted by blue and white accents, depicting an overall setting that resembled the actual island for which it was named.

Even Yanni couldn't believe the jolly mood we were in that night. He commented that this was the first time he had seen us looking so happy together. We were indeed happy beyond words about the way the night was progressing, considering that this was supposed to be our last hurrah as a couple. Instead, it was turning into an unforgettable experience that I was sure would revitalize our relationship, investing it with a stronger dose of understanding and caring for one another.

After Mykonos, we took Yanni home to New Jersey—but even then, Angela was not ready to call it a night. The Newark State College (later renamed "Kean" University) she had graduated from was only a few miles from where we dropped off Yanni. Angela wanted to take a nostalgic drive through the college campus. She became a little emotional as we slowly cruised the dark, narrow lanes, which held so many memories for her.

Just before we left the college grounds, Angela came close to me, hugged me, and gave me a long, passionate kiss. "I'm so happy, being with you tonight," she said, her eyes wet with tears of joy.

In the wee hours before dawn, we finally made it back to Angela's apartment. We looked deeply into each other's eyes, marveling over the complete turnaround of what we had thought was the end of us. At that moment, I remembered the sage words my friend, Paul, had said to me the day before: "When you do what you think is right, things usually fall into place."

Well, he was right! Everything I could ever hope for or dream about came true that night. This was unquestionably one of the most unforgettable nights of our relationship, a milestone that became the cornerstone of our bond.

THREE GRAINS OF WHEAT

After that fateful night, our romance blossomed without any serious arguments or major disagreements rearing their ugly heads. One of the most memorable days we spent together was when we drove toward the Catskill Mountains and ended up at a mountain top restaurant sometime in the late afternoon. It was a little early for dinner, so after we ordered two drinks, we played a few rounds of our favorite word game.

The rules of the crossword-like game are as follows: Each player draws twenty-five squares in rows of five on a piece of paper. The objective is to make as many words as possible in both vertical and horizontal directions. Each player calls one letter at a time, which must be used by both players as they take turns until all twenty-five squares are filled. Each letter has a value of one point. This simple but fun game was an excellent time-filler.

Our prime rib dinner that night was one of the most delicious meals we'd ever had. The entire evening was magical; I was head-over-heels in love with Angela and kept telling her so, over and over. We both felt close to one another. We were convinced that nothing could shake or damage the relationship we were rebuilding on the solid footing of love and understanding.

Chapter 42

What a Man Will Do for Love

During this period, when we went out to dinner or to some social function, we often invited Angela's friend, Rena, to join us, as she was not dating anyone regularly. I remember one night when the three of us left a nightclub in New York, driving toward the Lincoln Tunnel. It must have been after midnight when Angela said she had a craving for *keftedakia*—a Greek dish made of small meatballs fried in olive oil. Without missing a beat, I said, "I'll get them for you" and made a left turn, heading toward a Greek restaurant close to the Port Authority terminal. Both Rena and Angela scoffed, saying that I wouldn't possibly be able to find a Greek restaurant open at that late hour.

When I stopped in front of the restaurant, I saw that the front door was indeed locked, but that did not stop me. I asked the girls to wait in the car and ran around the building to the back door. I rushed in through the back door, but the staff told me that the place was closed and everything was already shut down.

When I pleaded with the manager that my "pregnant wife" (of course she was not pregnant—we weren't even married at the time) absolutely had to have *keftedakia* and I was not leaving the restaurant without them, he ordered one of the cooks to prepare an order. Angela and Rena could not believe it when they saw me emerge through the front door, holding a take-out plate full of *keftedakia* and grinning from ear to ear!

"What a guy!" Rena chortled to Angela as we all dived into the delicious treat. "He must love you very much to bend over backwards just to satisfy your craving!" I mention this little story because it has been brought up many times over the years as an example of how much you can do for, or give to, the one you unconditionally love.

During the summer months, Angela convinced me to go back to school. I took two courses, which I had to complete in one month. I can say that it was a demanding schedule, attending college every day from 8:30 a.m. to 3:00 p.m. and having to write an essay almost every day for the English course I was taking, all the while still working in the evenings. At any rate, I finished both courses with good marks.

On July 20, 1969, along with the rest of America and the world, Angela and I watched the first moon landing on television. The avuncular newsman Walter Cronkite spoke for everyone when he said, "Whew, boy!" with tears in his eyes and a huge grin on his face as Apollo 11 set down on the lunar surface. As Cronkite later commented, it was indeed the pinnacle of man's achievements in the twentieth century. I was so happy to witness it with my beloved Angela.

As for my job, I was not doing very well. My sales had dropped so low, my boss felt it was necessary to call Angela to his office to make her aware that, ever since I had met her, my work ethic had begun to deteriorate.

I knew Angela was the reason for my poor performance, because right from the start, she had believed the sales job was not suitable for me. This had been a frequent topic of discussion from the onset of our relationship. She was convinced I had hidden talents we should uncover, cultivate, and utilize in another area, so I could make the most of my gifts while getting paid at the same time.

Following the recommendation of a well-educated friend of the family, I took a three-day seminar at Stevens Institute of Technology in Hoboken, New Jersey, to determine the areas in which my talents or strengths could be best utilized. The results revealed an aptitude for social work, and I was advised to seek a vocation where I had the opportunity to help others.

One evening, Angela and I were walking through a small park in Jersey City, trying to decide what career I should pursue. We both realized that a career in the social work sector would not be profitable enough to support a family if Angela stopped working. So I brought up the subject of a computer school my coworker Jon was attending.

I told Angela that, according to Jon, computer programming was the choice career of the future. I honestly had no idea what computer programming was or even what computers did, but because Jon was so excited about this burgeoning field, I was willing to give it a look-see.

I was impressed with the International Institute of Technology in Edison, New Jersey. I met with the school director, who convinced me to enroll and embark on an intensive, seven-month schedule. I had to borrow a few thousand dollars to prepay the tuition expenses, a loan my bank would not give me unless someone with established credit would co-sign. Fortunately, Angela's sister, Katie, offered to co-sign the two-year loan.

For the new school year in September, Angela found another teaching position close to the area we were planning to live. You see, we were passionately in love, and the next logical step was for us to tie the knot. We found a garden apartment just across from a married couple, Kally and Alex, whom we already knew because Alex was the brother of Angela's good friend, Angie.

I remember the end of the baseball season in October when Alex and I watched the New York Mets, our beloved Cinderella team, win the 1969 World Series over the Baltimore Orioles. (Incidentally, Alex had an exceptional memory, a good sense of humor, and could tell a joke like a professional. He could memorize the monologue of a comedian on television and repeat it later without missing a word. His favorite was Jackie Vernon's slide presentation of his vacation to the Grand Canyon, a monologue in which Alex could perfectly impersonate using Vernon's dull, low-key delivery and self-deprecating humor.)

After we bought the bare minimum of furniture we could afford, plus using whatever Angela had in her old place, we furnished the one-bedroom apartment the best way we could. Without too much planning, we got married on Sunday, November 2, 1969.

A small gathering of the immediate family attended the religious ceremony, which was performed by Angela's brother-in-law, Rev. Dr. Father John Poulos, whose wife, Katie, had co-signed our loan. I could certainly write an entire book about Father Poulos' life and extraordinary accomplishments, as he was one of the most remarkable people I have ever met.

After the religious ceremony, with Angie as the maid of honor (our *koumbara*, as we say in Greek), we had dinner at a nearby restaurant without the traditional reception trappings. Neither Angela nor I believed we needed the hoopla of an extravagant wedding.

As far as jewelry was concerned, Angela did not want to have the diamond ring that traditionally symbolizes engagement; we only bought wedding bands, as we thought these would suffice to get us through the religious ceremony.

We stayed at the restaurant until about 8:00 p.m. We had already made plans to spend part of our honeymoon in Quebec City, so right after dinner, we began driving toward upstate New York on the throughway.

It was a foggy, misty, drizzling November night, which made driving a little difficult, so we decided to stop at a motor inn near Albany, where we spent our first night as a married couple. (In the interest of decorum, dear reader, I shall provide no intimate details here, except to say it was a night to remember!)

The next day, we arrived in Quebec City, a place I had promised myself I would definitely revisit someday. That day happened to be on my honeymoon, with my lovely wife, the heaven-sent *Angel*-a—the woman I adored and was so ecstatically happy with—at my side.

We explored some of the city's most interesting spots during the three days of our stay, although on the second day, Angela got a little sick and had to take antibiotics for some sort of sinus or ear infection. On our last night, we went to a lounge where we joined a sing-along crowd, most of whom sang French songs.

At one point, there was a solo singing round. When it was my turn, I chose the German song "Lili Marlene," which had been immensely popular during World War II and had become Marlene Dietrich's trademark song. Based on the rousing applause I received, I must have been pretty damn good!

That night, a distinguished gentleman came to our table and introduced himself as a doctor and an ex -professional hockey player. Apparently, he must have been impressed with Angela, because he promised he would send her flowers at the hotel where we were staying. Although we checked out around noon time, the flowers never came!

Our next stop was Montreal, where we stayed at the Holiday Inn downtown. We enjoyed the city's nightlife, and during the day, we visited some of the must-see places in the area. At one point, Angela convinced me to buy a sport outfit—a blue blazer with gray pants, a light purple shirt, and a matching tie. I was a smoker then and vividly recall the comment the girl behind the register made when I went to buy a pack of cigarettes: "Wow, I'm sure you must be a movie star!" Well, she made my day!

That evening, we went to a Greek nightclub where we had a wonderful time listening to familiar tunes that brought back memories of our homeland.

We headed back to our apartment in New Jersey, and Angela went to work the day after our return. Our honeymoon week happened to coincide with the teacher's convention, during which schools are closed. At the same time, I started school at the International Institute and, in the evenings, I was able to schedule some appointments for possible book sales.

Preparing dinner in the evenings fell to me, because Angela had never been exposed to the art of cooking. I took Angela under my culinary wing and she proved an apt pupil, learning the basics quickly.

She couldn't believe it when I told her that many people didn't know how to boil water to make a cup of tea. I explained what a French chef in

Switzerland had taught me regarding boiling water, either for tea or instant coffee. The ideal way is to let the water come to a boil and then turn it off after three seconds, just about when the boiling water has taken three turns. The chef claimed that if you let it boil longer, the water loses certain properties, thus affecting the taste of your tea. So don't take it as an insult if someone asks you if you know how to boil water!

During the first few months, we entertained some of our friends and family members. Although I was still doing most of the cooking, Angela was coming right along in that department. She was indeed determined to master the art of cooking so that—as she claimed—I wouldn't always get all the credit and praise from our guests

My friend, Yanni, the fellow I helped to come to America, started going out with a lady named Naomi, who happened to be the only child in a well-to-do family. It didn't take Naomi long to fall in love with Yanni, as he was a good-looking man. Plus, having worked as a waiter for many years, he had become a smooth operator who had a way with women.

A few months down the road, he informed us he was getting married to Naomi and he wanted me to be the best man. I gladly agreed. The wedding was scheduled to take place at an upscale hotel in New York City (the name of which I don't recall) within the next three months.

I occasionally reminded Yanni that he still owed me the expenses I had incurred for his trip to America, an amount I'd had to borrow from the bank. I emphasized to Yanni that, because I was going to school on a full-time basis, my funds were limited and it would be a great help if he would start paying me off. He apologized for neglecting to take care of the debt and agreed to pay $50.00 every two weeks.

Before the wedding, he made three payments, but that was where he stopped. It was ironic that my other friend, Minos, who owed me almost the same amount as Yanni, had also made the first few payments before he disappeared back to Greece.

Angela and I went to Yanni's wedding, a first-class affair on the seventh floor of the hotel, which was close to Carnegie Hall. Naomi's rich father could afford such a lavish event for his only daughter and had spared no expense. Some of the notable features of the affair were the cold seafood hors d'oeuvres section, where the bride's and groom's names were carved in an abstract ice sculpture. Next to the sculpture was a table with caviar of various colors (black, red, and brown). They had also hired two bands that played Greek, American, and Jewish songs during the entire evening.

Just before the start of the ceremony, Yanni came over to our table to inform me that, because of business reasons, he also had chosen another person as the best man, and if I didn't mind, he would be recognized during the announcements. However, he continued, I could still stand next to him during the ceremony.

Yanni went on to explain that his future father-in-law was planning to buy a restaurant in an upscale town in Bergen County of New Jersey for Yanni as a wedding gift, and the new "best man" had something to do with it, or he was the current restaurant owner.

"Listen, I will make it easy for you," I told Yanni. "Forget about me being extra baggage as a second best man and go ahead with your plans. As for me, I get the message loud and clear, so do what you think is right for your business."

"But Mike, you are my best friend!" Yanni protested apologetically. "You've done so much for me; please try to understand my position—"

"No, Yanni, *you* are the one who does not understand," I interrupted him. "You have no idea what friendship means. You really don't. Let's just leave it at that and go on with your wedding."

Angela and I were the first ones to leave, right after they served coffee. My last words to Yanni were, "Perhaps someday I will bump into you again."

Chapter 43

New and Unusual Passions

For the first time in my life, I was enjoying school immensely, despite the challenging computer programming courses. I approached the intricacies of programming like a game or a puzzle, and I didn't mind spending hours on end on my homework assignments, which seemed more like a fun and engaging hobby than drudgery.

It might sound strange, but on weekends, I couldn't wait for Monday so that I could go back to school! I was one of the top two students in my class of thirty, along with my good friend Bruce, who had come back from Vietnam after serving more than a year in the army. Fortunately, Bruce's veteran's benefits were enough to cover his school tuition.

As time went on, both our classmates and our instructors came to regard Bruce and me as computer whizzes. In fact, we frequently asked our instructors for extracurricular projects, because we finished our regular work ahead of everyone else.

Angela and I were happy with our decision for me to begin a career in the burgeoning computer field. Just about two weeks before I finished school, we found out that Angela was pregnant with our first child. Although the birth of the child was still more than seven months away, I was concerned about finding a job as soon as possible.

Bruce and I finished the course in June of 1970 with a grade point average of 98 percent. I immediately started looking for a job, and the school's job placement manager set up an appointment for an interview for me with an insurance company. After filling out the application paperwork, I took a written aptitude test, which I completed with ease, thinking that I did fairly well. I then met with the manager of the department, Steve

Johnson, who seemed impressed with me after I correctly answered every technical question he asked.

When I got home that day, I was certain I would get the job—until I received a phone call from Steve informing me that my test results were inadequate, especially in the math section. I was stunned, because the math problems were the easiest part of the multiple-choice test.

The next day, Steve got a copy of my test results. He called me later that evening. When I told him I was sure I had the correct solution to every math problem, he started going over the math questions and asked me to give him the answers.

To his surprise, Steve told me that I had answered all the questions correctly, but I had checked the wrong boxes! I was absolutely certain that Steve liked me and I knew he would do everything to convince the human resources manager to hire me. And so he did.

Steve had given me some details of the job I wasn't supposed to know, such as my starting date and annual salary. He also had told me that someone from Human Resources would be contacting me with all the details. Just before five o'clock, I received a call from the personnel manager, who basically repeated what Steve had already told me and said I would be getting a letter in the mail with all the remaining details and provisions of the job offer, including a medical exam and so forth.

Later that evening, during dinner, Angela and I celebrated the happy event with a bottle of red wine. My starting date was July 13 and the job location was in New York City, close to Wall Street, although the company had already committed to move to New Jersey within one year.

Once on board with the insurance company, I took the train to Newark, then the PATH (Port Authority Trans-Hudson Corporation) rapid-transit system to the World Trade Center station, and then I had another fifteen-minute walk to the office. Overall, my commute lasted about an hour and a half, but it was worth it. Most of the time, my boss, Steve, took the same train. He lived in the next town, close to the train station.

Early on, Steve sent a memo to the personnel manager indicating he was satisfied with my performance and saying that my contributions to the department were far greater than what was expected of a programmer trainee. Steve was taking care of me in all job-related aspects. Knowing he was looking for a new programmer, I recommended Bruce as an excellent candidate for the opening. I also emphasized that Bruce and I had finished with the top two grades in our class.

When I called Bruce to tell him about the job opportunity, he lamented the fact that, after going on a few interviews, he hadn't been able to find a job in the computer programming field and was toiling away at the same milk plant where his father had worked for many years. Bruce came in for an interview and, a week later, to the satisfaction of us both, he was hired. After three months, I received an outstanding job performance evaluation, accompanied by a 25 percent raise. I was now making $9,500 a year, which was a little above average in 1970.

Angela kept teaching her art classes in two different schools while her pregnancy progressed without any problems. We were both impatiently waiting for the birth of our first child, which was due around the second week of February, 1971.

During the Christmas holidays, our four-year-old niece, Athy, spent a few days with us in our apartment. Also, the day after Christmas, Rena and her friend, Anna, came over for an early dinner and spent the evening with us, enjoying the full pitcher of margaritas I had prepared. With everyone in a jolly mood, Anna asked Angela and me if we knew of any eligible bachelors to join us, since she and Rena were unattached. Offhand, the only one who came to mind was Bruce, so I decided to call him. I said there were two young, attractive, and vivacious girls with us in need of male companionship.

Bruce came over, sat down between the two bachelorettes, and joined the margarita party. While I played the guitar, Rena began her usual solo dancing routine, shaking her shapely tush in Bruce's face and mesmerizing the poor devil with her exotic movements. We all had a great time that evening. Fortunately, little Athy was occupied with a puzzle she was trying to put together, ignoring the adult antics going on around her.

Back at work, Bruce admitted he liked Rena and asked me if I could give him her phone number. I honestly had thought Bruce would have been more interested in Anna, because she was more reserved—unlike Rena, whose flamboyance said, "Hey, look at me, don't I look great?" In other words, her outgoingness and assertive nature were at odds with Bruce's quiet personality. Nevertheless, it was the beginning of their relationship. They had many ups and downs during the first few months, but in the end, they managed to make it work.

Chapter 44

Fatherhood

On January 30, 1971, Angela and I went to our favorite Madison Restaurant in Sayreville with my cousin, Andy, and his wife, Betty. It was a nostalgic event for Angela and me. This was the same restaurant where our relationship had begun to flourish after we bonded over the song "Those Were the Days" while driving over the Bayonne Bridge.

The manager gave us a table close to the stage, where the various entertainers would perform. We enjoyed the dinner as well as the two-hour show. A beautiful, voluptuous belly dancer was the highlight of the night, but the comedian was also funny. In fact, I still remember one of his best jokes, which went like this:

"A lady asked a doctor how she could improve her small breast size. The doctor suggested that she go to a cold place, such as Alaska, and stay there for two weeks. So she went to Alaska where she stayed for four weeks, twice as long as the doctor suggested. After a month, she came back like this." (Here the comedian curled the fingers of both hands in front of his chest, indicating a large cup size). Then, after a short pause, he added, "Arthritis in both hands."

With that joke, he ended the show around midnight. By the time we got home, it was almost 1:00 a.m. I don't think we had been asleep for more than four hours when Angela nudged me with her elbow and said, "My water just broke! I think we're having a baby!"

"Oh, my God, we're having a baby!" I shouted, jumping out of bed. "Yippee, we're going to have *our baby*!" Angela's suitcase wasn't packed yet, because we had another two weeks before the due date, according to her doctor. So we packed some essential items, called the doctor, and headed for the hospital, which was only a few miles away.

Checking Angela's condition, the obstetrician informed us we had a way to go, because she was hardly dilated. The doctor also informed us that the anesthesiologists were on strike and that she should be prepared for a natural childbirth. Before the doctor left, he said, "Since we don't expect the baby to arrive before late afternoon, I will go to church now and say a prayer for you."

After he had gone, Angela began shouting out loud about the unbearable pain she felt, especially in her back. She was having what is termed a "dry birth," a result of her water breaking too early. I held her hand while she screamed, "Oh, God, it hurts so much!"

She said she wanted to be left alone, so I went back to the waiting room, where I joined another expectant father who was facing a completely different problem. He explained that he had brought his wife to the hospital because she had severe stomach pains, but when she was examined, they found out she was pregnant and ready to deliver their second child! The father himself was a heavyset fellow, and, as he explained, his wife weighed more than 230 pounds. No doubt they assumed she had simply gained some extra pounds and never suspected she was pregnant.

Angela was given some mild painkillers, but for the most part, they were ineffective. Finally, at 4:34 p.m., Angela gave birth to our precious boy, whom we later named Alexander.

"Mike, we have a handsome boy," Angela told me as the nurses wheeled her to the recovery room. She was haggard from the ordeal, but to me, she was the most beautiful creature on earth. Her eyes had never looked so soulful or her smile more beatific. But she added pointedly, "No more children, darling. I can't go through this again."

I then went to a window, stared upward into the misty January sky, and, in my own way, I thanked God for giving me the most priceless gift anyone could possess. Thinking about the new life Angela and I had brought into the world, with God's grace guiding the miracle, I felt humbled and empowered at the same time. I couldn't help shedding a few tears of happiness for the awesome feelings I was experiencing for the first time in my life. I truly understood the concept of fatherhood overtaking my entire existence, a unique phenomenon whose mystifying effect on the psyche can't be expressed in words.

Later on, I went to see my son in the nursery room, where he was being kept along with the other newborns. Fortunately, he was near the glass partition, so I had a clear view of the beautiful baby face in his little bassinette. He was probably sleeping, as his eyes were closed at the time, but he was moving his lips hungrily, as if he were breastfeeding. My first sight of that little pink bundle of joy, so comical and adorable, stands as one of the most unforgettable moments of my life.

Kally and Alex, our neighbors from across the street, were the first to see our son when I brought Angela and the baby home to our apartment. Alex was thrilled and flattered when he learned we had named the baby Alexander, although Angela and I had considered many other masculine and feminine names, since we didn't know the baby's gender before he was born. We simply liked the name Alex, and we were certain he would like it as well when he grew up. (Interestingly, the name Alexander is of Greek origin and means "protector of men.")

We went through the first few months learning on the job, so to speak, about how to take care of a baby. Little Alex slept peacefully during the day and woke up many times at night. As his crib was in our bedroom, Angela and I both got an earful of his plaintive wails in the middle of the night. We tried all our pediatrician's suggestions for changing Alex's sleep pattern, to no avail. We decided we would just have to live with our son's "night owl" ways until he grew out of them.

When Alex started crawling, he wouldn't stay in one place for more than a few seconds. He was constantly exploring the entire apartment, so someone always had to watch every move he made. However, there was one occasion when the little rascal gave us a big scare.

We had several people over for dinner, including Angela's friend, Angie. While everyone was busy enjoying dessert, little Alex, who was sitting in his high chair near the cabinet on which an electric coffee pot was perched, apparently started pulling the cord. Unobserved, the pot of boiling liquid slid, inch by inch, toward the cabinet's ledge, where it began to tilt toward Alex's angelic face.

At that moment, Angela saw what was about to happen and shouted, "Oh, my God!" With blinding speed, she leaped towards the cabinet and grabbed the falling pot with her bare hands, a split second before the boiling coffee would have scalded the baby's face. Everyone stood there in silence, contemplating the disaster that Angela's quick reaction had narrowly averted.

Even in later years, we thanked God for preventing that accident, which would have left dear Alex with a permanently scarred face. Many times, Angela and I asked ourselves, "What if the pot had fallen on his face? What would his life be like? How would he handle it? How would we live with it?" These were scary thoughts. Fortunately, Alex's guardian angel had turned Angela's gaze in the direction of the coffee pot, prompting her to take the swift action that spared Alex a gruesome fate.

For the first vacation of our married life, we stayed with Angela's sister, Katie, whose house was half a block away from a small beach off the Long Island sound. We couldn't afford to go anywhere for a real vacation, so Katie was kind enough to let us stay with her family for a little change of scenery. We spent a week there sleeping in an enclosed porch attached to their living room, and I managed to complete an oil portrait of Angela holding baby Alex, a painting that today hangs above the piano in our living room.

It was around that time when—surprise, surprise—we found out that Angela was pregnant again. This was something we had not planned, as we were not ready to take care of two young children at the same time.

Our first priority became looking for another apartment with two bedrooms before the arrival of the second child, which was due around the end of March, 1972. Because the company I worked for was scheduled to relocate to Morristown, NJ, we searched for a new residence close to my new workplace.

As we looked for a bigger place, some of our relatives suggested that we should consider buying a small house. They even offered to help us with the down payment. So we began looking at one-family homes within a ten-mile radius of my new workplace, most of which were outside our price range.

Then my brother-in-law, Demo, pointed out that a two-family house—part of which we could rent out—would be a much better choice for us, providing an additional income source to help with the mortgage. Since my income at the time was less than $11,000 a year and Angela had already stopped teaching before Alex was born, it would have been difficult to maintain a single-family house. I had to agree with Demo's suggestion.

We then started searching for a two-family house, combing almost the entire northern New Jersey area. Angela found a new obstetrician, near the Morristown hospital. But in the end, we chose a two-family house in central New Jersey. It was a two-story duplex with each side having three bedrooms, a kitchen, a combination living room/dining room, and finished basement.

Demo lent me the required down payment, but I was still a little more than $1,000 short for the closing costs. In the meantime, we found a tenant: a family with four children, who signed a one-year lease.

A few days before the closing, I decided to call my friend, Yanni. With the help of his father-in-law, he had bought a restaurant that was doing very well. I asked him if he could lend me about $1000, which I would repay after I collected the first month's rent.

At first, he didn't recognize my voice; neither did he know who I was when I told him, "This is Mike from Rhodes." I was getting a little annoyed, so finally I said, "I'm the person who brought you to this country!"

When he finally realized who I was, he told me all about his restaurant and said that I should come over for dinner sometime. I then told him that I had called because I needed a short loan to cover part of the closing costs for the house I was buying. He said he was willing to give me the money, but it had to be at the end of the month.

"Yanni, I need the money now, because the closing is in two days," I replied. "I was hoping you would say yes, in which case I would drive down to your place and pick up the check."

Without missing a beat, Yanni responded, "I'm sorry. I have to wait for my accountant, who takes care of all my bills twice a month. If you stop over in two weeks, I will give you the money."

At that point, I was not only angry, but also hurt that I was getting the brush-off from someone who had once told me I was his savior and that he would do anything for me if I ever needed his help.

After pausing for a few seconds, I said heatedly, "Listen, Yanni, and listen good. I asked you for a favor and you downright refused to help me. The last time we met, on your wedding day, you treated me like garbage with that humiliating best man situation. When I left the reception, I thought I would never speak to you again, but I tried to give our friendship another chance by asking you to help me out. Well, this will probably be the last time you and I have a conversation, because you are not worthy of being called a friend. You are a pitiful excuse for a human being—a selfish, inconsiderate jerk. *Good-bye!*"

I hung up the phone without giving him an opportunity to reply—and although he could have called me back, he didn't. Fortunately, though, the combination of the security deposit and the first month's rent my tenant, Charles, gave me was sufficient to cover the closing costs.

On December 17, 1971, we moved to our new house. I remember Angela's humorous comment when we woke up the following morning and walked down the stairs: "Our furniture looks like an army unit formation!" Indeed, all the living room and dining room pieces were in a single row against the one long wall. I hadn't been previously aware that she did not particularly care for the two-family arrangement. But under the circumstances, this was our best choice, considering that another child was on the way.

The following day, Angela and I celebrated the completion of my company's office facilities in the new Morristown, New Jersey location. We had a great time with Bruce and Rena, who also were invited guests. We inspected our work office cubicles, which were arranged in an open floor setting except for the senior vice president's corner office. Bruce and I looked forward to driving to the office starting the following Monday, instead of taking the train to New York.

After a few hours of food and drink, Bruce followed me to our new house, where we continued to make merry about our exciting new office. I remember that evening that our little Alex, dressed in a light yellow outfit, tried to climb out of his playpen, as he was at the stage where he was able to take a few steps without any assistance. He walked from one end of the playpen to the other without holding onto the sides, which thrilled everyone to no end.

Angie, Alex's godmother, gave Angela a baby shower at her house with a gaggle of female friends and relatives in attendance. I was one of the few men present, as I was the packhorse responsible for hauling Angela's new loot home!

After Angela had opened all the presents, we loaded the car and headed home that evening. It was customary for us to play Scrabble right after dinner, and because we had already eaten at Angie's house, we immediately sat down to play a round of our favorite word game.

Somewhere in the middle of the game, Angela exclaimed, "Oh, *ugh!*"

"Did you drop a tile, darling?" I asked, scanning the floor for the wooden play piece.

"No, it's not that—my water just broke!"

Neither of us could believe what was happening because, once again, Angela's due date was two weeks away. Without losing any time, we called the doctor, packed all the things she needed, and headed for the Morristown hospital, which was thirty-five miles away. Our tenant, Shirley, was kind enough to watch little Alex until one of Angela's sisters could bring Koula, my mother-in-law, over to our house, either that evening or the next day.

At the hospital, Angela was not as uncomfortable during labor as she had been with Alex. When they took her to the delivery room around 3:00 a.m. on March 20, 1972, I was asked to wait in the main lobby. They said I would be called when Angela had delivered the baby.

I waited impatiently, pacing like a tiger in a cage and counting from one to 100 over and over before the receptionist finally motioned me to go upstairs. Too keyed-up to wait for the elevator, I vaulted up the stairs two at a time to the third floor, where I saw Angela in the hallway with a tiny baby swaddled next to her. I gazed in awe at the doll-like cherub with its squinched-shut eyes and little red mouth like two rose petals. Once again, I gloried in the miracle of birth.

"It's a boy, Mike," Angela said as a joyous smile lit up her face. "But this time, the delivery was so easy. It was not like the last time."

Although he was tiny—a little less than five pounds—the baby appeared to be of above-average length. The handsome babe had light-brown, almost blonde hair and hazel or green eyes. Angela said he was her "dream boy," as she had always wanted to have a child with these features.

The nurse explained our newborn son was a healthy little boy, despite his light weight. Also, as evidenced by his yellowish skin, she said he had jaundice, a condition that would be initially treated in the hospital. Because of this condition, she went on to say, he would be placed in a special nursery unit, which meant I would not be able to see him for a day or so.

I then accompanied Angela to her room, where I held her hand as we both thanked God for the birth of our second child. We had already decided that, if it were a boy, we would name him Paul. And so we did.

I stayed with Angela for a while and then I let her rest, as I had to go back home to take care of little Alex. During the forty-five minute ride home, I thought how blessed we were to have both Alex and Paul, who would grow up together as two good friends. At one point, I rolled down the window and cried out to the chill, pre-dawn morning, "Thank you, God, for this precious gift! Thank you, thank you, thank you!"

When I got home, my mother-in-law, Koula, was lying on the couch while little Alex was sleeping upstairs in his crib. Before I went to bed, I spent some time with Koula, talking pleasantly about the arrival of our baby boy, Paul, who would soon occupy the third bedroom in the house after spending a month or so in a bassinette in our bedroom.

I didn't go to work the next day. I went to the hospital in the afternoon, but I couldn't see Paul again because of his jaundice condition, which eventually cleared up. I spent a few hours with Angela, who seemed to be a little more rested. She jokingly said this time she didn't even feel like she had a baby, as the entire delivery process had been practically painless.

A few days later, we brought Paul home. He was the tiniest baby I had ever seen, weighing even less than he had a few days earlier in the hospital. We worried about whether this baby would ever grow up, because he refused to drink his formula milk. He was a long, skinny baby with little bones protruding all over his body.

To our relief, the pediatrician reassured us we needn't worry about Paul gaining weight and advancing normally through the stages of childhood. I remember the comments he made with respect to our concern about Paul's underweight problem: "Many children who don't look like the classic Gerber baby are nevertheless gaining weight just fine, so I'm not concerned about Paul."

Chapter 45

The Juggling Act

On the work front, everything was going swimmingly. My boss recognized my abilities and knowledge about the complicated application we were working on, which was already running in a production mode. About a year earlier, I had volunteered to undertake the reporting components of the system, a task that no one else wanted to deal with. This type of responsibility usually is assigned to the low-end or newest employees.

For me, this chore was a blessing in disguise. Having to deal with the reports the system was producing meant I was forced to learn all the detailed components of the programs with respect to their derivations. Because of that, within a year, I had learned more about the system's internal workings than anyone else on the team.

Because of my knowledge, after three years on the job, Steve promoted me to Project Leader, a position that usually is earned after no less than five years experience.

Of course, this promotion did not sit well with most of my coworkers, as they were now my subordinates. It was not an easy transition for me, either. But as time went on, things fell into place and my confidence soared to new heights. There was no task or problem I couldn't handle—even when the higher-ups called me at 2:00 a.m. to come to the office to help resolve a production problem.

Angela couldn't understand how I was able to jump out of bed after only a few hours of sleep, dash to the office, and work straight through until the following evening. I guess when you like what you're doing, as

I did, you don't consider it work, per se, but rather a hobby or a game you enjoy playing.

I truly enjoyed my work, to the point that I regarded myself as one of the company's most valuable assets and felt partly responsible for the robust health of the firm's bottom line. Whenever I waxed enthusiastic about my job to friends and coworkers, they told me I was lucky I liked my work, because hating one's job was the norm.

Angela's brother, Bob, who was successful in the corporate world, frequently reminded me that, despite my dedication, work ethic, and loyalty, I was not indispensable. He said anyone who works for a big company is just a number. In retrospect, he was right. But at the time, I was a dyed-in-the-wool company man who loved his job and extolled the virtues of corporate America. The thought that I might be fooling myself never occurred to me.

With our completed auto insurance application running in a production mode, the only programming involved was maintenance and inputting the individual states' auto insurance policy rules. I was then assigned a new responsibility: a project to develop a system for the homeowner insurance process. After purchasing a generic application from another insurance company, my boss, Steve, along with Ed Bailey, the underwriter, and I spent ten days in San Francisco, where we underwent basic training on the system's technical and functional components.

We were flown out in the ten-seater Falcon corporate jet, making one stop in Nebraska to refuel. No sooner had the plane landed at a small airport than two ladies dressed in matching red miniskirts (the *wow* type), strutted on board and proceeded to serve us the most delicious steak sandwiches I had ever tasted. After all, we were in Nebraska, the beef production capital of the Midwest. The pilot had radioed in the lunch order about twenty minutes before we landed.

"I want you fellows to taste the Nebraskan steak," he announced over the intercom. "It's so tender, it literally melts in your mouth." He wasn't just whistling Dixie!

In San Francisco, we stayed in a hotel within walking distance from the training facilities. We couldn't have asked for a better schedule—10:00 a.m. to 3:00 p.m.—leaving us free the rest of day to do whatever we wanted. It was absolutely an ideal situation to roam around the beautiful city on the bay, hitting all the points of interest and spending the evenings in trendy, well-known nightclubs.

One of those nights, we Three Musketeers—Steve, Ed, and I—went to a neighborhood lounge, sat at the bar, and ordered vodka gimlets, which had become our favorite cocktail since arriving in San Fran. At one point, a fetching young blonde with a tight, round caboose and legs that wouldn't quit sat down next to Steve, who told the bartender to put the lady's pleasure on our tab.

Although her low-cut blouse clearly revealed her well-endowed cleavage, the blonde looked otherwise like a normal neighborhood girl who had stopped to have a drink after work. However, she was displaying her assets each time she had an opportunity by slightly bending forward and resting her elbows on the counter. After thanking us for the free drink, she started chatting with Steve, who was clearly besotted with this beautiful stranger—and who could blame him!

I tried to encourage her to hook up with Steve because he was the only one among the three of us who was free, as he was in the process of getting a divorce. When Steve went to the men's room, the nubile lass cozied up to me and whispered in my ear, "I like you a lot, Mike. You know, we would be much more comfortable in the love seat over in that cozy corner." She gestured languidly toward the dimly lit sitting area on the opposite side of the bar, four steps up from the ground level.

Flattered, I cleared my throat and said, in a gentlemanly tone, "I can't do that, Miss. Steve approached you first and he should have that honor."

When Steve returned from the men's room, she said to him, "Listen, I know you're interested in me, but I like Mike. I'm sorry for being so direct, but that's how I am. So if you don't mind, Mike and I will go sit in the lounge area."

Steve was speechless for a few moments, but with his usual, agreeable tone, he commented, "That's all right, go ahead. Don't worry about me, Mike. Go with her and have fun."

Sheepishly, I went with the young lady to the lounge area, where we were alone for a while, enjoying our drinks. The more drinks she had, the closer she sidled up to me on the comfortable couch. At that point, I told her we should stop before the situation got out of hand.

"I'm sorry, but I can't continue," I said. "I'm a happily married man with two children, and I can't give you what you're looking for, so I'm going back to the bar to join my friends."

Her lovely face turned the most ominous shade of red and she started shouting, "So what if you're married! You're not the first one or the last, buster—*everybody* cheats on their spouse. You can't just walk away and leave me like this. I won't be treated this way!" She looked grotesque now, this woman scorned, with her face twisted in the agony of rejection.

After she stormed out of the lounge, I felt good about myself for having the moral principles to resist this most alluring temptation. Back at the bar, when I told Steve and Ed that I walked away on this bewitching creature, they thought I was out of my mind. I then brought up the analogy of how the Greek hero Odysseus had avoided the three Sirens—whose beautiful singing lured sailors to their death on the rocks surrounding their island—by ordering his crew to tie him to the mast of the boat so he couldn't escape and be seduced by the Sirens' promises of wisdom and knowledge.

Just as Odysseus had escaped from the alluring Sirens, so had I escaped from a mortal temptress. They still thought I was crazy to let an opportunity like that get away. However, I was satisfied that the decision I had made—as a devoted husband and father—was the only one possible.

We flew back to New Jersey, and Angela and our two boys were waiting for me as our company's private jet landed at the Morristown regional airport. I was so glad to see my beloved family after ten days apart—the longest I had been away from them. My sons wanted to see the plane up close, so I asked the pilot to show them the cockpit, where they stood looking at all the instruments in awe. Back home, I enjoyed the rest of the week being together with my family in our home.

Our first real vacation as a family was down along the Jersey shore, just before the summer season started, when the rent for an oceanfront cottage was only $95.00 a week. The following week, when school let out, the rates jumped to $400. So while our boys were at the pre-school age, we took advantage of a cheap vacation for the next few years.

I was doing quite a bit of traveling during this period with Ed and a new member of his underwriting team, Ted Brum. The three of us primarily visited the company's major regional branches, conducting basic training on the newly developed Homeowner's Insurance System. A frequent destination was Dallas, where we spent most of our evenings at Goldfinger's nightclub, whose nightly show featured a brief Greek segment, including a voluptuous belly dancer.

As part of her routine, the dancer would step offstage and gyrate her shapely hips right alongside the tables, so that customers could place dollar bills in her capacious cleavage or in her tiny bikini bottom, just below her sexy belly button. This was Ed and Ted's favorite part of the show and they always made sure they had an ample supply of one-dollar bills to tuck into these delightful crevices! Reminiscing about Goldfinger's, our favorite Dallas haunt, brought the three of us aging cohorts great joy in later years.

One year later, when my boss Steve was assigned to a different area in the department, I was certain I would be given Steve's managerial position. However, the vice president of the department decided to hire someone from the outside and put him in charge of both the auto and homeowner groups.

Our new boss, Howard, met with us, the three project leaders. We didn't think he had made a good impression; we characterized him as a Machiavellian character, a selfish schemer with a hidden agenda. He even pulled me aside to convince me to team up with him as his right-hand man (or, more to the point, his toady) and to backstab the other two project leaders. I flatly rejected his unsavory offer and let him know, in no uncertain terms, that he and I were starting off on shaky terms.

Alas, in those years, my virtuous ideology didn't win me any points in the corporate arena. When I was absolutely certain I was doing the right thing or making the right decision, I was not willing to back down from what seemed the best choice for the company, no matter what the other side wanted me to do— which was usually their way or the highway.

As a case in point, before the VP hired Howard, he gave all three project leaders an assignment to implement in our respective systems within a specific timeframe. When we presented the test results of our completed assignments, the VP observed that the other two project managers' designs had increased the system runtime by a full hour, whereas my solution only increased it by ten minutes. Long story short, even though my system was more efficient, the VP asked to bring my system in line with the other two in the interest of uniformity and expediency.

I flatly refused to do so, on the grounds that it was unethical. But my refusal to do what I was ordered was the reason I did not get a promotion or my scheduled salary raise. Instead, the VP hired Howard, with whom I continually crossed swords.

Within the next year or so, despite Howard's constant interference with my management style, my team successfully developed two spin-off property insurance applications. With Howard and me always at loggerheads, I sent my updated resume to a recruiter, who in turn started searching for a comparable position for me at another firm.

****

My mother-in-law, Koula, was one of the most beautiful people I had ever had the pleasure to know and I'm proud to say our relationship was warm and loving. I greatly admired the unbiased position she took when Angela and I had a disagreement. She was always fair and never criticized

either one of us, although she would occasionally bring up a story or proverb that illustrated her wise viewpoint.

Each time she visited, she doted on her grandchildren, who of course
adored their *yiaya* (which means "grandmother" or "granny" in Greek).
We had a special closeness that grew over time until I came to care for her
as I did for my own mother. It seemed as though I'd known her since I was
a little boy.

Koula loved music, and her favorite television shows were "The
Lawrence Welk Show" and "Sing Along with Mitch," featuring music im-
presario Mitch Miller. However, when we watched a movie, her limited
understanding of English greatly lessened her enjoyment. In these situations, I always volunteered to sit next to her and translate the dialogue
into Greek. She told me a few times how much she had appreciated my
animated and always accurate translations; the way she put it, my "performance" was entertaining and a whole lot better than watching a foreign
film with subtitles!

Koula certainly didn't fit the stereotypical notion of the mean, old,
battle-ax type of mother-in-law. She was a distinguished lady who made
everyone feel great when she was around, and my admiration for her knew
no bounds.

In 1977, she was hospitalized for the second time within a month, and
at the end of two weeks, we lost her. Not only did I lose a mother-in-law,
but I also lost a friend. Koula had been someone who possessed the gift of
kindness and who always kept a permanent smile on her face.

In February of 1979, we received a good offer from another Greek
family for our two-family house, although at the time, it was not up for
sale. Angela and I thought it was time for us to move to a single-family
house, so we accepted the offer with the stipulation that we would not
move out until we found or built a new house—even if we had to pay rent
after the closing process. The buyers agreed to these provisions and I immediately started looking for a lot to build our dream house, for which I
already had the blueprints.

Within a month, I had purchased a half-acre lot in a neighboring town
and I began making the preparations for the closing of the old house—so
that I could get the funds to finance the new house— and the required
building permits from the township.

I had a fairly good knowledge of the house-building process, which I
had obtained a few years earlier when two of my relatives and I had built
two new homes and sold them for a profit. We would have continued this
lucrative sideline, but the real estate sector took a dive, due to high interest

rates. In fact, in 1978, the mortgage rates had reached 18 percent, which slowed down the housing market tremendously.

Using what I had learned while building those two houses, I assumed the role of a general contractor. My cousin and friend, Steve Kontos, who was a seasoned builder, gave me a list of all his subcontractors. I contacted them and received quotes for every phase of the building process. I applied a project timeline method similar to the one I was using at work, specifically planning every phase carefully, so that the subcontractors didn't bump into one another or find that their materials weren't available, and so on.

My brother-in-law, Emmanuel (Katina's husband), who was a mason by trade, undertook all the masonry-related tasks, including laying the foundation and the construction of the basement.

During that phase, I took two weeks of vacation from my job and became the mason's assistant. My tasks included mixing the concrete and carrying it in a wheelbarrow close to where the mason was working with the cinderblocks. I must have carried more than 2,000 cinderblocks with my own two hands—but because my effort was an investment in my own house, I didn't mind the fatigue or the painful blisters that swelled up on both my hands.

I specifically remember one day around noon when I was carrying concrete from the cement truck to the furthest corner of the foundation. Not being used to this kind of manual labor, my arms simply gave out. I stopped for a moment, looked upward, and visualized that the family room of the completed house would be just above the spot where I was standing. That thought gave me enough energy to carry on until we had finished cementing all four sides of the foundation.

Both Angela and I were looking forward to moving into our new house, where we could make as much noise as we desired without having to consider the tenants in the next apartment. Angela and the two young boys visited the construction site almost every day; someone had to sign for and inspect the delivered materials, and this task fell to Angela. We enjoyed looking at the progress, especially when the framing and the roof were completed.

The house was completed fifteen days later than I had anticipated, according to my project plan. One of the reasons for the delay was the fact that, during that period, we had a gas shortage, which made it difficult for the subcontractors and delivery trucks to travel freely. The fact that drivers could only gas up on odd or even days, according to their license plate numbers, further complicated matters.

Chapter 46

Home at Last

At long last, on September 2, 1979, we moved into our new house. It was a big house with lots of room, plenty of closet space, and a big yard. I remember when Angela and I woke up the first morning; we thought we were guests in somebody else's house. We both thanked God for giving us the opportunity to own and enjoy our own slice of the American Dream.

As a result of some necessary upgrades, we had exceeded the overall budget, thus leaving us with little savings to use for the interior decor. Because we couldn't afford much, Angela and I learned how to make things instead of buying them, such as curtains, drapes, shades, and other decorative household necessities. To eliminate the labor expense, we even stained all the trim before the carpenter installed it. We had also tiled our kitchen floor, which was the last task before we moved in. So, in the end, we creatively accomplished many projects ourselves by paying only for the material we needed, thus eliminating the expense of hiring outside professionals.

My boss, Howard, and I were not getting along well. He announced during our weekly meeting that I was getting a promotion, only to inform me a week later that Mr. Butro, the senior vice president, would not approve it. Although I did not believe that Mr. Butro, who liked me very much, had stopped my promotion, I gave Howard the benefit of the doubt, as there was a slim possibility he was telling the truth.

Howard was conniving and diabolical, to be sure—but would he have gone so far as to influence Mr. Butro to vote against me? Well, it was possible. I didn't know what to say when my peers prematurely congratulated me on my new position. I felt like a fool. My canned response was, "What promotion? Go ask Howard, he'll explain."

After that incident, I was seriously determined to look for another job. I notified the recruiting agency to speed up the search. My assigned recruiter assured me during our first lunch meeting that it wouldn't be difficult finding another job for me, given my impressive resume, which reflected a host of accomplishments in a relatively short period. His comments made me feel a lot better, knowing how others viewed my strengths, and I realized I was more marketable than I had thought.

That December, we celebrated our first Christmas in our new house by inviting everyone from my side of the family over. My mother, father, my four sisters (Despina, Stacy, Katina, and Anna), and my brother, George, were invited, along with their spouses and their children. With a few close friends and cousins, the total number of guests was more than fifty. Fortunately, we now had enough space to accommodate and entertain everyone.

We had a jolly time decorating a live, seven-foot-tall Christmas tree, which we ultimately planted outside in the front yard after the holidays. Our two boys opened their presents on Christmas Eve in the living room next to the tree. We still have the pictures we took, capturing the delighted expressions on their innocent young faces when they realized what was in the gaily wrapped boxes.

The next day, when we gathered in the family room just before saying grace for our holiday meal, I took a few minutes to welcome everyone to our new house and began talking about my father, an only child who had lost his own father when he was only two years old. I told the gathering that eight children and many grandchildren had been born, starting with a single person—my dear father, whose mother had gotten married when she was just fourteen. My emotional tale made everyone's tears flow, even as the wondrous spirit of Christmas filled our new home, which Angela and I felt so blessed to share with the ones we loved.

In February of 1980, my recruiter called and informed me that he had scheduled an interview for me with a bank executive, Jim Morser, whom I was supposed to call to confirm the time and place of the interview. When I called Mr. Morser, he suggested that we meet at a restaurant and conduct the interview over dinner. While driving to work that morning, I listened to a radio talk show in which a British reporter was interviewing an Australian farmer. The dialogue went like this:

REPORTER: *"When my crew and I passed the big, semicircular sign bearing your farm's name, it took us another ten kilometers before we arrived here at the ranch. What a spread! Is all this acreage really yours?"*

FARMER: *"Yes, indeed, though a big portion is uncultivated and still remains in its natural form."*

REPORTER: *"I see. But I'm curious to know how you manage to contain all of your cattle so close to the ranch, as we did not see any fences anywhere during our ten-kilometer ride. Why didn't you put up any fences?"*

FARMER: *"Well, instead of putting up fences, I decided to dig wells around the ranch. Do you get my point?"*

REPORTER (after a long pause): "Ah, yes, I see what you mean! Yes, indeed!"

That little story stuck with me all day. I was visualizing the animals staying close to the ranch *where the water was*. In fact, no matter how far they would go to graze or explore, they would always come back to *where the water was*. What a simple concept, I thought to myself!

Jim Morser showed up on time at the restaurant and we were seated at a quiet, corner table. After ordering our drinks, Jim went right to the subject at hand. He first asked me the usual interview questions, such as why I was leaving my current job, how did I rate my manager, what were my major accomplishments, and other matters relevant to being a project manager. At one point, however, he caught me off guard with a question I didn't expect.

"As you know, Mike, the programming market is wide open right now, which is a key factor for the high turnover many companies experience," he said. "What would you use as an incentive to keep the employees satisfied and deter them from seeking another job?"

When he finished the question he rested his chin on his palm and stared at me quizzically, waiting for my answer. Immediately, I thought about the story I'd heard on the radio that morning. So, after a short pause I said, "I will answer your question with a true story," and related the anecdote, just as I had heard it on the radio. Then I elaborated further: "Just as the farmer dug wells instead of putting up fences, thereby keeping tabs on his cattle, my group had the lowest turnover of the programming department as a result of the scheduled weekly training I provided for all my employees."

"Very interesting," said Jim. "How did you do it—can you elaborate?"

"Certainly," I said confidently. "I was knowledgeable in both the technical and functional areas of my direct systems responsibilities. I scheduled two-hour sessions for specific topics tailored to the level or function of a particular group of individuals. Having experienced that training format firsthand for a number of years, I never ran out of material to teach. During those training sessions, I discovered that learning new things was more important to people than a salary increase."

"Wow, I'm impressed!" Jim enthused, taking a quick sip from his drink. "I liked the farmer's story and I like your style. You are my kind of guy, Mike. The job is yours if you want it."

He also specified the maximum amount he could offer me, which was 26 percent higher than my current salary. Furthermore, he told me I didn't have to give him an answer right away. Instead, he suggested I visit his office and meet with his other three managers to get a sense of the new environment and the people I'd be working with.

The following day, I took off in the afternoon and visited my potential new workplace. I liked all the people I met, but I was not particularly impressed with the physical accommodations of the entire fifth floor, which the systems and programming departments occupied. I was told that, within a year, we would be moving to a new office in the suburbs, only eight miles from my house. Under these terms, I thought I would be able to tolerate the train ride to the city of Newark, as well as the cramped office conditions.

Late that afternoon, on my way home from work, I listened to the hockey game between the USA and the Soviet Union at the 1980 Winter Olympics, held in Lake Placid, New York. I was about halfway home when I decided to accept the position, because the few negative factors were far outweighed by all the positive attributes and possibilities the new job offered.

When I got home, I discussed it with Angela, and we both agreed that I should accept the offer. I then called my recruiting agent to let him know I was agreeable with the terms of the offer and that I would submit my resignation to my current employer, giving a thirty-day notice. I thought that was sufficient time to transfer my knowledge to my successor, whomever it might be—although I had a pretty good idea that Howard had one of his underlings lurking in the background, waiting for my position.

Happy with my decision, I poured myself a drink to relax and enjoyed the third period of the medal-round hockey game, which the underdog Americans eventually won 4-3 over the Soviet powerhouse, pulling off the celebrated "Miracle on Ice"—the biggest upset in Olympic hockey history. It was a once-in-a-lifetime treat watching America's team of amateur and collegiate kids beat the seasoned, semi-professional Russian team, which

279

had been considered the best in the world. It was no less thrilling when the USA later went on to claim the gold medal over Finland.

That evening, Angela and I sat on the couch and discussed the pros and cons of my decision to accept the new job. We concluded that we could always make any undertaking work as long as we maintained a positive attitude. However, we were both aware of the risk we were taking by changing jobs right after we had built our new house, where the mortgage and upkeep were far more expensive than they had been for our previous two-family residence. Although we were confident we had made the right decision about taking the job, there was still a tinge of doubt in the backs of our minds.

As we wrestled with the question—"What if it's the wrong decision?"—Angela suddenly gave me a big hug and said to me soothingly, "Listen, my dear husband. I've known you for over ten years—you came out of nowhere and ended up being a successful professional in an exciting new technology you love and you're great at. And this is only the beginning! I have so much confidence in you, Mike—you can do anything, absolutely *anything* you put your brilliant mind to. So let's go for it—we'll be fine, I promise!"

I looked lovingly at my darling wife and wiped away the tears that trickled down her face. Then I held her hands and softly told her the words I felt at that moment.

"My darling wife, we have been married for over ten years, but I never opened my heart to tell you in simple words what you mean to me, the role you have played in my professional career and the confidence you have in me. You are the one who made me what I am today. You helped me build my self-esteem, but most of all, you were the only one who believed in me while everyone else doubted I would amount to anything worthwhile. And so, I owe everything to you, as you were my teacher whose faith, patience, and kindness taught me how to become the best I could be. Thank you, darling! Thank you from the bottom of my heart for your support and encouragement!"

Angela paused for a moment and said chokingly, "Oh, Mike darling, I don't deserve all the credit for your success. The one thing I'm sure of is the fact that you have the smarts—you have what it takes to reach as high as you want. I know the sky is the limit for you. The only role I played was to make you aware of the dormant strengths you possessed and helped you bring them to the surface. That's all—the rest you did it all by yourself!"

I clearly remember that Friday night of February 22, 1980, when we both felt so close to one another. We were reasonably optimistic about the future, while we pretty much defined success as being the respect and support for each other that we kept reinforcing throughout our marriage. I had always been of the opinion that getting married was like making a large deposit in the bank. As the years go by, you could withdraw part of the interest without touching the principal amount, which is analogous to the commitment we made when we got married.

In other words, I believed we should continuously protect and grow our investment in our marriage so that we would have enough interest left to last us through our lifetime, without breaking our commitment. And that's how I viewed my marriage. I was constantly making a conscious effort by being interested in an interesting person, who also happened to be my wife.

When Angela went to bed after our emotional conversation, I poured myself another drink and contemplated how lucky I was to have her as my partner. She was my wife, my lover, and my best friend, and I couldn't ask for anything more in a relationship. I also thanked God for our two boys, Alex and Paul, who were growing up so nicely—and rightly so, because they had a mother like Angela, who was the perfect role model during their tender years.

The boys had completely different personalities: Alex was a little introverted, whereas Paul was the outgoing type, taking more risks and getting into trouble more frequently. Paul constantly changed his mind about almost everything, including his original food choices at a restaurant or ice cream parlor.

From the time Paul was a baby, he enjoyed singing in bed every night for ten or fifteen minutes before he went to sleep. He had a natural gift for music and a lovely singing voice; he liked to bounce his head up and down on the pillow in time with the beat, singing every song he knew—including the National Anthem—as his closing tune before falling asleep.

Alex, on the other hand, was more of the introspective, creative type. He spent many hours making his own creations by disassembling several old and new toys to use their parts for the construction of a new one. This was Alex's passion, a trait he continued to cultivate in later years. At one point, our basement looked like Thomas Edison's lab, filled with a kinetic creation that made objects initiate a motion and then affect the movement of other objects, and so forth. The structure spanned for about fifteen feet and was made out of either broken toys or obsolete household items.

****

When I submitted my resignation on Monday morning, everyone was surprised with my decision, including Mr. Butro, the senior vice president. He immediately called me into his office to find out why I was leaving. His exact words were:

"Mike, you belong here! You are part of the furniture. I consider you one of the most valuable employees. What can I do to change your mind?"

"I like this company a whole lot," I replied. "But when I was up for promotion, my boss, Howard, said that you stopped it. He never gave me a good explanation why."

Livid, Mr. Butro banged his hand on the desk and exclaimed, "I did *what*? I assure you, Mike, I didn't stand in your way. And believe me, I'll take care of Howard—but good. Now listen, Mike—if you want to work in another group for another manager, you can choose anyone you want. I want to keep you here and keep you happy to boot."

"I appreciate that, but I'm sorry, Mr. Butro," I said. "I've already accepted the new position at the bank. I wish I had known that it wasn't you who killed my promotion. Things might have turned out differently."

Mr. Butro sighed deeply. "You're probably right, Mike. Thank you for being straight with me. And please do me the favor of not mentioning any of this to our friend Howard. I'll deal with him later."

During the next four weeks, I worked closely with my successor to transfer as much knowledge as time permitted. On my last day at work, I met with Howard, who wished me good luck, though deep down I was certain he was glad I was leaving. When we sat down in the conference room, he first told me he was sorry to see me go and queried me about the real reason I had taken another job. Then he asked what advice I would give him to manage the systems I was leaving behind.

I had been waiting for weeks for the opportunity to speak my mind to this nasty manipulator and get all the frustrations off my chest—albeit diplomatically, so as not to damage my reputation with the company. I took a deep, cleansing breath and said, "Well, I'm glad you asked. I will try to answer your questions honestly and right to the point. First, Howard, let's go back to the time you joined the company. You praised me as being the best among your managers, and then you tried to convince me to side with you against the others. In other words, you wanted me to be a sneak. When I rejected your tactics outright, you suddenly changed your opinion about me and treated me as if I were your enemy."

" I understand that I didn't always follow your suggestions—or, to put it more accurately, I didn't obey your *orders*—because in those cases," I said, "I was absolutely certain my approach was right for the system, the group, and the company.

"As intelligent as you are, Howard," I continued, watching as an arrogant smirk played upon his face, "your inconsistent management style hides an underlying selfish agenda by which you thought you were con-

282

trolling everything and everybody. But I have some news for you! All this time, you had no idea of the role I was playing, the problems I was solving, and my professional interaction with the user community. I just didn't want to bother you or report to you the solution of every problem so that you'd take notice of my accomplishments."

"You and the manager who will take my place have no clear understanding of the complexity of the applications I was in charge of," I finished. "I can assure you, though, that within a month, or maybe two, you will be begging me to come back, because your limited knowledge won't be sufficient to address the issues or resolve the problems that may arise."

Howard had remained silent all this time, but now the smirk left his face and I knew I had hit a nerve—probably several of them! "I know it will be difficult in the beginning, but we'll manage—don't worry about us!" he said with his usual bravado, although I think the implications of my departure scared him.

We shook hands and wished each other good luck. I did not mention any part of the conversation I'd had with Mr. Butro regarding my botched promotion. I respected Mr. Butro's request that I keep mum on the subject. I could only conjecture what grim fate lay in store for Howard!

After taking all my personal belongings from my desk, I went to a lounge in the neighborhood where some of my coworkers, as well as my entire group, were waiting for me for a farewell get-together. My two good friends from the underwriting department, Ed Bailey and Ted Brum, were also there.

Ed made the comment, "Don't worry Mike, what goes around comes around," referring to Howard's impending comeuppance. I was certain Howard had deliberately stopped my promotion because, behind the scenes, he was making plans to replace me with someone who was kissing up to him. He also assumed that not getting the promotion would anger me enough to leave the company. And in a way, he was right. It was the last straw that broke the camel's back.

Ed Bailey was also right. I found out a few months down the road that Mr. Butro demoted Howard three levels down, from assistant vice president to the title of programmer analyst.

We stayed at the lounge for a few hours, going over some of our most memorable moments with the company. One of the creative mementos that someone had brought to the lounge was the Pasta Fazool Award, a flip chart-sized pad on which many funny or infamously stupid events were recorded. When someone did or said something silly, we wrote it on the pad, which was then placed on the guilty party's desk until someone else committed an even more hilarious gaffe.

We had a lot of laughs reading the funny description of some of the blunders, such as, "Double your pleasure with coffee and tea," when Marianne, a bright young lady who worked for me as a programmer, poured hot coffee instead of water on top of the tea bag in her cup. There were comments about Bruce leaving his car running all day after parking it in front of my house one day when he rode with me to work.

Another time, Walter, a project leader in another programming group, received the Pasta Fazool Award when he came to work wearing one black shoe and one brown one! (As luck would have it, on that very same day as Walter's goof, I came to work wearing two different styles of black shoes—but fortunately, no one noticed, so I kept my mouth shut.)

We also got plenty of belly laughs from all the cartoons Bob Marazas drew on three-by-five index cards. No one was safe from his satirical drawings and punch lines. Fortunately, I made copies of all his drawings, which I have cherished to this day.

And so, that was the end of my employment at the insurance company, which had lasted for nine years and eight months. If I had waited for another four months before I resigned, I would have met the ten-year requirement to be fully vested in the pension program. I knew I was losing all the pension benefits I had accumulated up to that point, but I was simply unable to work there any longer— the emotional damage would have been too great. And besides, as this poor boy from Rhodes can attest, money isn't everything.

Chapter 47

Job after Job

On Monday morning, March 17, 1980, I reported for my new job in Newark, after a forty-five minute commute. I had a ten-minute drive from my house to the station, a twenty-five-minute train ride on the train, and a ten-minute walk to the office. It was St. Patrick's Day, and I remember I was wearing my gray suit with a red tie that day, although I should have observed the tradition of "the wearin' o' the green" as most people—of Irish descent or otherwise—did, to avoid getting pinched. (If memory serves, I avoided this fate, despite my fashion faux pas!)

I spent most of the day attending various orientation sessions as well as being introduced to my coworkers on the fifth floor, in addition to those I had already met the day after my interview. During the first week, I attended several meetings with my boss, Jim Morser, and the system users, to get acclimated to my new environment.

Except for two consultants, the rest of my limited staff were not as knowledgeable in the technical area as those in my previous group at the insurance company had been, so I had a lot of training work ahead of me. Besides the training, which my boss wholeheartedly endorsed, I also had to hire a few new people to either fill vacated positions or replace some of the highly paid consultants with permanent, full-time employees for the entire department.

Some of the systems my predecessor left behind were in bad shape, so I rolled up my sleeves and, together with a few other programmers, we managed to resolve most of the major problems that prevented the end users from receiving the correct financial reports. For clarification purposes for the non-technical readers, in information technology, the term *end user* is used to distinguish the person for whom a hardware or software product is designed from the developers, installers, and servicers of the product.

As time went on, I became more familiar with all the systems I was responsible for, and both Jim and my users seemed pleased with my performance. My peers—Dick, Jack, and Bill—were amiable, good-humored fellows. Our camaraderie allowed us to help one another without egos getting in the way, and we were always ready to lend a helping hand to anyone who needed it.

A few months later, my boss gave me the additional responsibility of overseeing two full-time, junior programmers who were slotted to play a key role in the upcoming major conversion of an especially complex system.

The company's annual outing in April of 1980 at a country club in Summit, New Jersey, coincided with the completion of another bank acquisition. During the day, some of us participated in outdoor sporting events such as softball, tennis, golf, and horseshoes. In the evening, there was an elaborate dinner reception where Mr. Malcolm Davis, the chairman of the board, announced that his dream had been fulfilled, because the acquisition of the new bank made our bank the largest in New Jersey.

I remember that statement well. I also remember the glowing expression on his face so vividly; it was the face of a man who had reached the pinnacle of his profession. Mingled pride, joy, and humility showed in his toothy grin. When he stepped down from the podium and walked toward his table, which was close to ours, I joined in the loud applause as this pillar of our company walked among us, his face beaming as a forest of hands reached out to clap for him, pat him on the back, and shake his hand.

Arriving at the office the following morning after this wonderful event, I heard the most disturbing news: our chairman had been killed instantly the night before in a head-on collision with a drunken teenager. What a shocker it was! Only the night before, he had been on top of the world. An hour later, cruel fate saw fit to punish him by taking away his bright future. His death was an enormous loss for our bank and a void that could not easily be filled, as Mr. Davis was considered a giant of a leader in the banking industry.

During the summer and fall months, after stabilizing some of the systems I had inherited, I concentrated on the conversion of the Corporate Trust application to a new IBM operating system, as well as continuing to hire and train full-time employees. Right after the holidays, we would be moving to our new office building in the suburbs. Jim gave me the first choice to select my office after he privately showed me the floor-seating plan. At least this time, there were five private offices—one of which was mine!

I was certain I was getting preferential treatment from Jim when, one evening, he asked me to meet with him at a bar on my way home from work. Over drinks, he commented that he thought I was doing a crackerjack job overall. He commended my successful recruitment efforts to reduce the number of consultants. But the main reason for our tête-à-tête, Jim said, was that he wanted me to evaluate my peers, especially the one he was considering firing before the move to the new office.

I told him emphatically that I thought this was not a good idea with respect to timing, because we were not sure how many employees would not make the move to the new location, due to probable commuting difficulties. Without any arguments, my boss gladly accepted my suggestion to wait until after we had settled down in the new office, at which time we would be in a better position to assess the overall situation and make any necessary staffing adjustments.

The move to the new location was a pleasant event for me, since I didn't have to take the train anymore, which reduced my commute by fifty minutes each way. Just before the move, several upper management changes were instituted. Jim, my boss, was transferred to another department and was replaced by Frank Mondelli, who had come from the bank we had recently merged with. Though Frank's management style was very different from Jim's, we saw he was a fair and affable gentleman and immediately showed him our approval and promised him our support.

Unlike Jim's controlling management style, Frank encouraged employee participation, an approach that improved employee commitment and empowerment. Right after the move, in February of 1981, one of my project groups was heavily involved with the conversion of a complex corporate trust system. Many of us had to work long days, nights, and weekends. But in the end, we were able to deliver a new version of a system that was favorably accepted by both the technical and user personnel. At home, Angela and I were using most of the free time we had working around the house, making some of the things we couldn't afford to buy. Housework notwithstanding, we made every effort to watch our boys play Little League baseball. Although Angela had never liked baseball and did not understand the rules, she hated to miss a game. When the boys were out on the diamond giving it their all, it was great entertainment, and she was their biggest cheerleader.

For most of their Little League years, Alex was a good first baseman. Paul was a good pitcher, but he frequently had difficulties catching the ball when the catcher was returning the ball to him.

The boys were growing up so nicely, doing well in school, and developing distinctive personalities that reflected their respective demeanors, talents, likes, and dislikes. When we baptized Alex, Angela's friend Angie, who had been maid of honor at our wedding, was the godmother. Paul's godmother was Rena, who had married Bruce in the early seventies. They had a son, Nicholas.

Back then, right after I got my promotion to project leader, Bruce decided to resign and accept another position with a chemical company. We maintained a close, friendly relationship with Bruce and Rena, visiting one another or going out to various functions. In fact, one summer our families went on vacation together to the Poconos, where we rented a lakefront house for a week. We had loads of fun, especially fishing on the lake, where the boys, as young as they were, managed to handle their own rods and caught a few fish as well—after I helped them untangle their lines, of course!

Speaking of the Poconos, one of the best vacations we had was at a lakefront house. It was completely private with a private beach and a rowboat. At that time, we had a one-year-old dog named Daphne, a white mutt resembling a Labrador, although her mother was a German shepherd and her father was a greyhound. We got Daphne from a neighbor when Paul brought her home as puppy, insisting he would only keep her overnight. We knew all along that he wanted her for a permanent pet, and we ended up adopting Daphne as our first dog.

We had no idea how to train a dog, so we allowed Daphne to be a free spirit who did anything she wanted. We were blissfully ignorant of the responsibilities of a dog owner, letting her out of the house to roam around the neighborhood and do "her business" all over—which, naturally, the neighbors complained about. She ended up training us about the dos and don'ts of dog ownership, instead of us training her!

Occasionally, we would foolishly leave the sliding patio door unlocked. Then Daphne, who had learned how to push the door open with her paws, would sneak out and go snooping around the neighborhood. What a Houdini! One evening, a neighbor called to tell us that Daphne wouldn't let her visiting cousin get out of the car!

The smart pooch was even able to turn knobs when we had to confine her in the laundry room, a long strip behind our garage. And Daphne was as talented as she was intelligent. Why, she could sing in perfect harmony with her human masters on cue—and with perfect pitch!

Daphne had the time of her life while we were in the Poconos. She was constantly in the water, either swimming or trying to catch the little fish in the shallow waters. In later years, we took Daphne with us every time we went there, because she was truly a member of the family.

The most significant aspect of our Poconos vacations for the boys was on the first day, when we always went grocery shopping. It was the only day of the year the boys were free to buy anything they wanted, without any restrictions. Besides their favorite sweetened cereal brand, they stacked the cart with pretzel and potato chip bags, as well as all sorts of sweets and sodas such as Hershey bars, M&M's, and licorices. They chose snacks which we, for the most part, never kept in our house. I believe they enjoyed this shopping spree more than any other event when we visited the Poconos or any other place with kitchen facilities. We always made sure that we had a barbecue grill to cook the store-bought chicken and other meats, as well as the fish we caught.

There was one occasion, though, when the facilities we rented in Virginia Beach did not have a grill, so we had to bring our own, securing it on the rack of our 1973 AMC Hornet. No one in the family liked this gaudily yellow car; in fact, we all hated the yellow color right from the day I drove it home for the first time. The yellow hue was exactly the same as a taxicab, although in the sample shown in the book we ordered the car from, it had looked more like a light yellow.

Anyway, after spending ten days in Virginia Beach, we reloaded the car, including tying the grill on the Hornet's rack. When we stopped for lunch after a few hours of driving, we noticed that the grill was no longer on the rack! I probably hadn't secured it tightly enough, and the wind must have blown it away—*oops!* Down through the years, the grill incident, always good for a few laughs, has loomed large in our family lore. We have always compared my ineptitude to the mishaps in those Chevy Chase *Vacation* movies.

In those days, we were on a tight budget, so we made every effort to save money in areas that were within our control, such as grilling our own food instead of eating out. The air conditioning in the car was a luxury instead of necessity. Fortunately, though, we all learned to live within our means, so we only borrowed money when it was absolutely necessary.

At the office, I thought I had everything under control until one day when my boss, Frank, wanted to see me in his office. He closed the door and confided to me that Bill, one of his managers, had resigned. He was in a bind with regard to who would assume his responsibilities, including the automated teller machine (ATM) project, which had started a week or so earlier. (Bill was the manager my previous boss, Jim, had wanted to fire and had asked my opinion about.)

Bill's ATM project was a major revamp of the existing, antiquated system, involving a complete rewrite and the introduction of an ATM switching network that would be able to communicate with other networks throughout the country. Based on a newspaper article resulting from an interview with a reporter, our chairman had already committed to a completion date for the project,

Having explained the magnitude of his predicament, Frank pleaded, "Mike, you have to help me get out of this jam. Please take over the ATM project. You can hire as many people you need, consultants or otherwise, as long as we can complete it by the projected date."

Cool and collected (and flattered by his offer), I asked Frank to turn over to me all the project information, including the specifications, so that I could study them for a few days before I gave him an educated assessment of whether the forecasted completion date was feasible.

I don't think I had ever turned down or walked away from a new challenge, no matter the difficulty. So a few days later, I told Frank that I would accept the project, although I could not guarantee completion on the date the chairman had committed to.

"After all, Frank," I commented, "we're dealing with a brand new technology and we have to get training in as well as hiring knowledgeable programmers—a process that takes time and effort, no matter how much money you offer for these positions."

Without further ado, I began learning the new technology and developing a detailed project plan. I also started the hiring process, with the help of human resources. We formed a team of about thirty people—a mix of programmers, analysts, consultants, and users—and the project forged ahead at full speed. After presenting the project schedule to our senior management, they were convinced that the original completion date was unrealistic, so we managed to negotiate a delivery date we all felt comfortable with.

In order to facilitate the introduction of a new ATM switching communication network, the bank decided to form a subsidiary company that would independently handle the hardware (the computers) that would communicate with other potential member networks. Our bank owned 51 percent of the newly developed company, leaving the balance of ownership to others who wanted to join the network, such as credit unions, other banks, and so on. The headquarters of the new company—which, for the purpose of preserving its anonymity, I will call "Switch"—were located within the same compound as the bank operations center, but in a separate building, close to ours.

During the development of my project, I was dealing with Switch's technical manager, a gentleman named Walter, to arrange when and how we were going to test the communication between the IBM mainframe application and Switch's two mini-computers, which in turn would control the ATMs. Around the beginning of December, I wrote a memo to Walter requesting a block of test time, day or night, anytime after February 1, 1982. I was certain my newly developed software would be ready for the beta test stage by that time.

Walter replied that he could not guarantee me any test time on the requested date because he had already made testing arrangements with another member of Switch. I then sent him another memo asking for any date in February, day or night, but his reply was similar to the first one. Although I had no proof, I had a pretty good idea why he had taken a hostile and uncooperative stance: he had failed twice when he tried to complete one of the three components of my project, and now he was purposefully hindering my efforts and threatening to undermine the project's success. As a result, I had to find a way to test my software without having to communicate with his computers.

While I was drinking my coffee one Sunday morning, a great idea just hit me. I had working for me an Ivy League "whiz kid" fresh out of Princeton named Robert, whose insistence that no one call him "Bob" had earned him a certain infamy around the office. I picked up the phone and asked him if he could develop the required software to simulate Switch's computers so that we would have total control of the testing within the IBM mainframe domain. In other words, I wanted to virtually replace Switch's computer behavior with a single program that would perform the exact same transaction error-checking process that Switch's software did.

Being a brainiac who thrived on technological puzzles, Robert dropped everything he was doing and went straight to the office, where he spent the day and most of the night working on the challenging assignment.

On Monday morning, when I got to the office, Robert was still there, chomping at the bit to show me the results of his creation. We began testing by using two IBM terminals, one representing the mainframe and the other simulating Switch. The third component in the mix was an ATM, used for testing purposes, that was located on our premises. After the initial, successful testing, I congratulated Robert for the ingenious way he had completed the development in less than a day. The real beauty of all this was the freedom we had to test everything without Walter's help or cooperation.

291

It took us a little more than a week in February to test the entire communication cycle and correct all the errors that cropped up. For example, at point A, we initiated an ATM transaction; at point B, Robert's program simulated Switch, receiving the transaction, such as a money withdrawal or transfer, a deposit, or a balance inquiry. Robert's program would then pass the transaction to point C, the IBM mainframe software, which accessed the customer's account and returned a response, following the same way back from C to B to A at the ATM machine.

Without getting into more technical details, we basically tested every possible scenario where the ATM transaction could be interrupted at any point during the process, either because of a system problem, customer intervention, power failure, or other causes.

After the successful testing, I gave my boss, Frank, a progress report and asked him not to mention anything to Walter or any other executives regarding the testing method we had developed. I told Frank that this was a matter between Walter and me and that, if Frank didn't have a problem with it, I wanted to resolve it myself, for my personal satisfaction.

Considering the Switch component completed, I turned all my efforts toward the other two project components, which needed a little more tweaking. It was around the beginning of March when I received a phone call from Walter, asking me when I was planning to begin testing the Switch component. He added ominously that my project was in jeopardy because I should have been testing back in February.

"Listen, Walter, stop playing games with me," I said. "I was ready to test a month ago, but you wouldn't even give me the time of the day."

"That's not true, Mike," he replied snidely. "I was just waiting for you to let me know when your software was ready to be tested."

"You know what, Walter? I actually need no more than an hour of testing from you so that you can sign off that my part of the project has passed your testing requirements. That's all, just one hour."

"You must be kidding! How could you possibly pass all of our demanding prerequisites within one hour? You're not serious, are you?"

I was eating up his incredulity and said with conviction, "I'm dead serious. If you want to see how serious I am, we can perform the testing process right now!"

I heard him snort contemptuously before he replied, "Okay, you're on! Get your group, I'll get mine, and let's get this thing started."

No sooner had the phone clicked in my ear than I snatched up Robert and took him with me to the ATM machine. Meanwhile, Walter and two of his technicians set up in the Switch computer room. Next to the ATM, we turned on the speakerphone, and we began performing the scripted, thirty-step test. Within half an hour, we had completed all the steps without incurring any errors. Toward the end of the scripted steps, I could hear Walter in the background mumbling, "This is not possible! How come they don't get any errors or rejections?"

Finally, Walter came storming into the ATM room and said angrily, "What are you, Papasavas, a wise guy? How did you do it? No one is capable of passing the test on the first try, but you … how in the hell did you do it?" His face was so red with rage and humiliation because I had put one over on him and I could almost see wisps of smoke coming off of it.

"Did my software pass the test—yes or no?" I asked evenly.

His complexion was returning to normal as he sighed and turned to leave. "Yes, congratulations," he said calmly. "But I'm just curious to know how you did it."

I smiled enigmatically. "Maybe I'll tell you later, Walter. For now, I want to let you know that your throwing a monkey wrench into the works was a blessing in disguise. Your stubbornness got my creative juices flowing, forcing me to find a novel way to climb the mountain you put in my way. Thank you for that."

Later that afternoon, when Walter came to my office, I finally told him how I had accomplished the error-free testing. When he had a good grasp of the process and the design concept of Robert's program, he politely asked me if he could have the program to use with future clients. I told him I would let him know after discussing the matter with my management.

When I met with my boss, I made him aware how eager Walter was to get hold of Robert's program. I also explained to Frank the real value of the program, whose use could save hundreds of man-hours of unnecessary testing. In the end, after Frank approached Switch's management with my recommendation, we gave them the program after they agreed to transfer $30,000 from their budget to ours. This "payback" was just a figure I came up with, on the spur of the moment, to serve as a memento of an accomplishment I would never forget.

Chapter 48

Vermont Vacation

After the project was completed, I was able to take a two-week vacation I desperately needed. We rented a house on Echo Lake in northern Vermont. For me, at least, it was an ideal location for a relaxing vacation after many months of long work hours and demanding responsibilities.

On the way to Vermont, we stopped in New Haven, Connecticut, to refuel and also to have our traditional first day of vacation breakfast at a nearby fast food restaurant. For this one occasion, we deviated from our normally healthy diet and all four of us ordered omelets with all the trimmings, including bacon, sausage, and hash brown potatoes. This rare breakfast treat, not to mention the traditional grocery shopping spree at the supermarket on the first day of our vacation, were memorably happy highlights for our two boys.

After we settled into the house by the lake, it took me a few days to unwind and truly enjoy the beautiful setting. I had a breathtaking view of the water from my perch on the deck. At first, it was difficult for me to detach myself from the work environment, as I worried about how my group at the office would handle any problems that might arise in my absence. However, a few days later, the surrounding beauty of nature vanquished my concerns and I realized there was more to life than my work.

The boys and I fished almost every day, using the minnows we caught in the shallow waters as bait. The most delicious catch was the lake trout that we usually caught right after sundown, when they came close to the shore to feed on the minnows, which we noticed disappeared from the shallow waters around that time every day. We also tried to go for bigger fish by taking the rowboat out into the deeper waters, but we were unsuccessful and had to settle for the trout and some other smaller fish.

The following weekend, Frances and Regis, our friends and neighbors from the previous house, visited with their two children and stayed over for two nights. We enjoyed a Saturday evening dinner of grilled steaks out on the deck. The full moon was shining and dancing over the lake's rippling waters. While the children played a game inside the house, we savored our second bottle of red wine with only the shrill, monotonous chirping of the crickets breaking the stillness of the night.

As we drove to a nearby town one day, it was as if we were explorers in the wilderness who had stumbled onto a pocket of civilization. Of course, the boys, especially Alex, went searching for places that had video games. Angela and I indulged Alex's mania for spending hours glued to game consoles because, on many occasions, he had declared convincingly that he wanted to know how the games worked and how they were created.

Another highlight of our Vermont vacation was the day we drove across the border into Canada and attended a small circus. Our boys enjoyed the antics of the human and animal performers. During the remaining few days of our vacation, we mainly took our ease, boating and fishing on the lake. Overall, it was an enjoyable and relaxing vacation, which I had needed to regain my sanity after spearheading such a grueling project at work.

Author's note: For personal reasons, I was unable to continue my writing for about two months. I decided to resume writing when I received an e-mail from the wife of my friend Richard (who was nicknamed Teddy). Here is a copy of the communication (in German and with the translation) I had initiated a few days earlier (October 2, 2008):

Guten Morgen Richard,
Die tatsache, dass ich nicht erhalten eine Antwort auf meine
letzte e-mail im April, ich bin senden diesem vermerk der hoff-
nung, dass alles ist gut mit dir und deine familie. Bitte e-mail ein
paar zeilen.
Danke,
Mike

Translated as:
Good morning, Richard,
The fact that I have not received a reply to my last e-mail in April,
I am sending this note hoping that everything is well with you and

your family. Please e-mail a few lines.
Thank you,
Mike

****

Hallo Mike, leider muss ich dir schreiben, dass Teddy im Juni ganz plötzlich verstorben ist. Ich wünsche dir und deiner familie alles gute.
Teddy's Frau, Doris

Translated as:

Hi Mike, unfortunately, I must write to you that in June Teddy suddenly died. I wish you and your family all the best.
Teddy's wife, Doris

I was truly shocked and saddened by this unpleasant news, which explained why he had not responded to my last e-mail.

Chapter 49

Dreams and Realities

One night, while I said my prayers before I went to bed, an impulsive thought flashed through my mind: "Is it possible that there is nothing after death?" I shrugged off this disconcerting thought and hit the hay. Somewhere in the wee hours of the morning, I had a most extraordinary dream:

I found myself elevated to a different plateau than my usual, earthly surroundings and onto an open field filled with wildflowers. The sun was shining on that late morning, the birds were singing, and the bees were buzzing busily to retrieve the nectar from the rainbow of blossoms. I stood in the middle of the field for a while, admiring the majestic scene and enjoying the serenity I felt.

All of a sudden, I saw a tall man dressed in denim coveralls. He was holding a saw and standing next to an unfinished wooden horse he was working on.

"Come to me, don't be afraid," he said as a wide smile spread over his gentle face. "I understand you had a question."

"Yes, I did but ... how did you know?" I replied with a trembling voice.

"It doesn't matter how I know, but I would like to answer your question," he replied, beckoning me to approach him. "Come, my friend, hop on behind me and take a short ride on my wooden horse."

Unafraid, I climbed aboard the wooden steed behind this kindly man. "Hold tight!" he cried, and at that point we whizzed through space at the speed of light. I was overtaken by an unusual sensation of contentment, ecstasy, and serenity: a unique feeling, beyond mortal exhilaration and the power of human words to describe.

"Don't stop, please don't stop!" I yelled as orgasmic waves of pleasure washed over me.

My guide laughed and said, "Ah, my friend, this is just a sample of what afterlife is like! I hope I've answered your question!"

I remember the man said he was taking me back. I awoke with a gasp and bolted upright to a sitting position in the bed. As I could not sleep anymore, I went downstairs, sat on the couch, and spent more than an hour contemplating this wonderful, phantasmagorical dream. It was the reassurance I had needed to strengthen my faith and, at the same time, to look at life with a more positive attitude. I couldn't have had a more profound answer to my doubting question. The dream convinced me that life is great, before and after death.

It was around this time when some of the new microcomputers on the marketplace became affordable to the general public, a phenomenon no one could possibly have imagined a few years earlier. So, one day after work, I went to an electronics store and bought a Commodore 64 personal computer. It was smaller than a toaster and had a capacity of 64k (kilobytes). To put it in a better perspective, the first IBM computer I had trained on, twelve years earlier, had been as big as three refrigerators and had a capacity of 30k.

As I was driving home, I couldn't believe I had a 64k computer in the trunk of my car! This was a surprise present for Alex for his birthday. He could use the machine to hone his burgeoning creative and technological skills.

Both Alex and Paul were ecstatic to realize they had their own personal computer on our kitchen table, where I showed them the fundamentals of the basic programming language. Alex was kind enough to tell Paul he would share the computer with him. I remember that I spent about an hour with them, writing a few simple commands, such as asking someone to enter his or her name.

I showed them how once the name was entered—let's say "John"—they could attach the name to another word and display both, such as "Hello, John." But then Alex wanted to know how we would handle the situation if we didn't want to say "Hello" to everyone. I then showed him in the manual how the "IF" statement is used. Once he mastered this, he was able to display different messages for different names.

This was the extent of the tutoring I provided for my boys. Using the manual, both Alex and Paul became proficient in the programming language, utilizing most of the computer's capabilities. Because Alex was spending much more time on the computer than Paul, after a while, he somehow took sole ownership and began developing his first computer game. It was similar to Pong, one of the earliest arcade video games that was popularized by the Atari company.

Paul, who recognized Alex's inclination in the programming of arcade games, had no problem with Alex being the sole owner of the computer. In fact, when we went to the Poconos for a one-week vacation, Alex spent most of his time in the house developing all sort of games. Angela and I realized Alex had a definite inclination toward computer programming and hoped he would be able to combine a hobby with a potential career in the video game industry, which was just taking off and promised to become a money tree in years to come.

As soon as my big project was completed, I was asked to undertake another challenging assignment that entailed the development of a corporate demand deposit application. I had to work closely with two other major banks, as this project was a co-development effort. My programming staff included several capable British consultants who ended up playing a major role in the successful completion of the project after one and a half years of long hours and hard work.

To celebrate the project's implementation, I arranged a party at my house for everyone involved in the highly successful effort. The name of project was F.U.N D.S, where each letter stood for a specific banking term. When I ordered the cake, I asked the baker to place the word "FUNDS" vertically, and then horizontally, next to each letter: "For Us Nothing Deters Success." The "name cake" was a huge hit with everyone, but the Bass pale ale—imported from England—was even more popular with my British guests, who drank the stuff like fishes. They had given me a friendly warning that I'd better not run out, so I had a second case in reserve.

For the food and all the trimmings, Angela did a superb job and received many compliments for being a great cook and a perfect hostess. The party was a smash celebration of our latest technological conquest, and everyone went home happy. (That Saturday night party on December 10 coincided with my birthday, but I hadn't told anyone beforehand, so they wouldn't feel obligated to bring a gift).

There was one incident I would like to write about that occurred a few days before the Christmas holidays, when we were getting ready to have my entire family (about fifty-five people) come to our house on Christmas Day. Although Angela described the event to me in detail right after it happened and asked me not to say anything about it to anybody, I think it is worthwhile to record it here for posterity.

Angela was in the supermarket, doing her usual grocery shopping, when she spotted an elderly gentleman holding a small basket with only one or two items in it. He was examining the tomatoes and other vegetables, but after weighing them and calculating the price, he was putting everything back. Out of curiosity, Angela followed him down each aisle as he shuffled along, checking the prices of various products. He put two cans of tuna in his basket, took a few steps forward, and turned around and put the items back on the shelf.

Angela knew his funds must have been limited, but she could not think of a way to help him. She did not want to insult him by simply offering him some money. Instead, as she pushed her cart behind him, she placed a $20 bill on the floor right next to the old man, but he did not notice it and kept staring at the shelves.

Angela then tapped his shoulder and said, "Sir, you dropped some money on the floor."

"No, Miss, I don't think so," he replied with a puzzled expression.

"Well, it has to be yours because I have all my money in my purse," Angela insisted. "Please take it, sir, or someone else will."

Although he knew it was not his money, he picked the bill up off the floor and continued his shopping. Interestingly, as Angela observed, he went back to the produce section, where this time he put the tomatoes and some other vegetables in his basket. In the end, his basket was almost full.

When Angela told me the story, I hugged her and congratulated her for the ingenious method she had used to help someone in need without expecting even a thank you. This deed was the "Spirit of Christmas in action," a small illustration of the true meaning of the holidays.

On Christmas Day, my entire side of the family came to our house, with each bunch bringing a festive dish to add to the feast. As was customary, before we formed a line at the buffet table, my father was designated to deliver a short speech in Greek about the holiday's true meaning and to say a prayer.

I also said a few words regarding the immense size of our family—young and old, spanning three generations—that filled our house to overflowing, and reminded our guests that all of this started with my father being the only child whose mother got married when she was fourteen years old. I reminded them that, right after my father was born, my grandfather had died during the Spanish flu pandemic of 1918.

I emphasized the fact that, whether we call it fate or the intervention of a higher power, "... all of us here today are alive and celebrating Christmas as a result of my father's fortitude under extraordinary circumstances." My father and mother just nodded, as if I'd revealed an epiphany.

As my father told me later, "I never thought of it the way you explained it; now you got me thinking ..." The wonderful evening even included a family sing-along with yours truly playing the guitar.

In the spring of 1984, I located a two-acre building lot in a desirable location in Holmdel, New Jersey. I immediately put up a deposit, signed the required papers making an offer of $73,000, and waited for the realtor to get back to me after he presented the offer to the lot's owner. On that same Saturday, we were invited to Angie's house for an afternoon cookout.

Let me say here that Angie was, and still is, one of my favorite people. She has a mystique, like an invisible aura of serenity, which has always made me feel great to be around her. She is compassionate to a fault and always finds goodness in everyone. I admire her outstanding listening skills most of all; she makes you feel important as she gives her undivided attention to whatever you're saying.

Bud, Angie's husband, was a high school math teacher and a football coach. Bud and Angie met in college, but their relationship went through a difficult period because Angie's father Eddie, a traditional Greek, wanted his daughter to marry a fellow of Greek descent. Bud's ancestors were from Italy, so Angie's father did his best to thwart their romance. However, in the end, Eddie gave in as Bud and Angie got married and stayed in the "being in love forever" stage.

Angie was not bothered by Bud's permanent limp, which was a result of a serious car accident that had severely damaged his leg. Bud's handicap had not affected Angie's love and caring for him; instead, it made their relationship even stronger. Both of them wanted their marriage to work, not only for their own happiness, but also to prove to Eddie that their choice to marry was the correct one.

That afternoon, Bud and I were having a beer when I told him that I had just put down a deposit for a building lot in an exclusive neighborhood. Bud paused for a moment and then he calmly said, "Mike, you have a nice, comfortable house. Why in the world do you want to go to the trouble of building another house?"

"Well, I want to move to an upscale location where the house values appreciate faster and have a much higher resale value than in my current location. ... you know what I mean," I responded with conviction.

Bud continued putting the scenario into perspective. "Look at my situation here. I have a modest house in a quiet neighborhood. I can afford my mortgage payments, both my sons are doing well in school, I'm happy with my teaching job, and Angie is pursuing her PhD in English literature. Bottom line, I can sleep at night without any worries. I have peace of mind!"

Without saying a word, I tried to digest what Bud had just said, but he continued with another litany of drawbacks. "Also, have you considered the fact that you will live in a rather wealthy neighborhood where your children won't have the things the kids next door have? You may be forced to replace your old beat-up car with a new one. In other words, you won't be able to afford the lifestyle that might be expected by your neighbors. Believe me, Mike, keeping up with the Joneses is a losing battle. Wouldn't you rather stay put and have peace of mind?"

Although what Bud said made a lot of sense, and I admit he planted seeds of doubts in my decision, I didn't back out of the pending deal. However, a few days later, the realtor informed me that the owner realized he could get more for his property and had raised the asking price from $73,000 to $95,000. He already had another buyer willing to pay more for the lot.

I tried to argue with the realtor, indicating that this was an absurd increase, since he had previously accepted the $73,000, but the deal fell through when the other buyer was not able to raise the money. The owner steadfastly resisted my many attempts to get him to reduce the inflated asking price, which, as the realtor explained, was based on the well-built homes in the neighborhood. The owner had only recently visited the area, after many years, and hadn't realized how upscale it had become.

I told the realtor to cancel the deal, because I could not afford the new asking price. Perhaps Bud was right with his evaluation of the situation, and the deal's falling through was a blessing in disguise.

I was disappointed, of course. But as the saying goes, when God closes a door, somewhere he opens a window. For the Papasavas family, that window was a well-deserved trip to Greece.

Chapter 50

When You Need a Vacation from Vacation

I called a travel agency and booked four tickets to Greece for June 30, 1984. We planned to stay a week in Athens at Angela brother's house and a little more than two weeks in Rhodes at my sister Mary's house. All of us were looking forward to this trip, especially Alex and Paul, who would have the opportunity to visit the places where their parents grew up before coming to America. Angela and I were sure that a lot of things must have changed in the sixteen years since we were last in Greece, which was in 1968.

We were already packed when we got up on Saturday morning, June 30. Our plan was to drive my car to the home of Angela's sister, Katie, in Queens, New York, and then Katie would take us to JFK Airport. It was raining when we left the house at 11:00 a.m., but we thought we had given ourselves plenty of time to make the 3:30 p.m. flight.

As we approached the George Washington Bridge, the rain was coming down in torrential sheets and we were forced to come to a complete stop at a police barricade before we reached the tollbooths. An officer informed us that the highway was flooded a few miles beyond the bridge and that we should find an alternate route to the airport.

I took the first exit after the bridge to locate a phone booth (not having the luxury of a cell phone in those days, of course) to call Katie and make different arrangements. It was a white-knuckle ride for Angela, sitting next to me, with the boys in the back seat. They were worried about the weather. I tried to put their minds at ease, although deep down, I knew the trip to the airport would be perilous.

With the strong winds swirling and the rain coming down even harder than ten minutes earlier, I stopped the car next to a telephone booth and got out to make the phone call to Katie. I stepped out of the car into a deep puddle, lost my balance, and hit my shin against the curb. Wincing in pain, I told Katie we would not be able to drive to her house and asked if it were possible for her to meet us at the airport with her daughter, so that they could drive our car back to their house.

When I got back to the car, Angela tried to stop my bleeding shin by pressing firmly on the wound with a clean cloth. As my injury was the least of my worries, I got back on the highway, heading towards the Triboro Bridge. Again, the police had set up a barricade just before the entrance to the tollbooths and told us that the other side of the bridge was also flooded. They advised us to take the Whitestone Bridge, using local streets because the Cross Bronx Expressway that would have taken us to the bridge was closed.

We exited the highway and began driving in the blinding rainfall, not knowing where the new highway would take us. At one point, a light truck from the opposite direction approached us with its high beams flashing and stopped next to our car. The driver stuck his head out the window and yelled that we were driving the wrong direction on the highway toward oncoming traffic!

"You could have gotten killed," he said, obviously concerned for our safety. "Where are you heading?"

When I told him we needed to go to the Whitestone Bridge, he told me to turn around and follow him because he was heading in the same direction. He drove through local streets as if he knew precisely how to avoid the flooded areas. Within twenty minutes, he guided us onto the Whitestone Bridge, where I briefly stopped the car next to his truck and thanked him many times for his kindness.

In retrospect, we tried to understand how this nice person happened to be there at the right time to save us from a potentially serious accident. Also, without his help, I wouldn't have been able to navigate through the local streets to find the bridge. Was he God-sent? I would like to believe he was, because his truck, with the flashing lights, had suddenly appeared next to my car as if it came out of nowhere.

In any case, we managed to drive to the home of Nina, Angela's other sister, which was only a mile away from the bridge, so we could use her phone to check on the status of our flight. By now, it was around 2:00 p.m. The airline representative told me our plane was still on schedule to depart on time at 3:30 p.m.

We got back in the car and began driving toward the airport on the Whitestone Expressway. Although it was still raining heavily, the traffic was light for a few miles—but then we almost came to a standstill.

It was a little before three o'clock when we heard on the radio that all flights in and out of JFK were suspended and the airport was closed, due to flooding conditions. This news made us sigh with relief, as we assumed that a lot of other people in the traffic jam had also been heading to the airport. Within two hours, we had probably covered less than three miles.

My gas gauge—full before we left the house—showed less than a quarter of a tank, which meant I only had two or three gallons left. Fortunately, a few minutes later, we spotted a gas station where we immediately pulled in to fill up the tank. I also called Katie's house to let them know where we were, as I was certain that they wouldn't be able to drive to the airport. Katie said that they had driven a few miles and turned right back because every road they tried was flooded.

I told her that we would keep them informed of our situation every time we had access to a telephone. At the gas station, most of the people confirmed that the airport was closed and said that there would be an announcement on the radio and television when it reopened.

Feeling a little more relaxed, we took a side street and stopped at a diner to have something to eat. We then drove around to find a hotel or motel where we could stay—either overnight or at least until the airport reopened. Unfortunately, most of the nearby hotels had no vacancies, which was understandable, as many people ahead of us were facing the same problem.

We finally located a rundown motel with vacancies, but it was one of those cheap, seedy places where you must book a room by the hour. When the receptionist saw my two young boys, she asked me if I were sure I wanted to stay in such a disreputable place. I said to her in a desperate tone, "Lady, at this point I don't really care. We're all exhausted and all we want is a reasonably clean room with a phone and a TV."

The first thing we did when we entered the room was to tune the TV to a local station, which was mainly reporting the flooding conditions in the surrounding areas of the five New York City boroughs. They reported that the airport was still closed and that they would announce when it had reopened.

We also made a few phone calls to let Katie and Nina know of our situation. I told Katie that I would call her from the airport to let her know where I had parked the car so that she could pick it up the following day.

Around 9:00 p.m. they announced that the airport was now open. We rushed out and got back on the highway, again driving at an almost bumper-to bumper pace. It again took us two hours to cover three miles. I drove up the departure ramp and, after taking the luggage out to the airline counter, I told Angela to go ahead with the check-in process.

The clerk at the counter said that our plane would depart in five minutes and that we should hurry up. In the meantime, I still had to park the car somewhere. As I was leaving, I heard Alex and Paul crying and pleading with the clerk: "Please wait for my daddy! Don't let the plane leave without my daddy!"

I took the car and tried to squeeze through the tight opening of the many cars that were dropping off passengers. I remember I drove next to a bus with only a one-inch clearance from the wall to my left. I entered the first parking lot, but there were no available parking spots. Desperate by now, I didn't care about the car, so I parked it on a sidewalk, placed the keys under the floor mat, locked it, but left one of the rear doors unlocked—knowing full well I was running a great risk of it being stolen or towed away.

Thinking of what I had gone through that day, I didn't give a hoot about the car. I then sprinted to the terminal, going up a set of steep stairs. Drenched in sweat, I made it to the security entrance and spotted Angela and the boys waiting for me on the other side. Both boys ran toward me and hugged me. "Daddy, we told the person at the counter not to let the plane take off before you came back," they reported with great self-satisfaction, obviously convinced their entreaty had kept the big silver bird on the ground.

Ah, 'twas a moment of many emotions, including both fatigue and elation! Before we boarded, at around 11:10 p.m., I called Katie and told her where I had parked the car and where I had put the keys. No sooner had we gotten settled in our seats than I asked the flight attendant to bring me a double Scotch. After our twelve-hour adventure, I needed a good, stiff drink, and the cocktail tasted like the nectar of the gods to my parched lips.

Although the airline clerk had told us that the plane would leave in five minutes, we stayed in the terminal for more than an hour, so the plane took off for Athens at around 12:45 a.m.

The following day, Katie found the car. However, she laughingly told us that the car was locked—but all the windows were rolled down! I then remembered that we had turned the air condition off so that the car did not overheat when we were driving bumper-to-bumper from the motel to the airport.

As first-time fliers, the boys were agog to see every cloud and land mass visible from the plane's windows and got an especially big kick from the Alps' snowcapped peaks, soaring impossibly high. I was keyed up and didn't sleep at all during the nine-hour flight. But as soon as we landed in Athens, I felt like I was on a real vacation and immediately forgot the previous day's ordeal and all my work-related worries. It was as if someone had turned one switch off and another one on, so I didn't need an unwinding period to adjust to the new environment, as I had on our American vacations.

Angela's brother, Maki, offered us a nice, comfortable two-bedroom apartment on the first floor in his house, where we planned on staying for ten days.

A few days later, Alex and Paul were playing in the basement, practicing their karate kicks on one another. At one point during this roughhousing, Paul apparently tried to block one of Alex's kicks with his palm and the impact broke his thumb. We immediately took him to the emergency room and then to the children's hospital, where he was given a bed in a single, large room shared with more than ten other children awaiting surgery. We had arrived at the hospital a little before 1:00 p.m. and waited until nine that night before Paul was finally taken to the operating room.

I was waiting in the hallway when I saw a father whose child had fallen through a glass door. The broken glass had severely damaged the arteries of his arm. The little boy had been brought to the hospital during the morning hours and it wasn't until 8:00 p.m. that the surgeon operated.

The child's father was crying hysterically because the doctor had told him his child wouldn't be fully able to use his arm. "They should have operated on him right away instead of waiting for more than nine hours before the surgeon saw him," he blubbered, blaming Greece's bureaucratic medical system. I found out later from the boy's father that most Greek doctors took bribes (euphemistically called "little envelopes") so that patients could get preferential treatment. He also explained that, if you didn't pay "under the table," you just had to wait at the end of the line.

When I learned about this medical corruption, I was infuriated. I just couldn't imagine that doctors who had taken the Hippocratic Oath could, in good conscience, allow their palms to be greased to speed the treatment of a patient. The boy's father, who happened to be unemployed at that time, told me that he could hardly afford to buy food for his family, let alone pay a bribe so that the doctor could afford a better vacation house on one of the islands. As a result, his little boy would probably be handicapped for the rest of his life, whereas his arm might have been restored to full health had a doctor operated on him immediately.

The doctor probably went home that night and slept without any guilt or regrets, perhaps justifying his actions because many others in the Greek medical community were just as corrupt. I don't think I will ever forget that case. I often wonder whatever happened to the helpless little boy who was not old enough to make his own choices, but instead had to depend on his family, the doctors, and the country's flawed medical system.

I was with Alex at Maki's house while Angela stayed with Paul all night, sitting and occasionally catnapping in a chair next to his bed. The hospital's overcrowded conditions made us appreciate the American accommodations in similar situations. When I went back to the hospital the next morning, Angela was physically and mentally exhausted from having to spend the night in that crowded room.

That Friday morning, the doctor came into the room to check on Paul and reported that he was healing fine. He recommended that Paul stay in the hospital over the weekend so he wouldn't accidentally fall and re-injure the same hand. When we insisted that we wanted to take Paul home, he made us sign a consent form indicating we were responsible for any consequences. We also made an appointment for x-rays on Thursday morning the following week.

That was also the day we were scheduled to fly to Rhodes in the early evening. We spent the rest of our stay in Athens, visiting various places of interest, such as the Parthenon on the Acropolis and the museum that were within walking distance from Maki's house. We also spent a lot of time at the famous "Plaka" area, a place that has shops, outdoor cafes, and restaurants. The area is considered as a Mecca for the tourists. Since Paul's hand was in a cast supported by a sling around his shoulder, every time we went to the beach, he could only walk in the shallow water that barely reached his waist.

When we went to the hospital for the follow-up examination on Thursday morning, the attending doctor could not locate our son's records. Discourteous and arrogant, he asked us over and over if we were certain this was the hospital where Paul had been treated. After we reassured him that Paul had indeed had surgery there the previous Friday, he made a few phone calls. Finally, Paul's file was located. Adding insult to injury, the doctor began playing the blame game, holding us responsible for Paul's misplaced records! His reasoning was that the files were lost because we took Paul home the day after the surgery, acting against the orders of the surgeon.

I couldn't reason with this type of logic, so I kept quiet and proceeded to the next phase of the follow-up, getting the x-rays. We waited for more than an hour before they took Paul to the radiology room. Ten minutes later, the power went off and Paul came out—but the nurse informed us that they had lost power while processing the films; therefore, we had to wait until the power was restored. Two hours later, the lights came back on and they were able to complete the x-ray process as well as the doctor's review.

The final step of the follow-up was to go to the cashier's department, which was a semi-circular counter with several clerks sitting behind windows. I must have signed four or five papers, but one event that amazed me was when a clerk stamped one of those papers and said, "Next window, please." I looked at the next window, but no one was behind it. Then the same clerk rolled his chair over and signed the same document he had previously stamped! After all this rigmarole, I ended up paying an insignificant amount of one hundred drachmas, which at the time was equal to less than half a dollar.

After we left the hospital, I concluded that, in the twenty-five years since I had first left the country, the bureaucratic process had become more convoluted instead of being simplified. Ordinary Greek citizens were now being smothered to death in miles of red tape.

The plane landed at the Rhodes airport on Thursday July 12, 1984, in the early evening. My sister, Mary, and my two nephews were waiting for us at the main gate. Mary had always been a sensitive soul and became emotional when she saw her big brother and his beautiful family; after all, it had been sixteen years since I had visited Rhodes, and I had been single at the time.

We went straight to Mary's house, where we met a few more relatives, including her two daughters. Although the house had three bedrooms, it became a little crowded with four new occupants, but Mary wouldn't even consider letting us go to a hotel.

During the same period, my brother, George, and his two sons were also in Rhodes, staying with his wife's relatives. We spent about two weeks on the island and took the children to all the "must-see" places, including spending one night in the village, where Paul had lots of fun chasing my sister Vasilia's chickens. Also, both boys paraded through the center of the village on the back of a donkey, a hilariously memorable scene preserved in several fond snapshots.

The following day, we decided to attend a festival at a neighboring village. I took a dirt road shortcut that saved us at least half the distance of the regularly traveled route. As luck would have it, a sudden rainstorm (an unusual event in the middle of July) had flooded many low spots—and in one of them, my car got stuck.

It took us a while to push the car out of the mud; in fact, the only way to get some traction in the muddy morass was by using a few bales of hay that were neatly piled in a garden next to the road. (I found out later that the garden and the hay belonged to my Aunt Katerina!)

At the festival, we joined some friends, ate all sorts of barbecued lamb and pork, and sampled the traditional local beverages, including the unadulterated (without anise) type of ouzo called *souma*. At around ten that night, we decided to leave, heading east toward the city of Lindos, where we planned to spend an entire day. However, first we needed a place to spend the night. At that late hour, we didn't think we would find a hotel with vacancies.

Just a few miles before Lindos, we stopped at a hotel, but the desk clerk said there were no rooms available. At that moment, the owner was passing by and, when he saw the two tired children staring at him with their sad eyes, he told us that he might be able to accommodate us for the night by placing a few cots in an empty apartment on the ground floor. The place was not bad at all; we had everything we needed for just one night and the boys looked on the impromptu accommodations as an adventure.

In the morning, while Angela and the boys were getting ready, I ordered breakfast for everyone. Enjoying our breakfast on the patio outside the kitchen was one of the most memorable moments of our Greek getaway; I felt perfectly at peace with myself and with everyone around me.

As the birds on the vines above the patio happily warbled and the rays of the rising sun coyly penetrated the thick foliage of the flowering shrubs, I savored the best cup of coffee I've ever had. Although the paradisiacal surroundings and my family were a contributing factor, I believe the essence of my happiness and peace of mind during those moments stemmed from within.

Departing right after breakfast, it took us less than ten minutes to drive to Lindos. The following overview of the village and the description of the Acropolis will give the reader a good idea of its storied history and how it looks today:

"*The modern village of Lindos: The entrance to the village is on the north, by its only square, which is now used as a car park and has a large tree in the middle and a small fountain with many features from the period of the Knights [of St. John]. Rocks behind and above it recall ancient aqueducts. The graveyard is also at the entrance to the village, containing the church of Phaneromeni. A little beyond and below the square are the remains of the Moslem cemetery, containing a few graves whose typical grave markers have been demolished. The school has been moved to the side of the Megalo Yialo and the old building, beside the church of the Panayia, built in the neoclassical style, is now used by a local society for various cultural events.*"

After we parked the car, we started heading for the Lindos Acropolis, situated on an elevated hill about one kilometer from the village square.

There were donkeys available that tourists could ride to get to the Acropolis, because of the steep steps. We spent about an hour on the plateau of the Acropolis where we took quite a few panoramic pictures and read most of the inscriptions with their modern explanations.

Our next stop was Lindos Beach, located at the foot of the Acropolis hill. We drove down a steep, narrow road and parked the car near a beachfront restaurant. Although I had visited the beach when I was a teenager, this time it seemed as if I were looking at the surroundings with a different pair of eyes. The overall setting, with a multitude of straw umbrellas sticking jauntily out of the sand like giant mushrooms, was just magnificent.

We sat underneath an umbrella and ordered cold drinks from a roving waiter. Most of the tourists who were roasting under the hot sun were from the northern countries of Europe, and their fair skin was taking a beating. A line of sunburned bodies, all trying to get a good tan, stretched down the beach, looking like a lobster convention!

Most ladies were topless, a common phenomenon on all the beaches during the summer months. These well-endowed beach bunnies paraded shamelessly back and forth along the seashore, exhibiting their assets— and they had plenty of admirers!

The water was so calm and warm that it felt as if we were bathing in a swimming pool. We also took a paddleboat out to the deeper waters, where we could see the pebbles at the bottom of the sea even at depths of thirty to forty feet, because the water was so crystal clear.

Around noon, Angela and I secured a table at the restaurant and ordered lunch for all four of us. In the meantime, we watched the boys, who were in line to use the outdoor shower. When Alex's turn came, he looked behind him and saw two tall, gorgeous, topless blondes! I always tease him about this incident by reminding him what a polite thirteen-year old boy he was, letting the ladies go first and shower in front of him so that he could enjoy the view. (By the way, the delicious lunch included many Greek delicacies, soft drinks for the boys, and two cold beers for Angela and me. This was indeed a day to remember!)

We got together a few times with my friend, Dimitri, and his wife, Sophia, at their summer house in Trianta, a suburb about five kilometers from the city. His property, which was filled with every fruit tree imaginable and huge vegetable gardens, spanned several acres, at the end of which was the beachfront where Dimitri took a healthful, twenty-minute swim almost every day before lunch.

The boys had a great time at Dimitri's summer house, using the swimming pool and climbing the fruit trees of their choice, although Paul was only able to use one arm, as the other was still supported by a shoulder sling.

Another memorable event was a family dinner we had at a secluded restaurant right on the water. We were told that only the locals knew about this particular restaurant and that the food was excellent. My brother, George, and I planned to treat about twenty people, so naturally we wanted to find the perfect place for this special dinner.

Angela and I went to check out the restaurant early in the afternoon. The owner/chef showed us around and had us taste some of the specials he was preparing. After seeing all the mouthwatering specialties, I asked him to prepare a platter of every item on the menu, including a few kilos of *barbounia,* a delectable Mediterranean red mullet, and steaks for the children.

When everyone arrived, a long, rectangular table—overflowing with platters, wine, beer, and soft drinks—was set at the end of the raised veranda, next to the water. The setting was just breathtaking and we would occasionally feel the refreshing mist of the water that gently splashed against the rocks and sprayed over the walls of the veranda.

We must have stayed there for more than three hours, having one of the most memorable dinners ever. (Would you believe the total bill was only $72.00, including the tip? Just for comparison, Angela and I revisited the same restaurant sixteen years later and paid more than $72.00 for a complete seafood dinner for two plus a bottle of domestic wine. My brother, George, and I recollect that vacation dinner party with extreme fondness and heartily agree that Greece was much better off before it joined the European Union.)

After we left Rhodes, we spent a few more days in Athens. We went out with Angela's friends, Rena and Antony, and spent our last evening at a restaurant called Dionysus. It was located across the street, just below the Acropolis, where we could clearly enjoy the illuminated Parthenon. We truly enjoyed the evening, carrying on an interesting conversation with two sophisticated and kind people whose humble opinions and ideas were of a higher caliber than the mainstream Greek mindset.

Chapter 51
Back to the Grind

Back in the United States, it took us a while to readjust to the American way of life after a halcyon month of carefree leisure in a country where the irrepressible sun shone every day on the turquoise water and sugary white beaches of paradise. The next day after our arrival was indeed a rude awakening.

We had been invited to a coworker's wedding. The day was dismal and cloudy, with a light mist falling amidst the fog. To make it worse, the reception was held in a gloomy hall without windows. What a contrast with the Shangri-La we had come from just a few days earlier! Daydreaming of the warm people, breathtaking scenic vistas, and historical and cultural richness of Greece, Angela and I could barely suppress our yawns as the wedding ritual played out to its ho-hum conclusion.

In the fall of 1984, the bank where I worked was purchased by and merged with a larger, more powerful bank. Although it was called a merger, in reality, it was more like an acquisition. In these situations, the stronger of the two has the upper hand and thus calls most of the shots. There were many meetings held with our counterparts to synchronize the plans of the merger, but their position on most of the issues prevailed.

At the time, I was assistant vice president in the systems and programming department. Just before the merger was finalized, all my counterparts in the other bank's respective department were promoted to vice president. We all realized that move was designed so they could take the higher management positions and have us as their subordinates. And that's exactly what actually happened.

I was forced to endure these topsy-turvy conditions for the next few years. It took senior management a while to recognize that the more talented employees were within our side of the bank, after which they began making better assignments. It became necessary to revamp F.U.N D.S., the project I had completed more than a year earlier, because the other bank used the exact same software to run their commercial demand deposit systems. It took us about a year to merge this and some other systems into a single entity that could handle more than double the corporate account base.

***

Back in 1978, we had joined St. George Greek Orthodox Church near our house, where Angela began teaching the Greek language a few hours in the afternoon. In the fall of 1984, I became a youth counselor and volleyball coach there. I dedicated many hours to practice sessions held right after work, as well as devoting Sunday afternoons to actual games with other communities in the state.

Another interesting annual event was the "Sights and Sounds" youth program for teenagers, which all seventeen Greek communities participated in during the first two weeks in March. The contest included fine arts, literature, music, theatre, and other creative arts and crafts.

There were two parts to this contest. All arts and crafts items (poetry, paintings, literature, etc.) were submitted a few weeks in advance so that the judges would have enough time to select the best three in each category. The winning pieces were displayed with the appropriate ribbon attached to differentiate first, second, and third place. In contrast, the performance categories took place in front of a live audience, which was mainly composed of students and counselors.

Alex and Paul participated every year of their eligibility. Both of them had won several trophies for their work in poetry, drawing, photography, and music. Angela and I were in charge of the original, fifteen-minute play, which we had to write, direct, and finally present on the day of the competition. The genre of every play was comedy, but we had to develop the characters in such a way that there was a moral to the story. All together, we wrote ten original plays in as many years. We won first place once and placed second or third for the remaining years.

I remember the moment in 1988 when one of the judges told me that our play had taken first place. Before the announcement was made, I went outside, looked upward, and said, "Thank you, God, for this joyful experience. This is a wonderful feeling I would not exchange for anything else in the world." I couldn't wait to see the expressions on our kid-actors' faces when they announced our collective triumph.

I only shared my advance knowledge with Angela, who held my hand as the actors from the best three plays were called to the stage. They were also holding hands, hoping their name wouldn't be called for third or second place. What excitement and elation when our young actors, jumping up and down and yelling for joy, realized they had won first place! Spilling from the stage in a rowdy mass, they hugged and kissed us and thanked us from the bottoms of their hearts for helping make this extraordinary dream come true.

The name of the award-winning play was *The Misunderstanding*. Taking place in a family's home, the parents receive a phone call from a veterinarian, who wants to talk to one of their daughters about the test results of a neighbor's sickly dog she was taking care of. The comedy results from the parents misunderstanding that the case had to do with their daughter being sick. The reader can imagine the funny dialogue that ensued from this farcical situation, especially since the parents were uneducated and naive. We knew we had a good chance of winning because the judges were doubled over from laughter throughout the entire play.

Things were rather quiet at work until March of 1986. Then Tom, my manager's boss, offered me the position of Information Center Manager. My new location would be twenty miles farther away from my home than my current workplace. However, because the new position was a promotion with many benefits and promising possibilities—as well as exposure to the newest technologies—I accepted the offer.

I would report directly to Tom, who was a senior vice president. Right from the start, I was exposed to and utilized technology that dealt mainly with microcomputers and networking. I was certain that Tom would advance me to the vice president level, but it never materialized; instead, he decided to resign and accepted a position in Michigan, his home state.

During Tom's last two weeks, I discovered that one of our consultants was double-billing for several systems he had developed and maintained. This practice had gone on for more than a year without anyone noticing it. I approached Tom, showed him the actual ledger entries, and asked him what steps I should take to rectify the situation.

After he reviewed the ledger report, Tom agreed with me, but said he was not sure if we should report it because there was a possibility that some other executives in high places might be involved in this scam. Given the short time frame before his separation from the bank, Tom didn't want to get involved. He warned me to be careful handling this sticky situation.

When I went home that evening, I discussed the matter with Angela, who felt the same way as Tom and advised me to think it through before I went to senior management. But by the time I got to the office the following morning, I had already made up my mind to report this blatant misappropriation of money.

I discussed the case with the executive vice president, who was pleased that I had taken the initiative to inform my management of someone's wrongdoing, regardless of who that "someone" was. I can still hear his sincere-sounding words: "I'm glad you came to me, Mike, and I commend you. I wish we had more people like you."

About a week later, the executive vice president—who was now my interim manager—called me into his office. At first, we made small talk about the conference I had recently attended in Washington. But he quickly got to the point.

"Mike, I have decided to transfer you to your previous department," he said quickly, tapping a pencil nervously on his desk. "You will be reporting to the same manager as before. I believe they need you there more, and I'm sure you will provide the support that's expected of you."

I remained silent for a moment, as I thought the ceiling was caving in. I asked why he was transferring me and inquired if his decision had anything to do with the double-billing issue I had reported earlier that week. I didn't expect him to admit it, even if it were true; I just wanted him to know that this was the first thing that crossed my mind.

He paused for a few seconds before he insisted that the decision to transfer me had been made for business reasons and that I would he more useful in the other department.

I was devastated when I left his office, because I viewed the transfer as a demotion, a sort of a punishment for something I had supposedly done—or was it something that someone feared I might do, if I had stayed in the same position? After all, I had proven to be a vigilant watchdog and whistleblower who had no qualms about doing the right thing, regardless of the consequences. That meant I couldn't be counted on to keep my mouth shut about any other corporate chicanery I might witness.

The demotion, for lack of a better word, was a huge blow to my career. This was the first time I had ever been punished for no good reason whatsoever, other than my refusal to compromise my principles and turn a blind eye to someone's wrongdoing. I was convinced that people like me, who defied the corporate culture, were branded as irrelevant and treated, or rather penalized, in a manner that only benefited those in power, who simply gave the orders without suffering any self-reproach for the consequences.

316

My ex-boss, Frank, was a good listener when we went out to lunch that day. I only had a few bites from the sandwich I ordered, but I quickly drank two glasses of wine, hoping to calm my nerves. Up until that day, I hadn't had a cigarette for three months, as I was trying to stop smoking. But the ugly episode made me buy a pack of cigarettes and I began lighting one after another. I was in a state of confusion and uncertain of my future career with the bank, and I'm sure my dejection was written all over my face.

Frank was the shoulder I needed to lean on at this difficult time, and he did everything in his power to try to lift my defeated spirit. He tried to convince me that the situation wasn't as bad as I perceived it. I don't remember the exact words he used, but he put it in such a way that it sounded like a paraphrased Chinese proverb: "There are two kinds of people: those who think there is a night between two days and the other who think there is a day between two nights. So, put yourself in the first category. It is night right now, but the day will be coming soon." Frank went on to emphasize that I should give it some time. He said I should be able to forget this incident because "the cream always rises to the top."

During the following few weeks, Frank defined my responsibilities by assigning a small group of analysts and programmers to me. Fortunately, my users in the Trust department welcomed me with a positive attitude, something I needed during this difficult period.

After working with my new group for almost a year, I was assigned to an additional major project that had to do with a system conversion from an outside vendor to in-house installation. The project was called Personal Trust, but it also processed estates and other functions for wealthy families.

In the summer of 1988, I hired Mary Haniotis, who ultimately became my right hand and one of my best friends. Mary was one of the Trust group's few full-time employees, whereas the other members of the technical staff were outside consultants. I was the technical manager, with Paul H. serving as the overall project manager. The scope of the project was so big that it required its own IBM mainframe, which was more powerful than the one that housed and processed all the other bank applications.

After a year of hard work involving late nights and weekends, the system was successfully implemented in 1989. During this period, there was another merger with a Philadelphia bank; that event added more projects and conversions to our already packed work schedule. Because I was averaging a seventy-five hour workweek for more than a year and a half, I regretfully neglected most of my social obligations, including my children's activities.

317

Paul, at the age of eighteen, was already proficient in the fields of computers and communications. He wanted to take airplane and helicopter flying lessons, as this was one of his passions. Because the $150-per-hour lessons were rather expensive for my budget—plus the fact that neither Angela nor I approved of this dangerous avocation—I utterly refused to foot the bill. My refusal, however, did not even make a dent in Paul's aerial ambitions. He found a job as a waiter and spent all his money for airplane flying lessons.

Later on, around 1992, when he started selling computers to the public and had a little more money to spare, he began taking helicopter lessons. Angela and I were already convinced that, when Paul wanted something badly enough, nothing could stop him. It took him about three years, but he managed to get his helicopter pilot license.

Alex, the budding computer genius, was placed in an elite group during his last year of high school, where he learned and used several programming languages, honing skills that came in handy when he attended college.

Angela and I were pleased with the way our children were progressing educationally, socially, and personally. We believed we had to earn their respect instead of taking the easy way of spoiling them with many presents or succumbing to their wishes and demands. We were good listeners and tried to reason with them, even when their emotions threatened to overpower our logical thinking. We always stood our ground, despite the temporary disappointment and hurt we inflicted on them by sometimes saying "no" to their whims and fancies. In the end, our way of raising our children made them strong and independent thinkers who realized that nothing is impossible if you put your mind to it.

I will never forget a little story called "The Cocoon," which I told to the boys to illustrate the importance of standing on your own two legs—or wings, as the case may be. It went like this:

"A man found a cocoon of a butterfly. One day, a small opening appeared. He sat and watched the butterfly for several hours as it struggled to force its body through that little hole. Then it seemed to stop making any progress. It appeared as if it had gotten as far as it could, and it could go no further.

So the man decided to help the butterfly. He took a pair of scissors and snipped off the remaining bit of the cocoon. The butterfly then emerged easily. But it had a swollen body and small, shriveled wings. The man continued to watch the butterfly because he expected that, at any moment, the wings would enlarge and expand to be able to support the body, which would contract in time.

Neither happened! In fact, the butterfly spent the rest of its life crawling around with a swollen body and shriveled wings. It never was able to fly.

What the man in his kindness and haste did not understand was that the restricting cocoon and the struggle required to get through the tiny opening were God's way of forcing fluid from the body of the butterfly into its wings so that it would be ready for flight once it achieved its freedom from the cocoon.

Sometimes struggles are exactly what we need in our lives. If God allowed us to go through our lives without any obstacles, it would cripple us. We would not be as strong as we might have been. We could never fly!"

Original Author Unknown

Angela and I both learned so much from this enduring parable and related it to our way of raising our boys. Their accomplishments reflected positively on us as parents, but our greatest reward has always been the respect they have shown us. We taught them that "a diamond was once a piece of coal that stuck to its job," an adage they believed in. As a result, they became not only two bright individuals, but also respectable human beings who care for their fellow man.

Chapter 52

Saying Good-bye to Mother

Early one morning in February of 1989, I was at the office when I received a call from a nurse informing me that my mother had suffered a possible stroke and was in the hospital. I immediately rushed to the hospital and saw my mother in the emergency room. My father was sitting on the end of the bed, his face ashen with worry.

As soon as I arrived, my mother recognized me and said weakly, her voice barely more than a whisper, "Good morning, my son. Make sure you take care of your father." And then she turned toward my father and beseeched him, "Please forgive me, if I have ever hurt you in any way, forgive me … please, forgive me."

It seemed as if she knew or saw signs of her impending mortality, because these were the last words she uttered before she fell into a coma. The doctors made us aware that the stroke had affected the "brain stem," the lower part of her brain, which controls most functions necessary for survival.

A few days later, after many tests, the doctors determined that the damage to her brain was irreversible. We had to decide whether to put her on a ventilator when she could no longer breathe on her own. Along with all the relatives, I visited my mother every day, but her condition remained the same during the entire month she stayed in the hospital. As a last hope, we brought in a specialist, who also informed us that—beyond putting her on the breathing apparatus when it became necessary—there was nothing medical science could do.

The immediate family, headed by my father, gathered at my brother George's house, a few miles from the hospital, to confer and agree upon a course of action. During a lengthy conversation, it seemed as though everyone expected me to make the final decision. I asked my father his opinion, and he pragmatically declared that he couldn't bear the thought of his wife living as "a vegetable."

At that time, I felt anxious and started shaking while everyone else stayed silent, as if they expected me to say the last word. I asked my brother, George, to bring me another drink, which I immediately gulped down as if it were a glass of water. I needed that stiff drink to calm my nerves, because I was about to tell everyone that I agreed with my father and that we should not let the doctors put my mother on a ventilator.

And so I did. I burst into tears, exclaiming, "Mother, please forgive me if this is the wrong choice, but someone must do it—you can't decide for yourself." I would never forget those gut-wrenching moments, which troubled me for years to come.

On March 19, 1989, I received a phone call from one of my sisters who sadly told me that we had just lost our mother. I remained silent for a few minutes while feeling an overpowering emptiness, realizing I would not be able to communicate with Mother anymore.

Over the following few days, my father and I made all the funeral arrangements, including the selection of two graves at the Fairview Cemetery in Westfield, New Jersey. The plots were side by side, and one of them would be reserved for my father. We held a two-day wake service while the funeral sacrament took place in the Greek Orthodox Church in Union, New Jersey.

At the end of the religious service, I stood next to the coffin and read a poem I had written for my mother as my final good-bye. The poem, presented here, was written in Greek and had eight verses, representing each of her eight children:

Οι Τελευαίοι Χαιρετισμοί
(Για τη μητέρα μου Τσαμπίκα)

The Last Goodbye
(For my mother Tsampika)

Με της αυγής το χάραμα
και το ψωμί στο χέρι
ξεκίνησες πρωΐ πρωΐ
με του νοτιά τ' αγέρι
πήγες μιά μέρα με σκοπό
γιά να καλλιεργήσεις
το περιβόλι της ζωής
το προίκισμα της φύσης.

At the crack of dawn
and a piece of bread in your hand
you set out early morning
with the south wind
You proceeded one day with a
purpose
of fostering the garden of life
the endowment of nature.

Έρριξες σπόρους μες τη γη
κάποτε να βλαστήσουν
γιά να γευθείς τα φρουτα τους
όταν καρποφορήσουν
και τότε όμως πίστευες
τα όνειρα κι' οι ελπίδες
πως μόνο εκπληρώνονται
με χρόνια και ρυτίδες.

You sowed seed in the land
so that once would germinate
so that you enjoy their fruits
when fruition occurs
But even then you believed
that dreams and hopes
can only be met after
many years and wrinkles.

Πέρασαν μπόρες και βροχές
λυώσαν τα πρώτα χιόνια
ήλθε η πρώτη ανοιξη
ήλθαν τα χελιδόνια
και μες στο περιβόλι σου
φυτρώναν τα βλαστάρια
με φύλλα καταπράσινα
και τρυφερά κλωνάρια.

There were storms and rains
melted the first snowfall
then came the first spring came the
swallows
and in your garden
the shoots began to grow
with bright-green leafs
and tender little branches.

Τ' αγάπησες τα δρόσισες
σε τόπο αγαπημένο
εστέριωσες τις ρίζες τους
σε χώμα ευλογιμένο
και όταν ήλθε η ξερασιά
κι' η στέγνωση της βρύσης
τα μάτια σου γίναν πηγή
τη δίψα τους να σβύσεις.

You loved them, you moistened
them
in a favorite place
you protected their roots
in blessed soil
and when the drought came about
and the spout went dry
your eyes became the source
to quench their thirst.

THREE GRAINS OF WHEAT

Προσκήνιο πλάϊ στα δέντρα σου
σκυφτή στα γόνατά σου
κι' η Παναγιά σου χάϊδευε
τα μαύρα τα μαλλιά σου
οι προσευχές σου ακούστηκαν
τα δέντρα μεγαλώσαν
απλώσαν τα κλωνάρια τους
τα φύλλα τους φουντώσαν.

Κι' η χειμωνιά σαν έπεφτε
η αγάπη σου η τόση
τα τύλιγε, τ' αγκάλιαζε
τη ζεστασιά να δώσει
μαζί τους σ' όλες τις χαρές
μαζί και στις οδύνες
πάντα αστήρευτη πηγή
στις φτώχιες και στις πείνες.

Και ήλθε η ώρα η καλή
τα φρούτα να ωριμάσουν
περήφανη καμάρωνες
τα έργα τα δικά σου
κάτι που βγήκε αληθινό
το καρποφόρο γεύμα
το όνειρο που έγραψες
με το δικό σου αίμα.

Έφυγες……μα η μνήμη σου
βαθειά' ναι χαραγμένη
μες τις καρδιές των δέντρων σου
χρυσοστεφανωμένη….
θά' σαι εικόνα αθάνατη
μέσα στην ύπαρξή τους
θά' σαι χυμός στις ρίζες τους
σε όλη τη ζωή τους.

Proscenium next to your trees
crouched on your knees
And the Virgin Mary was touching
your black hair.
Your prayers were heard
the trees grew taller
their branches were spread out
their leaves became denser.

And when the winter came
your never-ending love
wrapped them,, hugged them
to give them warmth.
Always with them in all the plea-
sures
together also in sufferings
always infinite source
in poverty and hunger.

And the good times have come
about
for the fruits to ripen
you had proudly admiring
your own accomplishments
something that came true
the fruitful meal
the dream you once inscribed
with your own blood.

You left ... ... but your memory
is deeply engraved
deep in the hearts of your trees
wrapped in a golden wreath...
you will be an immortal image
in their existence
you will be the fluid in their roots
throughout their lives.

It took a long time for the overpowering grief of my mother's loss to diminish; I felt as if I had been responsible for making the decision to let her go without life support. I often had nightmares in which we had supposedly buried her alive and she came out of the coffin, gazing accusingly at her family and demanding, "What am I doing in this cold, dark place?"

I was also greatly saddened that Mother never knew I had been promoted to vice president, a milestone that occurred during the period she was in a coma. I would have liked her to know how far her son's career had come since those miserable days in the village, where we were not even allowed to dream about such lofty successes.

After my mother was gone, I realized how unfairly I had treated her, especially during my teenage years, when she occasionally visited me in the city. I felt uncomfortable every time my friends saw me together with my mother, because she looked like a typical village woman.

As I grew older, my relationship with my mother had improved and I had come to realize she was a wonderful person, eager to please and help everybody around her. Although my demanding father was not the easiest person to live with, my mother never argued with him. Instead, she would often say, "Whatever you say, my dear husband," as this was her unique way of easing any tension in their relationship.

Even when Mother came to America, her values remained intact. She would help anyone in need, no matter the circumstances; she would always find the good qualities in people; and she would never talk behind anybody's back. These are just a small sample of the many qualities she possessed, but her overall attitude and belief was simply the notion that she had been brought into this world for the purpose of serving others. And that she did, more than anyone I've known.

Now I wish I had another chance to be with my mother, even for a few days, to tell her how I felt after I lost her, and how I feel now. I would like to hug her, kiss her, and tell her for the first time in my life—yes, you've heard me correctly, for the first time—"I love you, Mother," a phrase and an emotion I had never learned to either feel or express until I met Angela, who became my teacher, my friend, and my wonderful wife.

Chapter 53
Company Politics

The Personal Trust project went into the live production mode over the Fourth of July weekend, at which time all of us worked around the clock to complete its grueling installation. Even after the project was in full operation, we had several technical personnel working in shifts, providing around-the-clock coverage to ensure that any potential problems would be addressed and resolved immediately. We took this approach because the overnight processing of all the transactions that were entered each day took about nine to ten hours, so we only had a two-hour window to spare before the morning business day began.

Sometime in the middle of summer, my family and I managed to go away for a week down to the Jersey shore. In fact, our friends Bruce and Rena joined us, renting a two-bedroom apartment next to ours, located within walking distance from the boardwalk.

It was good to get away from the everyday stresses of the office, but even on vacation, I was not completely relaxed. I found myself calling the office several times to check on the status of the system. From the project's initial development through its successful completion, I never felt I had my own management's full support, as they had little understanding of the enormity and complexity of the application and the estate/trust products it processed. In my opinion, they mainly stayed on the sidelines because they didn't believe the project would succeed. If it failed, I would have been the scapegoat.

However, when the project was declared a success, my boss and his manager thought that the size of the project was too big to be managed by one person (me), so they proposed dividing the responsibilities into three sections to be led by three people. One of them would be Mary, who at that time reported directly to me.

Mary stood by my side, loyal as ever, and wanted to continue reporting to me. Her attitude reminded me of a quote by humorist Arnold Glasow: "A true friend never gets in your way unless you happen to be going down."

To make matters worse, I was shocked when my manager gave me an unfavorable (average) annual review, which detailed certain actions I had supposedly taken that were not in line with company policy. I told him I utterly disagreed with the report. When I asked him to give me an example of my incorrect actions, he could not come up with any specifics. As he was not willing to change the content or the tone of the review, I told him that I was going to write a rebuttal and submit it to human resources to be filed together with my annual review.

I was angry and hurt that my management had done an appraisal of my work "blindly." They were totally clueless about what I did all year and had left me alone to sink or swim. (I was certain that, when it came time to write the annual review, my boss had his girlfriend—who later became his wife—do the actual writing, since she had excellent writing skills. The vocabulary and the syntax used in my review were of a much higher level than my boss's writing abilities.)

After the review incident, Mary and I met outside the office to discuss a strategy regarding the pending division of my group. We came up with an outline of the paper we intended to write, which would strongly indicate we were against the group's breakup.

We submitted our proposal, and management agreed to leave the group structure intact. After all this commotion, I took solace in a comment made by Ann, another one of my associates. I remember it well, as this was the second time someone had applied this adage to me. "Mike, I know they did not treat you right," said Ann, "and you didn't get what you deserve. But be patient—the cream always rises to the top."

In September of 1989, Alex started college at Rutgers University's School of Engineering, the campus of which is about a mile from our house. But because he decided not to go away to other colleges that had accepted him, he wanted to live in the dorm. We went along with his request and he moved to the dorm, which was located less than two miles from our house.

At the end of the first semester, he breezed through his classes and got good grades. He didn't need to do too much studying because most of the subjects were a repetition of what he had taken in his honors classes during his senior year of high school. However, the rest of his freshman year was a little more challenging.

Having gone through the experience of dorm life, Alex decided to move back home as he started his sophomore year. Paul also started at Rutgers Engineering School, but after a few months, he realized this was the wrong curriculum for him and he transferred to Rutgers College to pursue a political science major.

***

Right after my mother died, my father's behavior and disposition began to deteriorate. He often made the comment that his life had no meaning without my mother in it. A little more than a year later, he started complaining about a persistent cough that wouldn't seem to go away, despite the many anti-cough remedies he tried. When we finally convinced him to go through some tests, it was determined that he had cancer of the lungs, just below the tracheal tube.

Following the doctor's recommendation, he had surgery, but because of the location of the cancer—right at the joint of the tracheal tube with the lungs—they couldn't do anything and ended up closing the incision. When I found out the results of the surgery, I asked the surgeon how I should tell my father that no cancer cells were removed.

"He will never ask, don't worry," was his reply.

After surgery, my father received the customary chemotherapy and radiation, a treatment that lasted three to four months. Following the treatment, we wanted him to know that the surgery and the treatments had eliminated whatever ailment he had. However, we never used the word "cancer" and, as the doctor had assured us, he never asked, either. For a period of three or four months, he felt much better. In fact, he danced at my niece's wedding, and I was encouraged to see my father so energized and full of joy—almost the way he had been before he became sick.

Alas, after a short while of this "almost back to normal" condition, he relapsed and had to be hospitalized. Several tests determined that the cancer had spread to other organs. By this time, my father must have known he had cancer, but again, he never called his ailment by its name—instead, he referred to his condition as "the bad disease."

He remained in the hospital while the doctors tried to make him more comfortable with pain medication. He was at the point of no return, so at least one member of our family was always by his bedside until one evening when my sister called me after midnight to inform me of our father's passing.

We made funeral arrangements similar to Mother's, using the same funeral home, and almost everyone who knew or had heard of my father was at the wake. The one person I was surprised to see entering the funeral home was Kay C., my boss' manager.

Ever since the merger of the banks, I had not been one of Kay's favorite people, and our relationship remained strictly on the professional level. Within a few years, Kay, who was part of the larger bank that acquired our bank, was elevated from assistant vice president to the senior vice president level. I told her how much I appreciated her visit as we shook hands. I introduced her to Angela, Paul, and Alex and she sat with them for several minutes, offering them words of comfort.

After the religious service in church, Paul eulogized his grandfather, saying a few words about his accomplishments and his intelligence. He emphasized the fact that his high schools teachers had recognized his brilliance and had advanced him from the first to the third level after only two months. My father was buried next to my mother, and their names and dates are engraved on the marble tombstone at the Fairview Cemetery.

It was only a few weeks after my father's death when Kay C. restructured her division and asked me to report directly to her. It seems that her opinion of me must have changed after meeting my family at the funeral home. Or was it me whose view of Kay had changed when Angela and our boys told me what a wonderful lady Kay was? In either case, Kay and I viewed one another as if we had just started a new and healthy relationship. The new reporting structure came as a pleasant surprise to me; not only did it elevate my career one extra notch, but my relationship with Kay C. took an almost 180-degree positive turn!

At the same time, our merger with a Philadelphia bank was proceeding at full speed. A new conversion division was put together to address almost every system that would have to be converted, changed, or eliminated. As for my trust application, it was decided the bank would go back to the outside vendor who had serviced the trust processing before we brought it in-house.

When I found out about this decision, I thought of the comments made by Bob R., who had strongly believed it would benefit the bank financially to continue the trust process with the outside vendor. Bob was one of the brightest consultants I'd ever come across during my professional career. His depth in systems analysis and his impeccable presentation skills made him extremely qualified when dealing with senior management.

Incidentally, Bob and I remained friends even after he worked for other financial firms. Sadly, Bob suffered a massive heart attack and died in

2004 at fifty-five years old, one day after he finished writing a book about "the art of consulting."

He had presented valid arguments about using the outside trust processor, but other executives—who would have benefited if we brought the system in-house—overrode Bob's recommendation. As a result, someone must have thought that Bob was a dangerous consultant, so they found a way to let him go. Yet here we were now, about to go back to what Bob had suggested in the first place; if the bank had followed his suggestion, we would have saved about thirty million dollars.

Under my direct supervision, we assembled a "de-conversion" group that analyzed, programmed, and finally accomplished a successful reverse-conversion. I'll never forget the glowing review my boss, Kay, gave me: "You handled your assignments very well; I'm proud of you!" I was not used to receiving such positive acknowledgements for my achievements, which further proved that Kay's opinion and perception of me must truly have changed.

Toward the end of the trust project, we arranged a farewell dinner for all the consultants who had worked with us. They worked for a firm called FTI, which had sold us the base system. As a surprise, Mary and I put together a "roast" in which we good-naturedly ridiculed every consultant who was present (only one was absent). I read these playful comments right after the main course.

Chapter 54

Puppy Love

At this point, it had already been one year since we lost our beloved first dog, Daphne, whose free-spirited shenanigans and uncanny intelligence had so endeared her to us. I remember it was December 13, a cloudy Sunday, when we had to put her to sleep after she became sick with cancer in many of her organs.

I missed Daphne terribly and tried to convince Angela to get another dog, but she did not want to go through another heartbreaking moment like the one when we said our last farewells to Daphne. Paul was my ally in my crusade and politely asked his mother to go to a pet store just to look at the dogs, and nothing more.

Paul had already put a $20.00 deposit on a yellow Lab puppy with the provision that if Angela didn't like it, he would get his deposit back. As Angela held the darling puppy in her arms, we all declared it the most beautiful creature we'd ever seen. Without batting an eye, we plunked down more than $850.00 and brought Daisy home that evening.

Paul promised he would help train the puppy and, indeed, he spent a lot of time teaching her the basic commands. We even enrolled Daisy in a puppy kindergarten training school, which she attended for ten sessions. Within a short period, she was house-trained and never had an accident in the house, no matter how long she was left alone.

However, during the first year, she was a terror! She chewed on everything in her way, including the stems of the vine around the outside deck. I was forced to install chicken wire in front of the vines and keep it in place until Daisy graduated from the chewing stage. The little rascal also chewed up the air conditioner's rubber hose, which I replaced and also wrapped with chicken wire.

Miraculously, exactly a year after we brought her home, Daisy became the best-behaved dog. It was as if a switch were turned on that activated an educated, obedient dog. As I mentioned earlier, it was true that Daphne had trained us, because we were so ignorant about the freewheeling behavior of dogs. With Daisy, it was different. Our training efforts paid off, as Daisy was a perfect dog who learned to stay within our property boundaries without any chains or electric fences.

The first year Daisy was with us, we took her to the Poconos to a lakefront house we rented for a week. As soon as I parked the car and opened the back door, Daisy jumped out of the car, ran towards the lake, jumped in the water, and started swimming! Now, this was the first time she had seen water, but since hunters have long used the Labrador breed for retrieving waterfowl, I guess her instincts drew her toward the lake.

All week, she moseyed into the lake whenever she wanted to cool off. She dog-paddled about, as happy as could be. We took Daisy on other trips, too, usually near a lake where she would use her strong, webbed paws to exercise and show off her amazing swimming skills.

When Daisy was a puppy, I promised her that I would do my best to train her, love her, and spend quality time with her, and so I did. We both enjoyed each other's company during our daily walks, no matter the weather conditions. It was just a pleasure having Daisy around. She became the new member of our family and she was treated as such. She truly gave us many years of joy and liveliness.

***

It was around this time that Paul finished his helicopter lessons and became a certified pilot. Later on, he also became certified as an instructor and was hired by an aviation company to train other pilots. He also had certification as an airplane pilot.

As I mentioned in an earlier chapter, Paul paid for his aviation training during his college years without my financial assistance. The way he went about it was ingenious. A budding entrepreneur, he set up shop in our basement and started his own computer business, ordering the required parts, assembling the computers, and selling them to the public. He became an expert on all available hardware and software technology and was able to customize and sell his desktop computers below retail store prices.

Paul began with 386-chip technology and continued through the 486 and up to the Pentium series, at which point he gave up the business, as his profit became marginal. He had decided to start a new business model in information technology consulting. However, he had managed to accumulate enough profit to pay for his flying lessons, which cost more than ten thousand dollars.

I can't say it enough: when Paul wanted to do something, nothing or nobody could stop him. His vision, persistence, and determination were the driving forces that motivated him to achieve his goals.

At this point in time, Alex formed a company named Reallis and began working on his own video game. I will cover this subject in a later chapter, but for now I would like to point out Alex's musical talent. After taking piano lessons for about ten years, he became a formidable pianist, especially after we bought him a synthesizer during his high school years. He used the keyboard to compose, edit, and save his creations on a linked computer.

Alex's musical interests ranged from classical to pop/rock and ultimately to jazz. His Ray Charles improvisations earned him the appreciation and admiration of friends and relatives. His musical talent became evident if one observed his bodily movements and facial expression when he played a piece of his liking on the piano. He was truly feeling every note, as well as the pauses between the notes.

Although his music has been his number one leisure activity, Angela and I are so proud of Alex's musical accomplishments. Besides the enjoyment he realized each time his fingers touched the keyboard, he also entertained others when the opportunity arose.

***

The bank where I worked acquired a new system from a vendor from Texas and I was assigned to manage its customization and installation. It was called the Risk Analysis System and had been designed to analyze the risk level of various loans made both nationally and internationally. The system weighed many factors, including political, social, or military conflicts in some countries, as well as projected energy costs. It then warned loan officers of possible dangers of the bank's exposure to those businesses or geographical sectors. We set up a development lab away from the main programming department, where we spent a year to complete the application's installation and operation.

During that period, our division was reorganized, and I ended up reporting to a new manager, Ken O'Hara, who came from a savings bank we had recently acquired. He had an unusual management style that seemed rather demanding, but at the same time, he didn't listen to what his direct reports told him. He seemed to be bitter about the acquisition of his former bank, where he had been a division executive; now he was a section manager with only a few people reporting to him. His manager, Mike Balanger, was a typically ruthless, New York-trained senior executive who, in my opinion, was only interested in his own advancement.

Ken and Mike Balanger were close friends who had previously worked together at a major New York bank. Ken and I were present at a meeting in which Mr. Balanger and the vice chairman had a major disagreement that had to do with the Risk Analysis System, which was already in operation. The fractious tone of the meeting intensified to the point that the two executives exchanged quite a few harsh words, including some of the four-letter variety, and they almost ended up in a fistfight. Mr. Balanger's Irish temper was getting the better of him and his red face, popping with veins, looked to me like a thermometer that was about to explode.

The argument stemmed from the fact that the vice chairman, who represented the user community, was a proponent of the Risk Analysis System and Mr. Balanger was not. In fact, Mr. Balanger had already fired Harry, the user project manager, claiming he had far exceeded the project's developmental budget.

Two days after that contentious meeting, Ken met with me in his office and delivered a disturbing ultimatum. "Listen, Papasavas, whatever we discuss here must stay between us," he said *sotto voce*. "If you tell anyone, I will flat out deny it. So, here's what you must do if you want to keep your job. You will write some virus-like software to be inserted in the Risk Analysis System to make it dysfunctional for at least a month."

I was struck dumb. After a long pause, I managed to reply, "Do you mean that you want me to intentionally sabotage the system for no reason whatsoever?"

"The reason is that our boss, Mr. Balanger, was humiliated by the vice chairman in front of all the people who attended that nasty meeting. He wants to punish him by making the system he uses inoperable. So you've got one of two choices: you either plant the virus or lose your job. What will it be?"

It took me a few seconds to digest the essence of the intention, but I responded firmly. "I was in a similar situation before where I was not willing to compromise my moral principles and I unjustifiably suffered a demotion. Here I am again, facing a similar situation, with you asking me to do something that is against my beliefs and work ethics. Well, let me also tell you, flat out: *No, I will not do it!*"

I knew Ken hadn't expected this answer. His eyes flared, his neck turned red, and his mouth was set in an angry line. "Okay, Papasavas, don't say I didn't warn you," he sneered. "You've made your bed and I won't be responsible for the consequences."

Two weeks passed, and all was quiet regarding Ken's diabolical scheme and his threats to my job. The incident never came up again, but afterwards, my relationship with Ken was always strained.

Then we received an announcement that our bank was about to be acquired by and merged with a North Carolina banking institution. This announcement must have been the main reason Ken's priorities had shifted. He was no longer concerned about me; instead, he and Mike Balanger were trying to save their own positions within the new organization.

There was great concern for the information technology personnel in terms of their jobs, because the computer hardware, as well as the programming division of the merged banks, would be located in North Carolina. It was assumed that several jobs would be eliminated, either because of duplication or the fact that some people would not want to relocate.

After an interview process that was conducted by the North Carolina executives, the selected candidates, including myself, were given job offers— provided we wanted to relocate. In fact, we were given the option to visit the new location for three or four days, all expenses paid, to check out the new city in terms of housing, neighborhoods, and other job-related aspects.

Angela and I went to Charlotte, North Carolina, in the beginning of January 1996. Jack, one of my direct reports, also came along with his wife, Mary. We saw some beautiful houses twice the size and half the price of our home in New Jersey. Angela and I had dinner with my potential manager, who tried to convince me to make the move by emphasizing that my expertise was truly needed in the bank's emerging client/server technical projects.

While we were in North Carolina, we were informed that a big snowstorm was going to hit the entire eastern seaboard, so we decided to leave one day early. On the last day of our stay, Saturday, January 6, we went to a Greek church to observe the Epiphany service, a holiday dedicated to Jesus Christ's baptism. When the church service was over, the snow had already started covering the grassy areas.

I called the airline and arranged for a flight early that afternoon. When we arrived in New Jersey, everyone was preparing for the biggest snowstorm in twenty years. Fortunately, Angela managed to go grocery shopping before the heavy snow arrived. By the end of Sunday night, the accumulation was about thirty inches. I was lucky enough to own a small snow-blower, which came in handy, not only for my own driveway, but also for a few of my neighbors who were trying to dig their cars out with snow shovels.

After we came back from North Carolina, I had two weeks to let our management know whether I was willing to accept the relocation option. However, Angela had already made up her mind that she wouldn't possibly make the move and leave friends and relatives behind. I agreed with her, although I wouldn't have minded getting involved in another adventure or new start, as I was overdue—since my last real adventure had been my move to America during my younger years.

I communicated my decision to management and they, in turn, determined June 30 would be the last day of my employment with the bank. I would receive my severance pay as well as my accumulated pension benefits, which they generously recalculated. They awarded me an additional three years of service, which brought my total years with the bank to twenty, and they also added another three years to my age. And so, with the combination of service and age, I just made it over the threshold that brought my pension percentage to 85 percent instead of the 50 percent I would have received with only nineteen years of service.

When I finally understood all the permutations they used to calculate the pension benefits, it dawned on me that, when I left the insurance company in March of 1980, I had forfeited all benefits because I needed another four months to be fully vested. However, had I stayed with the insurance company for three more months, thus starting with the bank in the middle of July, I would not have enough time during 1980 to be counted as a full year of service in my new job. In that case, my total years of service with the bank would have been nineteen.

I mentioned earlier in the book that some people told me I was crazy to resign my position before I was fully vested, since I only would have had to stay for three more months to complete the required ten years. Although not obvious then, my decision was a blessing in disguise. No one, not even me, could have predicted my bank retirement benefits would dwarf what my pension with the insurance company would have been.

Although I was getting a good severance and pension, I still had to find another job, so I started sending out resumes as well as attending various job fairs. Fortunately, I was offered a position by one of my ex-consultant associates who was an executive with a major insurance company. At the same time, I made sure that my friend, Mary Haniotis, would also be offered a job—and so she was.

I was thrilled when Paul came into our bedroom one morning and woke us up, teasingly waving a Federal Express envelope, which I asked him to open. Inside was an offer for the position of vice president with a salary almost double what I had made at the bank. I felt like I had won the lottery!

When I called Mary with the wonderful news, she told me she had also received a similar envelope with a generous offer. We congratulated each other on our respective triumphs and were elated we would still be working together.

The next day, I filled out the job acceptance form and indicated on the form that my starting day would be September 3, 1996. When I contacted Bill, my future manager, he had no problem with my starting date.

Right after I secured my new job, I began making arrangements for a six-week trip to Greece. I got in touch with my friend, Dimitri, in Rhodes, who insisted that we stay in one of his vacant apartments. He did not want to accept the option of us staying in a hotel or even at my sister Mary's house, where it would have been a tight squeeze, given her family's large size.

My last day at the bank was Friday, June 28, 1996. As I walked down the hallway toward the exit, all the memories of my many years in that building came flooding back and my eyes welled with tears. It was hard to close this chapter of my life, but my association with the bank had to come to an end so that my next occupational adventure could get underway.

A few days later, my friend, Mary, and Angela arranged a surprise farewell dinner in one of my favorite restaurants. The invitees were a selective group of associates with whom I'd had a good rapport during the later years at the bank. I was truly touched by the appreciation that bunch of great guys had shown me, as everyone gave me a gift along with their good wishes for my new endeavor.

Chapter 55

Summer Fun

Our flight to Greece was scheduled for July 5, so on Sunday, June 30, we invited a few close friends over to our house and we had a barbecue cookout on the deck, where we spent all afternoon having a great time. Our guests included Mary and her husband; he worked for the airline we were taking, and he promised to upgrade our tickets to business class. So it seemed that, without even trying, everything was falling into place: going on a six-week vacation and returning home to a new, exciting, and lucrative job. Life didn't get any better!

Flying business class from New York to Athens was a great experience, starting at the VIP lounge at JFK Airport. The nine-hour flight was comfortable in the wider seats, and the service from the flight attendants was excellent.

In Athens, we stayed for a week in the first floor apartment at the house belonging to Angela's brother, Maki, just as we had in 1984 when we'd had the children with us. I don't recall much of how we spent our time in Athens except for a few trips to the beach and meeting Angela's friend, Rena. However, the five weeks we stayed in Rhodes was probably the best vacation we have ever had.

Instead of describing some of the highlights of this great vacation, I would rather translate a sixteen-page vacation review I wrote to Dimitri and his wife when we returned to the States. I intended to write a one-page letter thanking them for their hospitality, but it ended up being a sixteen-page chronological travelogue of the trip's many highlights.

Titled "Our Stay in Rhodes," here is an excerpt from the translation, as well as some clarifications for the reader

Our dearest friends Dimitri and Sophia,

We cannot find the appropriate words to thank you nor adequately to describe what we really felt during the time we spent with you. Naturally, for many reasons, this trip will definitely be an unforgettable event, but we especially want to thank you for all the love and friendship you showed us and for everything you did for us with so much care and finesse. So, the only things we brought back with us are the memories, especially those we spent and lived with you. And ... what memories! I don't know where to begin.

Arrival in Rhodes

The reception we received at the airport—not to mention the apartment you had prepared for us, the food-filled refrigerator, and the other details you had thought of and prepared—was something that we have recognized and valued so very much. Come on, guys, you surpassed all of our expectations.

First Sunday in Trianta

Trianta is a little town where Dimitri's summer house is located. In Trianta, we shared some unforgettable moments—evenings and late nights spent having a great time without any care in the world. We called Dimitri's property "The Garden of Eden," a parcel of several acres filled with all kinds of fruit trees and vegetable gardens. It spanned all the way to the beachfront, where Dimitri took his daily swims.

On our first day in Trianta, we joined Dimitri for a short swim. When we returned from the beach, Sophia had already prepared many Greek delicacies, while Halili (Dimitri's gardener), who was a lively, cheerful fellow with a big smile, was ready to share with us the fruits and vegetables he had gathered from the garden.

Halili was an incredible man. He even had some artistic talents. This can be proven from the selection of vegetables and fruits and the arrangement he created in the middle of the wooden table. Of course, we took a picture of the arrangement, enlarged it, and made three copies, one of which is hanging on our kitchen wall, labeled "Trianta 1996." I hope Halili appreciates his copy and your copy stays hung as we left it, under the eaves of the Trianta house.

First Sunday Night in Haraki

On Sunday night, we drove to Haraki, a little resort beachfront village. We enjoyed our walk along the beachfront, where the reflection of the dancing lights on the calm waters of the inlet made a spectacular pan-

338

orama. On the way back to the city, Sophia realized that she had lost her favorite silk scarf; probably the wind had blown it away. However, Bill and Billitsa (Sophia's cats) love Sophia and they appreciate all the care she provides for them, and they made sure that lost scarf was replaced. (We bought a new scarf and gift-wrapped it. The note inside said it was a present from Bill and Billitsa. By the way, they named their cats after Bill Clinton, whom they liked very much!)

The Night the Lights Went Out

The lights went out one evening. The entire city of Rhodes was without electricity! We went to the apartment and began searching for either a flashlight or a candle, but we didn't find either. In fact, we were surprised, because Sophia had thought of almost everything—except for a candle. We later discovered that she had put a few candles in one of the cabinets, but in the darkness, we had failed to locate them.

We took the car and drove downtown, but even there, it was as dark as everywhere else. Finally, the lights came back on around 10:30 p.m. We went to an outdoor restaurant named Alexandros in a park-like setting, where we had dinner in a cozy, private spot that was surrounded by flowery bushes. In fact, I knew the owner and his family, who were born in the same village as I was.

At one point, the wind picked up and Angela felt a little cold. The waiter noticed that she was somewhat uncomfortable and the best he could do was to bring a white tablecloth, which she wrapped around her shoulders. When we got back to the apartment, we learned that Dimitri had been searching all over, trying to find us.

First Trip to the Village

The following Sunday, we set out for the village Agios Isidoros. When we passed the Monastery of St. John (Artamiti), every location reminded me of my childhood memories and events; I thought they had occurred in another lifetime. It seemed as though all the liveliness that existed when we were young had faded away, and what I saw now while driving by the familiar locations—Milo ... Atria ... Kaminia ... Souloutrana—are simply shadows of a distant reality. Back then, there was lots of noise; there was movement of people and animals everywhere; we could hear voices all around us. And now ... all is quiet! I wonder, though, if everything has changed, or maybe it is I who changed. Even the trees and the bushes seemed somewhat depressed ... and quiet. I was thinking that perhaps I need to live again close to those trees and the overall local nature around the village, and perhaps then I might be able to see them livelier and more real, like it was back in my younger years.

When we were driving through Campus, about one kilometer from our destination, we saw the village from a distance. This view was an extraordinary image that unfolded in front of me, something I hadn't seen since 1984. That moment I thanked God who granted me the opportunity to revisit my village, the place where I was born and had spent the first twelve years of my life.

In the village, we met the rest of the relatives, acquaintances, and all the old women, who kissed us on both cheeks every time they met us because they assumed that we were all related. Together with my sister, Vasilia, we visited the house where I was born. This time, it looked much smaller than it had in 1984. I marveled that there had been twelve people living in this little house and a few animals kept in the back room during the winter months. We endured a Spartan kind of life, the limitations of which we had inherited from our forebears. We learned to live with what we had without complaining, but we were continually searching and hoping for something new and of superior quality. Did we find it? Who knows!

We returned to the city after dropping off my Aunt Katerina in one of the villages (Salako). She went there to sell some handmade tablecloths and jars filled with pure honey, the source of which was the bees that gathered the nectar from the aromatic thyme plants. Aunt Katerina had friends in almost every village on the island of Rhodes, whom she visited from time to time while selling various products to support herself, thus avoiding becoming a burden to her relatives. However, she never gives up. Although her vision has reached a point that she can hardly recognize faces, she still moves around pretty sure-footedly from village to village. Perhaps this is what keeps her steady on her feet, despite her age and all her infirmities.

Sophia in Athens

During this period, Sophia went to Athens for a few days. The truth is, we were a little worried because of the unexpected urgency to fly to Athens, but Dimitri made us aware that everything was fine. We assumed she was getting some sort of therapy or treatment, but Dimitri did not divulge anything. In the meantime, everyone and everything around Dimitri's residence, people and cats, were like fish that had just jumped out of the water. Even Dimitri admitted the void and said how much he missed Sophia.

"But why didn't you tell her so, Dimitri?" We (men) take many things for granted, but women are more sensitive in this area and they want to hear it from us … every day! Anyway, we then realized what Sophia's presence meant. That was when Billitsa (the cat) started visiting our apartment and began getting used to us. She later continued her daily visits when Dimitri and Sophia were not around, as if we were her second choice.

The Garden Watering in Trianta

One day around noontime in Trianta, I devoured an overabundance of figs, which happen to be my favorite fruit, especially when I can pick them directly off the fig tree. I had them before lunch and then I had them again after lunch. White figs, dark figs, purple figs …. almost every known variety! Right after lunch, Dimitri and I started watering the vegetable gardens because Halili, his gardener, was away on another island, visiting relatives.

After Dimitri left for work, I continued watering the tomato plants. They were professionally planted in many rows of parallel furrows in almost perfect alignment. I'm sure this was the work of Halili, whom we regarded as an artist and a perfectionist. I often used a hoe to change the flow of the water from one furrow to another, just the way we did it in the village when we were young. What an enjoyable chore it was that unforgettable afternoon!

I even took off my sandals and felt more comfortable and unrestrained with my bare feet in the muddy furrows. It was just an incredible sensation! I felt as if I were a little boy who was playing in mud puddles. It took me until 8:30 p.m. to finish watering the entire garden—almost four hours—but I truly felt great. It was something I would never forget. I had once considered it to be an undignified and laborious chore, but now the same task was indeed a pleasurable and leisurely activity.

Wedding in the Village

We all started getting ready for the wedding ceremonies in the village. (I don't remember whose wedding it was, but almost everyone in the village was invited to these types of events.) Dimitri's orders were mainly for Angela to get a good night's sleep on Friday night so that she would be able to stay up the entire night on Saturday.

We set off for the village on Saturday afternoon. We stopped at a beachfront restaurant, where we had lunch on the porch adjacent to the seafront. The reason I remember this detail is because the setting and the food were just magnificent. When we arrived in the village, the usual late afternoon "northern wind" was becoming stronger and stronger. As we walked toward my sister Vasilia's house, Angela had to hold on to me because of the strong wind gusts. At my sister's, we had an early dinner, a soup-like dish called *patsas* (tripe soup), a delicacy for those of us who don't have the opportunity to enjoy it often.

After dinner, together with my two nephews, we went to the village hall where the wedding festivities had already begun. The dancing was at its peak when we entered the hall. Dimitri and Sophia arrived around midnight and joined us at the table where we sat with my nephew, George, and his wife, Dina. With us also was an old friend, Kyriako, with his wife, Meritsa, a fun couple with an interesting background regarding the way they bonded, or rather eloped, before they got married. We drank plenty of wine and whiskey and danced to the bouzouki music my other nephew, Savas, was playing.

Sophia left at 1:30 a.m., but we stayed until the music stopped in the pre-dawn hours of the morning. At that time, I tried to play the bouzouki and sang one of my favorite songs, but due to fatigue and my alcohol consumption, my fingers did not have the dexterity to press firmly on the instrument's strings, thus the sound must have been a little off. In the end, however, I got a nice round of applause when I finished singing.

When we left the hall, we all realized that we were hungry. I remembered that my sister had plenty of *patsas* left, so my nephew, George, went to her house and took the whole pot to Kyriako's house. When Meritsa started warming up the soup, she said that she did not have any lemons in the house. When Greeks eat patsas, there must be fresh lemons available, for almost everyone likes their soup sour. Another member of the band, Thanasi, who had also joined us, said that earlier in the afternoon, he had seen a lemon on a nearby lemon tree. He dashed out and, in a few minutes, he came back with a fresh-picked one. Everyone enjoyed the soup and bestowed many kudos upon Vasilia.

And then Kyriako started describing the events related to his love affair and adventures with Meritsa: the development of their so-called forbidden relationship—according to her strict parents—who believed that Kyriako had kidnapped their daughter. Before Kyriako finished his story, Dimitri observed that Angela's eyes were closing, so it was decided we should continue the story another time.

When we went outside at 7:00 a.m., Dimitri commented that we had managed to stay up all night and that now we should get a few hours of sleep before the next celebration began. We slept at my sister Mary's village house, which was vacant since her primary residence was in the city. At 12:30 p.m., we heard Dimitri outside the house yelling, "Hey, guys, wake up! It's raining hard, get your umbrellas and come out!" Of course, he was joking, because it almost never rains in Greece in the summer.

While Angela was getting ready with her morning routine, I joined Dimitri and some other people at the café who had already started drinking ouzo and munching from an assortment of appetizers. When Angela joined us, we all mingled with the wedding crowd outside the church. As is customary, the wedding party began dancing to the traditional tunes the band was playing. Somewhere in the crowd, Dimitri pointed out a lady standing close to me named Sevasti. I wouldn't have recognized her, as her wrinkled face made her look at least fifteen years older than me. I approached her and introduced her to Angela.

"This is Sevasti, the first girl I had a crush on. Dimitri and Elias were also in love with her."

Without missing a beat, Sevasti replied, "But there was another fellow who was also in love with me: Pete."

"Oh, yes, I forgot about him," I grinned.

"But I was the most beautiful girl in the village, wasn't I?" asked Sevasti with a wide smile on her face.

"Of course, you were stunningly attractive!" I concurred. "You were the prettiest girl in the village."

Sevasti laughed and said, "Ah, but someone else was smarter than all four of you. Emanuel acted swiftly and ended up marrying me." She sighed wistfully, because Emanuel had died at a relatively young age.

I was sure she was pleased with our playful conversation, which reminded her that somewhere in the past she had been a pretty girl who was aware that several boys were interested in her. For a brief moment, deep in the shadow of her smile, I visualized the innocent—or was it shrewd?—little girl she had been.

After dinner, Dimitri and Sophia left for the city. Angela and I also went home (to my sister Mary's house) and sat on the front porch to enjoy the quiet night with a sky full of bright stars and the singing of the crickets. Without exchanging any words, Angela and I held hands, reveling in our oneness as only true soul mates can. I looked up at the sky and silently thanked Him for my good fortune: "Thank you, God, for you making it possible for me to be here this very moment, with my wife Angelica, the one You gave me as a gift, the woman I love very much."

At that moment, I remembered the poem I had written in February of 1969, right after we made up following our brief separation. Here is a rough translation from the Greek version:

Thank You, God

When the almond trees began flowering
And the birds built their nests
While I was also building
My own nest
The skies opened up
And I heard a voice
And it was the answer
To my request
Then, flowering spring
Spread before me.

Thank you, Creator
Thank you, God!
You've heard the prayer
I sent to You …
And the angels caressed her
With their white wings
You told them to give her
Their own name—Angel-ica
You brought her in Your world
And awarded her to me
As it was meant to be
A dream that came true
God I owe much gratitude
And many thanks
I have saved for You.

And so I spent a beautiful and unforgettable evening together with the
lady of my dreams, my wife!

Chapter 56

Travelogue

O n Monday, after the wedding, I decided to visit some locations of importance, places of which I had significant memories. I first drove to the closest place, where once we had a garden and a few fruit trees: a fig tree, an orange tree, and a tangerine tree. I remembered my younger years, when I frequently watered the vegetable gardens my father planted. In those days, all the gardens were huge in size, full of walnut and fig trees. They seemed like paradise. Now they seemed so small and abandoned, with a few scrubby trees here and there, surrounded by wild growth.

Next I stopped at my favorite place, called Pithana, a location featuring a spring water fountain as well as the many vegetable gardens, fruit trees, and the narrow, winding paths I once took to get to our parcel of land. I had a hard time finding the two properties we owned because the natural, wild growth had taken over, thus altering the terrain which was once was so familiar. Everything had changed, as if someone had shrunk the entire location.

I finally located one of our larger properties, and there stood the cactus tree I had planted when I was ten years old. It was around noon and the sun was blazing, but fortunately, I was driving in an air-conditioned car. I stopped near some pine trees and walked on a narrow path through the foliage.

At one point, I observed the needles of the pine trees swaying back and forth, stirred by a slight breeze. At that moment, I sensed someone was talking to me. It was almost as if God were communicating with me. I felt as if I were an extension of the nature around me. It was a beautiful moment that I will always remember.

I drove back past the village for the purpose of visiting a place where we had a sizable property with many olive trees and a stable that housed tools and other necessities for overnight stays. That's where my grand-mother kept the flock of sheep for part of the year. At one point, I turned my head and concentrated on the trunk of an olive tree, and at that moment I visualized my mother, just the way she looked when she was young and full of life, with her long, black hair tousled by the light breeze.

I remember that day very well. She appeared to me surrounded by the sheep and little spring lambs. She sang, with her beautiful voice, while the bleating lambs sounded as if they were accompanying her with their high-pitched *baas*. The bees were buzzing around, too, while collecting the nectar from the abundance of thyme bushes.

I considered that day a true delight, a blissful interlude. But with deep sadness I thought, "Where is my mother now?"

Gimouki Family

One of the pre-planned events each time I am in Rhodes is to visit the Gimouki sisters, one of which is Bemba, who was the girl of my dreams when I was in high school. The first sister I met was Georgia, whom I ran across the last time I was in the village. Next I met Eleftheria, with her husband Emanuel, and then I visited Marina in her house. Based on their deep facial wrinkles, I have to say the years had not been kind to the once comely sisters.

When I was at Marina's house, she gave me two poems I had written back in 1957. I wrote one specifically for Marina on her name day—the feast of a saint after whom a person is named. The other, entitled "Gimouki Family," I wrote solely for Bemba to see—but since I hadn't had the cour-age to give it to her, I'd decided to write a few verses for each of her sisters as well. This way, in that the entire family would read the poem, I knew Bemba would definitely see it. It was sort of a cowardly approach, but shrewd on my part, given my limited (almost nonexistent!) experience with girls.

Marina commented that she had saved these two poems as a note-worthy remembrance of our younger years. In fact, she told me she had memorized them after reading them so many times. One night in Trianta, we read those two poems and, at the same time, we also reviewed my vis-its and commented on each of the six Gimouki sisters.

A few days later, Angela and I visited Bemba at her parents' house. Both her mother and father had aged a great deal since the last time I'd seen them, in 1984. In fact, her mother was completely blind, but she recognized my voice. Bemba had lost some of the freshness she'd had twelve years earlier, but she was still attractive and younger-looking than her sisters.

We stayed for more than two hours with the center of conversation being her daughter and her grandchild, as well as her son-in-law, who was a pediatrician. Bemba was proud of all of them and never stopped talking about their successes. I didn't blame her for being so enthusiastic, because since her husband had died at a young age, she had sacrificed her life and focused only on her daughter's successful upbringing. It was a true sacrifice for a nineteen-year-old widow to forfeit everything in life except for her family! It seemed unbelievable for such a beauty to stay a single parent for all her life.

Nevertheless, judging from the results, she has accomplished her goal and she now enjoys the rewards of her sacrifice. She totally convinced me that she never second-guessed herself with her decision "to live only for her daughter." Struggling uphill against the wind, Bemba met or exceeded her own expectations. As one Greek philosopher said (τα αγαθά εν κώπεις κτώνται) which means: "Hard work yields the goods we seek." Enough said about Bemba.

Professor Fotis Varelis

One of the most enjoyable days was when I visited my professor, Fotis Varelis, an exceptional man and teacher whom none of his students has likely forgotten. He was the kind of teacher who allowed us to think and express our opinions freely. When we made mistakes, he didn't tell us in a superior way, "This is wrong." Instead, with a calm temperament and a big smile, he showed us not only how to correct our misstep, but how to improve on it.

It was Prof. Varelis whose positive influence convinced me to believe in my talent for writing poetry. I may not be the greatest poet, but once in a while, when the right moment or the right person is the subject, I can definitely write a few clever verses. Prof. Varelis, I thank you for being my greatest influence during my school years, and I truly wish there were a few more teachers like you among today's educators.

As soon as I entered the gate of his house, Prof. Varelis met me with a wide, beautiful smile, just the way I remembered him. Over a cup of coffee, he gave me an overview of his interesting life after retiring from the teaching profession. Starting in 1970, he had concentrated on his writing, which became his most important activity. He possesses a unique philosophy of life, and I admire in general how he develops and analyzes thoughts on almost any subject.

It was a great achievement for him to write about fourteen books between 1970 and 1992. He gave me six of his books, five of which I had already read within a few weeks after returning to America in August 1996. I particularly liked this passage from his poem "When we were young:" *"Those days, when life was simpler, if we were not hungry and if we didn't hurt, then we were happy."*

I'm glad I had a chance to spend a few hours with Prof. Varelis and I would like to thank him for giving me the opportunity to meet face to face, because he was truly the personification of peacefulness—and, in his own humble way, he epitomized the definition of human kindness. Prof. Varelis' philosophy and the man himself have been an enduring inspiration for my creative life.

Festival in Fanes

Another memorable event was the day of the festival in Fanes, a village about twenty kilometers from the city. We arrived there late in the afternoon and joined the crowd in the town square, where all the activities were taking place. We walked up and down the main street where we met many people we knew, including my Aunt Katerina, who had a hard time identifying us because of her poor vision. All the vendors on both sides of the street displayed an assortment of games and a smorgasbord of food items, including sweet delicacies.

I was thinking how wonderful it would have been if I were eight years old and had all these delicacies at my disposal! Unfortunately, this is how life is: when we get older, we have the means to buy those things that only young people enjoy. What an irony! We also spent some time with my sister, Vasilia, and my two nephews at an outdoor restaurant, where we had a few beers and barbecued eats while the band played on a temporary stage.

On the way back to the city, when we passed Dimitri's house in Trianta, we noticed all the lights in the front of the house were on, the gate was wide open, and Sophia and Dimitri were sitting on the veranda. I immediately made a U-turn and parked the car on a side street. We then joined them for a supposedly brief visit, but we ended up staying until 2:30 a.m.

Dimitri explained, "We were waiting for you—that's why I left all the lights on and the gate open, so that you would see us."

That evening and those moments we spent together will remain special indeed, because everything just happened without planning—an impromptu meeting of the minds! We carried on an interesting conversation, touching on many subjects of deep philosophical substance. When we left, Angela said it had been one of the most beautiful nights we'd ever spent together with our friends.

Full Moon in Kalyva Restaurant

Angela always wanted to go back to the Kalyva Restaurant to relive those moments in 1984 when we first went there and had dinner next to the splashing waves. Dimitri was waiting for the full moon so that the setting would depict exactly the same ambience as the last time we were there. So we went to Kalyva on the "full moon" evening in August and our table was again located right on the beach, close to the water.

The moon was shining on the calm waters of the sea and we could clearly see the Monte Smith knoll—the site of the Acropolis of ancient Rhodes—located above the semi-circular coastline that stretched from Trianta all the way to the city of Rhodes. The majestic scene made me truly happy. I contemplated whether I would be able to recall those moments in the future to remind myself how contented I was. Why is it that we appreciate the value of something only when we lose it or cannot get it at will?

Farewell Dinner at Trianta

We arrived at Dimitri's summer house in Trianta around 9:00 p.m. The enlarged, framed photograph of Halili's fruit arrangement hung on the wall under the rear eaves of the house, directly below the spotlight. A few guests had already arrived, some of whom I met for the first time. My sister, Anna, arrived with her husband, Emanuel, who had come to Rhodes from America a few days earlier. Dimitri's in-laws, Christos and Eleni, whom we had met several times, were also among the guests.

Speaking of Christos, I remember the silly joke he told us one evening, an old chestnut that made my father laugh his heart out every time he heard it. It goes like this: "Once upon a time, there were two people. When the one departed, there was only one person left. When he also departed, there was nobody left."

Yanni, his wife, and their dog, Rocky, also showed up. A month after we returned to America, we learned that Yanni passed away after suffering a massive heart attack. He was in his early fifties. We missed him terribly.

Believe it or not, everyone was there, sitting at a long banquet table, except for Dimitri! He had a problem with his car, but he finally arrived, half an hour late. We feasted on the many dishes and delicacies that were spread out over the entire length of the table, as well as a sea of drinks of all kinds. We laughed over many jokes, but we had to keep their content

G-rated because there was also a youngster sitting with us. At one point, I read the satirical poem I had written in 1961, when I went on a survival outing to a deserted beach with my friend Postoli. To my great satisfaction, some of the guests were able to understand the village dialect it was written in.

At this juncture, I would like to mention a subject we touched upon each time we got together with Dimitri and Sophia. The first time we had lunch together, Dimitri said that he had a surprise for all of us, which had to do with a letter dating back to the early sixties. He added that the letter would be read at the appropriate time, so every time we were together, Angela, Sophia, and I all begged him to show it to us, but Dimitri would not yield to our pleas. His usual response was, "It's not the right time yet."

After that night's dinner, we were hoping he would read the letter, because our curiosity had been piqued beyond the limits of our patience. Well, you've guessed it: it was not the right time yet!

Last Time at Trianta

It was Friday, August 9, and again we went to Trianta, but this time only Kyriako and Meritsa had joined us. During dinner, Kyriako resumed telling the love story we had interrupted a week or so ago because Angela was falling asleep after the all-nighter on the day of the wedding.

Having been a bus driver before he retired, Kyriako began describing some funny episodes resulting from his interaction with some of his passengers. He admitted he was bothered when he was called "Pops" or "Uncle," especially by riders who were almost as old as he was. Bottom line, Kyriako was a fun guy to be with.

At last, the moment had arrived when Dimitri took out the letter and asked me to read it. Sophia and Angela assumed comfortable, seated positions and listened with their mouths wide open. It turned out I had sent this letter to Dimitri in 1962 when I lived in Manheim, Germany, although I couldn't remember having written it. The gist of the letter was the fact that I knew a Swedish girl who was planning to go to Rhodes and I had asked her to meet Dimitri. Here's an excerpt of the actual text:

I'm sending you a Swedish bombshell, completely trained and with excellent references. She has outstanding experience and she is ready for almost anything. The only thing you have to do is to welcome her and the rest will take its natural course.

The rest of the letter continued in a similarly flippant vein. The women were somewhat disappointed because they were expecting something more dramatic. Anyway, I curiously asked Dimitri to tell us whatever happened with the Swedish girl. He explained that he met her, they went out to dinner and to the beach, but he always took someone else (a friend from Cyprus) with him. No wonder Sophia, Angela, and Meritsa were disappointed; they emphasized that Dimitri should understand the term "three is a crowd!"

Last Saturday in Rhodes

On Saturday night, we went to my sister Mary's house to have dinner and see everyone one last time before our departure the following day. All the nephews and nieces were also there, but the overall mood was not as jolly as on the first evening of our arrival in Rhodes. My sister was saddened by the fact that we would be leaving the next day; she always had a hard time accepting the departure of relatives.

When we finished dinner, we started an interesting conversation, primarily about how high people can reach or how much they can accomplish when they have dreams and hopes, and if they always believe in themselves and never lose sight of their dreams, which must be deeply engraved in their psyche. Unfortunately, there are some people who don't even dare hope for something better because they don't believe they have what it takes to compete in a cruel society.

It's almost like those years when we were in high school. We were the low-class villagers as opposed to the city boys, who enjoyed the better things in life and had all the privileges. On the other hand, we couldn't even imagine having any expectations, as if we were destined to remain our whole lives in a much lower class than those city boys. Perhaps poverty forced us to live that way. For example, we wore the same pair of pants for months and did not have any extra money to buy a candy bar from the vendor (Ali) who was stationed in the schoolyard.

We didn't think we were good enough to play ball with the city boys and we believed everything they told us, because they were the true "Rhodians." They wanted us to believe they were more intelligent than we were. Little did we know! We should not have yielded to their presumed superiority, nor should we have behaved as if we were the losers before the competition had even started.

We should have insisted that we also had rights; we should have believed in our abilities and ourselves. But we didn't know any better; no one had taught us how to play and nobody told us that we might have been better equipped, mentally and physically, than the city boys. The one thing we lacked was the social education. So, these were the underlying thoughts of our conversation.

351

The next day, around noontime, Sophia invited us to have lunch with her and Dimitri before we left for the airport. Depressed that our next stop would be the airport, it was difficult for Angela and me to swallow the small bites of the light lunch Sophia had prepared. In a few hours, we would leave behind our friends, with whom we'd spent more than a month. During that time, our friendships had grown continuously stronger. Every one of us tried silently to hide the melancholy of our upcoming separation.

The drive to the airport seemed so short. I didn't want the ride to end; we wanted to avoid the end of a good thing. But I knew that everything in life has a beginning and an end, and we hoped the time we spent with our friends would remain forever as unforgettably good memories.

At the airport, we also met my sister, Mary, and her family. We finally hugged everyone, said our last good-byes, and proceeded to the entrance of the plane. For one last time as the plane took off, I tried to enjoy myself by visually embracing the beautiful beaches of Trianta, the hill of Monte Smith, and everything else I was able to see through the small window of the plane. It was then that I remembered a small poem I once had written about the island of Rhodes.

Here is the original poem in Greek and a rough English translation:

<u>Ρόδος, Πατρίδα μου</u>   <u>Rhodes, my Hometown</u>

Μ' ευχές λουσμένα   Drenched with wishes
λόγια που νοιώθω   Words that I feel
λόγια γραμμένα   Written words
μ' αγάπη και πόθο   With love and longing

Πιστή η λατρεία μου   Faithful is my adoration
πικρός ο πόνος   With bittersweet yearning
μικρή πατριδα μου   My little hometown
γλυκειά μου Ρόδος   My sweetest Rhodes

Μακρυά σου βρίσκομαι   I am far away from you
μακρυά στα ξένα   Away in a foreign land
μα συλλογίζωμαι   But I contemplate
πάντα εσένα   Always your image

Λουλούδι αμάραντο   Perennial flower
μικρό νησί μου   My small island
μείνε αθάνατο   Remain immortal
μες τη ψυχή μου.   In my soul

352

THREE GRAINS OF WHEAT

It was around 2:00 a.m. Greek time in September of 1996 when Dimitri called me to comment about the delightful travelogue he had received. Both Sophia and Dimitri thought it was an excellent piece, something they appreciated and vowed to keep as a valuable memento of our friendship. In fact, he said that, even as we spoke, some of the people I'd mentioned in the writing were there with him, enjoying the travelogue and basking in the limelight I'd shed on them.

Chapter 57

At Death's Door

In September, right after Labor Day, I started my new job. My manager was Bill B., who was indeed an outstanding individual, both personally and professionally. The only negative aspect of the job was the hellacious sixty-four mile commute—*each way*—to the office in Eastern Pennsylvania. The first few days, I was discouraged about the long drive, but eventually I got used to it.

Mary Haniotis started working there two weeks later. We tried to carpool for a while, but it didn't work out, as my schedule forced me to stay longer than the regular nine-to-five shift. The project I was assigned to was already in the last stages of development and beta testing. I had to learn the overall system functionality quickly. A month later, I was given direct management responsibilities of all reporting components.

While operating on a live production mode, we stayed in the Pennsylvania location. Then, in February of the following year, we moved to a nice office complex in Newark, New Jersey. My spacious office had a view of the New York skyline, but more importantly, my commute had been cut in half.

My boss was pleased with both my personal performance and that of my team. I was pleasantly surprised when I found out the resulting bonus I received was 40 percent of my salary. When I also was given my own parking space in the executive garage next to our building, I thought to myself that times had changed, as my career was reaching new heights. In the ensuing months, I hired two more ex-associates from the bank. I also hired my friend Bruce, who was given the title of director and a salary almost twice as much as his previous job.

THREE GRAINS OF WHEAT

I continued strengthening my team by hiring more qualified people, including a redoubtable fellow named Oscar, who—along with Mary and Jack—ultimately became the backbone of my group. It should be noted that Oscar was practically indispensable. His loyalty, hard work, and excellent technical problem-solving abilities were recognized not only by me, but also by my manager and his coworkers. All of us enjoyed our high-paying jobs and got along well with our management and the rest of the people in the department that Bill and I had built from scratch.

For our summer vacation in 1997, we went to Aruba, where Angela and I had a spectacular time at a resort hotel. When we came back, Alex convinced me to get involved in golf, a sport I thought was boring and somewhat silly—chasing a small ball across a well-manicured cow pasture! However, one Saturday afternoon, Alex and I went to the "pitch and putt" area of a golf course, where I learned the basics of the game.

The following weekend, we went back and practiced one more time before we played a round on the real golf course. I remember my first score was an embarrassing 129, but during my second game, I got my first birdie! Since then, I've never looked back, and hitting the links has become a favorite pastime. I enjoy golf every chance I get.

In the late nineties, I mostly teamed up with my friend and former neighbor, Regis Byrnes, at a regulation, nine-hole course called Tara Greens. We would go around twice in order to complete an official game. (Regis and his wife, Frances, remained good friends with whom we met often, either for dinner at a restaurant, or at each other's homes.)

As I teed off early in the morning, I would occasionally feel a discomfort around the upper part of my stomach when I carried my golf clubs from my car to the clubhouse—but after a while, the feeling would go away. In fact, similar episodes had happened in the previous few years during my short morning walks from the parking lot to my office. Again, the pain would subside after I started my routine. As a precaution, my doctor outfitted me with a heart monitor, which I wore for twenty-four hours. The device didn't reveal any abnormalities, but when the same symptoms kept occurring on the golf course, I followed my doctor's advice to go for a stress test.

I was shaken when the cardiologist informed me that the stress test showed one artery had a significant blockage. In order to determine the extent of the blockage, a few weeks later, the doctor performed an angiogram at a nearby hospital. The results revealed an approximately 70 percent blockage in one artery. It was recommended I should have a balloon angioplasty, a procedure in which the artery wall is expanded using a balloon attached to a catheter that the doctor inserts through the femoral artery in the groin area.

After a family meeting, we decided to get a second opinion from another cardiologist. The new doctor reviewed the angiogram pictures and suggested that I should have the balloon procedure. In fact, he described my condition as "a textbook case."

So, I went ahead with the angioplasty, and it seemed to eliminate the morning discomfort after I went back to work. However, a month later, I began to feel even worse than before I'd had the procedure. I went back to the cardiologist who, after another stress test, recommended I have another angioplasty, because the ballooning procedure could have caused significant scar tissue built-up.

In the operating room, the doctor informed me that he had to put in a stent, because the blockage was now above the 90 percent range. This procedure took place on my birthday, December 10, and I waggishly told the nurses stationed around the operating table, "I will remember this birthday because I'm getting my own balloons!" They got a big chuckle out of my jest, but in truth, I was one nervous son-of-a-gun.

As I was going through these medical woes, I didn't enjoy the Christmas holiday, which fell a few weeks after my second angioplasty, as much as I had all the other years. However, I took the time to write the following heartfelt letter:

My Christmas Message to my Wife:
I know that God and my guardian angel have always been with me, especially during the recent difficult times I'm experiencing. Unfortunately, I must go through this process and hope that soon all problems will be behind us. I wish I could share with you the spirit of the holidays as I did in past years, but what I'm asking this time is your patience and understanding until I rebound back to normal. I know it's not easy for everyone around me to tolerate my moody attitude, the way I interact and the way I handle even the small stuff. One thing I know for sure is that you are with me all the time (in spirit when not present), the thought of which is a comforting remedy. At times I believe you are my guardian angel. I need you more now than ever before. I need to lean on you and draw the energy that will help me go on. Please be patient with me a little while longer.
Merry Christmas!

With all my love,
Mike

After the second procedure, I felt better for a few weeks. But I had the disconcerting feeling that something still wasn't right. After yet another (the third) balloon angioplasty in February of 1998, I learned to live with the uncomfortable chest pains, taking my nitroglycerin medication when the pain was unbearable.

Then, one morning in May of 1998, the pain struck when I was driving to work. At the office, my chest pains became so severe I asked my boss, Bill, to take me to the emergency room. This time, I was certain that I would end up having open-heart surgery because, in my humble opinion, the balloon angioplasties and the stent procedure had just made my condition worse! I was admitted in the hospital on a Monday, May 4, and had a double bypass on Friday, May 8, 1998.

I remember the few moments I spent with Angela before they took me to the operating room. Holding her hand, I told her, with a trembling voice, "Darling, even if don't come out alive after the surgery, I wanted you to know that I love you so much and I have no regrets. Despite my medical situation, you gave me the best years of my life—or to put it more bluntly, I started living only after I met you." The last thought I remember before the anesthesia took affect was Angela's image flashing through my closing eyes, until both the image and I faded away.

When I was in the recovery room after the surgery, just about the time the anesthesia started to wear off, I could hear voices as if they were coming from far away. When I tried to lift my heavy eyelids, I saw a few figures in white uniforms and what I thought was my sister, Despina, standing alongside the bed. I closed my eyes and after I assembled some scrambled thoughts, I assumed I had died and the white uniformed, fuzzy figures were angels. I was almost sure about my assumption because, if I were alive, Angela would have been with me instead of my sister.

When Angela came to see me at 6:00 a.m., she told me that the surgeon had instructed her to go home and get a few hours of sleep because it would be a while before I would come out of the anesthesia. Well, later on, when I was fully awake, everything was put in some perspective, although the discomfort and pain were unbearable for the following thirty-six hours.

It was not a pleasant stay, especially for the first few days, being attached to so many tubes and monitors, with nurses taking blood samples throughout the day and night, like insatiable vampires. When my friend, Dimitri, from Rhodes found the number of the hospital room and called me, I broke down in tears of joy, simply because my good friend had made it his business to find a way to get in touch with me during that trying time.

357

I was discharged on Thursday, May 14, a significant day for me because it happened to be the same day we celebrate the memory of Saint Isidore, who is the patron saint of the village of Agios Isidoros.

I went through an entire month of recovery and rehabilitation at home. I began taking short walks, gradually increasing their length until I could do an entire mile without any discomfort. During the first few weeks after I went back to work, both my emotional and physical energy were somewhat weaker than before I'd had the surgery.

A few months later, I also noticed I was experiencing some sort of depression, a condition that often occurs after major surgery, as my doctors informed me. Thankfully, my depression improved after taking a prescribed medication for a few months.

Unfortunately, when I went back for a follow-up visit after the bypass, I was told there was a residual blockage at the graft joint of the two arteries as a result of scar tissue accumulation. I remember that day I was beside myself with worry, outrage, and despair. I was not sure if there were any options left.

On the way home, Angela and I stopped at a mall to withdraw cash from the ATM. Suddenly, I recalled an earlier occasion when Angela had admired a diamond pendant at the jewelry store just across the street from the bank where we were parked. Taking Angela's hand, I guided her to the jewelry store, saying, "Listen, sweetheart, despite all the bad news we learned today, I want to buy you the pendant you liked so much. After all, tomorrow is your birthday ... and life still goes on."

She remained speechless for a while, and then she told me how bad she felt, getting a present under those circumstances. I bought her the pendant anyway. Down through the years, the recollection of those juxtaposed events—the heartbreak of my latest health setback and the *joie de vivre* of buying a special gift for my precious wife—always brought a bittersweet smile to our lips.

After these disappointing findings, I switched to another cardiologist who had been highly recommended by a relative who was a doctor himself. The cardiologist, Dr. Kostis, used a more conservative approach and began treating my condition with medication instead of invasive methods.

In late August, Angela and I drove down to High Point, North Carolina, a city renowned as a marketplace for high quality furniture at discount prices. We stayed in High Point for a few days, where we bought furniture to our liking, and then we headed for the Carolina coast, intending to spend several relaxing days there. However, our mini-vacation was cut short by a few days when we learned that an approaching hurricane was expected to hit hard, right in the place where we were staying. To avoid the massive exodus, we hit the road two days before the hurricane's predicted arrival.

Back at home, we watched TV coverage of the devastating damage that Hurricane Bonnie caused to the Carolina coast when it moved ashore early on August 27, including a frightening shot of the beachfront hotel where we had stayed getting bombarded by huge waves that surged over the five-story building's rooftop. We assumed everyone in the hotel must have been evacuated the day before.

We were hoping to have our furniture delivered before Christmas, but as it often happens with items that have to be special-ordered or manufactured, the shipment was delayed because one of the bed pieces had been incorrectly constructed.

The family Christmas get-together was celebrated in our house, where we had more than fifty guests. Everyone had a wonderful time, except for me. Owing to my health problems, I was a real Scrooge. In contrast with previous years, when I had embraced the holidays with the gusto of a little kid, my recent botched surgeries had me in a real "bah, humbug" mood—especially since my new cardiologist had publicly avowed that all the procedures, including the open-heart surgery, had been unnecessary and that they should have treated my case only with medication.

I remembered that one day at the hospital, I had overheard my doctor, who was the hospital's chief cardiologist, yelling at the bumbling doctor who did all the angioplasties: "You're not a doctor, you're a plumber!" That had given me a much-needed laugh

But what was done was done, and I could not turn the clock back. I had to accept my prognosis and let things take their natural course, and never forget to live life to the fullest, while I could. Angela often reminded me of the adage, "We should count our blessings." Truer words were never spoken. Blessed with a wonderful wife, two handsome and talented kids, more faithful friends than I could count, and a pretty darn good career, I didn't have all that much to complain about!

While I was coping with my health concerns, our department at work relocated from Newark to Edison, a convenient location that was only eight miles from my house. A humorous anecdote concerning a young lady named Maria, whom I was scheduled to interview at the new Edison location, bears mentioning.

An hour after the time Maria was supposed to arrive for the interview, her agent, Erica, called and told me there had been some kind of a mix-up and that Maria would not be able to make it to my office. What actually had happened was a classic misunderstanding. Maria and Erica were supposed to meet at Penn Station at 9:00 a.m., but Maria went to the Penn

Station in *New York* while Erica was waiting for Maria at the Penn Station in *Newark*.

I thought it was an amusing episode, so I asked Erica to reschedule the interview. Erica called me again the morning of the interview, apologizing for Maria, who wouldn't be able to make it because her grandfather had passed away.

By now, my curiosity was piqued and I wanted to see Maria in the flesh. I wondered if she still dared to come for an interview after the mishaps she had gone through in such a short period. The third time's the charm, as they say. Maria showed up and sat in a chair across from my desk, looking nervous and a bit shaken.

During the interview, she was able to answer most of the technical questions. But at one point, this bright, young, pretty girl said in a faltering voice, "I won't b-blame you if you d-don't hire me, Mr. Papasavas, because I messed up the first two appointments. I know you were p-patient with me, but I don't deserve it."

After she left my office, I was certain about her technical ability as well as her overall strength of character. I saw a hidden talent waiting to be nudged to emerge from its dormant state—she just needed someone to believe in her abilities and give her the opportunity to prove herself.

I hired Maria. Right from the start, she blended well within my group. Oscar became her mentor for the next several months when she was assigned to work in his unit. Somewhere along the line, their mentor/pupil relationship blossomed into a hot and heavy romance, culminating in a marriage made in heaven! I won't say much more about Oscar and Maria, other than they are at the top of the list of my favorite folks. They frequently send me greeting cards and emails in which they express their gratitude for bringing them together.

Matchmaker Mike, that's me!

Chapter 58

The Later Years

In the summer of 1995, when he was twenty-four years old, Alex began working on his own computer-action video game—called *Rogue Wars*—with a few other part-time developers in an office down in the basement of our house. This has long been Alex's dream, and he now had the opportunity to complete and market his game in a fiercely competitive industry.

While the game was still at the beta stage, he attended a few conferences in California, where he presented his idea to agents and executives, hoping to receive positive endorsements that would ultimately lead to the additional funding necessary to bring the project to fruition. Alex needed to hire a few more people, but he didn't have the financial means without the sponsorship of a big company, such as Microsoft or Sony.

Working as the only full-time developer, he finally recognized his underdog status and realized he couldn't compete with other gaming companies whose technical and manpower resources dwarfed his own. Nevertheless, Alex's extensive experience in the gaming sector was not wasted; it had earned him a great reputation, an attribute that helped him get a good job with a local video game company.

Alex stayed with that company (Quartix) for a few years, during which time he moved out of our house and into his own apartment, close to his studio. Regrettably, the small firm he worked for couldn't compete with the larger companies and was forced to declare bankruptcy. He then joined the New York City studio of Trauma Studio, which was acquired by Electronic Arts. This was one of the largest gaming companies, and he became the lead developer on one of the most successful video games of all time—*Batllefield 2*. He was even asked to spend three to four months in Sweden to help a group of developers meet their responsibilities, which were critical to the project's timeline.

After the game's successful completion, the company decided to close down the New York studio and allowed the employees to move either to California or Sweden. No one accepted these options; therefore, the alternative was termination with a small severance. In the meantime, another company acquired Alex's entire group from the New York studio and funded a new project that was slated to take two to three years to complete.

Although Paul's major had been political science, at the age of 24, he continued pursuing and enhancing his computer skills on his own and began working as a networking consultant. Even though we did not totally endorse his decision, he made an unsuccessful attempt to join the United States Air Force Academy. Then he set his sights on the New Jersey State Police force, which offered numerous specialized details throughout the state, including a helicopter/aviation unit.

Because he had already received his helicopter pilot certification, Paul saw a career as a state trooper as the shortest route to putting his passion for flying into professional practice. Despite our objections, he decided to go through with the state police basic training. He had to report to the base by noon on Mother's Day, May 11, 1997. Angela was crushed when just she, Alex, and I went out to dinner without Paul, for the first time ever.

Fortunately, after three weeks in basic training, Paul realized this line of work was not for him. After we gave him our approval, he decided to quit the academy and return to the computer technology field. Although Paul had not taken any computer courses in college, his knowledge in most areas of computer technology (networking, Internet, programming, and so forth) was much more advanced than the content of the subjects they were teaching at that time.

For his next job assignment, he worked as a consultant at a pharmaceutical firm. After two years there, he decided to go on his own and formed a consulting firm. He also managed to buy his own house, only seven minutes from us. Little by little, he built and grew his business clientele to the point where he was able to support himself comfortably. One of his clients who owned a jet plane paid for Paul's aviation jet training so that he could fly the ten-seater to the Caribbean, Mexico, and other resort locations.

While conducting his consulting business, in 2003, Paul started flying a news helicopter on a part-time basis in the New York metropolitan area. Despite his successful business model, Paul's number one priority was flying, so he decided to join a company that provided helicopter Medevac (the transport of severely injured people to a hospital via helicopter) services in New Jersey. In fact, Paul and another pilot convinced the Louisiana-based company PHI to expand their Medivac services to New Jersey, and that's where he's been situated from 2005 to the present.

He works a twelve-hour day shift for seven straight days, followed by a week off, then works a twelve-hour night shift for a week, followed by a week off, and so on. Even with this demanding schedule, he has been able to retain and run his business without any difficulties, as there is no conflict of interest between his Medivac responsibilities and his consulting business.

The realization of his dreams sometimes makes Paul declare out loud: "What a great job I have! They pay me for something I consider a hobby." However, after Paul started flying, Angela and I went through several worrisome moments, especially during inclement weather conditions or long-distance flights on either the jet plane or the helicopter.

Back in May of 2004, the NBC Channel 4 news helicopter crashed on a rooftop in Brooklyn, NY. Paul had been scheduled to fly that helicopter, but at the last minute, another pilot was assigned for the flight. Although nobody was seriously injured, Paul often wondered how he would have handled that situation if he had been the pilot.

Angela was content teaching the Greek language to children on a part-time basis at the seven-year school at St. George Greek Orthodox Church in Piscataway, New Jersey. This was and continues to be an undertaking that requires many hours of preparation, in addition to the time she spends in class.

Our relationship grew stronger as the years went by, especially after all my alarming medical problems, which I had finally managed to keep under control with diet, exercise, stress reduction, and medication. I truly appreciated Angela's patience and the emotional support she gave me during those difficult times.

Chapter 59

Unspoken Words

Over the next few pages, I would like to share some of the writings I have composed for Angela on various milestones and occasions, beginning with this anniversary letter:

> *To My Wife*
> *On Our 29ᵗʰ Wedding Anniversary*
> *November 2, 1998*
> *Darling,*
> *It is so easy for me to write about you because the thoughts I make and the feelings I have for you are so sincere and always triggered by the deep-rooted love both of us have built through the years of our married life.*
> *The caring for one another, the respect, and our strong bond are some of the basic ingredients that kept us together for twenty-nine years. My love for you has penetrated deep in my existence and is becoming stronger and unshakeable with each year that goes by. I'm certainly a lucky man because I have a partner, a friend, and a wife like you!*
> *I know that at times I take you for granted, but I would like you to know that during my work day there is that vivid image of you flashing in front of my eyes. It creates unusually pleasant thoughts—like the rainbow after the storm—and then, I look forward to coming home to you! What a great feeling!*

Yes, if I had to do it all over again, I wouldn't hesitate for a minute to marry you again, for you are God-sent to be my sole and precious gift, someone who is the inexhaustible source of pleasure, goodness, and kindness, enough for me and plenty left over for our children, relatives, strangers ... and Daisy, too! No one can ever take your place; you have secured a permanent corner in my existence and you will be part of me forever ... and I mean forever!

We should be thankful for what we are and what we have. I always thank God for giving you the "Angelic attributes" and bringing you into my life as if I were rewarded for some great deed I had done.

Thank you, darling, for being my real-life "guardian angel," and if I don't remember to tell you more often how much I care for you, many a time my non-vocal attitude and inner voice says more than the words "I love you." It whispers: "I adore you."

Happy Anniversary,
Mike

To My Wife for Her Birthday
8/2/1999
Darling,

Here we are again, celebrating another birthday for a person who is trying to be everything to everybody. Well, you come close to achieving this—that is, taking care of every "living" thing and everything else in the house, being the best social coordinator and counselor, the best mother for our children, and above all, the ideal wife and my best friend.

At times, I don't seem to show you or express my appreciation for what I have, but I'm going to make every effort to get even closer to you and remind myself to tell you more frequently how much you mean to me. Without you, life would be meaningless, as if a bird trying to survive and go on flying with broken wings.

We are inseparable! Most people would only dream to have what we have and what we are. Let's enjoy every day, enjoy every moment, give whatever we can to others because we have built enough love and caring for one another and we are certainly able to weather every storm and face difficult situations together.

I feel you are the energy that keeps me afloat and gives me a reason to go on and enjoy you, our children ... and Daisy, too!

As I told you many times, you are the only woman for me, whom I'm still in love with, and no one could ever take your place. How many people, after thirty years of marriage, can say that the most attractive woman is their wife? Well, you are ... inside and out the most precious gift that I could ever have.

At this point, while writing this letter, I was interrupted and had to face an unpleasant work-related situation that affected my mood. However, getting back to this letter and continuing the thoughts about you, made this problem not so significant. You're so right when you remind me that we should count our blessings and shouldn't sweat the small stuff!

I'm so lucky having you on my side as someone I can always count on, someone who will support me no matter what the circumstances are. In return, I will always love you, adore you, and be proud of you as my wife, friend, and above all a wonderful and unique human being.

Happy Birthday, Darling!
With all my love,
Mike

Only "YOU"

My mind wanders in the skies,
In the mountains and valleys
And ... among nature's beauty
There's you ... blending so nicely
With all those beautiful things
I connect with nature and you're there.
I smell the flowers and I sense your presence
I hear music, I hear humming and ...
There are the angels whispering your name
Angelica, Angelica!
What a beautiful name, what a beautiful person
A blend of everything with kindness,
Understanding and selfless loving care ...
Giving, giving, giving
More than she ever receives.

But once, I was told that I had the right to dream
That I can have a partner, a wife like that person.
Am I still dreaming?
What is the difference between dream and reality?
Mine is "YOU"

****

Happy 30ᵗʰ Anniversary, Darling,
With all my love
Mike
11-2-1999

These were not just empty words written to my wife on special occasions out of a sense of obligation. Far from it: they were the simple, true feelings and sincere thoughts I kept inside myself, waiting for the right moment to surface. A spontaneous e-mail I sent Angela one morning went like this:

Creative writing is a simple function of transferring thoughts into words by isolating these thoughts, separating them from other irrelevancies, extracting them and transforming them into words. These words represent one's feelings and should be as pure and sincere as the spawning of the initial thought. Unless we have some inner peace, we cannot be completely truthful with what we're thinking, saying, or doing. For this reason, when we use the word "love" we should mean it; it should come from the deepest part of our soul: our sacred self. This is why, right now, this very moment, I truly feel like saying "I love you," but it's not just the words, it's the thought of you, the feeling, the relaxing and sooth-ing sensation that's running through me ...
So, this is how I started my day ... full of love!!!

For You, Of Course
Angela has been the inspiration I needed each time I attempted to climb another step. By believing in me, she supplied me with ample en-ergy to boost my confidence, which in turn became the fueling agent for my success. I owe her almost everything that made me what I am today in terms of my social, economic, and professional status. She has polite-ly pointed out my mistakes or failures in an indirect way, using a gentle

approach reminiscent of this quote from Tony Roberts, the renowned self-help author and life strategist:

"I've come to believe that all my past failures and frustrations were actually laying the foundation for the understandings that have created the new level of living I now enjoy."

Using an even-tempered approach, she often points out the lessons we can learn from our successes as well as our failures. With sincere intentions, she always keeps her part of our conversations at a mature and dignified level, regardless of whether she agrees with me or not.

Angela was indeed the source from which I drew the nourishment that ultimately strengthened the roots of my potentiality, as well as the bond in our marriage. She taught me to believe that the only limit to my success is my imagination, a reassuring notion that has kept me shooting for the moon all the years we've been together.

I'm not the only poet in the family. Our son Paul has been known to put his thoughts into verse, as in this beautiful, freeform birthday greeting to his Mom:

> *"The Perfect Person"*
> *While on a trip back from California, I was thinking of the essential characteristics that make the Perfect Person.*
> *First, the person has to be kind to all creatures, big and small, funny or furry (Daisy), and ugly or cute.*
> *Second, this person has to care about others' feelings and often put the other person before her.*
> *Third, this person has to have a way of soothing the tensions, worries, and fears of people around her.*
> *Fourth, this person has to have a giving nature, for no perfect person can be greedy.*
> *Fifth, this person has to have class and composure and must possess the qualities that make her appear like royalty to others.*
> *Sixth, this person must be an excellent listener and a wise adviser.*
> *Seventh, this person must be sharp and should be able to know what is on the other people's minds without even being told.*
> *Eighth, this person should raise children and generously donate precious parts of her life to enrich her children's experience.*
> *Ninth, this person should be liked and often envied by others, as this is the type of individual most people only dream of having around them.*
> *Tenth, this person is often a role model for others. Her good-*

ness and generosity uplift the spirits of people around her.

To most, the ten items above would have been difficult to come up with, because they probably don't have anyone around them who fits this mold. For me, it was a little easier to come up with: after all, I simply described my mom!

Mom, my words are but a petty excuse for the love, affection, and feelings I have for you. Over the years, I have grown attached to you and have realized all that you have sacrificed through your life to bring Alex and me into this world. Believe me, you work comes with much reward, as you have children who forever will remember you for the admirable qualities not found in any other mother.

Every night I go to sleep, I thank God for being so lucky ... so lucky that I was brought into this world by you! I wouldn't have wanted it any other way.

> *Happy Birthday, Mom!*
> *Paul*

Over the years we've come to realize that Alex is a deep thinker who usually expresses his feelings with a few words that carry a significant message and deep meaning. Probably his engineering background has molded his thinking process toward a direction where he always focuses on the essentials of the situation at hand, and he always manages to come up with the best possible solution.

At an early age, it was evident that he possessed a God-given gift: a creative mind that helped him excel in areas such as music and drawing as well as in his professional career.

I often recall Alex's reaction when, during a conversation, one of us made a negative comment about someone else. He immediately intervened by emphasizing that we should not criticize people who are not present to defend themselves. We always admired his honesty and genuine kindness for others, especially those close to him.

Here is a sample of Alex's expression and feelings for his mother:

Mom,

I am so fortunate to be part of a family where love, caring and understanding for one another are the predominant traits in our everyday life. I feel blessed to have a mother like you who always goes out of her way to give us any help we need.

When I hurt, I know you hurt more; I can feel your pain is greater than mine. Often I feel sad, as many children in the world

cannot experience the gift of your unconditional motherly love.
You certainly deserve all the happiness life could offer you, but
most importantly, I'm grateful for all the love you've given me,
and I send some back to you.
  Happy Birthday, Mom
  Love,
  Alex

Fortunately, Angela has saved everything Alex, Paul, and I have written about her. When we're in a sentimental mood, Angela and I review these writings and count our blessings for having raised two wonderful and exceptional sons who, in turn, have rewarded us with their love and the deep, abiding respect they have for us. We are so proud of them for being such good, caring, and honest individuals who have strengthened their inherent quality of compassion to treat and interact with everyone around them with dignity and respect.

Chapter 60

Trouble in Paradise

While surfing the Web one evening, I came across a chat room whose intelligent content, as posted by the members, convinced me to join and share my views on several nonfiction books I had read. After a while, a lady named Melinda started a private conversation with me, during which we exchanged personal information about ourselves, including that we were both married with children. I was intrigued by the fact that she was of Greek origin and lived in Adelaide, Australia.

A few days later, we exchanged e-mail addresses and began corresponding on a frequent basis. We kept the substance of our correspondence on a purely innocent and friendly basis—to my mind at least. However, after Angela read some of the e-mails, she saw it differently and assumed that my relationship with Melinda was heading beyond the friendship level.

Melinda commented that I had inspired her to renew her dream of writing a novel and lavished compliments on me for my wit, humor, and intelligence. She also made reference to some marital discord with her husband. I admit, being thought of so highly by another woman was flattering, but as long as we kept our correspondence on an intellectual level, I saw no harm in it. As platonic pals, I also saw no harm in our talking on the phone from time to time, which we did, much to Angela's disapproval.

I realized Angela was greatly bothered by this situation. She was convinced that, below the surface of the supposedly innocent communication, an emotional connection was blossoming. I often disagreed with these assumptions, but she was not about to change her view on the subject. At work, I discussed the issue with my friend, Mary, who thought my long distance correspondence with Melinda was harmless. In fact, Mary talked to Angela and offered her assessment of the situation. Still, Angela was unwavering.

Although I was totally convinced that my attraction to Melinda was purely platonic, I understood how Angela felt. With her strong woman's intuition, perhaps she recognized in our e-mails an emotional subtext I was unaware of, or which, in my manly vanity, I chose to ignore.

In the end, I realized that my wife was above anyone and anything else in my life. I did not want to hurt her or cause her anguish over an insignificant situation. So, one morning, I sent the following e-mail to Melinda:

Subject: C'est La Vie - Hope I Made a Difference
Sent: Thursday, February 01, 2001 7:44 a.m.

> *Dear Friend Melinda,*
> *After re-reading your e-mail of 1/29, I want you to know how pleased I was to see that you are considering making an attempt to rebuild your relationship with your husband. You have binds that cannot—and should not—be easily broken.*
> *It is upon these binds that your relationship will be built anew. I believe that doing so will result in a stronger and more satisfying relationship than you may have had previously.*
>
> *I hope that in some small way I was instrumental in your taking this positive step. However, at this time, I believe that any further continuation of our correspondence will only be detrimental for both of us.*
> *My wife has expressed concern regarding our association, and as I explained to you, I have a healthy and wonderful relationship with my wife. Believe me, I certainly don't want to do anything (right, wrong, or indifferent) to jeopardize it. Our marriage is too precious to me.*
> *So in closing, I want to wish you the best of luck in every aspect of your life. I hope you will view our short association as a pleasant and positive one, and perhaps I will even warrant a brief mention in the book that you will write.*
> *Best regards,*
> *Mike*

Within an hour after receiving my e-mail, Melinda sent me an emotional reply in which she expressed her regret over being perceived as "the other woman" and lamented that our correspondence, which she cherished, must come to an end. She closed with the remark that, if I ever went into a bookshop and saw a book entitled *Dear Mike*, I would know who the author was.

As soon as I received Melinda's response, I sent a copy to Angela at home, but I also printed both e-mails, in case she didn't have a chance to read them.

We had planned to take Alex out to dinner that evening for his birthday, and I was naturally concerned about this delicate subject being discussed in front of the children, who were blissfully unaware of any parental discord. When I got home that evening, I gave Angela the printed copies of the e-mails and asked her to read them.

To my surprise, she didn't show any reaction. She also kept mum in the car on the way to the restaurant and directed her dinner conversation toward Alex and Paul. However, as soon as we got home, both of us let our guards down and fell into each other's arms, realizing that this unpleasant episode was over and a new chapter was about to begin. The night was just a wonderful finish to a day full of emotional turbulence.

On Friday morning, while still drinking my first cup of coffee at the office, I received a touching e-mail from Angela:

It's Thursday morning and the events of the last days have left me emotionally drained and exhausted. I feel like I am in a cyclone that is spinning me around and throwing me into different places at different times. I cannot stop feeling so many different and mixed emotions. It has become almost a nightmarish experience and I'm trying to make some sense out of all these overwhelming feelings.

Last night, when I went to bed, I was trying, at least for a while, to push away all these thoughts and feelings that have engulfed my whole existence like flames. I had to resort to a tranquilizer so that I could get some sleep and rest my mind. Even that didn't help much! Anyway, I'll try hard to put into words how I feel about the situation.

Your "association" with Melinda started as an innocent conversation that even I, in the beginning, thought was just harmless chat. However, I couldn't help but notice that, as the days went on, this was gradually changing from a friendly conversation to a more intense one. It started to occupy your time and your mind more and more. You started in the chat room, you moved into the whispering area, and then to emailing and finally to telephone conversations. I guess I'll never finish this e-mail today..........

It's a day later, Friday, and after what took place last night, I feel that the frantic spinning has finally ended. The cyclone threw me back into your arms. My Odyssey has ended, I'm back to Ithaca, I'm back home. I'm resting peacefully in your arms. Please keep me there, close to your heart, and I will stay and love you forever!
Your Angela

And then, my answer was this:

My Sweet Darling,
This past week will remain one of the most memorable milestones in our married life. We've experienced all sorts of emotions but in the end the events that took place were a true awakening for both of us, reaffirming how much we love and care for one another and how close we can be if we keep each other warm in our hearts.
I'm sorry if I hurt you. It wasn't intentional. It just happened, but this incident made me feel so much closer to you, as you showed me over the weekend how wonderful you were, the attention you gave me, the warmth I felt being close to you. Even when you were silent, I could hear you loud and clear. I could sense your inner world being overwhelmed, joyful, and delightful! Let this last for a long time, let this closeness last forever ... and ever!
I love you, my sweetheart!!!!

It was indeed the beginning of a new chapter, as my bond with Angela became ever so strong. We both felt content and happy. We expressed our feelings to one another on a daily basis, either in writing or verbally when we were together. Angela and I experienced a period of blissfulness during which we realized our marriage had reached its zenith in terms of unabashed sincerity and openness. It was a period of true connectedness between us; we frequently sent e-mails to one another to express our feelings about the day or the moment.

Chapter 61

Rekindling Romance

For our summer vacation in 2001, Angela and I revisited Greece, first spending a few days on the island of Santorini and then flying to Rhodes, where we stayed in one of Dimitri's apartments. This time, however, as soon as we entered the apartment, we did not feel as excited as we had back in 1996. We were expecting to relive the moments we had enjoyed so much in 1996, but unfortunately, this time the magic just wasn't there.

On the second day, our vacation was spoiled by an accident that occurred when we were going to dinner at a restaurant downtown. My brother, George, who was also vacationing in Rhodes, was driving a rented car when he failed to see a stop sign and struck a teenager who was riding his motorbike. The youth was thrown over the hood of the car and onto the pavement, where he lay motionless.

At first we thought he was dead, but on closer inspection, we thanked God he was alive, although he was badly injured. As bystanders from the immediate neighborhood crowded the scene, the teen's father started yelling at my brother for ignoring the stop sign. In my brother's defense, we explained that, first of all, tree branches that had grown too low covered the stop sign and second, the youth's motorbike had no lights.

It was an awful evening that ultimately cast a pall over our vacation, although we did spend some time with relatives in both the village and in the city, and we rallied our spirits to have the best time possible under the downbeat circumstances. My brother visited the youth at the hospital several times. The boy's condition improved to an ultimately full recovery.

One of the trip's highlights was a get-together Dimitri arranged at his house in Trianta. He invited the Polichronis family, most of whom had come from Brisbane, Australia, to have dinner and celebrate a reunion with those relatives who lived in Rhodes. Both Dimitri and I knew the older Australians, because they had been born and raised in Agios Isidoros before leaving the country during the '50s and '60s.

The party started at three in the afternoon and didn't wrap up until after midnight. It was there that I met an Australian-born economics professor named John Polichronis. He and I later played a few rounds of golf on a nine-hole course that was located near a beach, fifteen kilometers from the city.

Dimitri was kind enough to take us back to the Kalyva restaurant on the night of the full moon, so that we might relive the romantic splendor of our previous visit. Alas, although the majestic, panoramic setting had not changed and the food was divine, we just couldn't recapture that elusive vibe that dwelled in our memories.

At this juncture, Angela and I realized our vacation was no longer enjoyable, so we decided to leave a week early. We stayed in Athens for a few days, at a hotel near the Acropolis, which was also within walking distance from the home of Angela's brother, Maki.

One evening, we had dinner at the hotel Divani's rooftop restaurant with Angela's childhood friend, Rena, and her husband, Antony. It was one of the most beautiful settings I'd ever seen: the illuminated Parthenon seemed as if it were hanging from the ledge of the rooftop. It was indeed an enjoyable evening.

Office Scandals

A little more than a month after we came back from vacation, our office was rocked by a scandal that ultimately had dire consequences for someone near and dear to me: my boss, Bill. The accusation was made that one of Bill's managers owned a consulting firm whose employees worked in our department, a practice that was against company policy and was considered unethical.

We all knew that Bill was the most honest person in the department, someone who would never compromise company policies. But in the end, despite his valiant efforts to convince human resources of his innocence, he lost the battle. On the morning after the annual division picnic, the company's security personnel escorted Bill out of his office. It was a terrible scene, a bad day for all of us, as Bill was the best boss anyone could ever have and he didn't deserve this mortifying treatment.

Rick K., who was Bill's counterpart in the retirement services department next door, took over Bill's position. During the first week, Rick met with his direct reports and made us aware of his expectations and management style. After a few months, however, I observed that Rick was micromanaging the department, a practice that was becoming a hindrance to my daily project and personnel responsibilities.

To my consternation, he questioned my estimate of the time and effort needed to complete a high-profile project I was working on. He took the position that my estimate was 75 percent higher than he thought it should be. When the analysis was completed, all the parties involved met to review the assigned tasks. One of the project participants was a Wall Street investment bank, whose representatives at the meeting expressed concern regarding the tight schedule and the limited time that was allocated for the completion of the project. Subsequently, Rick acknowledged he had underestimated the project's scope and allowed me to obtain the necessary resources.

This is only one example of Rick's micromanagement style, but there were other, similar occasions where he tried to dictate how to run a project or how to interact with the user community. It appeared that Rick had more enemies than friends in the department. I remember one occasion when I reminded him that his subordinates might be more important than his superiors, as he was more likely to be dragged down by the people below him if he didn't treat them right than he was to be pulled up by the people above him with whom he sought to curry favor. Nevertheless, he kept ignoring some of our suggestions and chose to keep his distance from almost everyone in the department. I say "almost" because there were a few people with whom he teamed up and whom he used as his patsies against the rest of us.

As my relationship with Rick began to deteriorate, I no longer looked forward to going to the office. The enthusiasm I'd had during Bill's tenure was quickly diminishing. I was just waiting to reach my retirement age and call it quits. I kept in close contact with Bill, who had been out of work for almost a year and was still looking for another job.

To help him with his job search, one Saturday night I arranged a dinner at my house with a few executives I thought might either offer Bill a position or at least help him expand his networking contacts. Everyone brought their spouses, and we all had a nice sit-down dinner consisting of a variety of delicious dishes Angela had prepared. It was a delightful evening and everyone had a great time.

Eventually, Bill landed a job in the Information Technology division with another major insurance company. After he started working, some of his friends and I got together for a round of golf. In his new job, Bill had to do a lot of traveling, because most of his assigned staff members were located in four different locations throughout the country.

After two years, the traveling was probably the main reason Bill had to resign from that job and take a consulting position in New York City. We have been keeping in touch, either by phone or e-mail, but we never managed to get together after he left the insurance company.

In the summer of 2002, Angela and I spent ten days on the West Coast. First, we went to Napa Valley, where we visited a few wineries, including Cakebread Cellars, a small firm whose Cabernet Sauvignon is a top choice among wine connoisseurs. Then we drove to San Francisco, which Angela was visiting for the first time. Angela's favorite place was Sausalito, where we spent an entire day visiting art galleries and novelty stores.

Staying within walking distance from Fisherman's Warf, Angela enjoyed this unique setting by the bay with its Pier 39 shopping area, the many street vendors, and the various seafood restaurants. We also spent an entire day at the Golden Gate Park. The Conservatory of Flowers and the Japanese Tea Garden were among the notable areas we visited.

We had a great time in the City by the Bay, a town I could never get tired of, despite the many times I'd been there during the '70s and '80s. We then flew to Las Vegas, where we spent a few days before returning home.

Fortunately, Paul was taking care of our dog, Daisy, while we were away. We all had become so attached to Daisy, a creature we regarded as the perfect dog. On our daily walks, I enjoyed the side benefit of listening to nonfiction audio books. Within a period of four years, between the gym and Daisy's walks, I must have listened to more than 150 books, most of which were of the self-development/self-help, philosophical and spiritual varieties. Some of my favorite authors include Wayne Dyer, Deepak Chopra, Eckhart Tolle, Tom Friedman, Malcolm Gladwell, and of course, Elizabeth Gilbert.

When the weather was nice, I drove Daisy to an open field, where she was able to run free without a leash. That was where I met Beata, the owner of a Great Dane named Crash. It turned out that Beata lived in our neighborhood with her husband, Mark, and her daughter, Ava. Subsequently, we took our dogs for "walkies," as the British say, on many happy occasions.

One summer, Beata's mother had suddenly passed away and the entire family flew to Poland for the funeral. The short notice made it impossible for Beata to put the dog in a kennel or make any other arrangements, so I had to take care of Crash for two weeks. It was not an easy task handling an oversized dog. Crash was kept in their house with the kitchen door wide open so he could go in and out as he pleased, into a fenced yard. One evening, after Paul and I had walked and fed the humongous beast, we saw him bounding after us on his stilt-like legs just before we turned into our driveway! We assumed he must have jumped the fence—an easy feat for him—and took him back. But ten minutes later, he was standing at our front door again, the poor, lonesome fellow.

We finally let Crash in the house, hoping he would stay in the kitchen all night. However, when he saw Daisy go upstairs to our bedroom, he started whining and barking and attempted to follow her. At that point, I took Crash back to Beata's house, but this time I closed the kitchen door so that he couldn't get out and jump the fence again.

When I went to feed him in the morning, I opened the kitchen door to a messy scene of dog poop all over the floor, the cabinets, and the refrigerator. I suspected the brute did it on purpose as payback for us locking him up all night. During this period, I kept Beata updated via email of all the developments, as well as sending her some pictures I took of Crash and Daisy together. Miraculously, I survived those two weeks, but I was relieved when Beata's husband, Mark, returned and took over.

In the spring of 2003, our department went through reorganization as a result of an acquisition that had been finalized at the end of the previous year. It affected all of Rick's direct reports (five vice presidents) as well as those who reported to the five vice presidents. Another management level of three new people from the acquired company had been inserted between the vice presidents and Rick's position.

I was now reporting to Helen, who seemed to be a nice person. However, soon after the reorganization, the company issued a division bulletin announcing a workforce reduction, which had been expected after the acquisition of the new company. The reduction affected both companies in areas where duplicate job functions were unnecessary.

As a result of this so-called job redundancy, I was offered a severance option as a supplement to my retirement, which happened to coincide with the proposed separation date. Although this new development was a blessing in disguise, as it coincided with my approaching my 65th birthday, I felt sort of disappointed, because it was not my choice to retire. I was indirectly told that I had to take that option, which was almost like being fired for the first time in my career. What I wanted was to retire on my own time, with dignity. I wanted leaving to be my own decision; I probably would have resigned by the end of the year anyway, but at least it would have been my choice.

My impending job loss took a significant emotional toll on me. It was difficult to handle the anger, sadness, fear, and a sense of betrayal that initially overwhelmed me. I was made aware that my new responsibilities between April and December of 2003 were considered "support duties"— in other words, I had no specific assignments for the next seven or eight months. I was not used to this type of work arrangement, where I just had to show up every day and pretend I was working on something. Taking it one day at a time, I survived the unplanned and unpleasant monotony of this extremely boring period.

In September, Paul and Alex expressed an interest in all of us going on vacation together to the Poconos. Perhaps they wanted to relive the great times we had experienced in the resort Mecca when they were teenagers. It was a splendid idea, so we rented a lakefront house where our dog, Daisy, would have another chance to practice her swimming skills.

The sun was out when we arrived one Saturday afternoon. Alex took a paddleboat ride and Daisy took a lazy swim in the lake. It seemed as if she just wanted to please us, because her old age must have made it more difficult for her to swim the way she had in her younger years. Alex and I went to the supermarket to renew the first-day ritual of our past Poconos vacations. Our grocery shopping brought back many good memories of past shopping sprees, where the boys were allowed to get anything they wished, including junk food.

When we came back from shopping, we drove to a nearby airport to pick up Paul, who was flying a small, single-engine plane he now owned. Later that evening, it started raining hard, and the weather forecast for the next several days did not look promising. As we had no other choice, we spent the following two days in the house watching movies and playing games. No golf for me, either, this time around!

The boys left on Tuesday evening as the rain continued to come down with a vengeance. Even Daisy was restless and unhappy at being locked inside for days. On Wednesday, we decided to leave, because the rain didn't seem to be letting up. While I was taking the suitcases to the car, Daisy followed me in the rain and jumped into the back seat. Although we were not ready to leave for at least another twenty minutes, Daisy wasn't willing to get out of the car. We assumed she was trying to tell us she couldn't wait to get home and would rather wait in the car than stay cooped up in the rented house. We get a kick every time we recall this incident with Daisy.

My last day at the office was December 19, 2003. They allowed me to leave ten days earlier than my official separation day. I had already accepted the fact that my seven-year employment with the company had come to an end. One of the bright or positive consequences during this "winding down" period was the fact I was able to help many people to start or boost their careers.

380

Besides Mary Haniotis, I had hired three other people who used to work for me at the bank and who had been out of a job after the bank merger in 1996. Also, Oscar's and Maria's careers were progressing well above their expectations. All those people enjoyed lucrative careers, including the benefits and the camaraderie of a family-like environment.

The disconcerting reality of being out of work began to sink in right after the holidays, but at least my anger was slowly diminishing. I set about repairing my wounded self-esteem by learning to accept change and embracing the positive attributes of my new, semi-retired lifestyle. Once I went through this initial stage, I started to think about what to do next.

***

Back in 2003, the SARS (Severe Acute Respiratory Syndrome) epidemic hit China. The outbreak scared away tourists and investors in droves, dealing the country a monumental economic blow. Alex and Paul had taken advantage of the opportunity and bought two inexpensive tickets to China for a trip they were slated to take in March of 2004. The brothers left in the middle of March and flew to Chicago as the first stop on their long flight to Beijing. They were at the gate and about to change planes when they heard an announcement promising free tickets anywhere in the continental United States to anyone willing to take a flight leaving three hours later. Both of them jumped at the chance, got the free ticket vouchers, and boarded another plane. As an additional benefit, they were put in business class!

Many hours later, they arrived in China, where they had a wonderful time, judging from the pictures they took and the interesting stories they told us when they came back. However, the China episode doesn't end here. As a result of that trip, there were subsequent events that occurred as if there were a plan that had to be executed in some orderly means.

Chapter 62

Death as a Part of Life

t the end of April of 2004, Angela's nephew, Spiro, called us from
Athens with the bad news that Angela's brother, Maki, had passed
away. We immediately made arrangements for both of us, as well
as Angela's brother, Bob, to fly to Athens the following day. The nine-hour
flight seemed interminable, and understandably so, because our purpose
this time was not a vacation, but a sad occasion.

Coincidently, my sister, Mary, was scheduled for an operation at a
hospital in Athens during the same period. She had been diagnosed with
stomach cancer, an ailment that should have been detected by her doctor a
year earlier when she started complaining of severe stomach pain. It was
my other sister, Stacy, who had convinced Mary to have additional tests to
pinpoint the cause of the pain. Unfortunately, the cause was determined to
be cancer. Stacy had already gone through a similar process when she also
had been diagnosed with stomach cancer.

Mary had the operation, followed by several chemotherapy and radiation treatments, and in the end, she beat the cancer. If not for Stacy's
persistence, Mary's condition might have been diagnosed too late for any
medical intervention. Our initial lack of information about the severity
of Mary's condition and the uncertain outcome of her upcoming surgery
made our visit to Athens more stressful.

Maki's funeral service was held in the church of one of the well-known
cemeteries in Athens. Family and friends gathered in a private viewing
area, with Maki's coffin situated in the middle of the room. As I commiser-

ated with the assembled guests, I couldn't help but notice the profoundly grief-stricken expression on Bob's face.

As the eldest brother in Angela's family, Bob was no doubt trying to come to grips with his younger brother's senseless death after a simple hernia operation. The tragedy had to be the result of blatant medical neglect on the part of the attending nurses, who had not noticed the heart monitor's alarm until it was too late. Alas, we all know how difficult it is to prove that a death is the result of medical negligence. Maki's children, Bessie and Spiro, did not want to pursue legal action, since they knew nothing could bring their father back.

We all attended a beautiful funeral service in the small church where several cantors harmonized on the traditional funeral lamentations. When the service was over, the pallbearers carried the casket to the designated grave, where we said our last good-bye to Maki by placing a carnation on his coffin.

After the funeral, Angela and I went to the hospital where we saw my sister, Mary, who was scheduled to have surgery the following day. Mary's husband, Paraskevas, was distraught, because he thought there was only a slim chance for his wife's recovery after such an invasive stomach operation. In fact, when he saw us for the first time in the hospital hallway, he exclaimed, "I'm losing Mary! I'm losing my wife!" To console Paraskevas, we reminded him that this was the time he had to stay strong and positive, in order to reinforce the emotional and physical strength Mary needed to withstand her ordeal.

Lying in the narrow hospital bed, Mary was overjoyed to see us for the first time in three years and greeted us with a wide smile. The first words she uttered were, "I know I will be fine because God arranged it this way, so that you had to come to Athens to be near me at one of the most critical crossroads of my life." Noticing the tear that ran down my cheek, she added bravely, "Don't worry, Manoli, (her nickname for me) everything will go well—I just know it! God knows what He is doing."

Later on, I spoke to the surgeon, who explained that, depending on how far the cancer had spread, he might have to remove most, if not all, of Mary's stomach as a worst-case scenario. The following day, May 5, was a feast day set aside to honor Saint Irene, so before we went to the hospital, we bought a little icon depicting the brave fourth-century martyr, which we intended to give to Mary on the day of her surgery.

With Saint Irene perhaps watching over her, Mary's surgery went better than expected, according to the doctor's assessment. The surgical team removed three fourths of her stomach as well as the surrounding lymph nodes affected by the cancer, and her prognosis was encouraging.

However, she still had to go through the chemotherapy and radiation therapy as soon as she stabilized after the surgery.

When we returned to the States, I was in constant communication with Mary to help her find the best hospital and doctors for the follow-up therapy. With the help of Angela's cousin, Toula Stamou, we selected a highly recommended oncologist who ultimately performed all the necessary treatments within a six-month period. Although Toula did not know Mary, she was the one who went out of her way to help us find one of the best doctors in Athens. Mary made a remarkable recovery, with all subsequent test results indicating the disease was under control.

Angela's Siblings

I would be remiss if I didn't provide a brief mention of Angela's siblings, although I have made some sporadic references throughout the book. Her older brother, Bob, and his wife, Alice, had two children, Don and Christa. Bob was an executive in a large shipping company. He was enjoying a comfortable living in Connecticut until one night (a Good Friday), Alice had a massive heart attack and died at age fifty-two. Suddenly, his dreams and aspirations were shattered. It took him almost ten years before he began to regain some of the zest for life he'd always had.

Don married Tabatha and both of them managed to get their MBA degrees during a relatively short period in which their five children were born. We still don't know how they manage to juggle their responsibilities.

Christa, despite many difficulties—including the absence of her mother—pursued and successfully completed a medical education. She is now a pediatric cardiologist, married to Scott; they have a beautiful daughter.

Maki, who was an electrical engineer, spent all his life in Athens and had two children, Bessie and Spiro. In fact, Spiro had come to America and stayed with us for three years while attending high school. Subsequently, when he started college in New York, he stayed with Angela's sister, Nina, in Queens. Ultimately, he received his master's degree and moved back to Greece. He is now married to Nonie.

Bessie pursued a career in the corporate sector; she married Dimitri and, after many attempts and much patience, when she realized she was nearing the threshold of the child-bearing years, she got pregnant and gave birth to a baby boy named Mario.

Katie, who was mentioned a few times in earlier chapters, was married to Fr. Dr. John Poulos, a well-known personality among the religious and political circles throughout the New York metropolitan area. Katie served as a schoolteacher until she retired when Fr. John started showing the first signs of Alzheimer's disease. Several years later, Fr. John succumbed to the fateful illness. They have two daughters, Athy and Maria, both of whom are successful business women.

Athy is a corporate lawyer and partner with a prestigious New York firm. She also has a beautiful daughter, Katherine. Athy went through a rough marriage and a painful divorce and now she is engaged to Jimmy, a wonderful person who has brought her much love and happiness.

I took Maria under my wings when she didn't know what career to pursue and steered her toward the technical computer field, where she found her niche. After a few management positions, she is now an executive with one of the largest computer companies.

Nina was the first of Angela's family to come to America. She began and completed her studies in English literature at Hunter College in New York. She then married James Pappas, who had studied music but ended up managing a real estate business with his brother. Nina's many talents include painting and poetry; in fact, she published a poetry book called "The Healing Mirage." They have two daughters, Leah and Christina, who are both lawyers managing their own law firm in Queens, NY.

Toward the end of June, Angela and I took a cruise liner—the same one we had patronized a few years back—from New York City to Florida and then the Bahamas. We just wanted to get away after our stressful trip to Greece, where we'd had to face several unpleasant events. Perhaps the most significant event of our relaxing, weeklong cruise was my hitting the jackpot—more than two grand!—on a video poker machine after spinning a royal flush, the highest hand in standard poker. Just call me Mr. Lucky!

In 2005, Alex and Paul decided to spend Easter in Greece with two other friends. They stayed in Athens for a few days and then flew to Rhodes. The first order of business, according to Paul, was to visit Aunt Katerina, who was in a nursing home twenty kilometers from the city. Aunt Katerina was so pleased to see them, although her vision was so poor that she was categorized as legally blind. They participated in the midnight Easter Mass with my sister Mary's family.

Later, at Mary's house, they had *magiritsa*, a Greek soup made from lamb offal that is traditionally eaten after the midnight liturgy. The following day, Easter Sunday, they met with my friend, Dimitri, with whom they took a few pictures, including a close-up in which Dimitri is holding a photo of him and me when we were both fourteen years old. I don't know what I did with my copy of that picture, but it brought back some bittersweet memories of our younger years.

Their next stop was the village, where they spent the day and night with the rest of the relatives. If the pictures and videos they took are any indication, they must have had a heck of a good time! My sister, Vasilia, took especially good care of the boys, fattening them up with her Greek food specialties.

While in Greece, Alex sent me an e-mail indicating that an administrator at a local hospital close to our house wanted to rewrite an application that Alex had once developed. But now, he said, the language he had written it in was becoming obsolete and was not supported by the current operating systems. As Alex did not have any free time to devote to this project, he asked me if I wanted to take a stab at it.

Because Paul had an established consulting firm, when he came back from Greece, we met with Joan, the administrator. I finally agreed to take on the project, although I had to learn some parts of the new technology that were necessary for the system's redevelopment. Joan also requested that, since the hospital could not pay individuals for any services, the billing and payments would have to go through Paul's company.

At first, I was discouraged. I was working without any specifications, which meant I had to decipher the old code, comprehend the functionality, and then rewrite it, using a modern, Windows-like language. It took me about six months, but I completed the project, an accomplishment I didn't think I was capable of.

Although most of the development was done during the summer months—an undertaking that regrettably interfered with my golf outings!—I truly enjoyed the hands-on process and the sense of accomplishment. I was happy, and Joan was satisfied as well.

As a sort of reward, Angela and I took a ten-day vacation in late July, spending a few days in Seattle followed by a cruise to Alaska, which was one of the unforgettable cruises we'd taken. As the ship sailed through the narrow waterways of inside passage, we enjoyed the calm waters and the spectacular scenery, from Ketchikan to Juneau and all the way north to Skagway. The most spectacular setting was the Glacier Bay, where snow-covered mountains melt into turquoise-colored waters. I remember that sunny afternoon, sitting on the balcony of our cabin, and the many pictures I took of the floating glaciers.

Another interesting event was the three-hour train ride we took at Skagway into the Northern Canadian wilderness, riding between two tall mountains, where we occasionally spotted a few bears. Even with all the Caribbean cruises we took, Alaska was indeed the most memorable.

Chapter 63

Man's Best Friend

My dog, Daisy, and I were inseparable. Every day, no matter the weather, we took our walks around the neighborhood or in the open fields. Meanwhile, Beata's dog, Crash, had died at the relatively young age (in canine terms) of eight. I knew that Beata was devastated when I chanced to see her one day, walking forlornly along the same path we always took our dogs when Crash was alive. I told her that I sincerely missed our walks and wished her all the best with the new dog she planned to get. In fact, Beata gave me a reason to write an e-mail to her and to my friend Mary, my former colleague. Here is a copy of that message, which I entitled, "A Job and a Dog—The Broken Links":

My Dear Friends,

In December of 2003, I lost my job and said good-bye to Mary, a person with whom I shared a good portion of my professional and social life.

In January 2005, Beata lost Crash, a dog who was, to Beata, probably bigger than life. That loss terminated (at least temporarily) our evening walks, an event that I always looked forward to.

I remember the morning coffee and the numerous conversations Mary and I had every day before we tackled our daily work in the office. I miss her kindness and the warmth in her voice; the sincerity and the silence in her smile; all the things we had in common and all the other ways we were so different; her understanding, her simplicity, her humor, and the power of her promise. I was taking all these things for granted, but now that I don't see her every day, I realize the impact of that void. But you know, everything happens for a reason, and perhaps someday we'll find out what that underlying reason was.

I remember the countless walks Beata and I took with Crash and Daisy, as well as our efforts to solve every problem around the globe through lengthy conversations. Almost every evening, there was a change of pace from the daily work routine, out on the paths and fields enjoying nature, our dogs, and our conversations. I miss the summer and winter nights, our dogs' anticipation of the Milk-Bone moments. I miss her extraordinary intellectual ability and the way she formed an opinion on almost every subject.

I remember the many times I reminded her of her underestimated ability and the level she could possibly reach. But on the other hand, I admired her European charm, her simple approach to life, her toughness, and her survival instinct. I remember when I first saw her, I simply thought that she just existed. When I saw her again, I knew that she was truly an animal lover. Now I think I know the purpose of her existence.

The rule that every beginning has an end may not be true in all cases. Certain situations are destined to remain endless, such as true friendship and true love ...

Love,
Mike

Some months later, Beata got another Great Dane and the training started all over again. This time it was more intensive, as the young dog was a little more aggressive than Crash had been.

Speaking of dogs, my son, Paul, was also close to Daisy, as evidenced by his phone calls to us. Before he even said "hello," he demanded to know, "Where is Daisy?" In fact, he was so fond of Daisy that, on Father's Day one year, he was the ghostwriter for a hilarious message supposedly composed by our lovable Lab. We all got a good chuckle out of that! Here's the complete text of Daisy's Father's Day wish, ty*paws* and all (well, what other kind of mistake would a typing dog make?):

> *"WOOF"*
> *Dear Daddy ... this is your loyal dog DaIsY*
> *I jUst wAnTed to Wish YoU a Very happy FaTHEr's day anD menTiOn*
> *A few ThIngS to YOU tHat I May nOT hAVe MentIoned.*
> *First My PAwS keep HitTTING THE ShIFT KeY SorrY and My MAsTer DIdN'T TEACH me To USE ThE BACKsPSACE Key SO*

*I maY nOt SpeLL PrOprley SOMEtImes (WOOOOOF)
ANyWAYS eVen thoUGH YoU ArE NOT TeChNicaLLY my DAD
You HAVE Been BETTAR Than A DAD TO mE. YoU HAvE
AlWaYs FeD Me, Pet Me, SET Me UP oN bLiND DAtEs With
OTHeR naiberhood DAWGS, yOu tOOk me To THE FIeLD so I
CAN keep YoU KomPANY on YOUR WalKS, anD you EVeN LeT
me DRiNk Some OF yOur MilK. YoU TooK ME To THE DAWG
DoCToR SO HE CaN ADmIRE My FUR CoAT. ThaT WuZ
VErRY NiCE OF YOU. BuT MoST OF all YoU havE Been My
BEST FRIEND FoR MY EnTIRe Life. I don't WANT to ImAGiNE
LiFE wItHOUT You SItTiNg Next To ME EATiNG PeaNUTS On
YouR LoUNGE ChaIR as you Sister (OR Is she Your WIFE ? I
haveEN'T FIGuRED IT OUT YET) KeEPS Naggin YOU About
WatchING Too MUCH TV.
AnyWAY, I'm GoinG To Rest MY FlOPPY EaRS NOW but I'll BE
ThInKiNG OF you AS I ChASE DUCKS In my DREAMS. Much
LUV ALWAyS FrOM your FAithFUL AND Scruffly DAWG.
DAISY
p.s. I JuST WISH yOu COuLD TuRN the Air ConDITIoNER oN A
LiTTLE BiT MORE BeCauSE I'm DAmN HOT LatElY!*

This is the type of humor Paul can combine with a simple wit and get away with it, because he's known for his witty talent and the practical jokes he plays on friends or strangers. Paul is a remarkable writer and poet whose work appears on the Web site Poetheart (www.poetheart.com) as well as his personal Web site (www.pauly.us). (Paul's personal site also includes several of his original piano compositions—at Angela's and my urging, he studied classical piano as a youth—with Paul himself singing the inspirational lyrics in his soulful tenor voice.) Here is one of my favorite poems:

"A Talk with my Heart"
By Paul Papasavas

I suppose I should listen to you
Everyone proclaiming you're not true
Not worth a cent and not for a thought
Most people will tell me you're just
An emotion ... something that won't last
Nothing you can live with
And something you have to live without

But I tell you tonight and forever
You are the magic that few see
You defy the greedy norm
And help me to look past
What rages in others
You're the water and air
That lift my soul
To a cosmic elevation
A place most can't fathom
And at the lonely times
I look to you for my answers
The ones I cannot reason
I look to you to remove the anger
And you have carried me through
With footsteps of your own
You have wrapped your arms around
And gently touched my soul
You have colored all that was gray
And revealed a peace that exists nowhere
I don't know how I can repay you
Or thank you for your foundation
But to keep on listening

In September of 2005, Alex and Paul decided to use the two free tickets they were given in exchange for taking a later flight to China back in 2004. They had to use those tickets within one year, before they expired. For no particular reason—although my extolling the city's virtues may have had something to do with their decision—they booked a trip to San Francisco over the Labor Day weekend.

One night during their trip, Paul went to bed a little early, but Alex wanted to go to a place with some nightlife action. He took a taxi and told the driver to take him "where the action is." When the taxi stopped in a rather seedy neighborhood, Alex told the driver that this was *not* the type action he meant. Instead, he was looking for a respectable lounge where he could meet nice girls to dance with—that is, an upscale establishment catering to business people.

So, after spending $20.00 for the cab ride, the driver took him back where they started: the hotel next to where he was staying! Ironically, he could have saved the twenty bucks by walking to the lounge, but as some of us believe, everything happens for a reason—even if fate sometimes takes a roundabout route.

At the bar, Alex approached two girls who were having drinks alone with no male companions in sight. He started a conversation first with the brunette and then with the blonde, whom he liked better than her friend, as I learned later when all the parties involved filled in the details of the story.

Sara, the brunette, lived in San Francisco, whereas Stacia, the blonde, lived and worked in Palm Springs, seven hours away by car. Stacia had planned to visit another friend in Lake Tahoe, but the day before, her friend had canceled their plans, so she decided to visit Sara in San Francisco instead. Stacia liked Alex, but she assumed a laidback attitude; she didn't want to spoil a potential romance for Sara, who was also attracted to Alex.

At the end of the night, Alex asked the girls if they wanted to hang out again the following evening. Sara agreed and gave Alex her phone number. The following evening, all three of them met again, but this time it was Sara who graciously backed off, as she realized there was a true "love connection" between Stacia and Alex.

Right after the trio separated, each heading for their respective home base, Stacia had doubts about a serious relationship developing from long distance. Her doubts evaporated, however, when Alex called her as soon as he landed in New York and they talked on the phone for seven hours. Maybe, Stacia thought, a bicoastal romance could work after all!

Angela and I were happy for Alex when he told us about his encounter with Stacia. The way he put it—"This could be the girl of my dreams!"—we were certain he must have already been in love. They kept in touch on a daily basis until Stacia decided to visit Alex in New Jersey. After spending an entire weekend together, they had a better understanding of each other's character in terms of behavior, likes, and dislikes. All indications pointed to a definite match, for there was nothing that would keep them away from one another except for the distance between New Jersey and California.

We finally met Stacia on Thanksgiving Day. Alex had shown us some pictures of her, but when we saw her walking into our house, we immediately realized what a beautiful young lady she was. Beginning when she was fifteen years old, Stacia had taken advantage of her beauty (long, blond hair, perfect smile, and blue eyes) and had done some modeling for magazines and other publications.

As expected, she was a bit reserved when we sat down and engaged in a little small talk. We then went to the home of my sister, Despina, who traditionally hosted our family's Thanksgiving dinner get-togethers where, in addition to the customary roasted turkey, we always enjoyed the authentic Greek dishes.

After many coast-to-coast trips to see one another, Stacia decided to move to New Jersey into Alex's new, waterfront apartment by the Hudson River, along with her small Yorkshire terrier, Milla. It was a convenient location for Alex, as he only had to take the ferry across the Hudson to midtown Manhattan, where his office was located. After a while, Stacia found a job with a pharmaceutical company in northern New Jersey. In the meantime, they started looking for a house along the Hudson part of New Jersey, but the prices in that neighborhood for a two-bedroom condominium or townhouse were rather high.

The next significant event was the surprise marriage proposal that Alex had planned at the Ritz-Carlton Hotel in New York City. He rented a luxury suite, arranged roses galore throughout the space, and then he invited Stacia to inspect the suite, supposedly for future reference. That's where he gave her the diamond engagement ring and asked her to marry him.

Well, it didn't take long before they decided to get married, but not in the traditional way. Instead, they flew to California and arranged for their marriage ceremony to take place at a Malibu beach with just the two of them, a violinist, and a priest. The Malibu beach location was Stacia's suggestion, because it was close to Pepperdine University, from which she had graduated with a degree in Advertising and Applied Communication.

Chapter 64

Our Granddaughter on the Way

A few months later, we received a phone call from Alex informing us that Stacia was pregnant. For a few moments Angela and I were speechless, but when it finally registered that we would be grandparents, the news sent us into transports of delight, as if a miracle was in the offing—which it was!

The due date was in late November, so they still had enough time to resume their house-hunting efforts. We helped the newlyweds as much as we could in that area, as they wanted to find a house before their apartment lease came due for renewal. After looking at many houses in surrounding counties, they finally located and bought a condominium in a good location in New Jersey's Essex County.

The closing date was in September of 2007, a significant milestone for me as well, because it was the day when I first started writing my memoir.

At the eighteenth week of Stacia's pregnancy, we found out that she was going to have a girl. I don't know if subconsciously I had wanted their firstborn to be a boy, but Angela certainly got her wish: she had always wanted a little girl, and now she would have the opportunity to have one in her life.

Shortly after the baby shower—which was arranged by Angela and Stacia's mother, Ellen—Stacia gave birth to a beautiful girl named Ashlin. When Angela and I entered the maternity ward, we saw Ashlin for the first time in Alex's arms. Our granddaughter was gently moving her lips up and down and, with her beautiful brown eyes wide open and long eyelashes, she appeared to be examining her new world and its surroundings after her comfortable habitat in her mother's tummy.

Compared to other newborns, who usually have their eyes closed during the first day or two, she seemed to be alert. The joyousness of Ashlin's birth was even greater than when Alex was born, which substantiated what Angela's mother has always said: "Your son's child is two times your own child."

The following day, we picked up Stacia's mother from the airport and took her to the hospital, where Stacia, Alex, and Ashlin were happily situated in a private room. Ellen was planning to stay with Stacia and the baby for a little while before returning home to Florida. Because Stacia was more than a week past her due date, Paul had taken a flight to Greece the day before the birth. He missed all the excitement, but as he had his trusty laptop with him, we were able to e-mail him quite a few pictures of the newborn, which he shared with all our relatives in both locations, Athens and Rhodes. And who can blame him—he was a proud uncle for the first time!

Ashlin was growing up so nicely. She seemed intensely aware of her surroundings and the people around her. She seemed to be preternaturally alert, like a curious little scientist studying anything and everything within her sight. When she stared at me while sitting in my lap, her eyes were not just looking *at* me; I was certain, by her concentration, that she was looking *through* me!

Daisy's Final Moments

Sadly, around this same time, Daisy's condition had deteriorated to the point where she could no longer climb the stairs to the second floor without being helped, nor jump into the back seat of the car when I took her for a ride to the open fields. For the first time since we had gotten Daisy, fourteen years earlier, she began losing control of her bowels, despite her efforts to run to the door so that we could let her out. She had also suffered a few seizures that lasted fifteen to twenty seconds and left her disoriented when she tried to stand up.

Over a two-month period, I took her to the veterinarian several times to assess her condition and determine the best course of action for treating it. Although she had no appetite, her belly was getting bloated, as if she had drunk a few gallons of water. In late April, the vet suggested draining the excessive fluid being produced by her liver and accumulating in her abdomen. She stayed overnight at the facility, where the vet repeated the procedure several times to extract as much fluid as possible.

When I picked Daisy up late the following afternoon, she was wobbling when she tried to walk toward me. Once I got her home, she was restless, as if she were in pain, probably from the small incision in her belly that was slowly oozing the residual fluid from her abdomen. She had no appetite, refusing to eat even her favorite sliced turkey snack. Through the entire evening, the only thing she ingested was a little water.

That night, I stayed with her downstairs in the family room. I lay down on the couch as she was rested on the carpet next to me. I could hear her labored breathing until 5:00 a.m., when she got up and walked toward the front door. I went out with her to the backyard, where she managed to walk slowly all the way to the end of the property in front of the privet hedge. There she stood motionless, gazing upwards as if she were pleading for someone to mercifully end her life. She was far away from me, hoping that her miserable condition would not sadden me any further. That was why she had refused to eat: she knew that the end was near and she wanted to tell me she did not want to go on under these conditions.

Looking at her from afar, I experienced many emotions. Thoughts ran through my mind, beginning with memories from the time she was a puppy and continuing up until that very moment, as she stood there so helpless and disillusioned. I had kept my promise, though, when I told her when she was a puppy that I would take good care of her. I certainly had taken care of all her needs, and in turn, she became my best, most loyal friend for fourteen years.

I went close to her, picked her up, and brought her inside the house. I put my head next to hers while my tears dampened her face, telling her that I did not know what else I could do for her. I asked her to tell me, to give me a sign, so that I could make the right decision. Her only response was to fix her beautiful brown eyes on mine, and we stared at one another, soul to soul, for several heartbreaking minutes. I couldn't tell if she was saying good-bye or if she was asking me to help her. Perhaps she just wanted me to know how much she loved me for taking good care of her all her life.

Alex and baby Ashlin had spent the night at our house. Paul was vacationing in Scotland. Late in the morning, I called the vet, explained Daisy's condition, and asked his opinion in terms of the options we had. He indicated that her condition was not likely to improve. He also added that, if Daisy were his dog, he would have put her to sleep because he was certain she was suffering.

Alex, Angela, and I reviewed our options; we also called Paul in Scotland for his opinion. In the end, we all agreed that we should have put Daisy to sleep. Since someone had to stay with little Ashlin, Angela hugged Daisy, saying her last good-byes while shedding a few tears over the dog's furry face. She softly whispered in her ear, "Thank you for giving us so much love and devotion. Thank you for being a perfect dog for us. Thank you for being a true companion to all of us. I will never forget you … good-bye, my sweet Daisy, good-bye!"

On the way to the vet, Alex sat next to Daisy in the back seat. While Daisy was on the examination table, we called Paul again on my cell phone and put him on speaker. Paul started talking to Daisy in a sobbing voice, telling her how much he had loved her and that she was going to a better place. Alex and I stared mournfully at Daisy, who was breathing heavily. Her tongue was hanging down and touching the slick tabletop.

She probably sensed that the end was coming and looked as if she wanted to fight it, almost as if she wanted another chance to continue living with us. Both Alex and I hugged and kissed Daisy for the last time while Paul talked softly to her on the phone, which I placed near her ear. As we could not watch Daisy suffer any longer, we called in the doctor to give her the shot. She slowly closed her eyes until she became motionless, stretched out on the cold, steel tabletop.

After she was gone, we took a last glimpse at her, took her leash and her collar, and went home. We left Daisy's body with the vet with the agreement that it would be cremated.

When we got home, we noticed that her tags, which had been firmly attached to the collar, were missing. We called the vet immediately to see if we might have dropped them in the examination room, but he couldn't find anything. We retraced our steps, trying to locate the tags, but to no avail. This was another unexplained phenomenon. Daisy had always worn her tags everywhere we went, even on vacation, and had never lost one throughout her fourteen years. Then on the vet's table, her tags disappeared. Ah, another unsolved mystery that will haunt me to my grave.

Since Angela was babysitting for little Ashlin at our house, later in the evening, I went to church alone to attend the Good Friday service, but the thought of Daisy's passing prevented me from concentrating on the traditional singing of the lamentations, so I left before the service was over.

****

It was not easy to get over Daisy's loss, and I knew I had to let the grieving process run its natural course. Alex and Stacia convinced us to join them for a short vacation in Florida at a beach house in Naples, owned by T.K, her mother's companion. The setting of the property was just breathtaking, offering a private beach with comfortable sitting areas along

396

the sandy beachfront. We stayed on the second floor while Alex, Stacia, Ashlin, T.K., and Ellen were on the first floor.

I had been hesitant to go away after the loss of Daisy, but this short vacation proved to be therapeutic. We enjoyed being with our granddaughter, Ashlin, who was already a little more than six months old. Angela and I spent a lot of time with her, as our love and caring for our precious granddaughter grew by leaps and bounds. It seemed as though we couldn't get enough of her presence, as she was a bundle of inexhaustible joy.

I truly felt that Ashlin had replaced part of the void Daisy left behind; we bonded as only a grandfather and granddaughter can, delighting in silly games and cultivating a singular love that would only deepen as time went on. I was certain she understood how much I loved her and, at the same time, I knew she cared about me as well. In fact, the first person she learned to call by name was me! She learned to say *pappou*, which is the Greek word for grandfather.

After the Florida trip, we began making arrangements for Ashlin's christening in terms of the religious ceremony and the reception venue. Since Alex and Stacia had been married in a private wedding in California, they decided to have a formal christening celebration with all the relatives present.

I wanted to do something special for my granddaughter, something she would have for the rest of her life to remind her of her grandfather, who considered her the most precious gift anyone could ever have. And so, working with pastel crayons, I painted a portrait of Ashlin in the style of the Renaissance masters, attempting to capture her cherubic mystique. In the final portrait, Ashlin, surrounded by billowy clouds, looks remarkably like one of Raphael's famous angels.

The religious ceremony, attended by both sides of the family, took place at a Greek Orthodox Church. At the reception, we displayed the portrait—which was still a secret at that point—on a table at the entrance to the hall. We took a picture of Stacia when she first saw the portrait of her daughter. "Oh, my God, this is beautiful!" she said as she stood stock-still with her mouth wide open for several awestruck moments. We had a great time, sitting at a table with Stacia's father, Ed, and his family, who had come from Chicago, where they permanently reside.

A few weeks after the christening, Angela and I took Ashlin to our church, where she received her second communion after the Sunday liturgy. Ashlin was staying at our house more frequently, thus giving Stacia and Alex some free time to do the things they couldn't accomplish when the baby was around. Our relationship with Stacia also has blossomed; we truly consider her Ashlin's "supermom" and the daughter we never had.

We are sure she feels the same way about us. Stacia is comfortable leaving Ashlin with us, trusting that we will take care of her with the utmost tender loving care.

The more time we spend with Ashlin, the stronger our bond with our precious granddaughter becomes. We often wonder how Ashlin perceives spending several nights at a time at our house. Does she perhaps consider it her vacation house? Whatever the case, we enjoy every minute we spend with her, teaching her new words, playing games, and watching videos of nursery rhymes on the computer. I have to confess that my granddaughter is the reason I've learned most of the popular nursery tunes I should have known when my own children were young!

Now that she is walking and running through the house, she needs constant attention and care. But the joy of having her near us overshadows any weariness we experience running after her.

My final words are that life is beautiful with Ashlin. She constantly calls me "*Pappou, Pappou,*" and when I hear her say the word so clearly, I melt! I will never forget the first sentence she learned, by putting two words together when she wanted to touch or take an object, large or small. Pointing to the object, she says: "*Oh hold it.*" We all get a few chuckles, and this has become our favorite expression to occasionally mimic Ashlin's grammar skills.

My relationship with Ashlin is a bond like no other. At this point of my life, I discovered, I fell in love again, with *my little Ashlin.* This unconditional form of love has a unique, magical sensation that I'm certain will grow even stronger as time goes on. Every day, I pray to God to keep her safe and keep me healthy as well, so that I can experience the joy of seeing her growing up graciously during her toddler years and beyond.

Conclusion

In this final part of the book, I would first like to clarify some vague assumptions or fill in certain omissions.

Throughout the first half of the book, many readers may wonder why I never referred to my name, or specifically what people called me during a conversation, either one-on-one or in group discussions. To me, a name signifies an identity, and my birth name shaped who I was at the beginning of my life journey. But over the course of the years, my name changed as I changed. Although I briefly provided a short explanation, I would like to chronologically go over the name variations I was called from childhood and up to the current time.

So what's in a name?

When I was born, my parents named me Emmanuel, which was my grandfather's name. My parents, friends, and relatives called me "Manoli," which is the common Greek, short derivative of Emmanuel.

When I went to Germany, I automatically inherited the name "Manuel," a name I felt was more or less synonymous to "Manoli" used in Greece. In Canada, my Greek friends used the "Manoli" version, whereas the Canadians called me Manuel.

In the United States, my immigration papers were filled out by Eve, who assumed the English translation of Emmanuel was Michael, since her brother, who was born in America, was called Michael but had been baptized as Emmanuel. For reasons I discovered later, I didn't make any attempts to change my name back to Emmanuel and continued using the name "Mike," which I liked very much.

It was when I met Angela that I realized I was really a different person, a transformed individual. Angela managed to evoke many of my dormant talents that helped me reach new realms of success on the personal, social, and professional levels. I wanted to forget about the old "me" and I wanted to forget the name Emmanuel and its derivations—a life void of adventure and passion. I wanted to erase that part of my past, especially up to my high school years, which were filled with failures and disappointments, a period during which nobody thought I would ever succeed in anything of substance.

I liked and I wanted to keep my new name, Mike, as the representation of a person with elevated values and ideals, the person Angela discovered, the person I accepted for the first time in my life, the person I was at peace with.

The last line of my poem in the 1965 *Union Leader* newspaper article was "I have the picture but I need the frame." I had a picture in mind of who I was and wanted to be, but I simply needed the frame—a name—to complete the "me" I wanted to be. As the reporter explained, the picture was the talent, but I needed a break or the opportunity to apply my talent. Unexpectedly, my *frame* was Angela, who identified my potential and "framed my talent" with her reassurance, which refueled the determination I needed to reach my potential.

I am so grateful for my good fortune, but more importantly, I feel blessed for my very special family and all my lifelong friends, who have been there for me every time I needed a shoulder to lean on. However, I often ask myself if the achievements I have realized through the "Mike" years made me the successful person I had imagined when I put the *three grains of wheat* under a stone on the side of that path, so long ago.

Being critical of myself, I was never convinced I had reached my potential, for there are so many areas of interest that remain unexplored, including my own inner world. I have begun to realize that material possessions or external factors cannot be the definition of true happiness. Instead, the peace within us is the unshakeable force that can overcome any obstacles and diminish all negative thoughts. It is only with this peace, this ability to take into consideration perspective, the evolution of greater patience, and an unwavering compassion for others, that true happiness and "success" can be found.

If, when I was ten years old, someone had shown me a two-minute clip of what I would become fifty years later, I would have thought it was utterly impossible for me to realize a feat of this magnitude. However, as I gradually climbed the ladder of life one rung at a time, I didn't question how I got there. Instead, I accepted the phenomenon of my attainment as a natural law of life's progression.

I was fortunate to live and work in America where everyone has equal opportunities to succeed and reach any goals they set for themselves. Throughout my professional career, I always attained the level I sought and knew when to avoid higher positions that would have negatively affected my personal life, or would have forced me to spend less time with my family and at the same time increase the level of stress I had become accustomed to dealing with in the corporate sector.

It took me many years of hard work to build a career that afforded me the opportunity to enjoy a comfortable lifestyle. Is it possible, however, that the priority of "work" within the American culture tops all other aspects of our everyday life?

When Angela and I took a Caribbean cruise more than twenty years ago, we met a couple from Greece who were spending their honeymoon on the same cruise ship. One afternoon, we began comparing the standard of living between Greece and America. At that time, I was convinced my lifestyle was at a much higher level than the European standard of living, because of our overall economic superiority. And then the gentleman, whose name I don't recall, asked me a simple question:

"Besides your work routine, could you describe in a few words what else you did last week in terms of recreation?"

I certainly had not expected such a question, but I had to pause for a few moments to recollect the highlights of the week before I gave him an answer. When I realized that during the week I had just gone through my regular routine—work, home, watch TV at night, and then off to bed—I could only come up with the weekend dinner Angela and I had at a restaurant.

I clearly understood where he was going with that question because, even during the week, the Europeans find time to engage in recreational activities. Along those lines, I'm questioning the idea that has been sold to the American public in that, in order to be successful, above everything else in life, your number one priority must be your work. Is this really the answer?

Now, being in the retirement phase of my life, I have ample time to reflect on my past years, trying to assemble my understanding of who I was when I left the village and who I ended up being after a vigorous journey filled with diverse experiences. As Odysseus averted many obstacles and temptations before he finally reached Ithaca, I also have gone through an analogous lifetime trek, which has been the ideal teacher, especially in the area of "knowing the real me."

I am finally convinced that the knowledge I gained during my life-journey helped me realize there is still so much I don't know and so much I have to learn. I wish I had another lifetime to explore some of my uncompleted proclivities in the areas of music, painting, poetry, philosophy, and many other interests.

Writing a book of my memoirs was a cathartic experience, during which I had the opportunity to relive some of the profound moments, from childhood all the way to adulthood. I recognize the invaluable education I acquired while attending the "school of hard knocks" without a safety net. I've learned lessons that could not have been taught through formal education, whose structural methodology often diminishes creativity and independence while it constricts the free thinking process.

Always ready to take a pop quiz, and after realizing many failures, I had an optimistic mindset and was certain I could accomplish anything that could be perceived by the human mind. I've learned to follow the simple, logical rule of life that goes like this: *When you have a passion, you hope; when you hope, you learn to wait; when you wait, you persist; when you persist, you win.*

But winning is not the end. We need to cultivate the ability to enjoy the entire process up until it's time to plan the next goal.

Above all achievements, however, my family is the most significant aspect of my life. I've never stopped being in love with my wife, and I thank God for helping us raise two wonderfully gifted sons who possess all the moral qualities that define worthwhile individuals. Angela, Alex, and Paul—as well as our newly acquired, wonderful daughter, Stacia, and our precious granddaughter, Ashlin—are the joys of my everyday life. They are the ones with whom I would like to spend quality time during my remaining years.

As I conclude the chapters of my life thus far, I can clearly see the dawning of a new day, which I intend to live to the fullest. But this time, I will be playing a new role. As one who has experienced much, I have embraced a role as teacher, all the while still learning like a wide-eyed student when I encounter new life lessons. I eagerly look forward to each new chapter of my life as it is filled with fresh passion, faithful love, and life-changing revelations, from one day to the next.

CPSIA information can be obtained at www.ICGtesting.com
Printed in the USA
LVOW090243160312

273346LV00001B/165/P